Shojo Beat

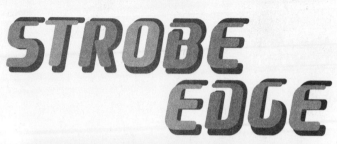

STROBE EDGE

Vol. 3

Story & Art by
Io Sakisaka

STROBE EDGE

Volume 3
CONTENTS

Story Thus Far

Ninako is a down-to-earth high school freshman who doesn't know much about love. She knows her classmate Daiki has feelings for her, but she only thinks of him as a friend. When she meets Ren Ichinose, however, she falls in love for the first time. Even after she learns that Ren already has a girlfriend, and even though Daiki tells her he's in love with her, Ninako can't deny her feelings for Ren.

After Ninako gathers the courage to tell Ren how she feels and he turns her down, she asks him if they can still be friends. Meanwhile, Takumi Ando begins to fall for Ninako. After Ando chews Ren out for giving Ninako false hope by being so friendly to her, Ren starts avoiding her in order to not hurt her further. Confused by the sudden change in Ren's attitude, Ninako can't help crying. Ando reacts by kissing her on the forehead, shocking her into running away. And then someone pulls her into a corner to help hide her...

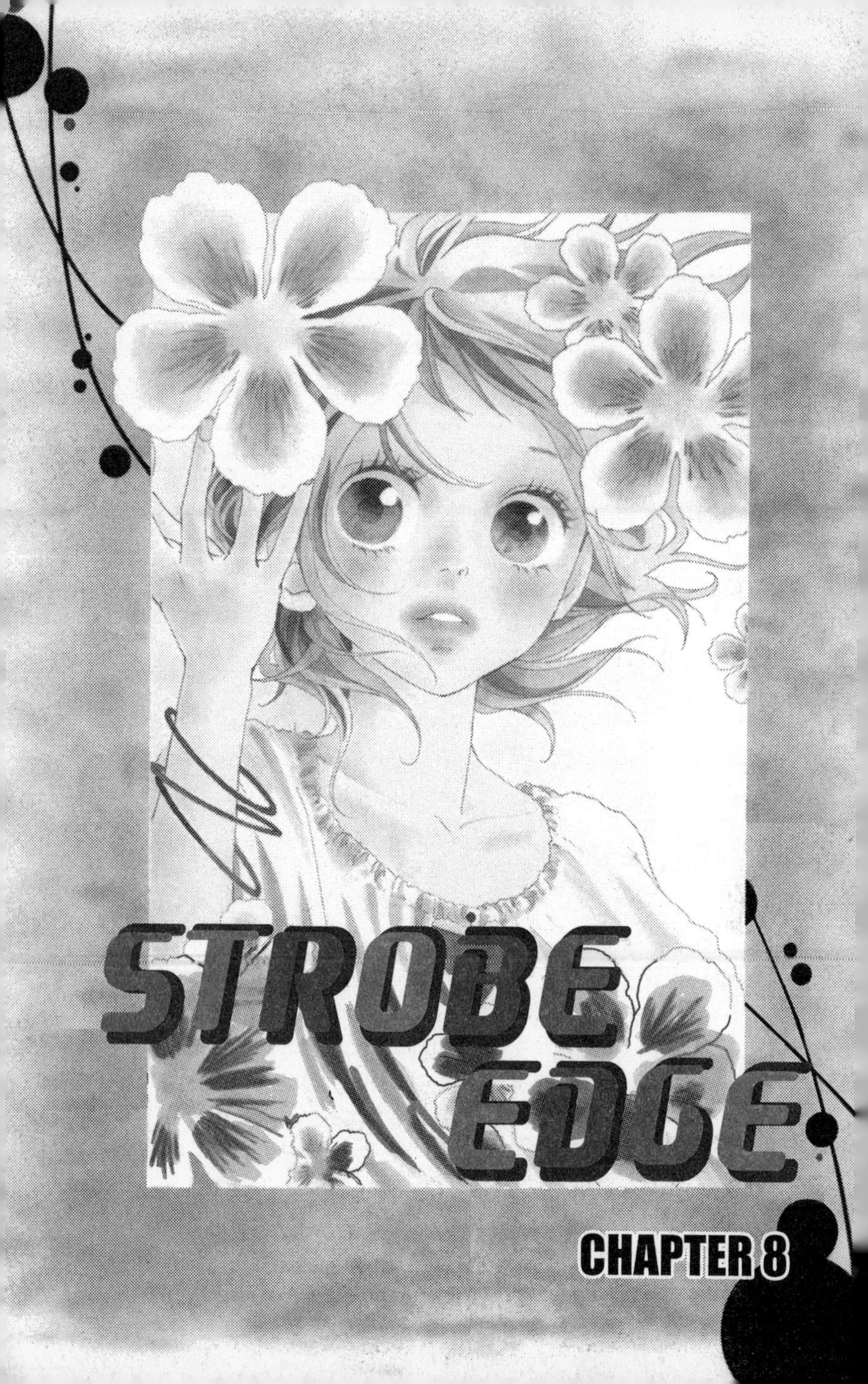
STROBE EDGE
CHAPTER 8

INTRO

Hello! Io Sakisaka here! Thank you so much for reading this book. I can't believe volume 3 has come out! This is my longest-running series to date, and I'm thrilled. If my story and characters touch your hearts even a little bit, all my work will be worthwhile. It'll encourage me to keep going!

I'm generally sort of noncommittal and easygoing, but since beginning this series I've really come to understand what it means to give something my all. With readers, assistants and publishers supporting me, how could I not? (But I probably could still do more...)

I'm grateful to be in a position to ponder things like that. Thank you so much! But aside from work, I still aim to be laid-back and easygoing.

And now, on to *Strobe Edge 3*!

★ Io Sakisaka ★

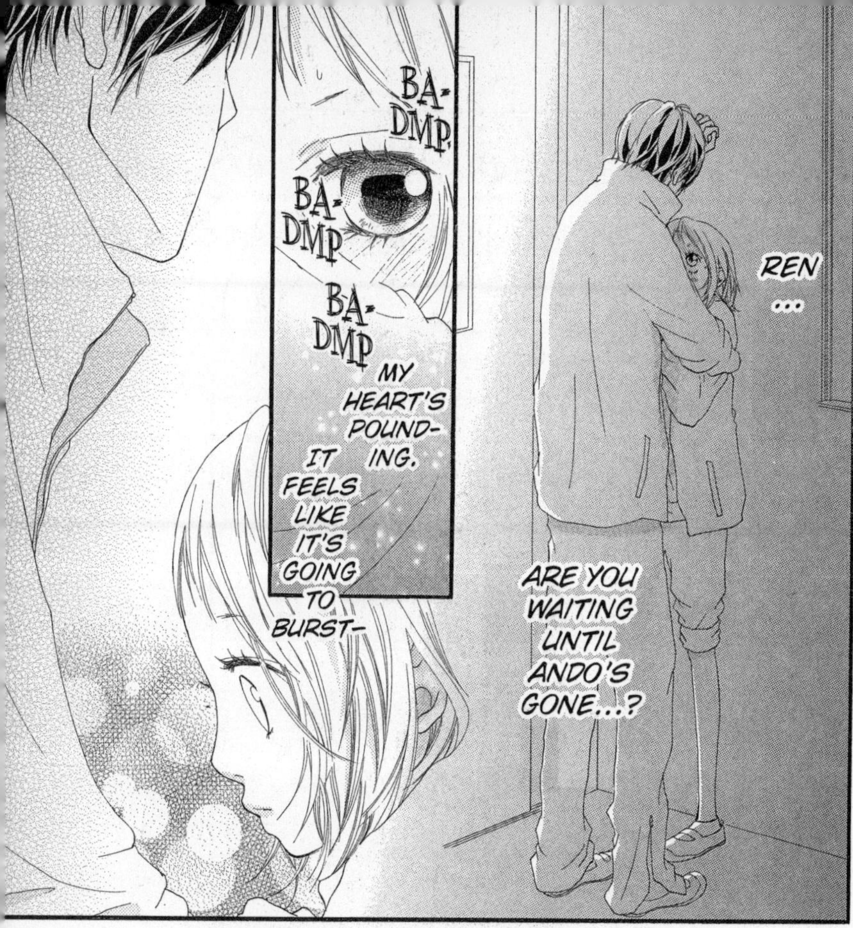
REN...
ARE YOU WAITING UNTIL ANDO'S GONE...?
BA-DMP
BA-DMP
BA-DMP
MY HEART'S POUNDING.
IT FEELS LIKE IT'S GOING TO BURST-

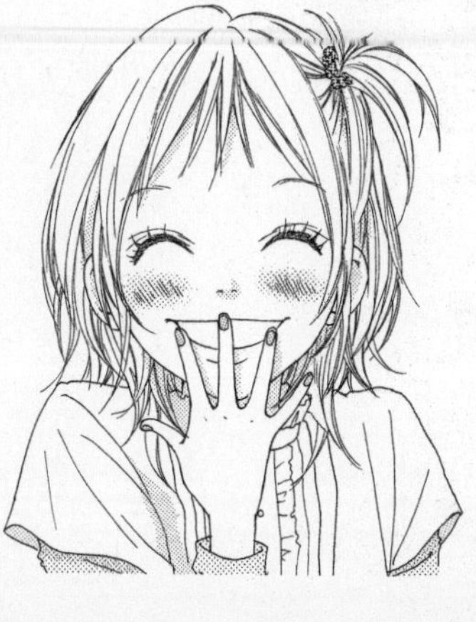

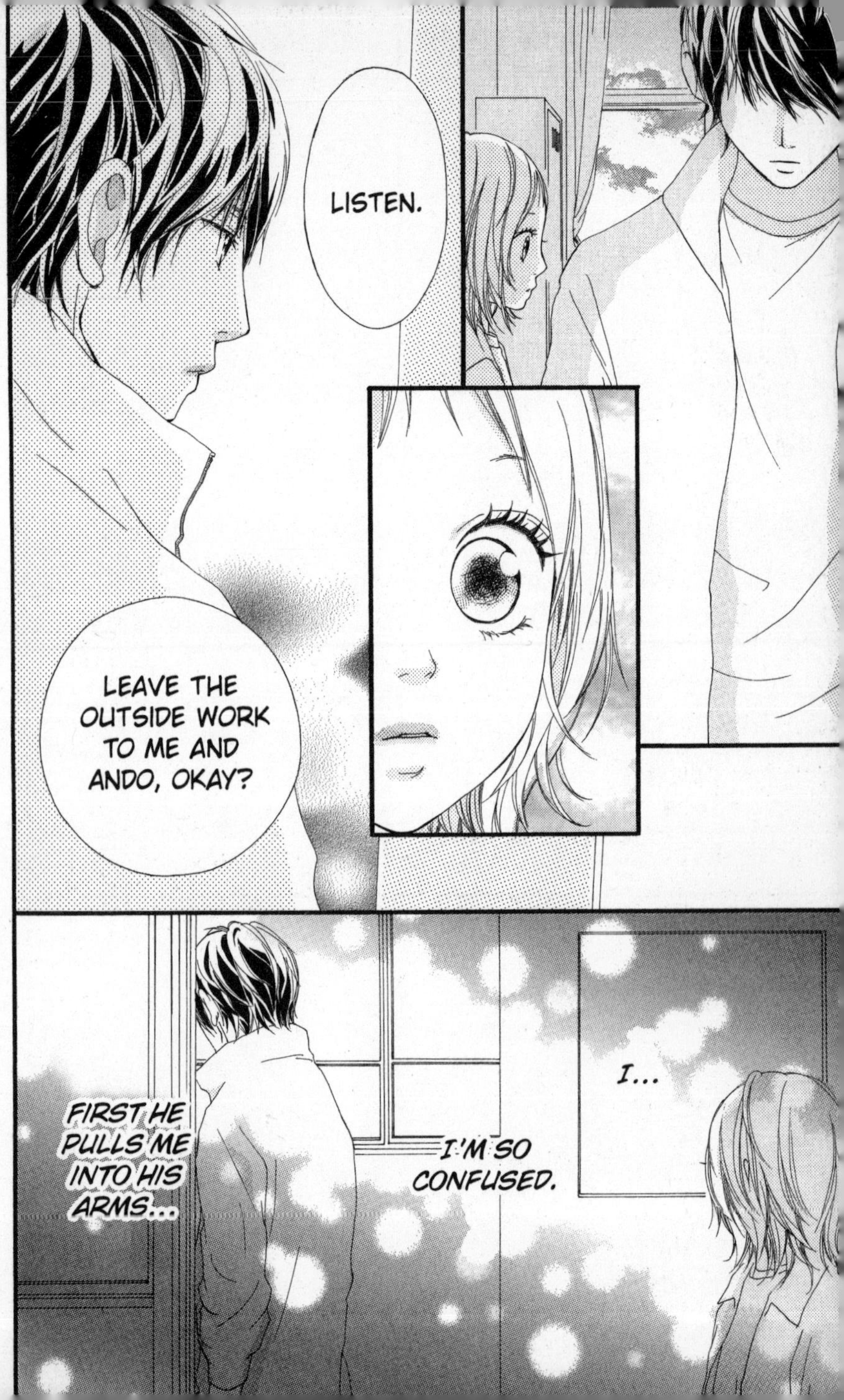
LISTEN.
LEAVE THE OUTSIDE WORK TO ME AND ANDO, OKAY?
I...
I'M SO CONFUSED.
FIRST HE PULLS ME INTO HIS ARMS...

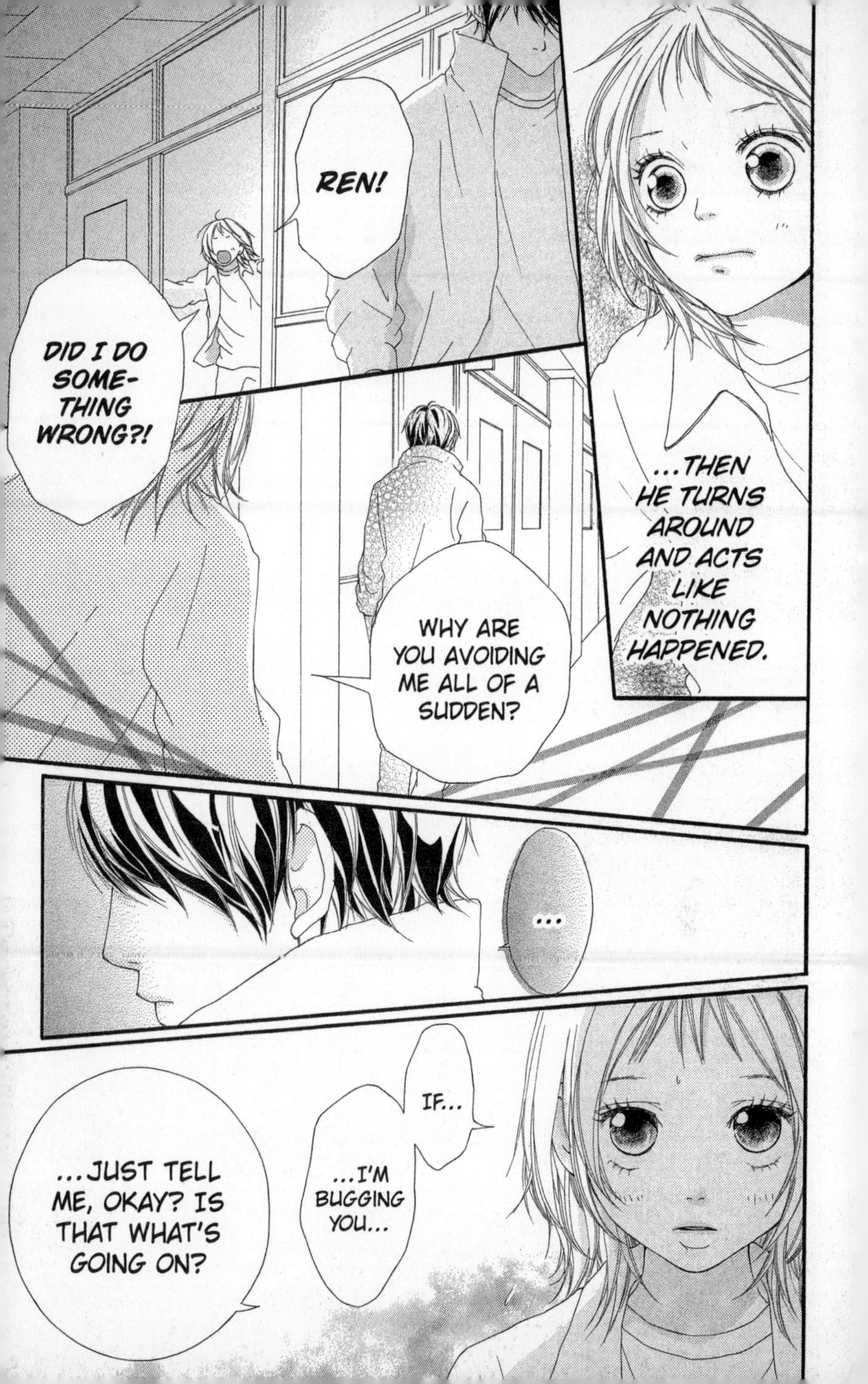
...THEN HE TURNS AROUND AND ACTS LIKE NOTHING HAPPENED.
REN!
DID I DO SOME-THING WRONG?!
WHY ARE YOU AVOIDING ME ALL OF A SUDDEN?
...
IF...
...I'M BUGGING YOU...
...JUST TELL ME, OKAY? IS THAT WHAT'S GOING ON?

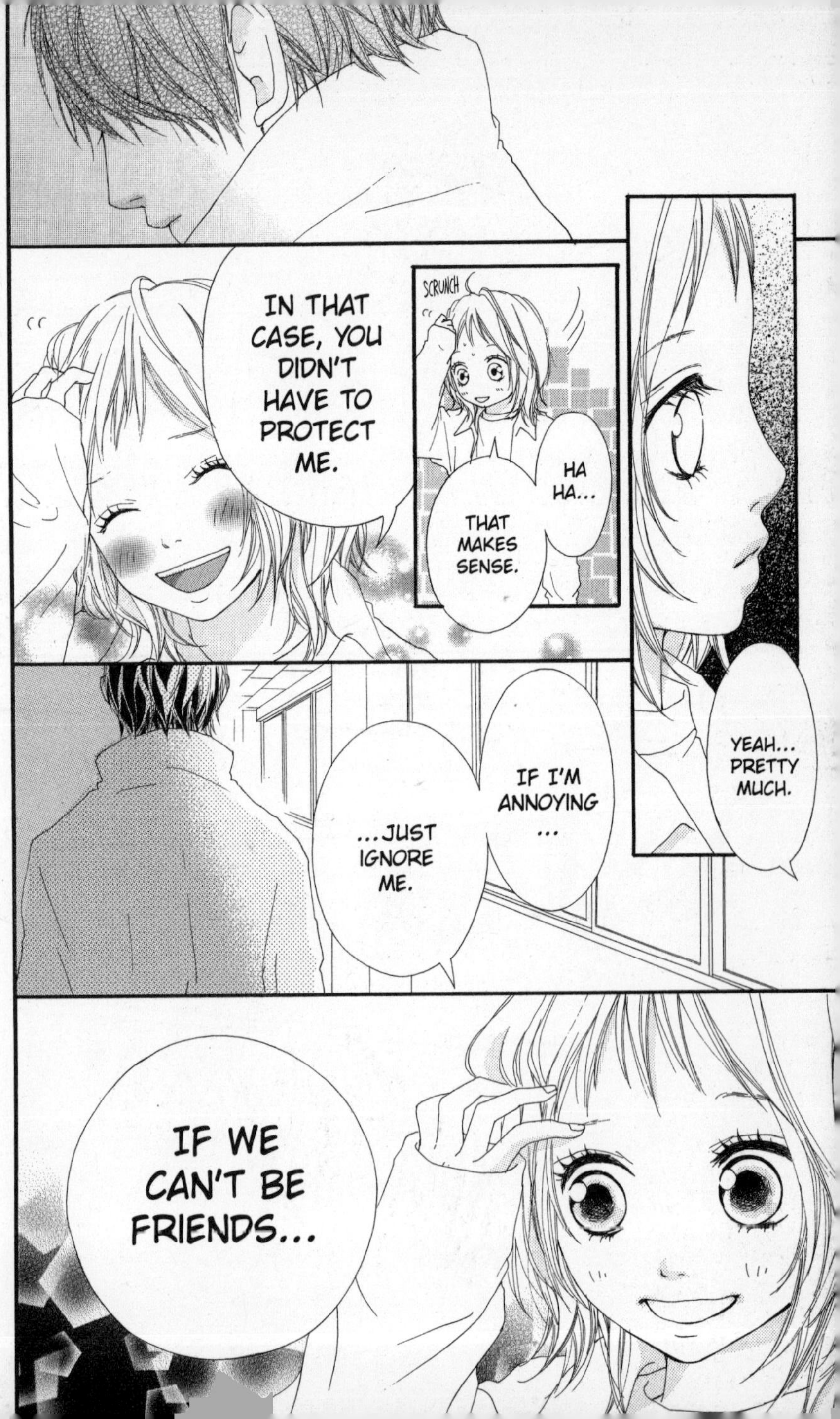
YEAH... PRETTY MUCH.
SCRUNCH
HA HA...
THAT MAKES SENSE.
IN THAT CASE, YOU DIDN'T HAVE TO PROTECT ME.
IF I'M ANNOYING...
...JUST IGNORE ME.
IF WE CAN'T BE FRIENDS...

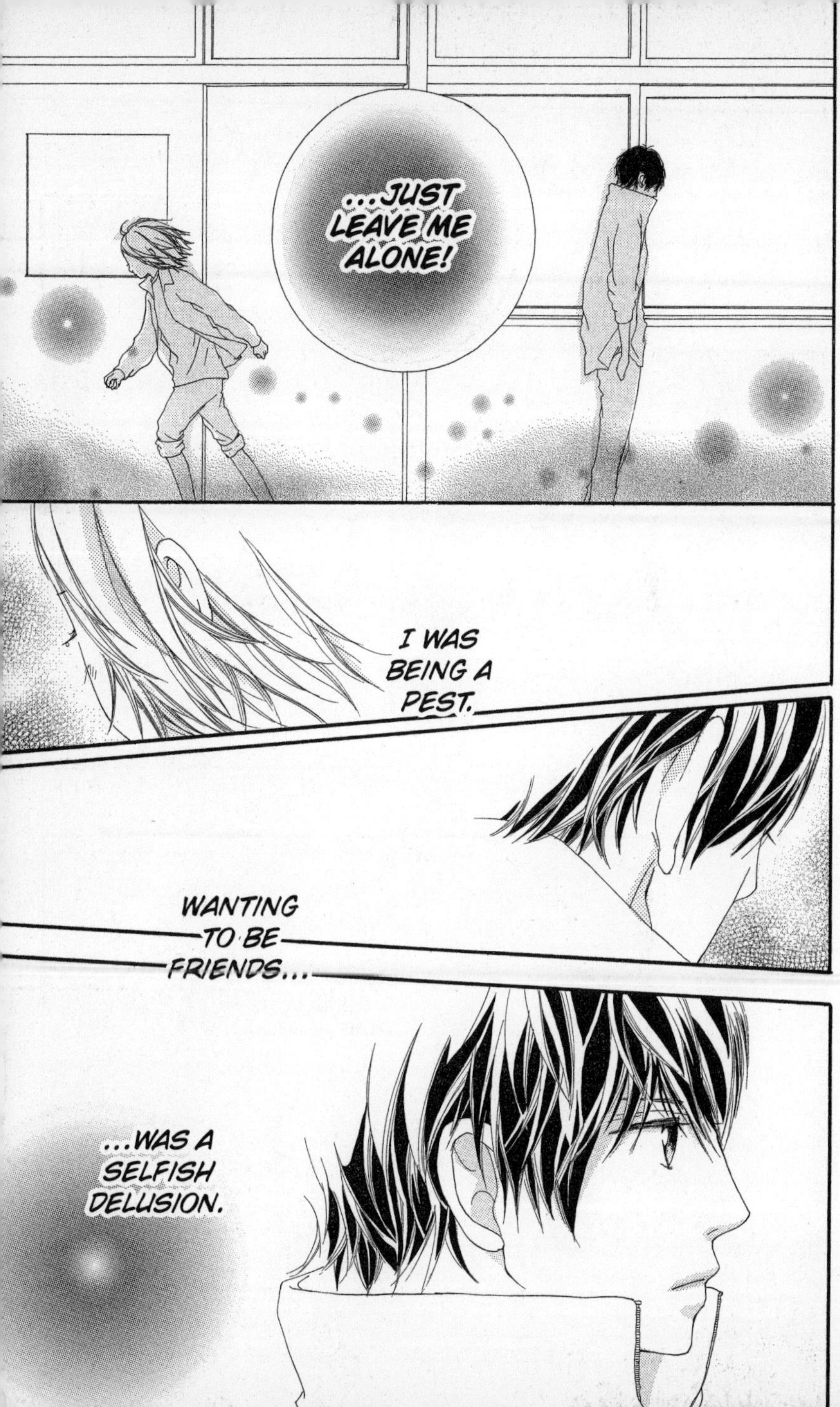
...JUST LEAVE ME ALONE!
I WAS BEING A PEST.
WANTING TO BE FRIENDS...
...WAS A SELFISH DELUSION.

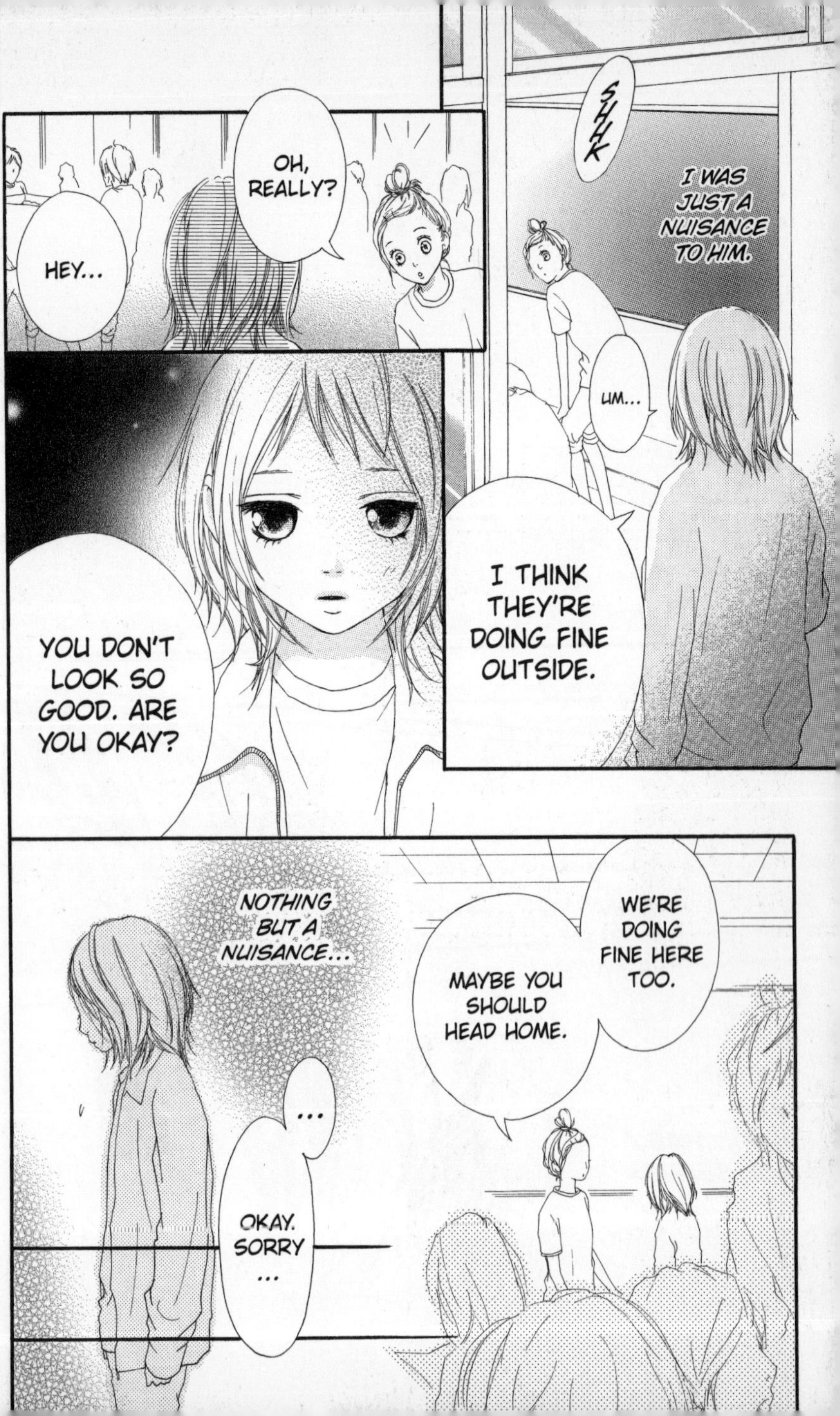
SHHK
I WAS JUST A NUISANCE TO HIM.
UM...
I THINK THEY'RE DOING FINE OUTSIDE.
OH, REALLY?
HEY...
YOU DON'T LOOK SO GOOD. ARE YOU OKAY?
WE'RE DOING FINE HERE TOO.
MAYBE YOU SHOULD HEAD HOME.
NOTHING BUT A NUISANCE...
...
OKAY. SORRY ...

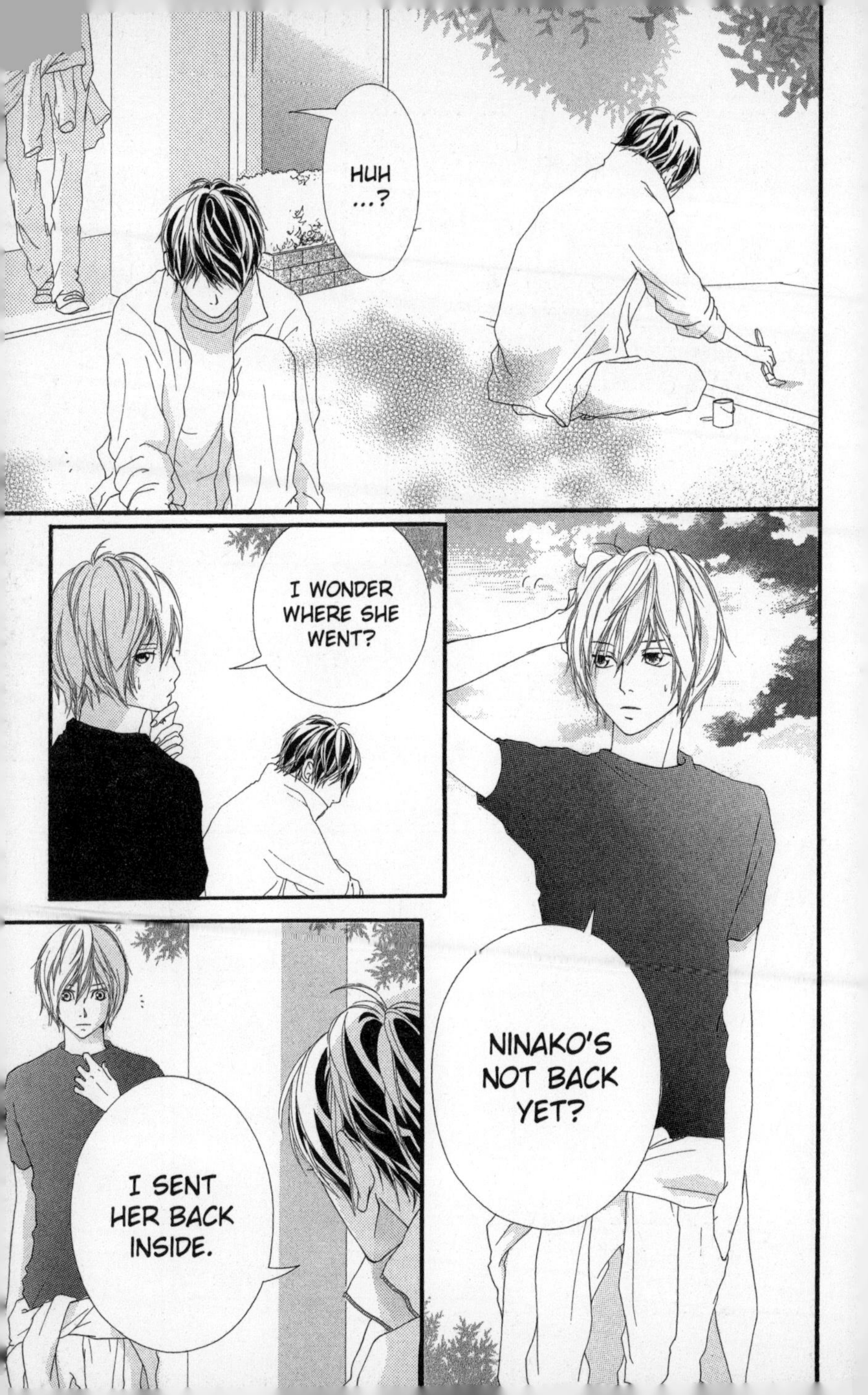
HUH ...?
NINAKO'S NOT BACK YET?
I WONDER WHERE SHE WENT?
I SENT HER BACK INSIDE.

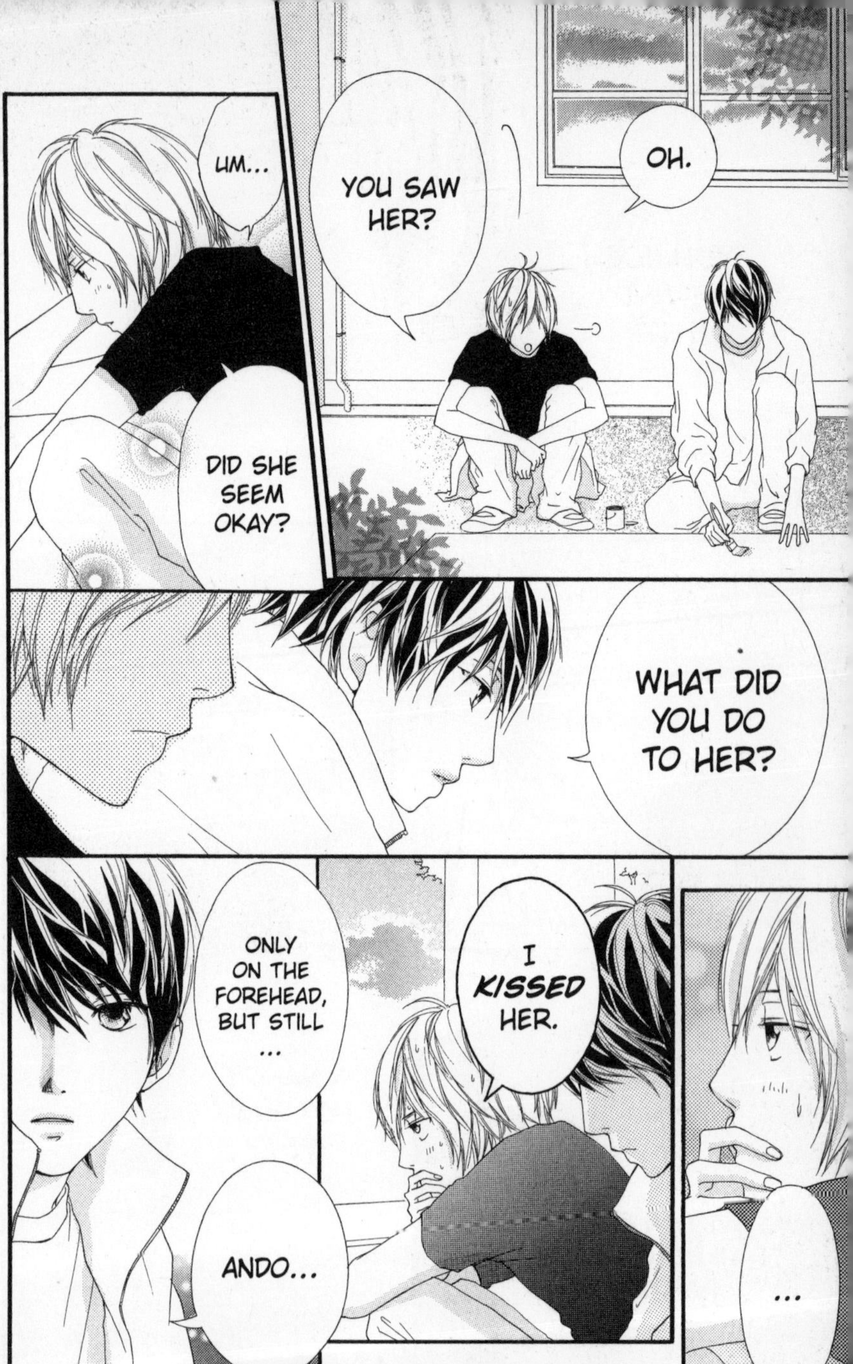
OH.
YOU SAW HER?
UM...
DID SHE SEEM OKAY?
WHAT DID YOU DO TO HER?
...
I *KISSED* HER.
ONLY ON THE FOREHEAD, BUT STILL ...
ANDO...

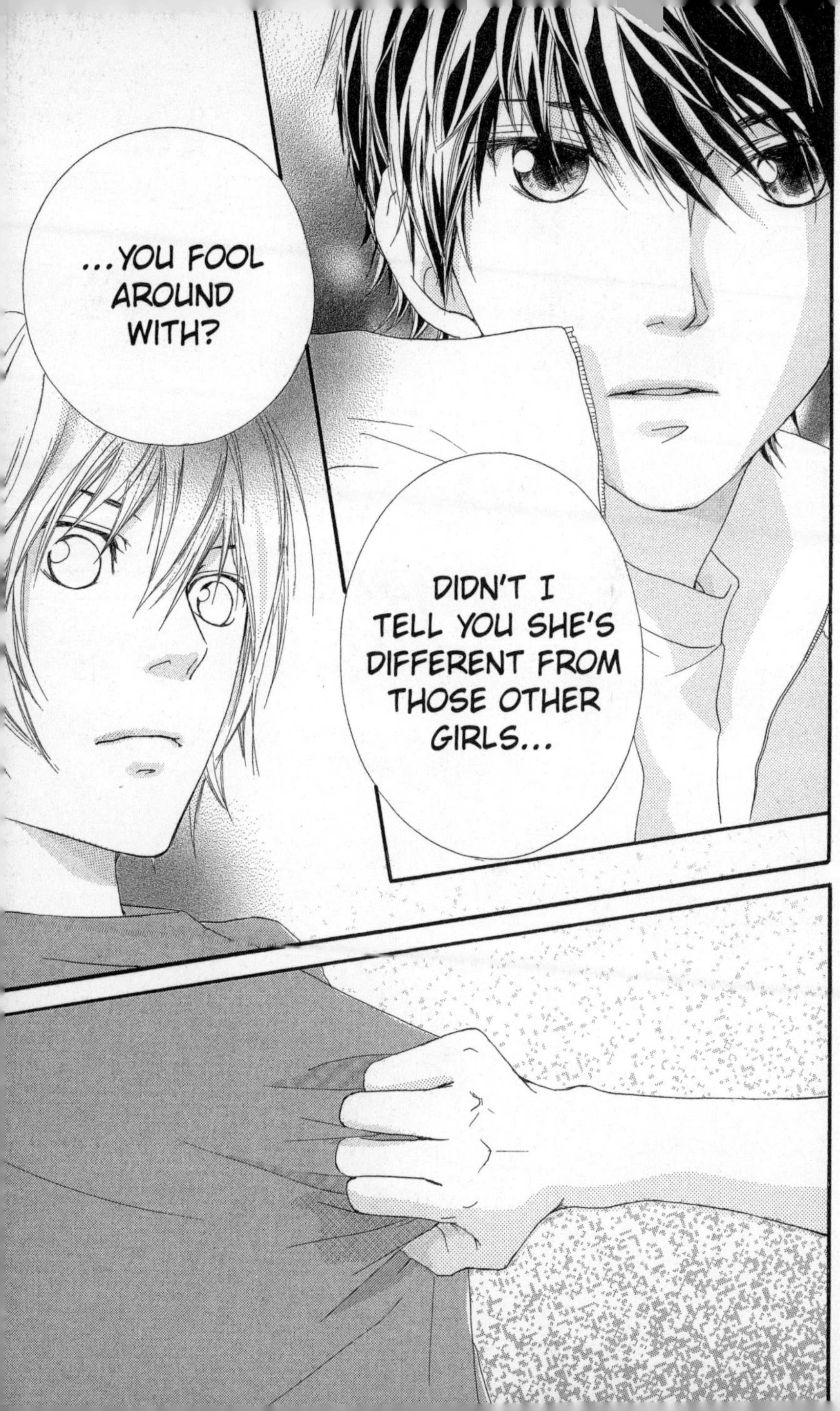
DIDN'T I TELL YOU SHE'S DIFFERENT FROM THOSE OTHER GIRLS...
...YOU FOOL AROUND WITH?

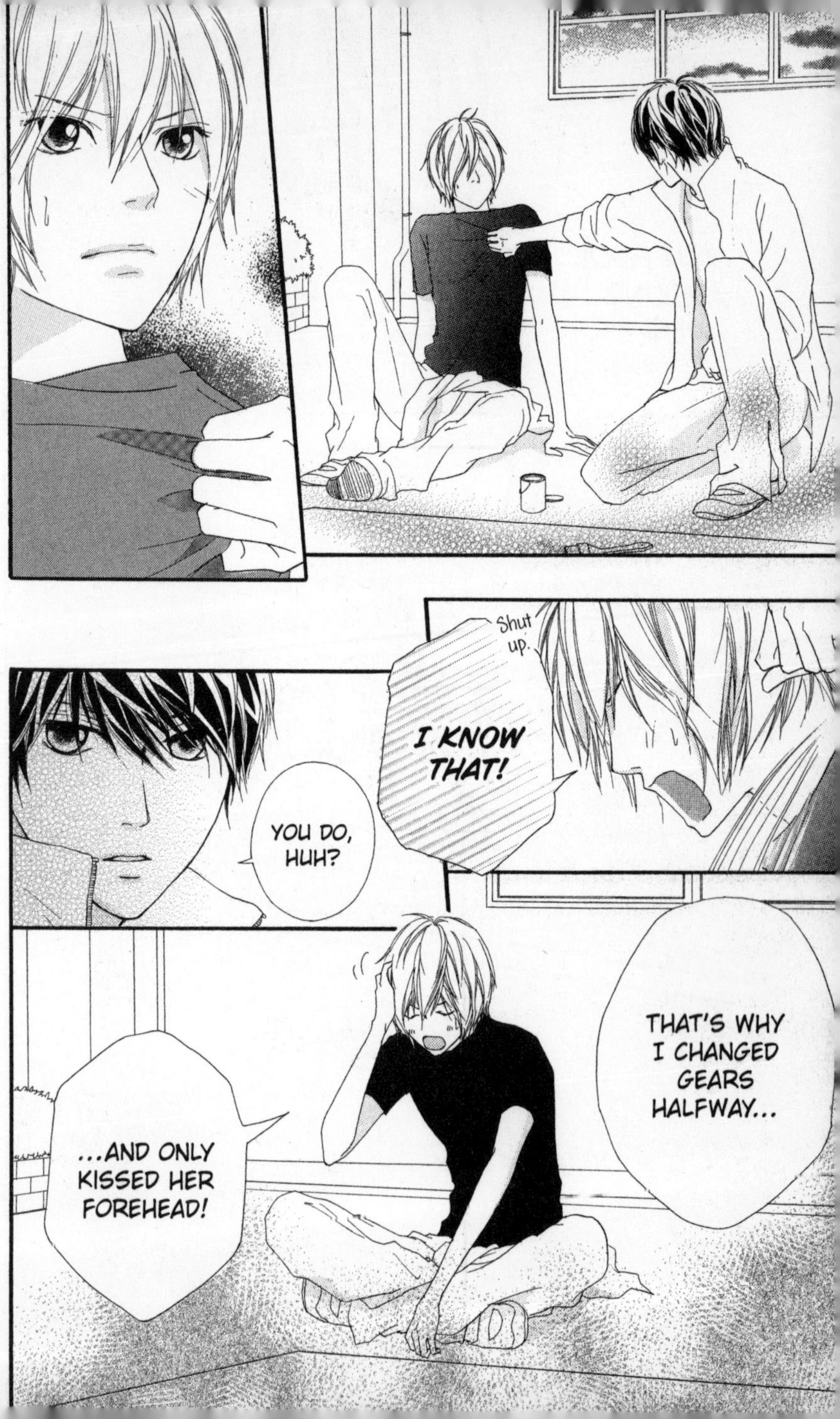
Shut up.
I KNOW THAT!
YOU DO, HUH?
THAT'S WHY I CHANGED GEARS HALFWAY...
...AND ONLY KISSED HER FOREHEAD!

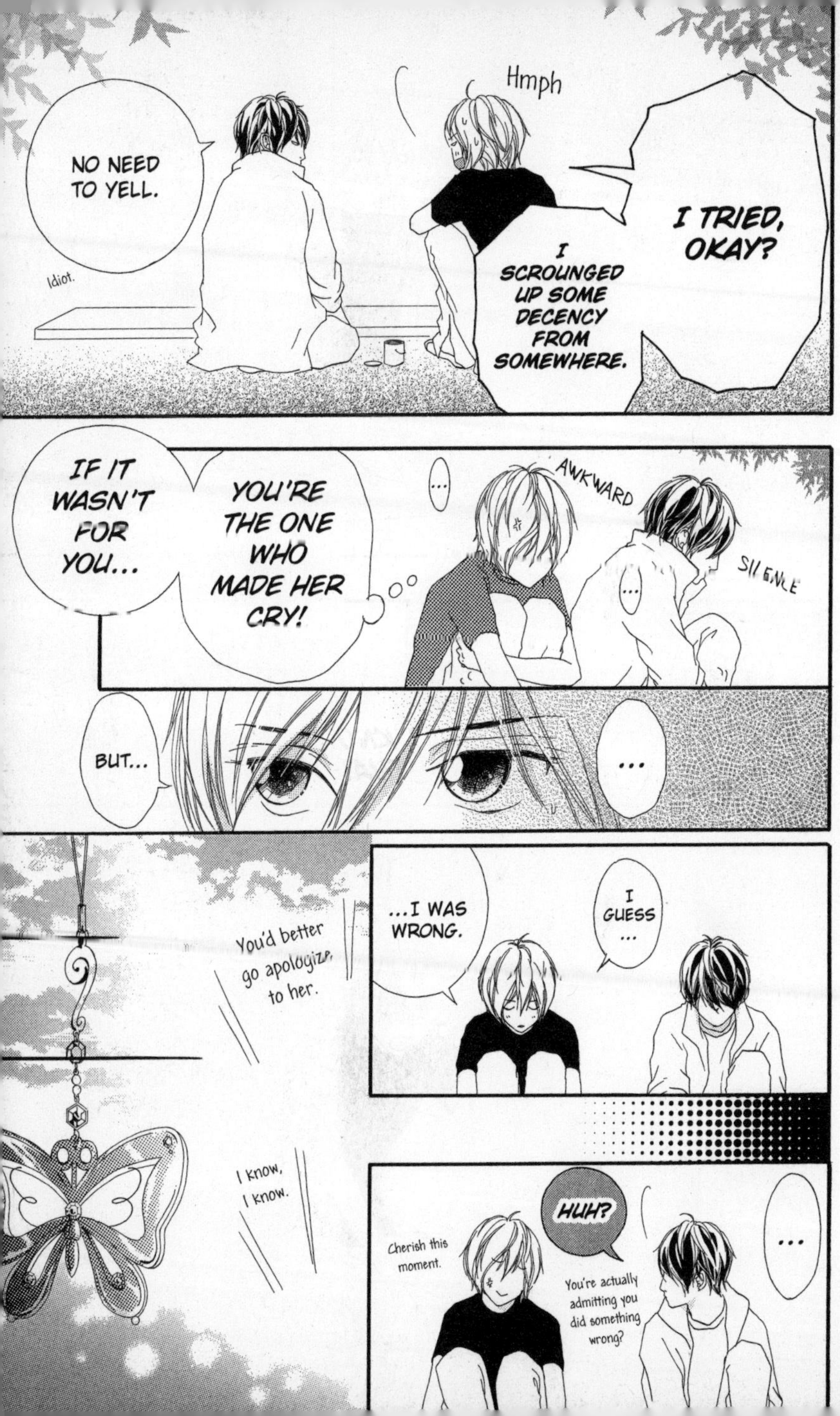
I TRIED, OKAY?
I SCROUNGED UP SOME DECENCY FROM SOMEWHERE.
Hmph
NO NEED TO YELL.
Idiot.
SILENCE
...
AWKWARD
...
YOU'RE THE ONE WHO MADE HER CRY!
IF IT WASN'T FOR YOU...
...
BUT...
I GUESS...
...I WAS WRONG.
You'd better go apologize to her.
...
You're actually admitting you did something wrong?
HUH?
Cherish this moment.
I know, I know.

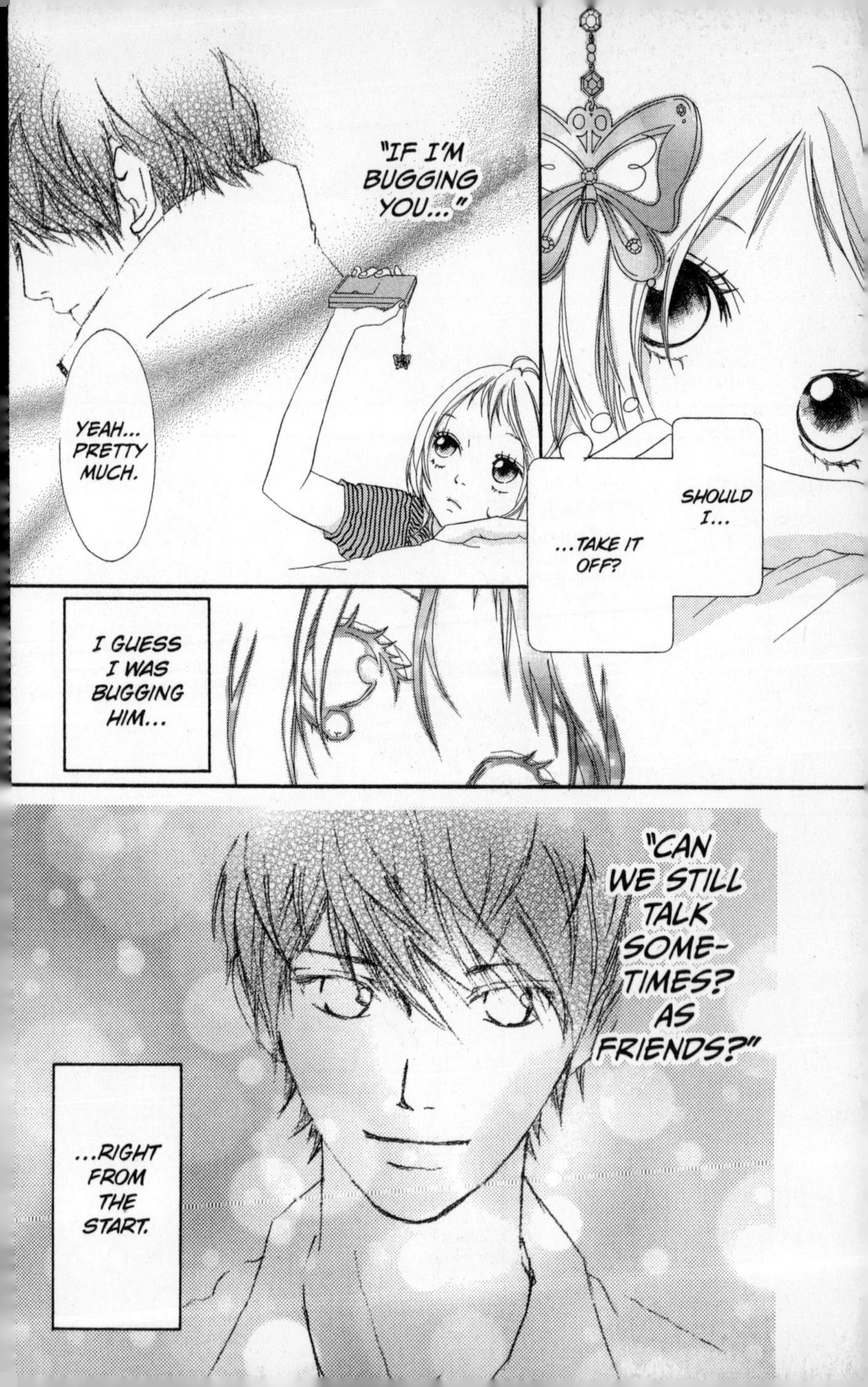
SHOULD I...
...TAKE IT OFF?
"IF I'M BUGGING YOU..."
YEAH... PRETTY MUCH.
I GUESS I WAS BUGGING HIM...
"CAN WE STILL TALK SOME-TIMES? AS FRIENDS?"
...RIGHT FROM THE START.

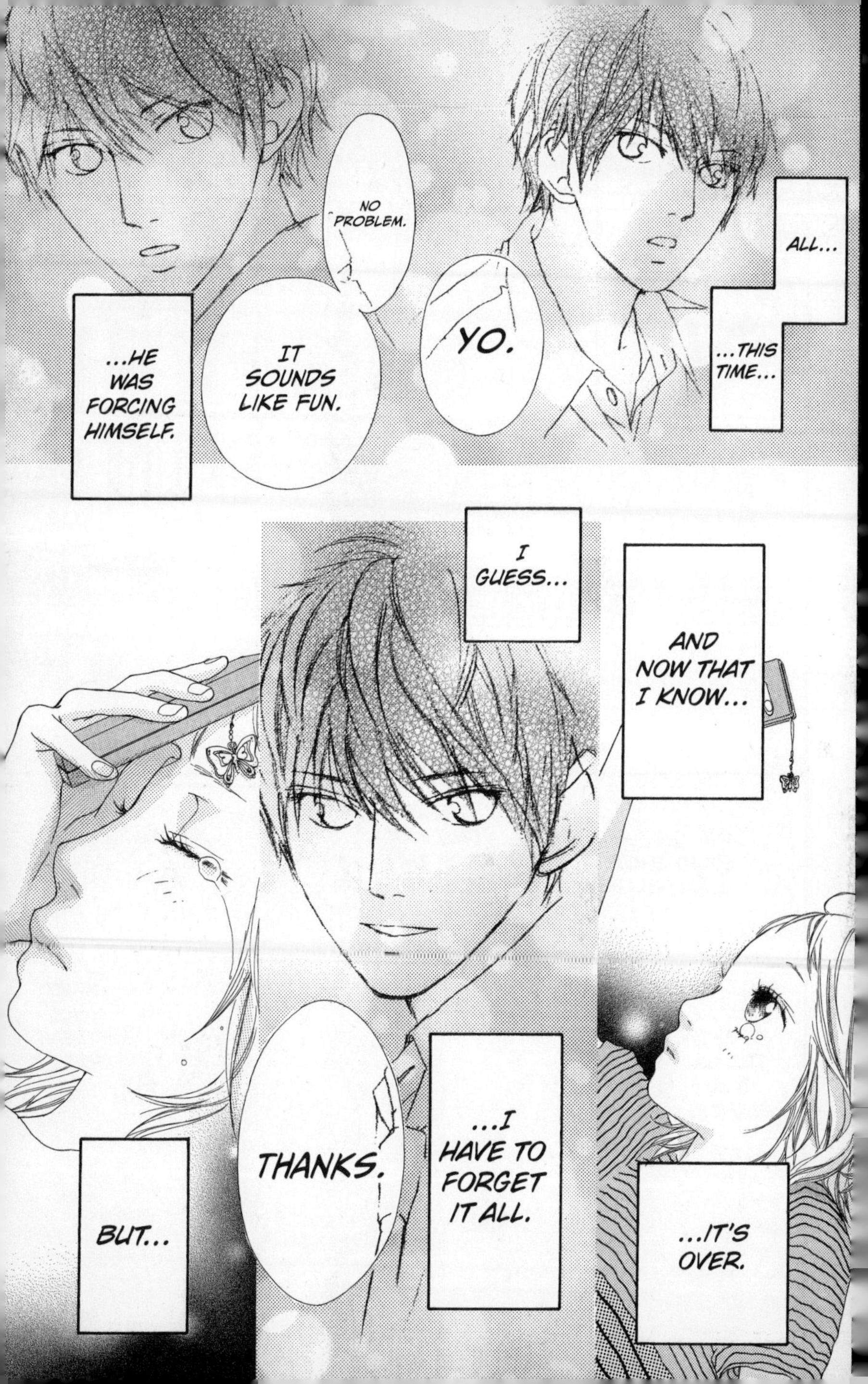
ALL...
...THIS TIME...
YO.
NO PROBLEM.
IT SOUNDS LIKE FUN.
...HE WAS FORCING HIMSELF.
AND NOW THAT I KNOW...
...IT'S OVER.
I GUESS...
...I HAVE TO FORGET IT ALL.
THANKS.
BUT...

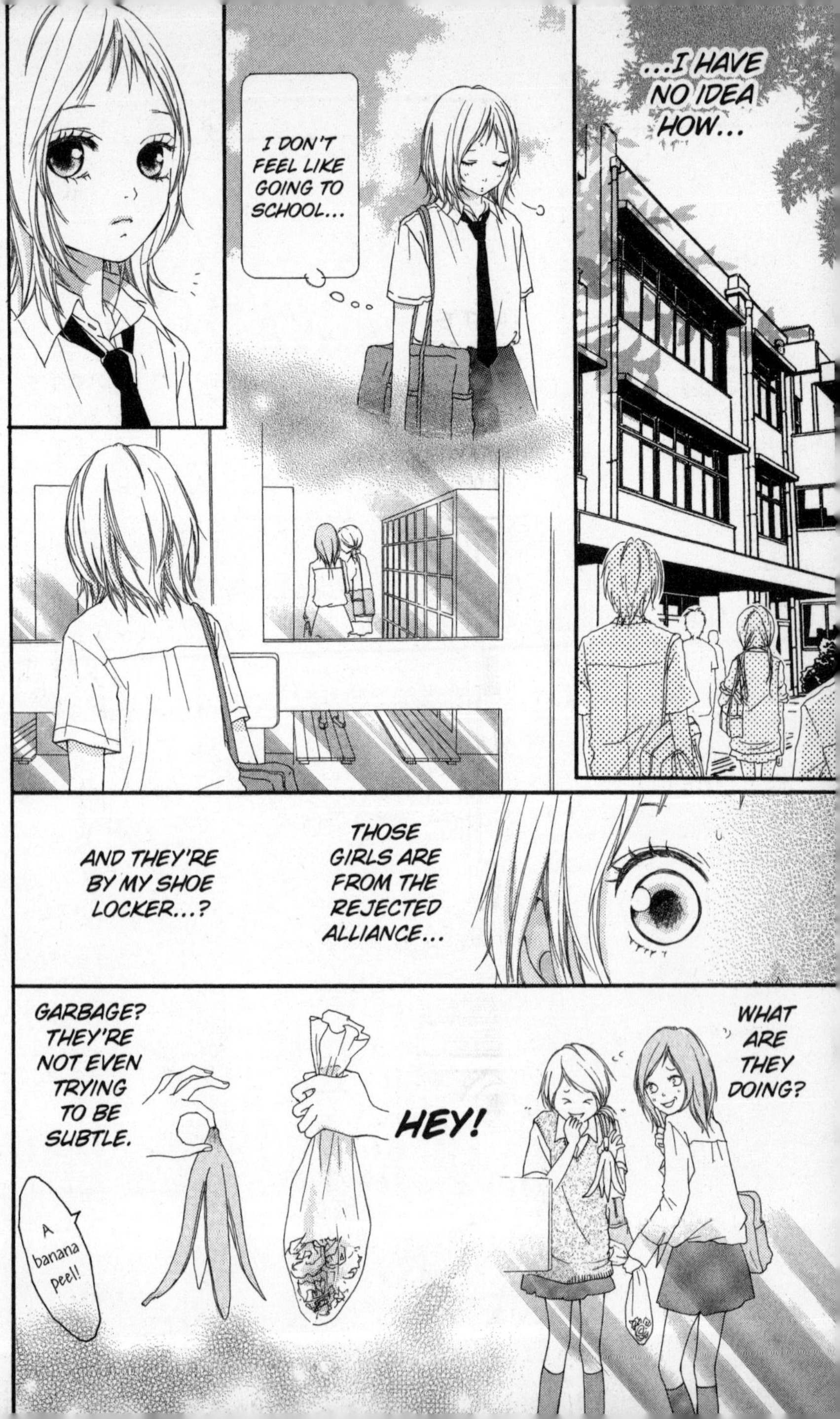
...I HAVE NO IDEA HOW...
I DON'T FEEL LIKE GOING TO SCHOOL...
THOSE GIRLS ARE FROM THE REJECTED ALLIANCE...
AND THEY'RE BY MY SHOE LOCKER...?
WHAT ARE THEY DOING?
HEY!
GARBAGE? THEY'RE NOT EVEN TRYING TO BE SUBTLE.
A banana peel!

WORKFLOW

~My Particular Method~

① THE VISION

If a single scene or line comes to mind, I try to imagine the character acting it out. Then I fill the story in.

② THE OUTLINE

I sketch a rough draft of the vision flowing through my head, but it's so messy that only I can understand it. Sometimes I panic because I can't read my own writing!

③ THE PLOT

At this point, I'm starting to record things in my notebook in greater detail. I write down each character's lines and thoughts so it's easier to plan out the pages later on.

← To be continued

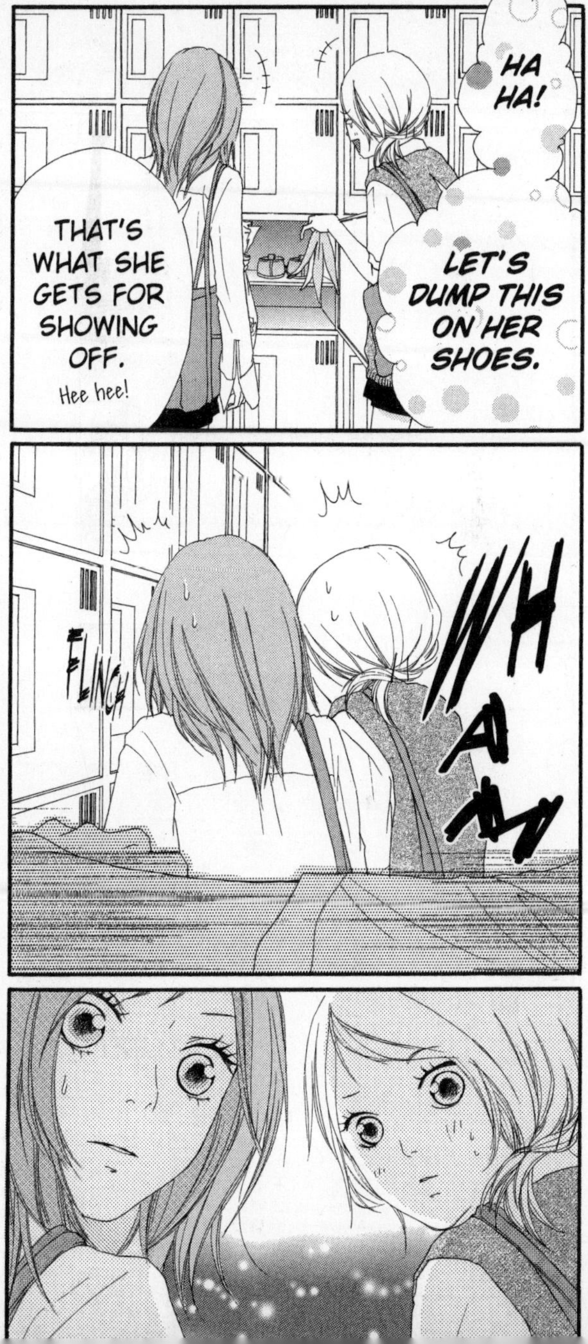
HA HA!
LET'S DUMP THIS ON HER SHOES.
THAT'S WHAT SHE GETS FOR SHOWING OFF.
Hee hee!
WHAM
FLINCH

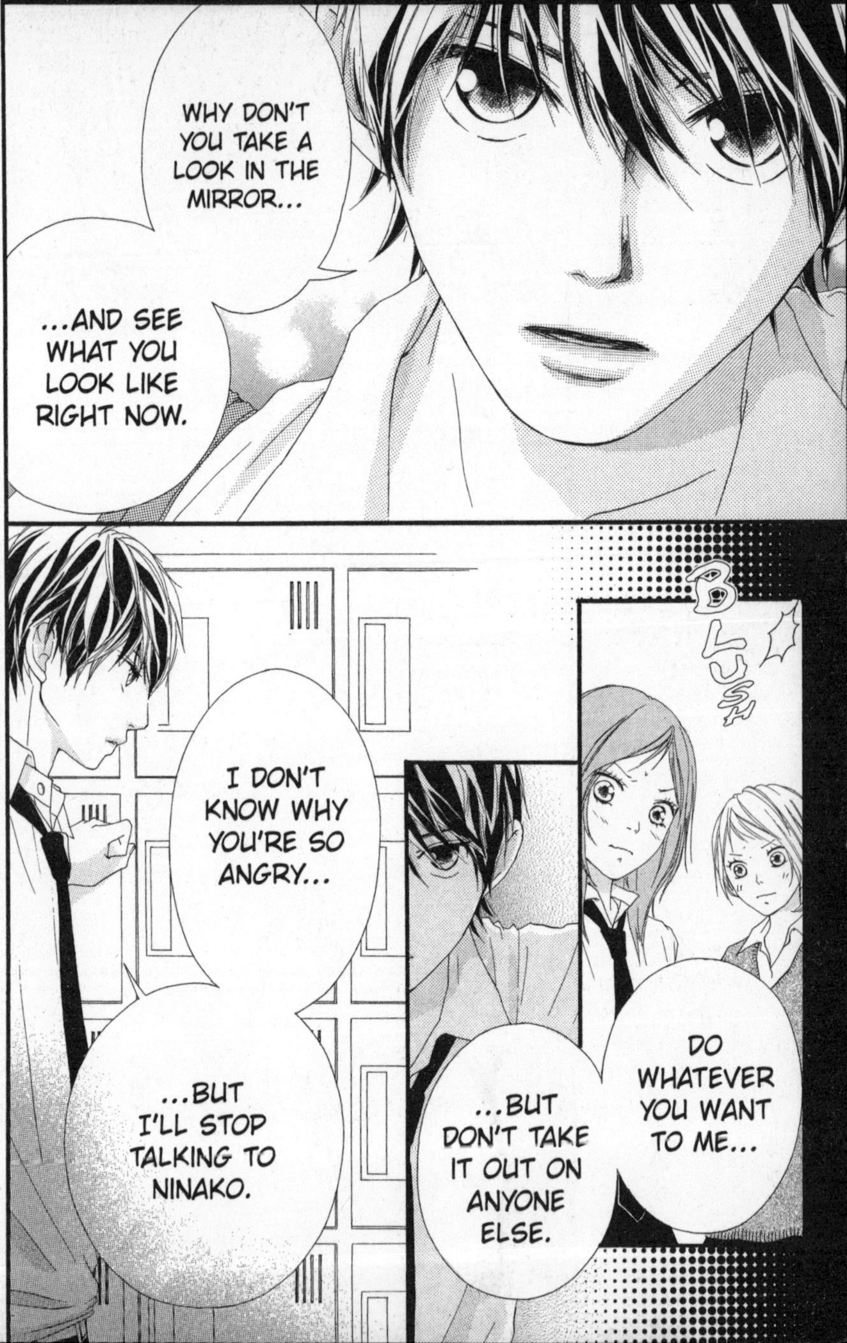
WHY DON'T YOU TAKE A LOOK IN THE MIRROR...
...AND SEE WHAT YOU LOOK LIKE RIGHT NOW.
BLUSH
DO WHATEVER YOU WANT TO ME...
...BUT DON'T TAKE IT OUT ON ANYONE ELSE.
I DON'T KNOW WHY YOU'RE SO ANGRY...
...BUT I'LL STOP TALKING TO NINAKO.

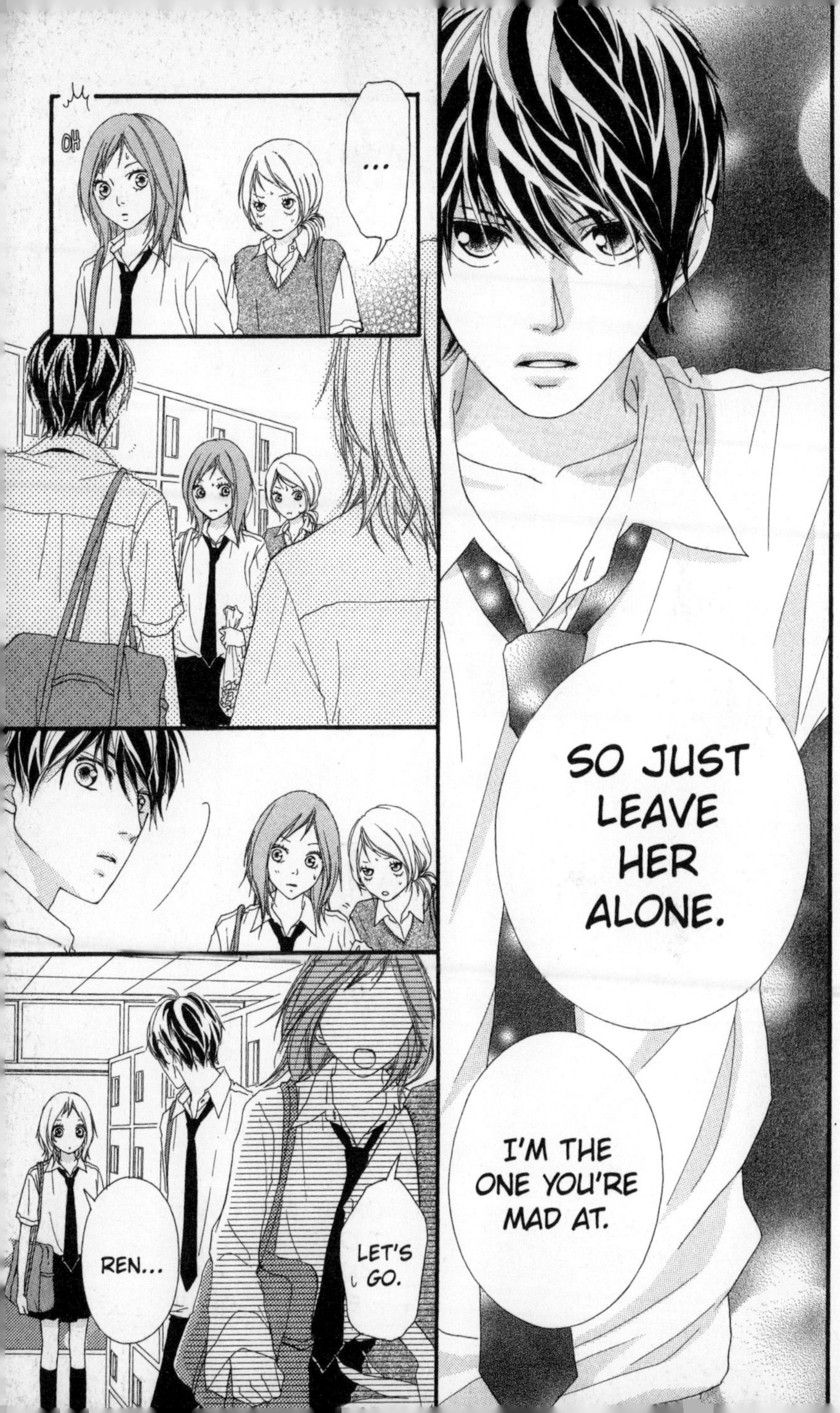
SO JUST LEAVE HER ALONE.
I'M THE ONE YOU'RE MAD AT.
...
OH
LET'S GO.
REN...

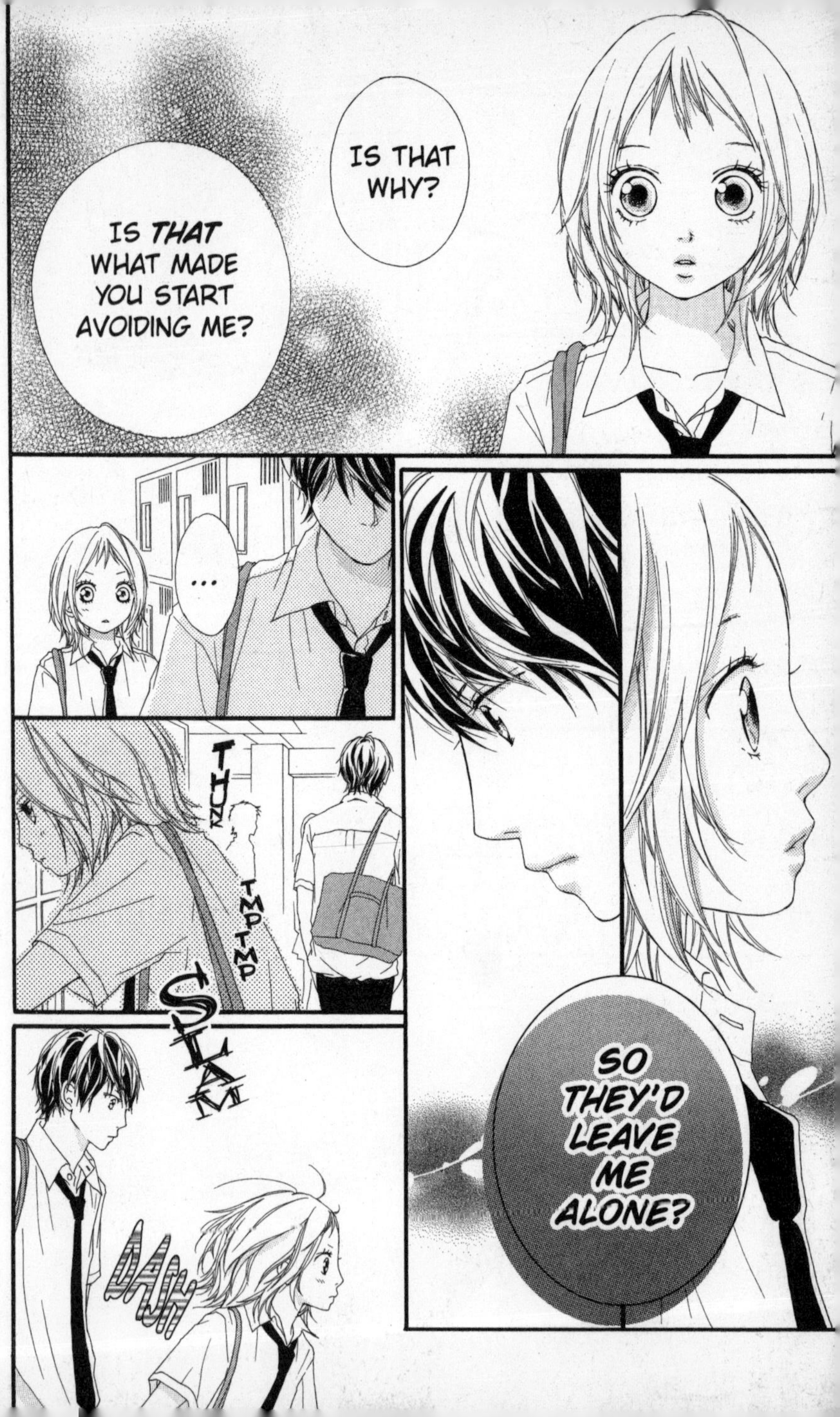
IS THAT WHY?
IS *THAT* WHAT MADE YOU START AVOIDING ME?
SO THEY'D LEAVE ME ALONE?
...
THUNK
TMP TMP
SLAM
DASH

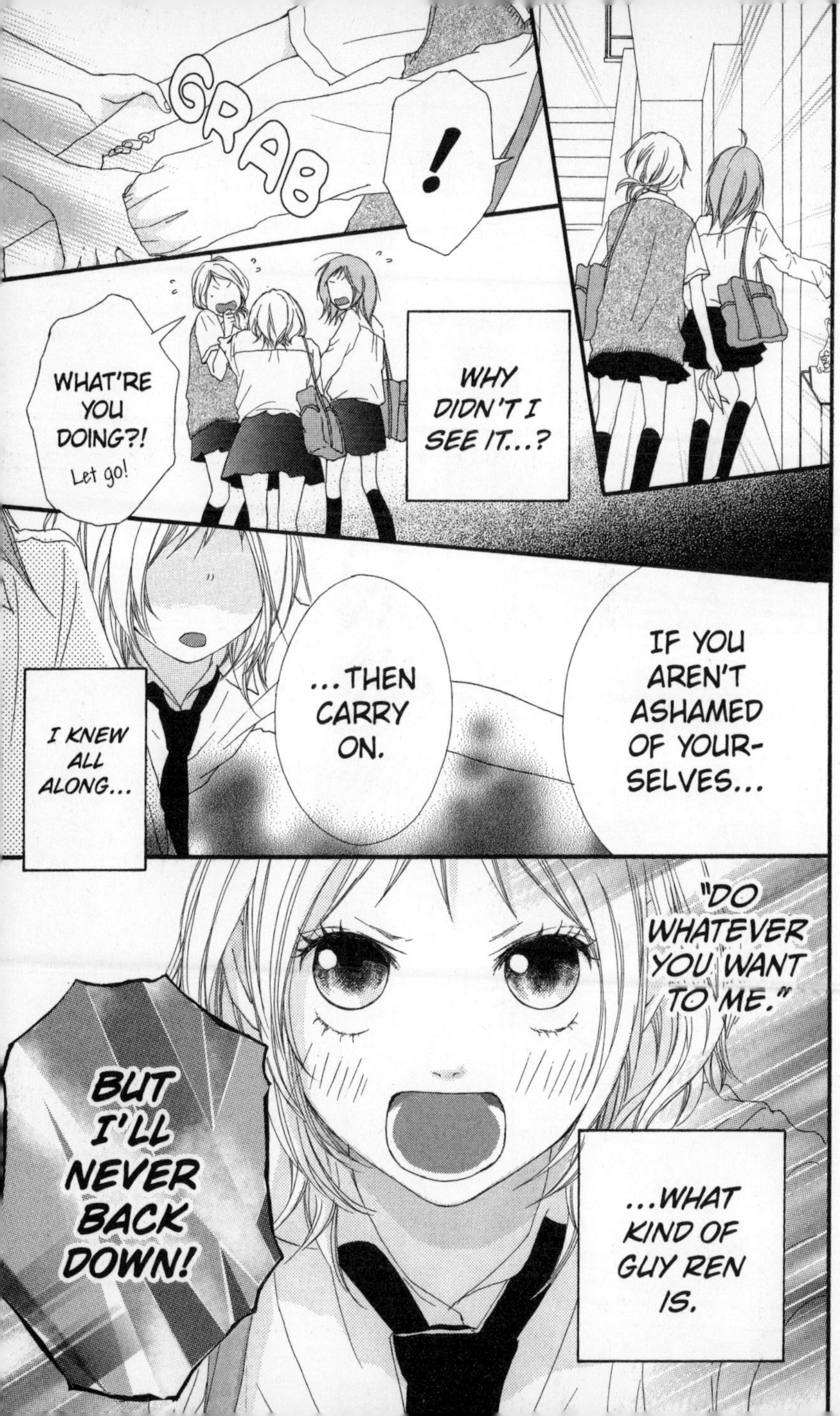
GRAB
!
WHY DIDN'T I SEE IT...?
WHAT'RE YOU DOING?! Let go!
IF YOU AREN'T ASHAMED OF YOUR-SELVES...
...THEN CARRY ON.
I KNEW ALL ALONG...
"DO WHATEVER YOU WANT TO ME."
...WHAT KIND OF GUY REN IS.
BUT I'LL NEVER BACK DOWN!

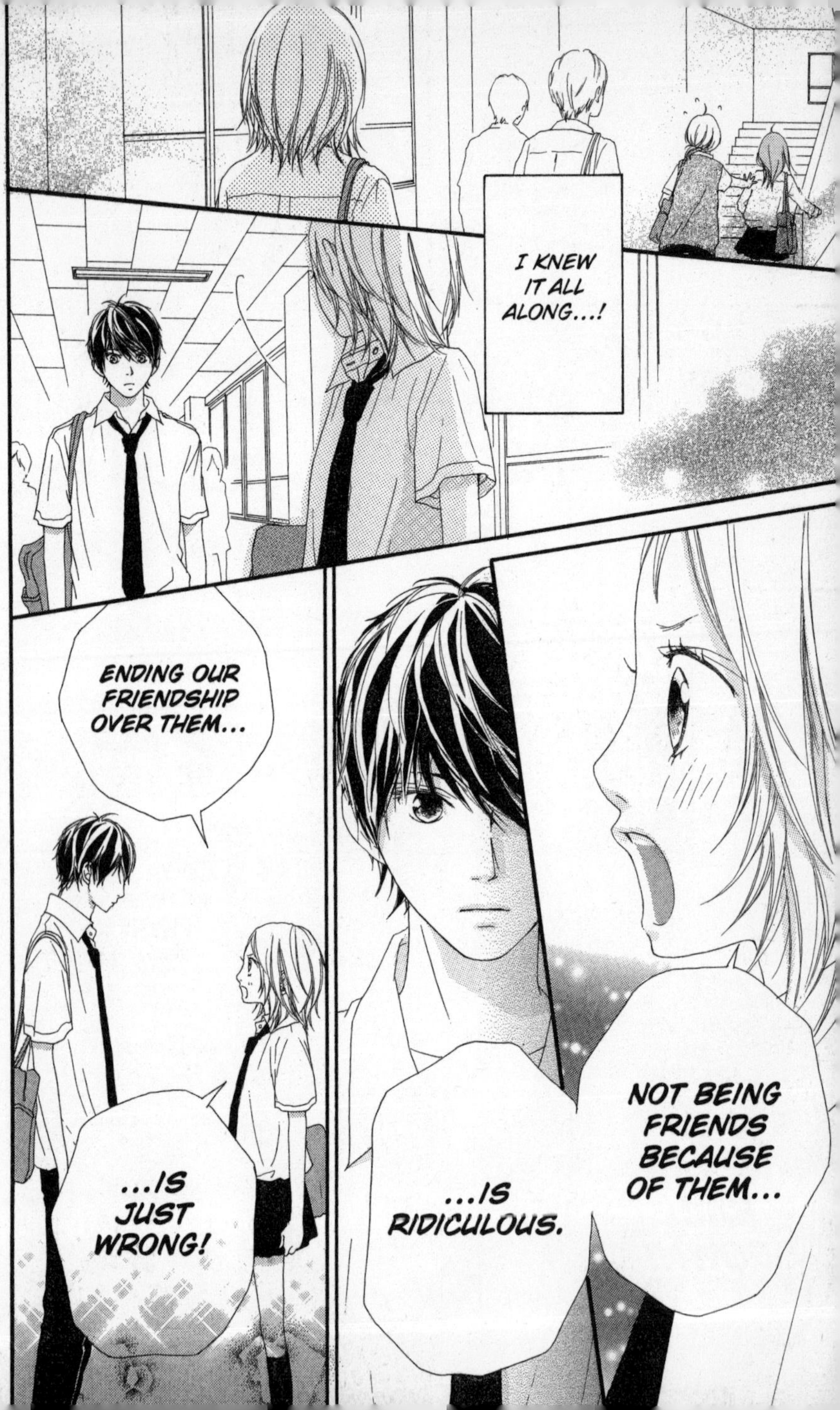
I KNEW IT ALL ALONG...!
NOT BEING FRIENDS BECAUSE OF THEM...
...IS RIDICULOUS.
ENDING OUR FRIENDSHIP OVER THEM...
...IS JUST WRONG!

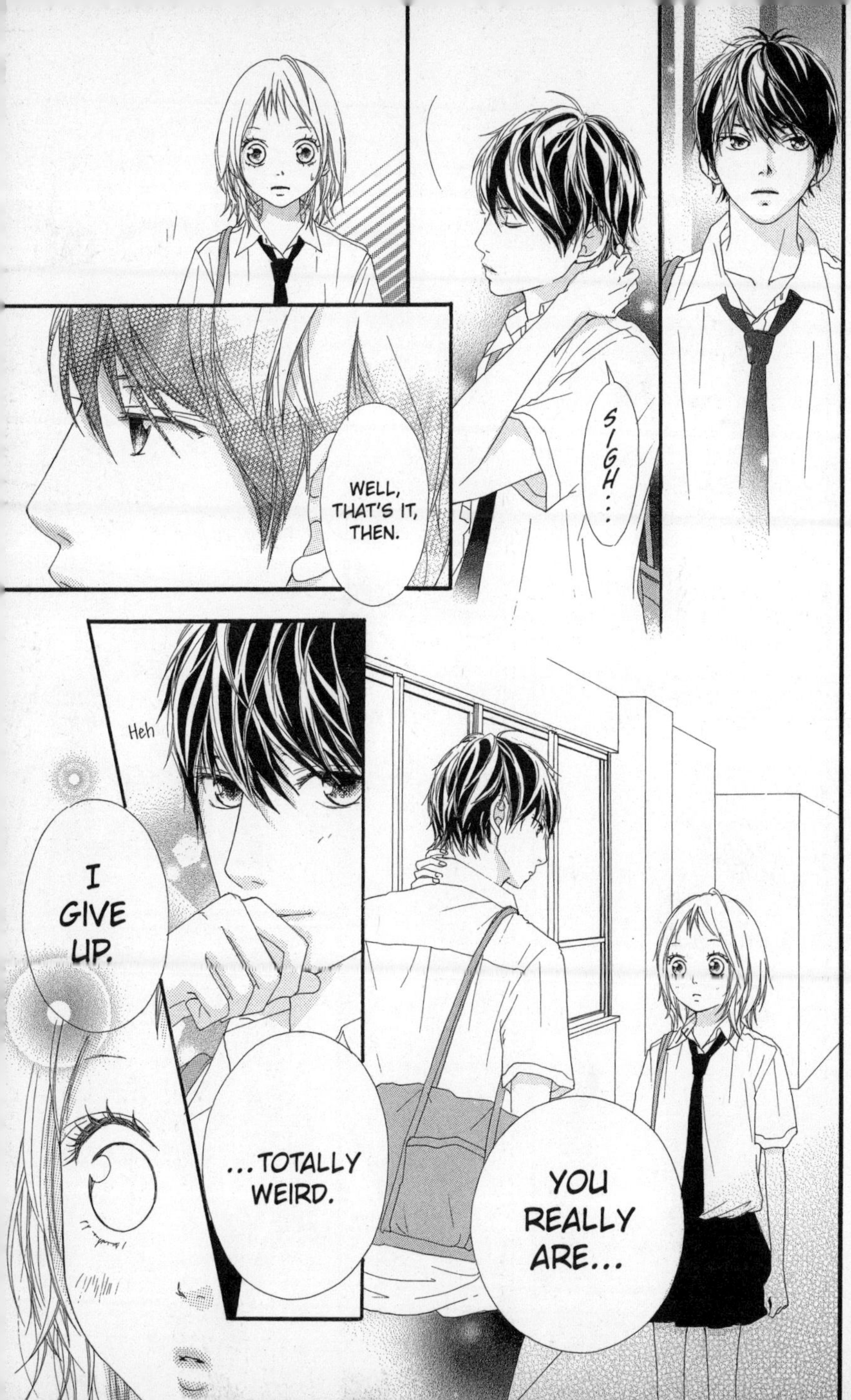
SIGH...
WELL, THAT'S IT, THEN.
YOU REALLY ARE...
...TOTALLY WEIRD.
Heh
I GIVE UP.

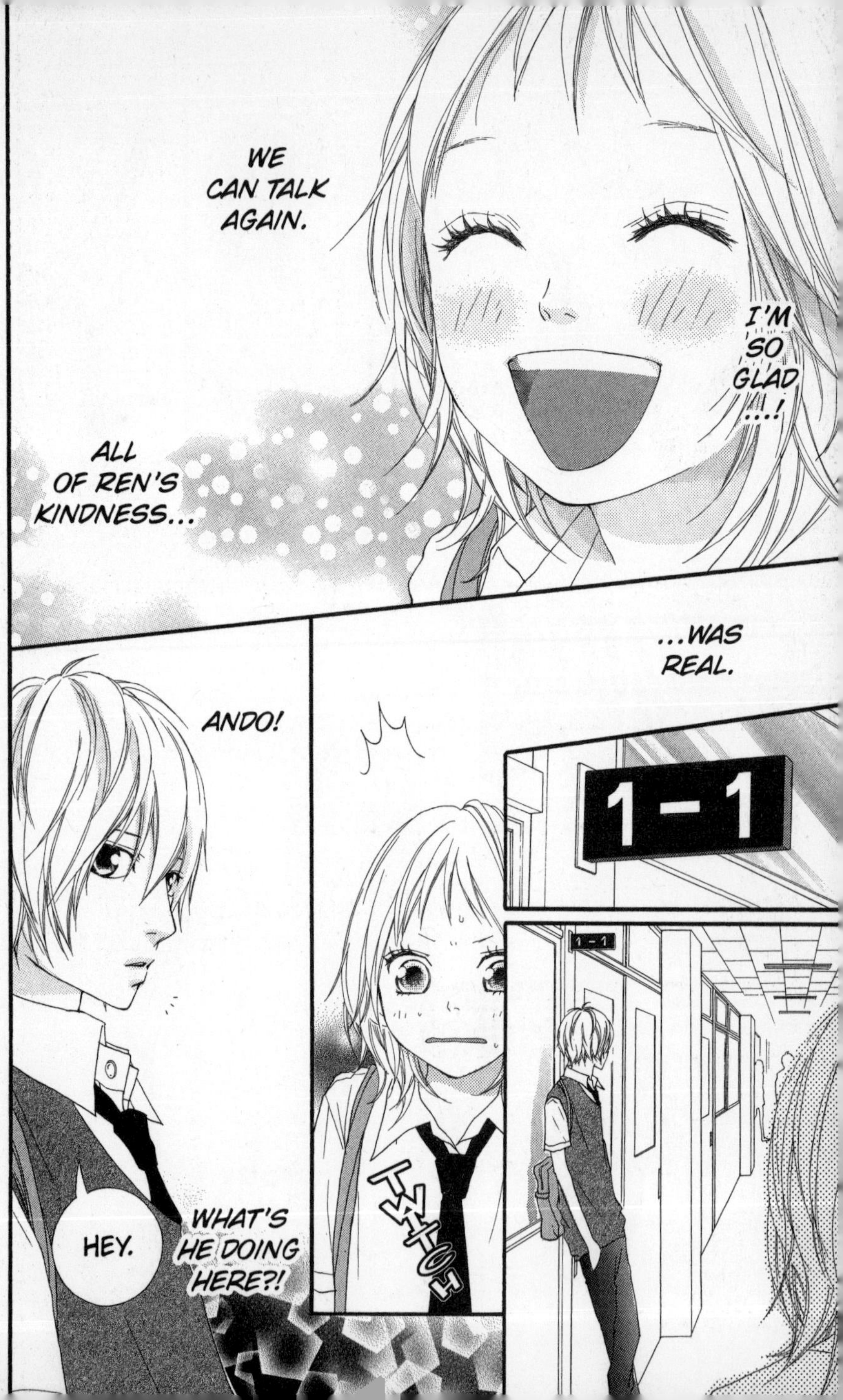
WE CAN TALK AGAIN.
I'M SO GLAD...!
ALL OF REN'S KINDNESS...
1 - 1
1 - 1
...WAS REAL.
TWITCH
ANDO!
HEY.
WHAT'S HE DOING HERE?!

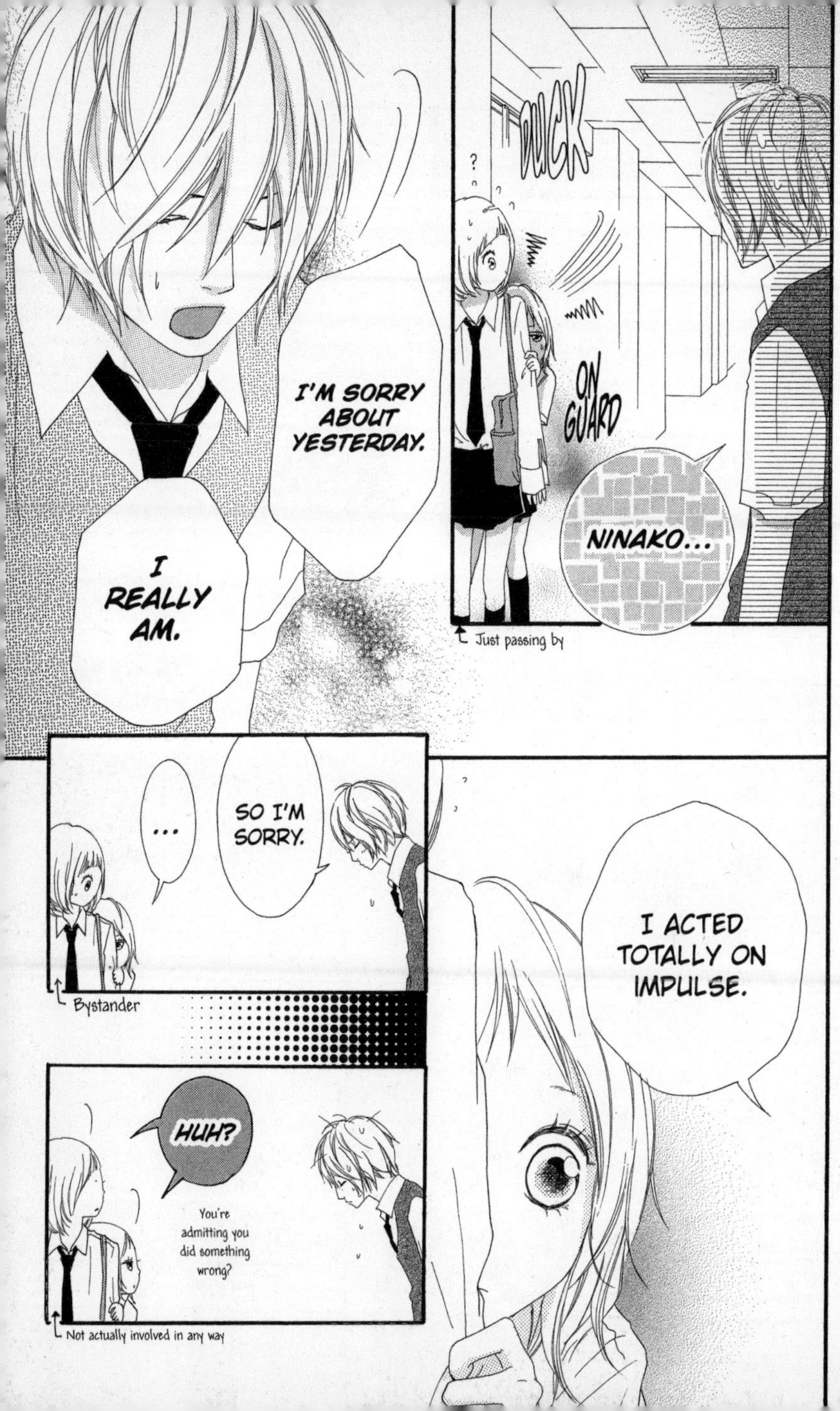
DUCK
?
WWW
WWW
ON GUARD
NINAKO...
Just passing by
I'M SORRY ABOUT YESTERDAY.
I REALLY AM.
I ACTED TOTALLY ON IMPULSE.
SO I'M SORRY.
...
Bystander
HUH?
You're admitting you did something wrong?
Not actually involved in any way

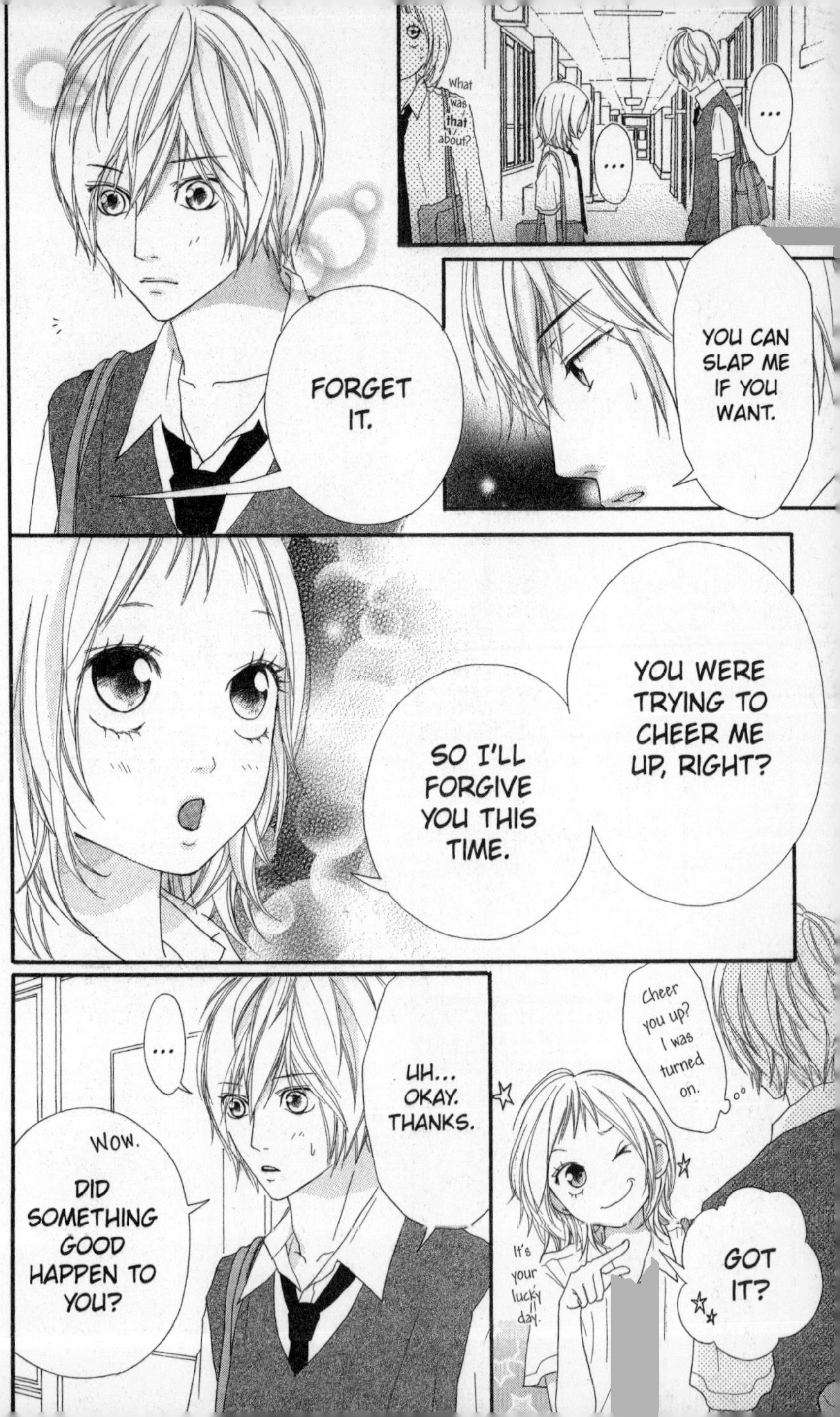
...
...
What was that about?
YOU CAN SLAP ME IF YOU WANT.
FORGET IT.
YOU WERE TRYING TO CHEER ME UP, RIGHT?
SO I'LL FORGIVE YOU THIS TIME.
Cheer you up? I was turned on.
GOT IT?
It's your lucky day.
UH... OKAY. THANKS.
...
WOW.
DID SOMETHING GOOD HAPPEN TO YOU?

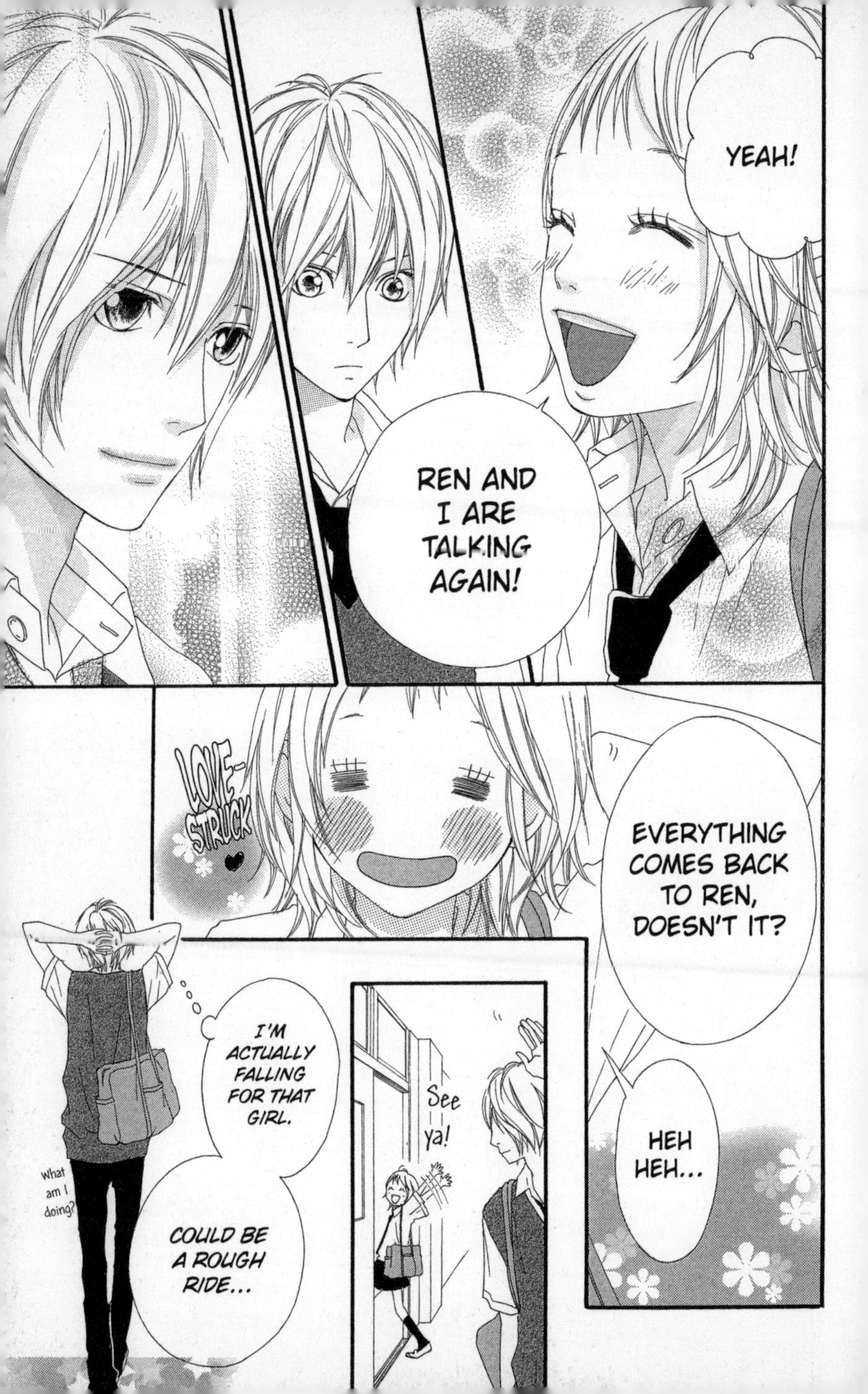

YEAH!
REN AND I ARE TALKING AGAIN!
EVERYTHING COMES BACK TO REN, DOESN'T IT?
LOVE-STRUCK
HEH HEH...
See ya!
I'M ACTUALLY FALLING FOR THAT GIRL.
COULD BE A ROUGH RIDE...
What am I doing?

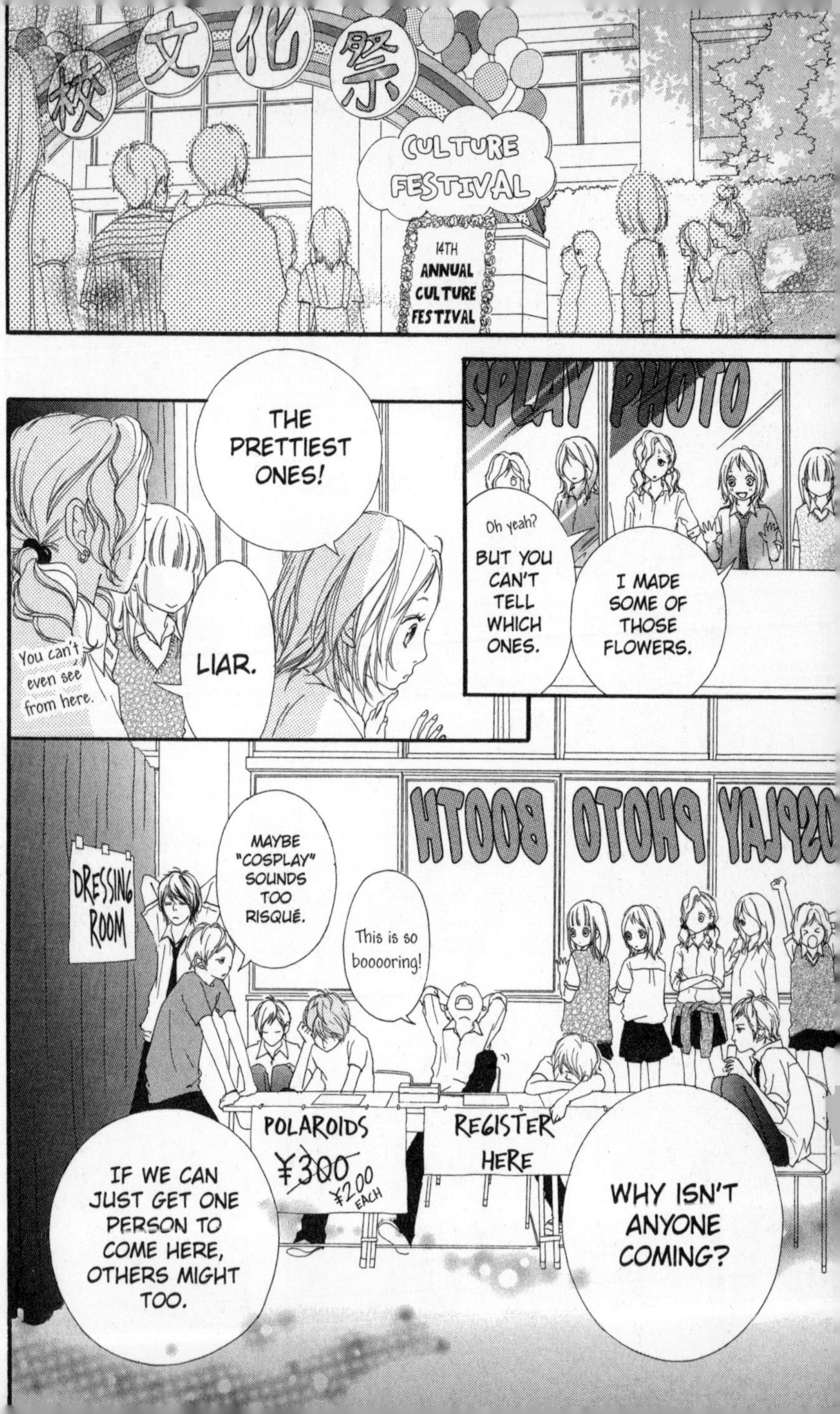

文化祭
CULTURE FESTIVAL
14TH ANNUAL CULTURE FESTIVAL
SPLAY PHOTO
I MADE SOME OF THOSE FLOWERS.
Oh yeah?
BUT YOU CAN'T TELL WHICH ONES.
THE PRETTIEST ONES!
LIAR.
You can't even see from here.
WHY ISN'T ANYONE COMING?
REGISTER HERE
POLAROIDS ¥300 ¥200 EACH
This is so booooring!
MAYBE "COSPLAY" SOUNDS TOO RISQUÉ.
DRESSING ROOM
IF WE CAN JUST GET ONE PERSON TO COME HERE, OTHERS MIGHT TOO.

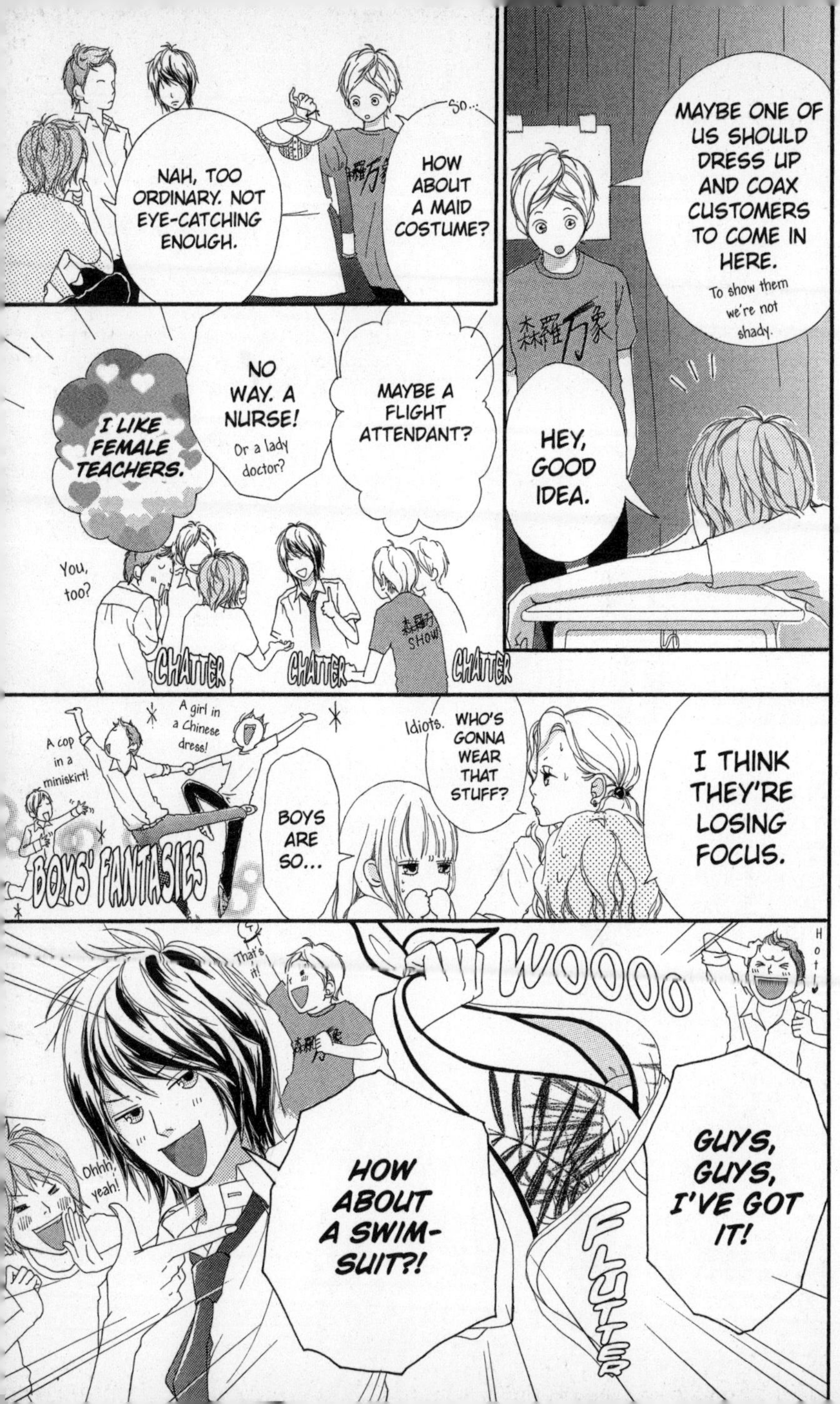
MAYBE ONE OF US SHOULD DRESS UP AND COAX CUSTOMERS TO COME IN HERE.
To show them we're not shady.
HEY, GOOD IDEA.
So...
HOW ABOUT A MAID COSTUME?
NAH, TOO ORDINARY. NOT EYE-CATCHING ENOUGH.
MAYBE A FLIGHT ATTENDANT?
NO WAY. A NURSE!
Or a lady doctor?
I LIKE FEMALE TEACHERS.
You, too?
CHATTER
CHATTER
CHATTER
I THINK THEY'RE LOSING FOCUS.
WHO'S GONNA WEAR THAT STUFF?
Idiots.
BOYS ARE SO...
A girl in a Chinese dress!
A cop in a miniskirt!
BOYS' FANTASIES
GUYS, GUYS, I'VE GOT IT!
Hot!
WOOOO
FLUTTER
HOW ABOUT A SWIMSUIT?!
That's it!
Ohhh, yeah!

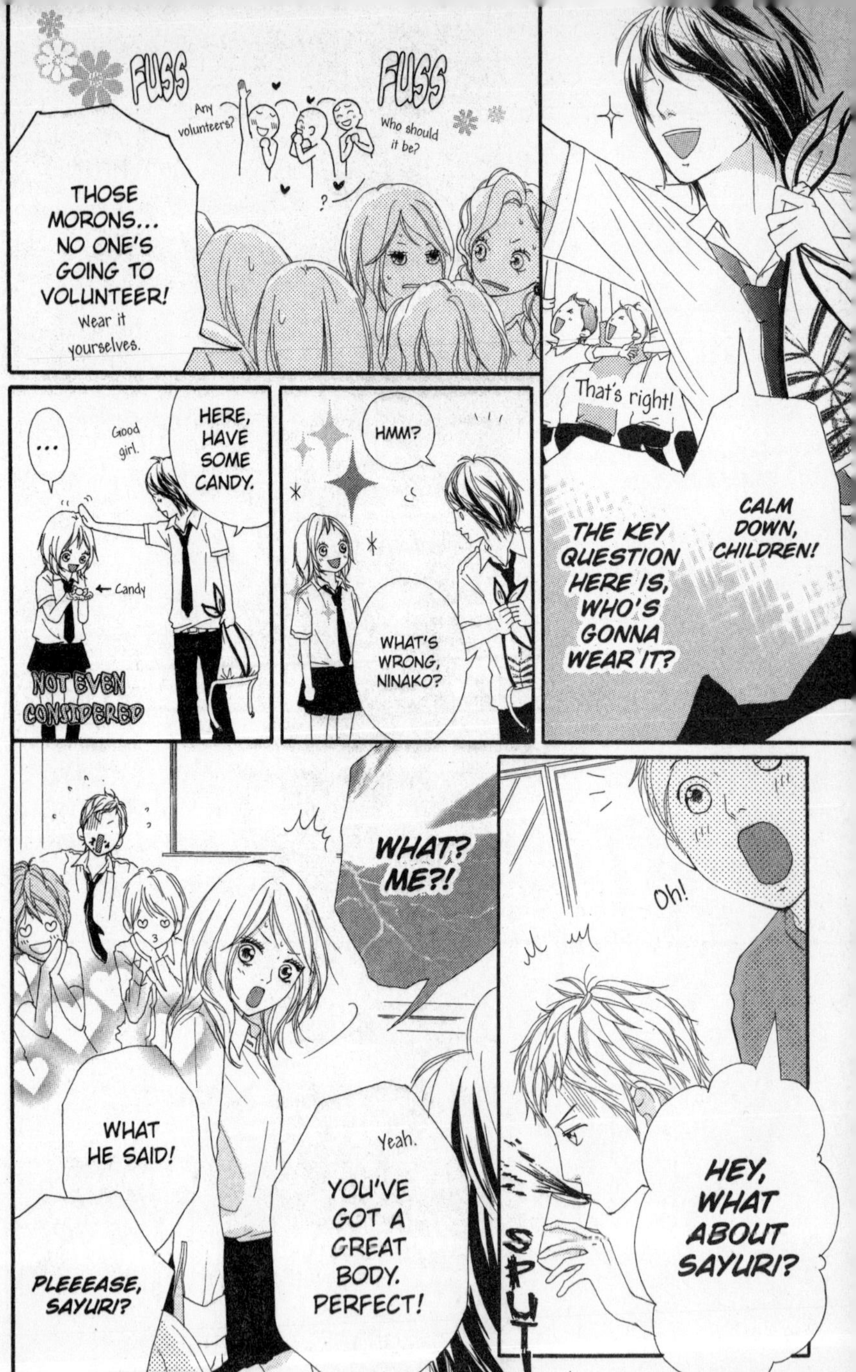
CALM DOWN, CHILDREN!
THE KEY QUESTION HERE IS, WHO'S GONNA WEAR IT?
That's right!
FUSS
Who should it be?
Any volunteers?
FUSS
THOSE MORONS... NO ONE'S GOING TO VOLUNTEER!
Wear it yourselves.
HMM?
WHAT'S WRONG, NINAKO?
HERE, HAVE SOME CANDY.
Good girl.
...
Candy
NOT EVEN CONSIDERED
Oh!
HEY, WHAT ABOUT SAYURI?
SPUT!
WHAT? ME?!
Yeah.
YOU'VE GOT A GREAT BODY. PERFECT!
WHAT HE SAID!
PLEEEASE, SAYURI?

PLEASE! (ALL IN A ROW)

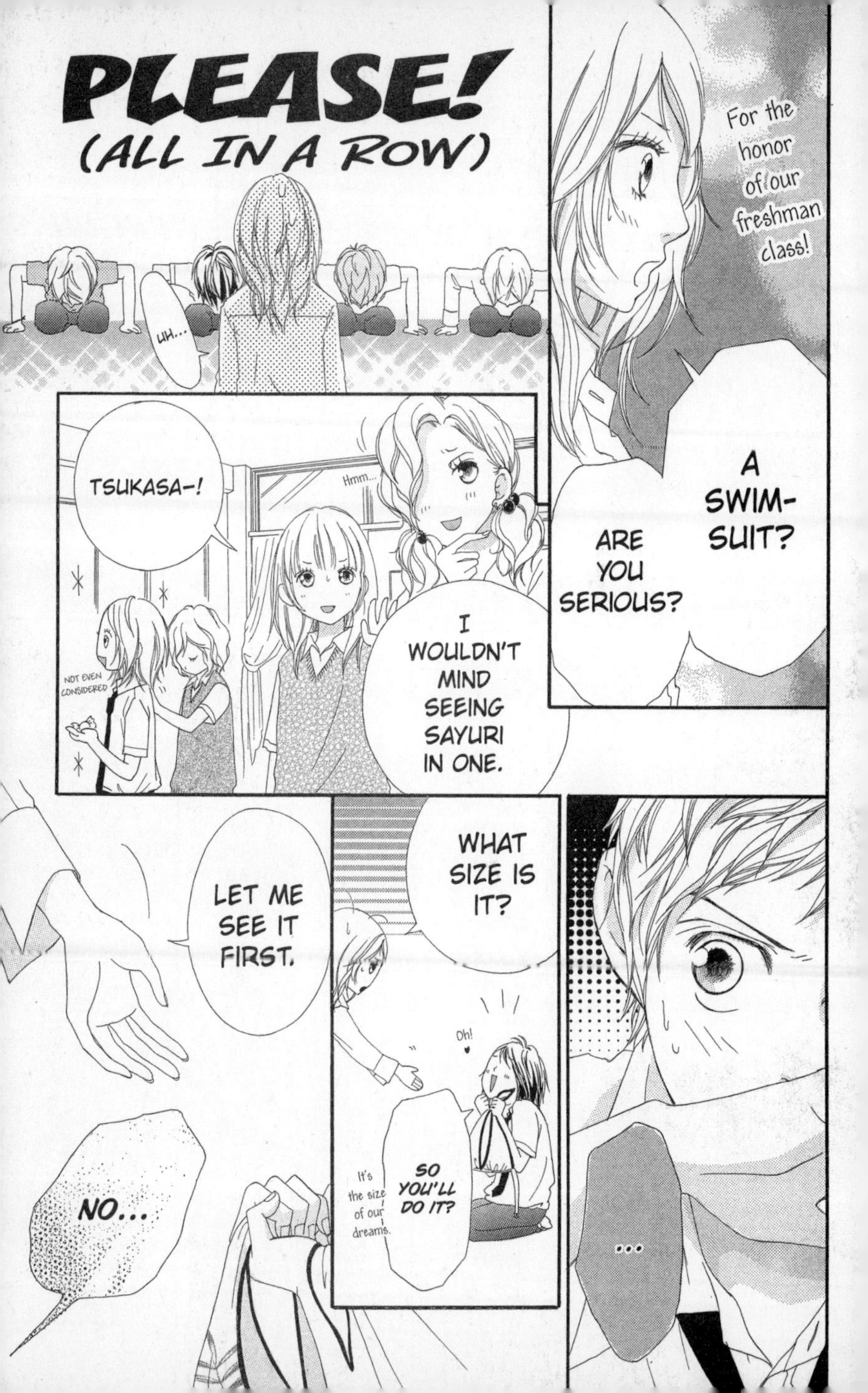

For the honor of our freshman class!
A SWIM-SUIT? ARE YOU SERIOUS?
UH...
I WOULDN'T MIND SEEING SAYURI IN ONE.
Hmm...
TSUKASA-!
NOT EVEN CONSIDERED
...
WHAT SIZE IS IT?
Oh!
SO YOU'LL DO IT?
It's the size of our dreams.
LET ME SEE IT FIRST.
NO...

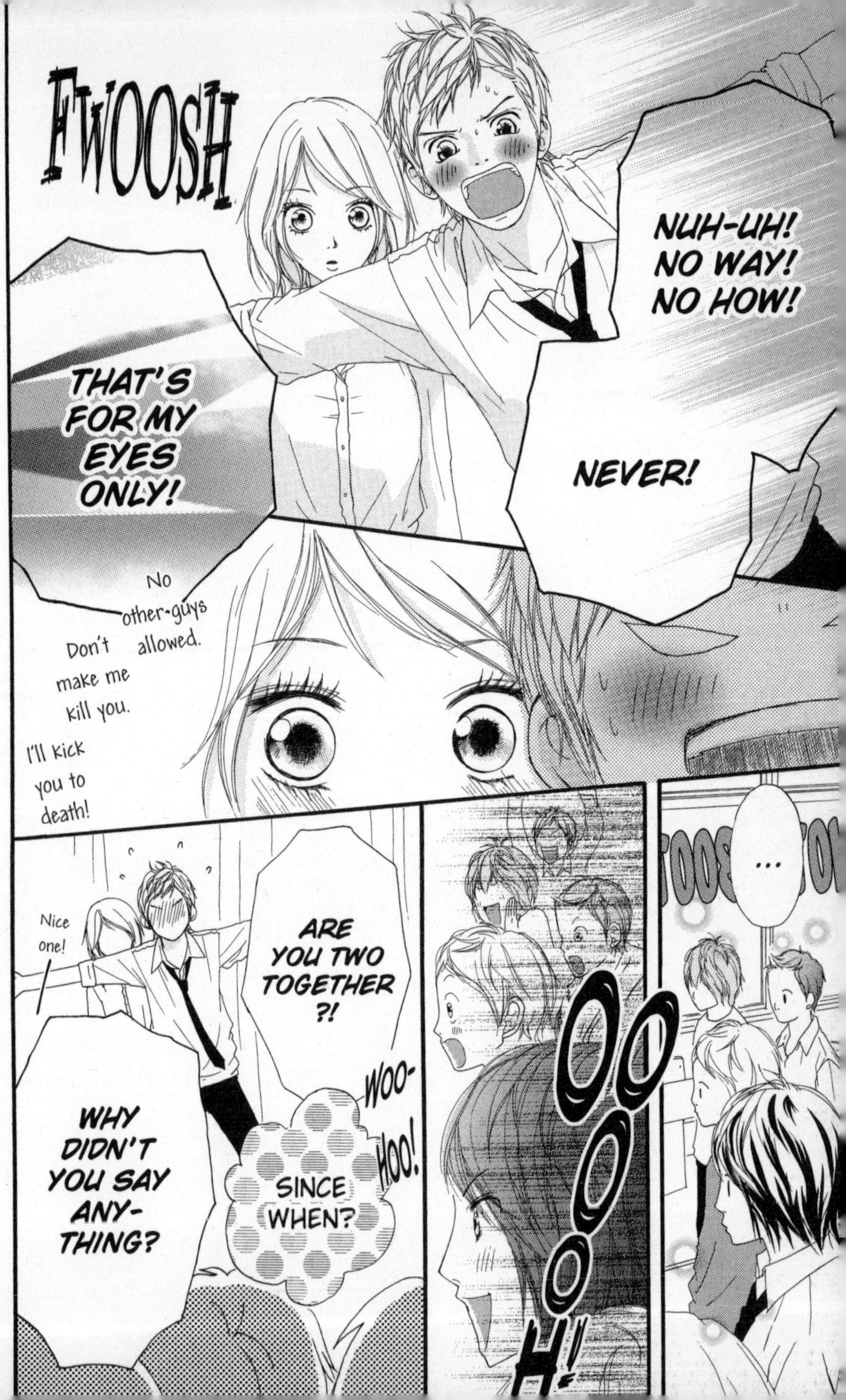
FWOOSH
NUH-UH! NO WAY! NO HOW!
NEVER!
THAT'S FOR MY EYES ONLY!
No other-guys allowed.
Don't make me kill you.
I'll kick you to death!
...
OOOOOOH!
ARE YOU TWO TOGETHER?!
WOO-HOO!
SINCE WHEN?
WHY DIDN'T YOU SAY ANY-THING?
Nice one!

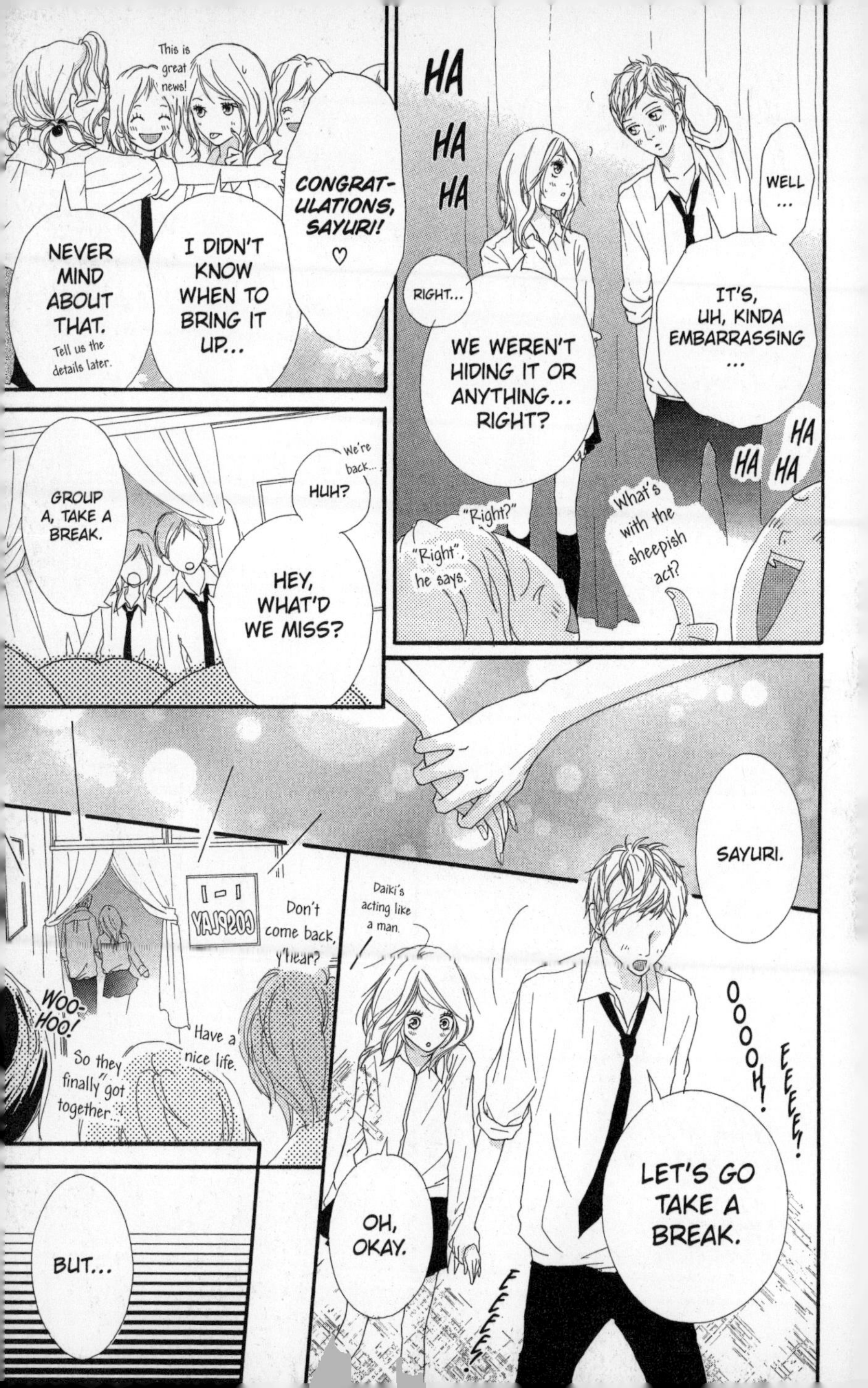
WELL...
IT'S, UH, KINDA EMBARRASSING...
HA HA HA
RIGHT...
WE WEREN'T HIDING IT OR ANYTHING... RIGHT?
HA HA HA
What's with the sheepish act?
"Right?"
"Right", he says.
CONGRAT-ULATIONS, SAYURI! ♡
This is great news!
I DIDN'T KNOW WHEN TO BRING IT UP...
NEVER MIND ABOUT THAT.
Tell us the details later.
We're back...
HUH?
HEY, WHAT'D WE MISS?
GROUP A, TAKE A BREAK.
SAYURI.
OOOOH!
EEEEE!
LET'S GO TAKE A BREAK.
Daiki's acting like a man.
OH, OKAY.
EEEEE.
Don't come back, y'hear?
COSPLAY
Have a nice life.
WOO-HOO!
So they finally got together...
BUT...

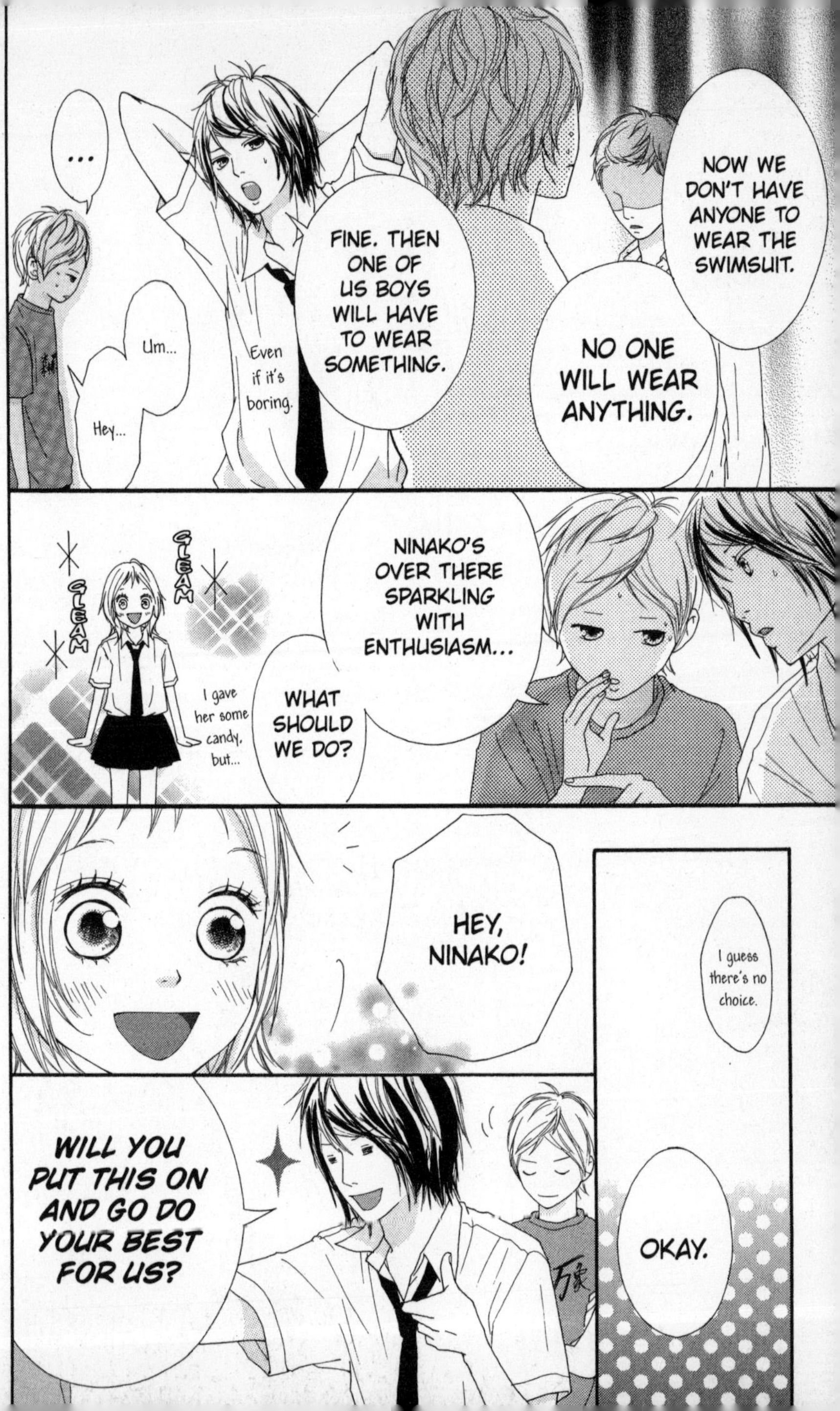
NOW WE DON'T HAVE ANYONE TO WEAR THE SWIMSUIT.
NO ONE WILL WEAR ANYTHING.
FINE. THEN ONE OF US BOYS WILL HAVE TO WEAR SOMETHING.
Even if it's boring.
Um... Hey...
...
NINAKO'S OVER THERE SPARKLING WITH ENTHUSIASM...
WHAT SHOULD WE DO?
I gave her some candy, but...
GLEAM
GLEAM
I guess there's no choice.
OKAY.
HEY, NINAKO!
WILL YOU PUT THIS ON AND GO DO YOUR BEST FOR US?

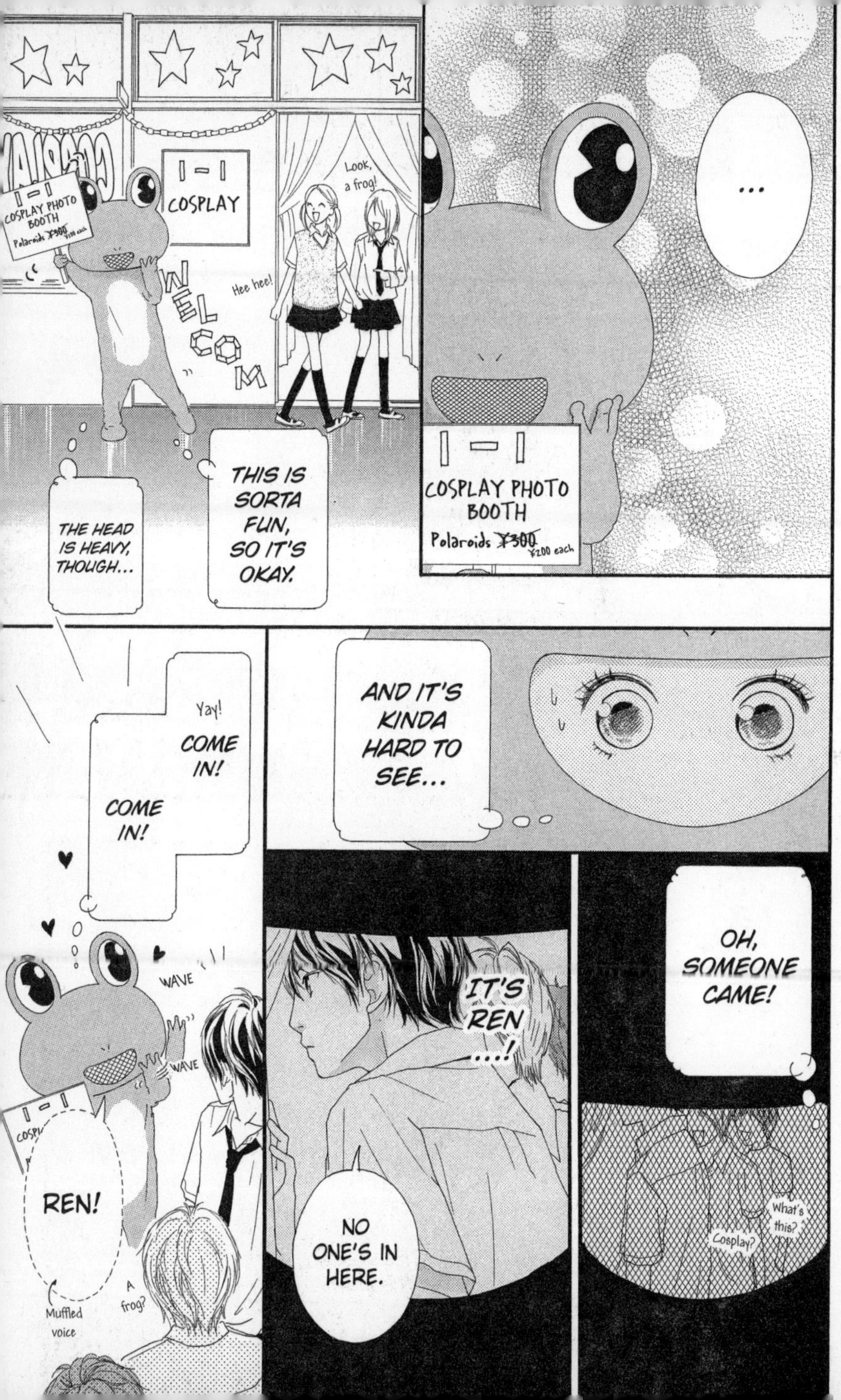
...
1-1
COSPLAY PHOTO BOOTH
Polaroids ¥300 ¥200 each
1-1
COSPLAY PHOTO BOOTH
Polaroids ¥300 ¥200 each
1-1
COSPLAY
WELCOM
Look, a frog!
Hee hee!
THIS IS SORTA FUN, SO IT'S OKAY.
THE HEAD IS HEAVY, THOUGH...
AND IT'S KINDA HARD TO SEE...
OH, SOMEONE CAME!
What's this?
Cosplay?
IT'S REN...!
NO ONE'S IN HERE.
Yay! COME IN!
COME IN!
WAVE
WAVE
REN!
Muffled voice
A frog?

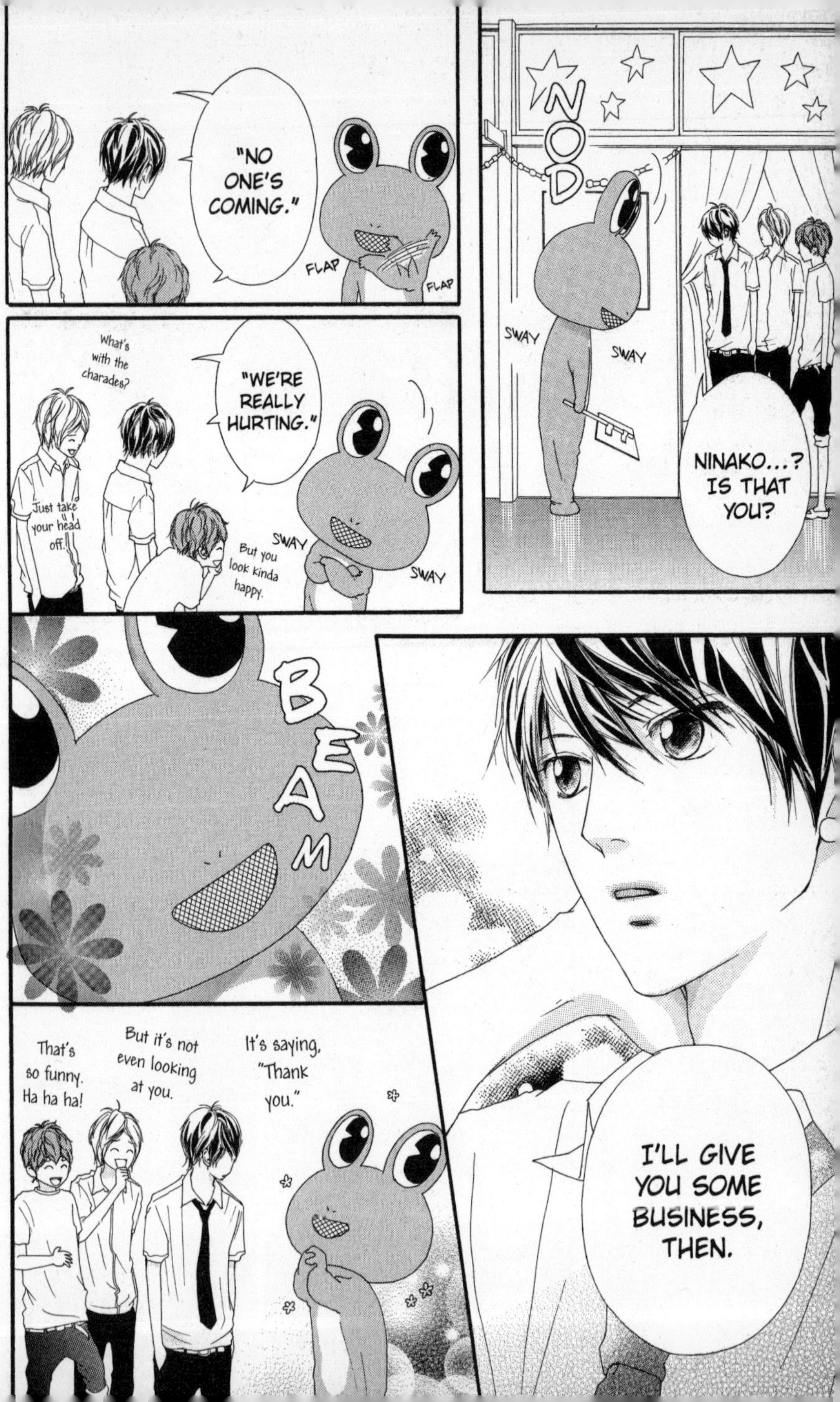
NOD
SWAY
SWAY
NINAKO...? IS THAT YOU?
"NO ONE'S COMING."
FLAP
FLAP
"WE'RE REALLY HURTING."
What's with the charades?
SWAY
SWAY
But you look kinda happy.
Just take your head off.
I'LL GIVE YOU SOME BUSINESS, THEN.
BEAM
It's saying, "Thank you."
But it's not even looking at you.
That's so funny. Ha ha ha!

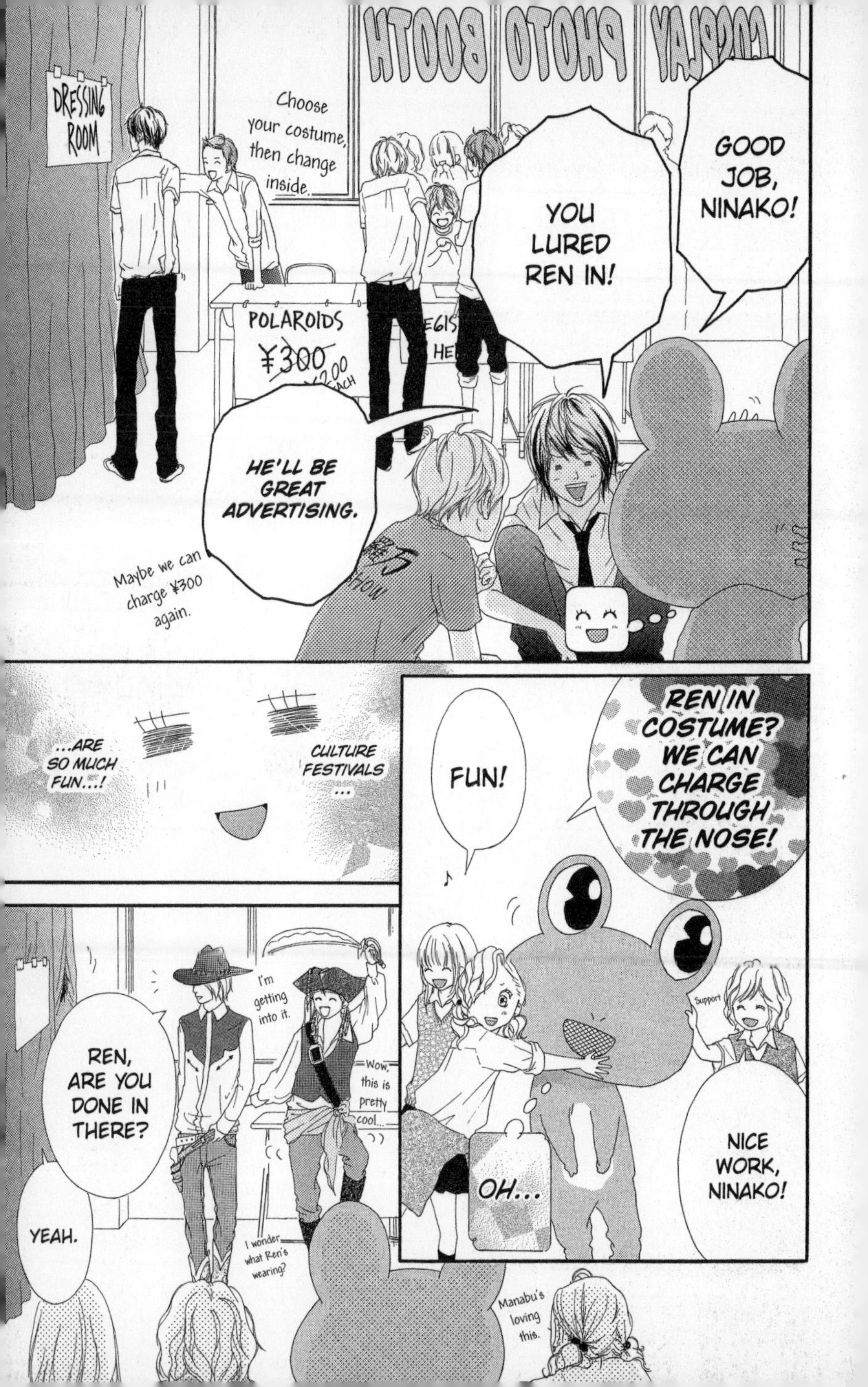
COSPLAY PHOTO BOOTH
GOOD JOB, NINAKO!
YOU LURED REN IN!
DRESSING ROOM
Choose your costume, then change inside.
POLAROIDS
¥300
¥200 EACH
HE'LL BE GREAT ADVERTISING.
Maybe we can charge ¥300 again.
REN IN COSTUME? WE CAN CHARGE THROUGH THE NOSE!
FUN!
Support
NICE WORK, NINAKO!
OH...
CULTURE FESTIVALS...
...ARE SO MUCH FUN...!
I'm getting into it.
Wow, this is pretty cool...
REN, ARE YOU DONE IN THERE?
YEAH.
I wonder what Ren's wearing?
Manabu's loving this.

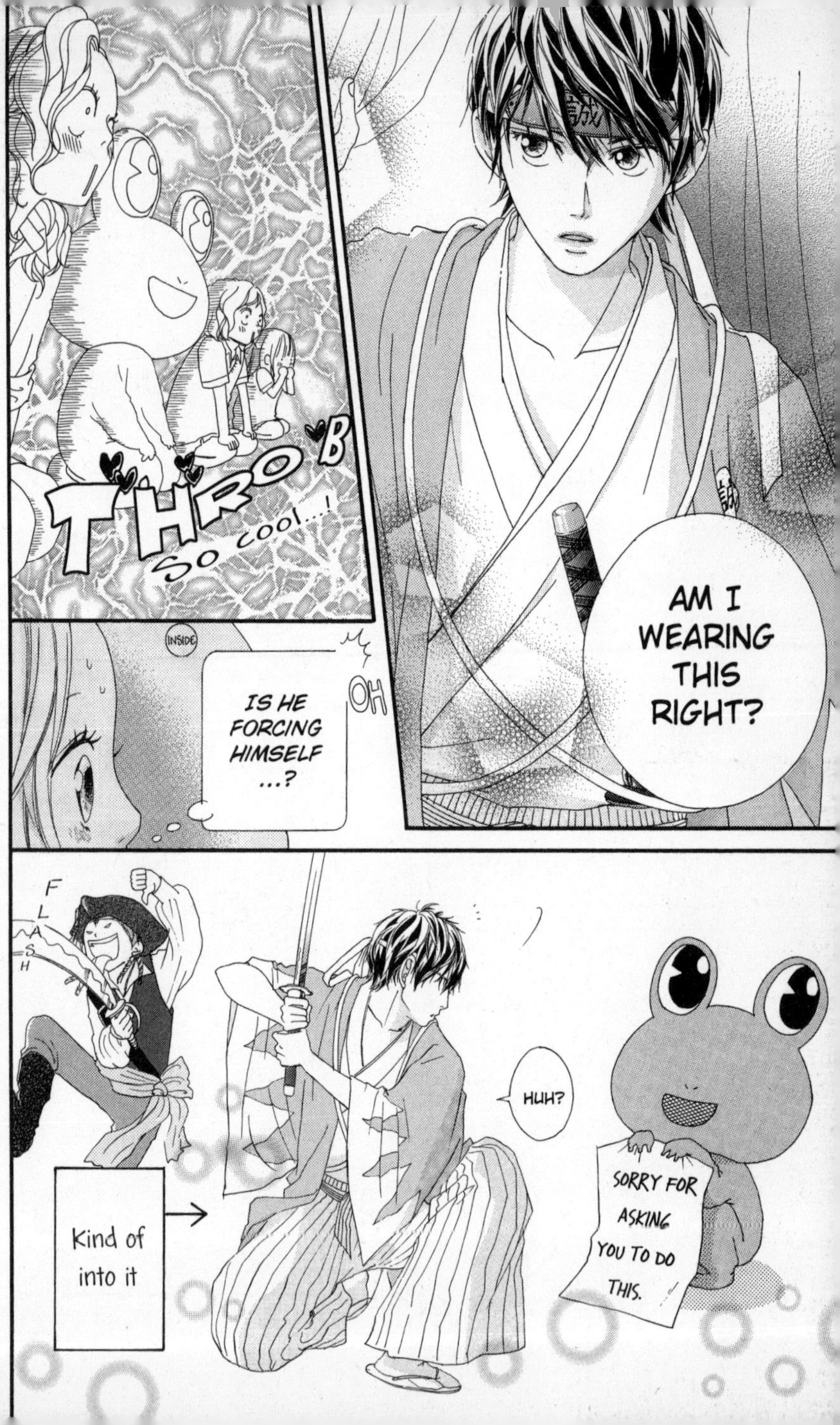
AM I WEARING THIS RIGHT?
THROB
So cool...!
INSIDE
IS HE FORCING HIMSELF ...?
OH
HUH?
SORRY FOR ASKING YOU TO DO THIS.
Kind of into it
FLASH

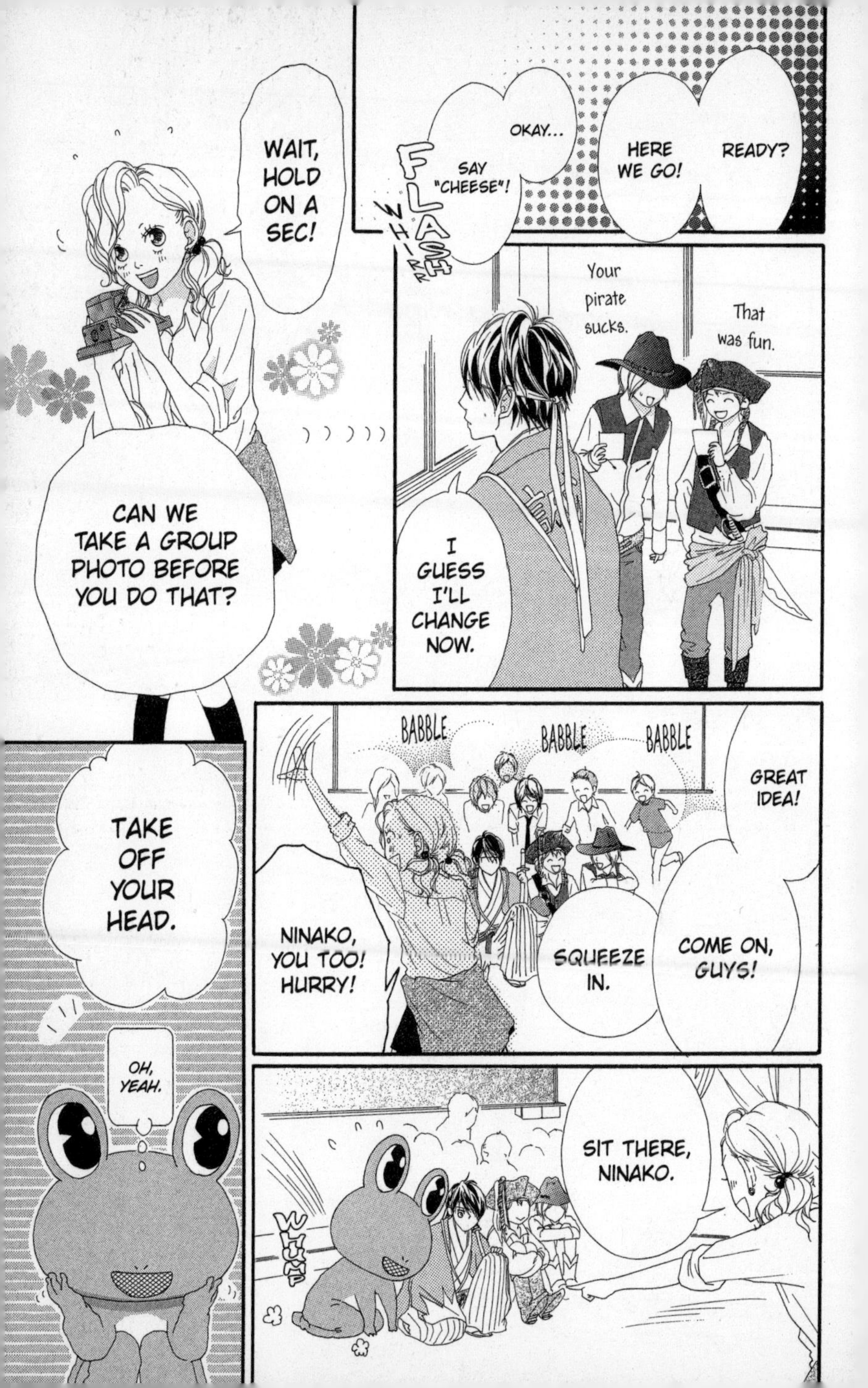
READY?
HERE WE GO!
OKAY...
SAY "CHEESE"!
FLASH
WHIRR
That was fun.
Your pirate sucks.
I GUESS I'LL CHANGE NOW.
WAIT, HOLD ON A SEC!
CAN WE TAKE A GROUP PHOTO BEFORE YOU DO THAT?
GREAT IDEA!
BABBLE
BABBLE
BABBLE
COME ON, GUYS!
SQUEEZE IN.
NINAKO, YOU TOO! HURRY!
SIT THERE, NINAKO.
WHUMP
TAKE OFF YOUR HEAD.
OH, YEAH.

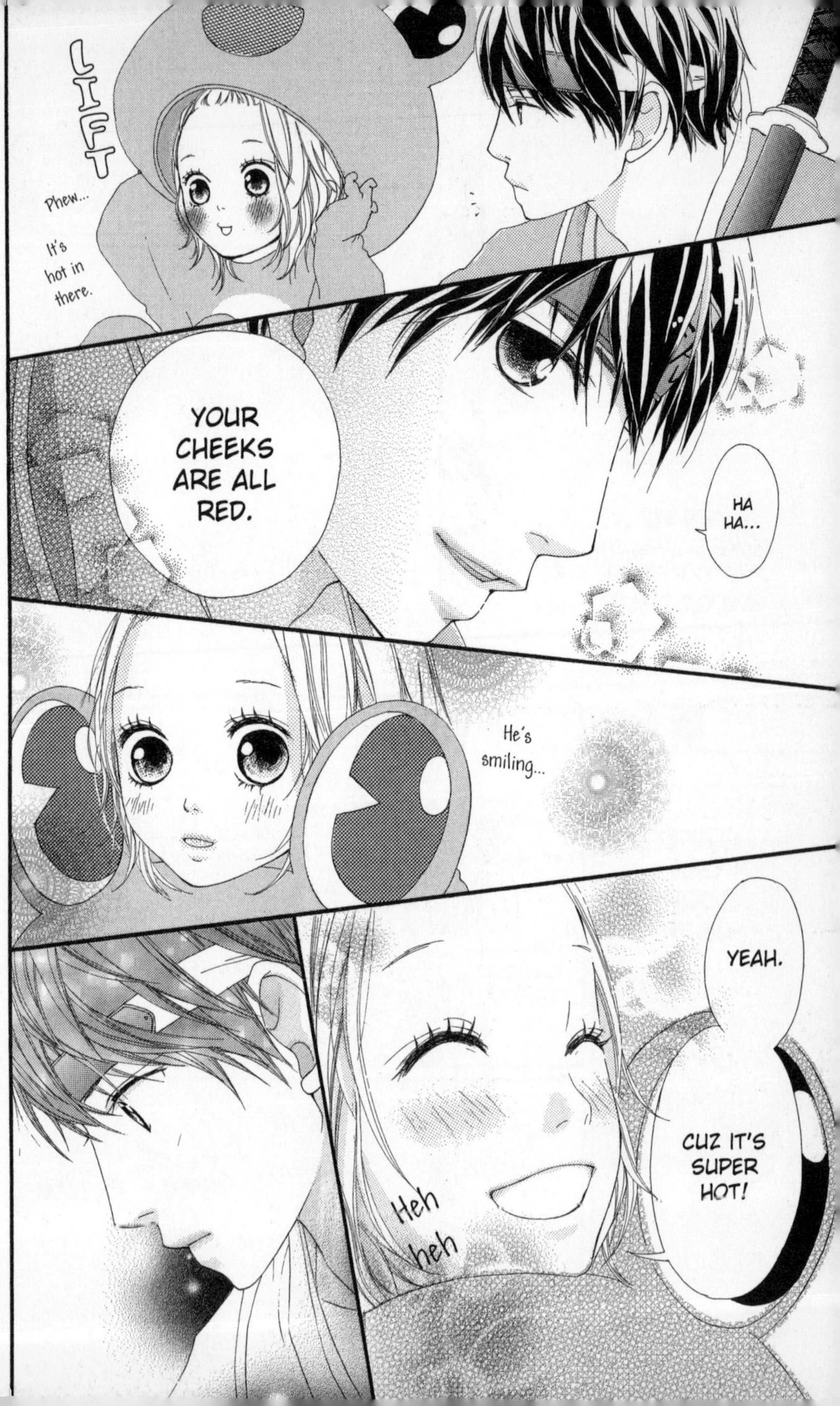
LIFT
Phew...
It's hot in there.
HA HA...
YOUR CHEEKS ARE ALL RED.
He's smiling...
YEAH.
CUZ IT'S SUPER HOT!
Heh heh

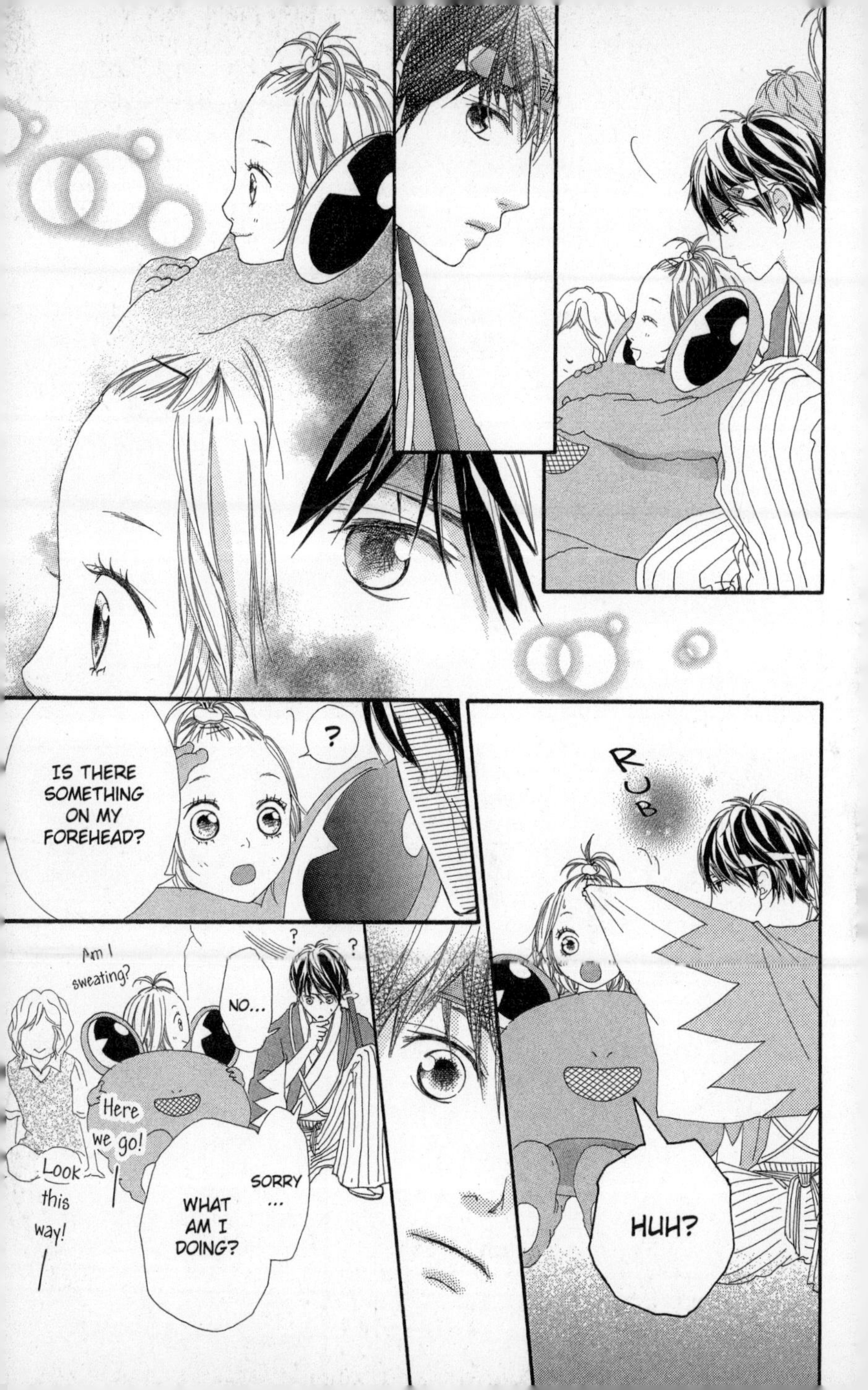
RUB
HUH?
?
IS THERE SOMETHING ON MY FOREHEAD?
NO...
Am I sweating?
Here we go!
Look this way!
SORRY ...
WHAT AM I DOING?

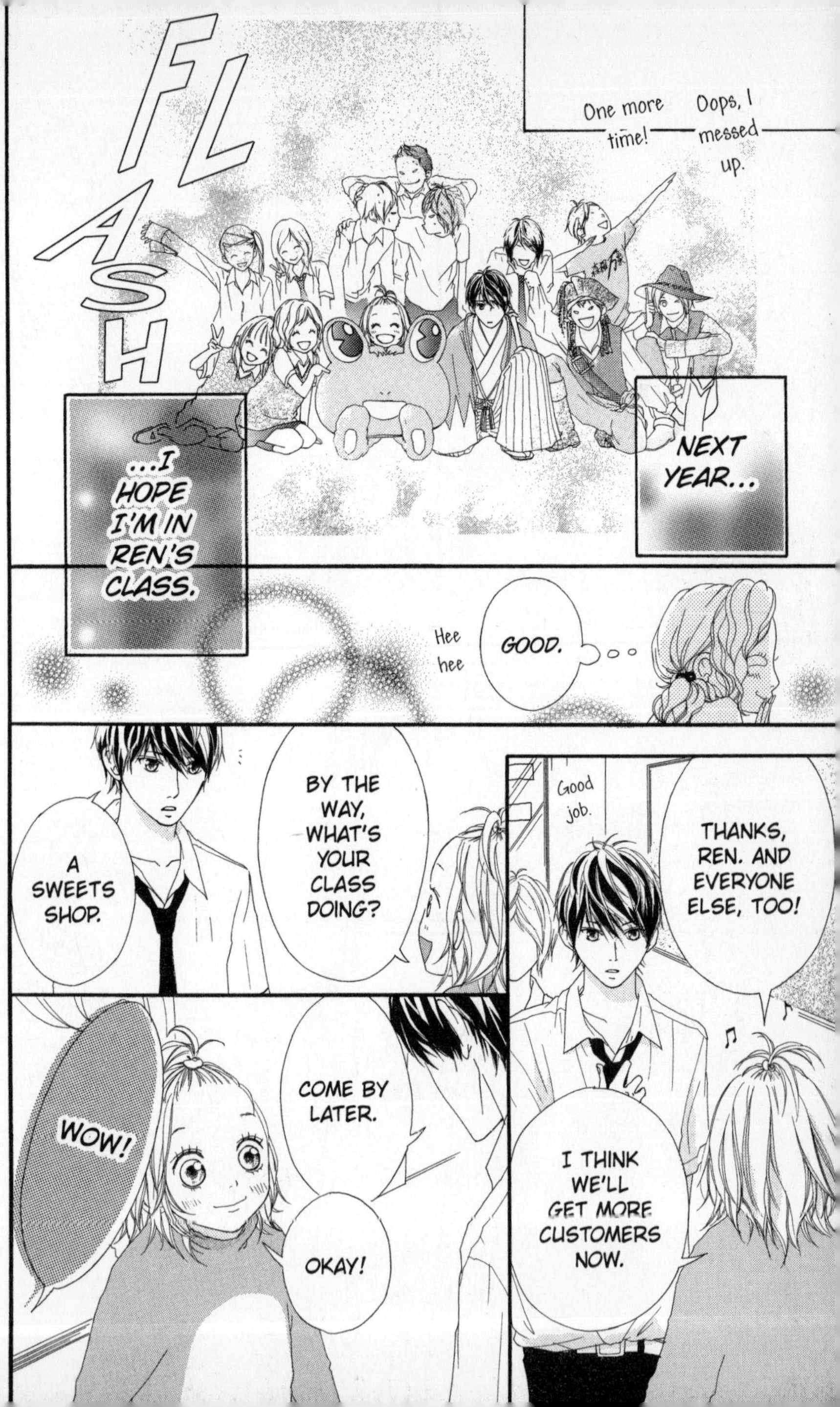
Oops, I messed up.
One more time!
FLASH
NEXT YEAR...
...I HOPE I'M IN REN'S CLASS.
GOOD.
Hee hee
THANKS, REN. AND EVERYONE ELSE, TOO!
Good job.
I THINK WE'LL GET MORE CUSTOMERS NOW.
BY THE WAY, WHAT'S YOUR CLASS DOING?
A SWEETS SHOP.
COME BY LATER.
OKAY!
WOW!

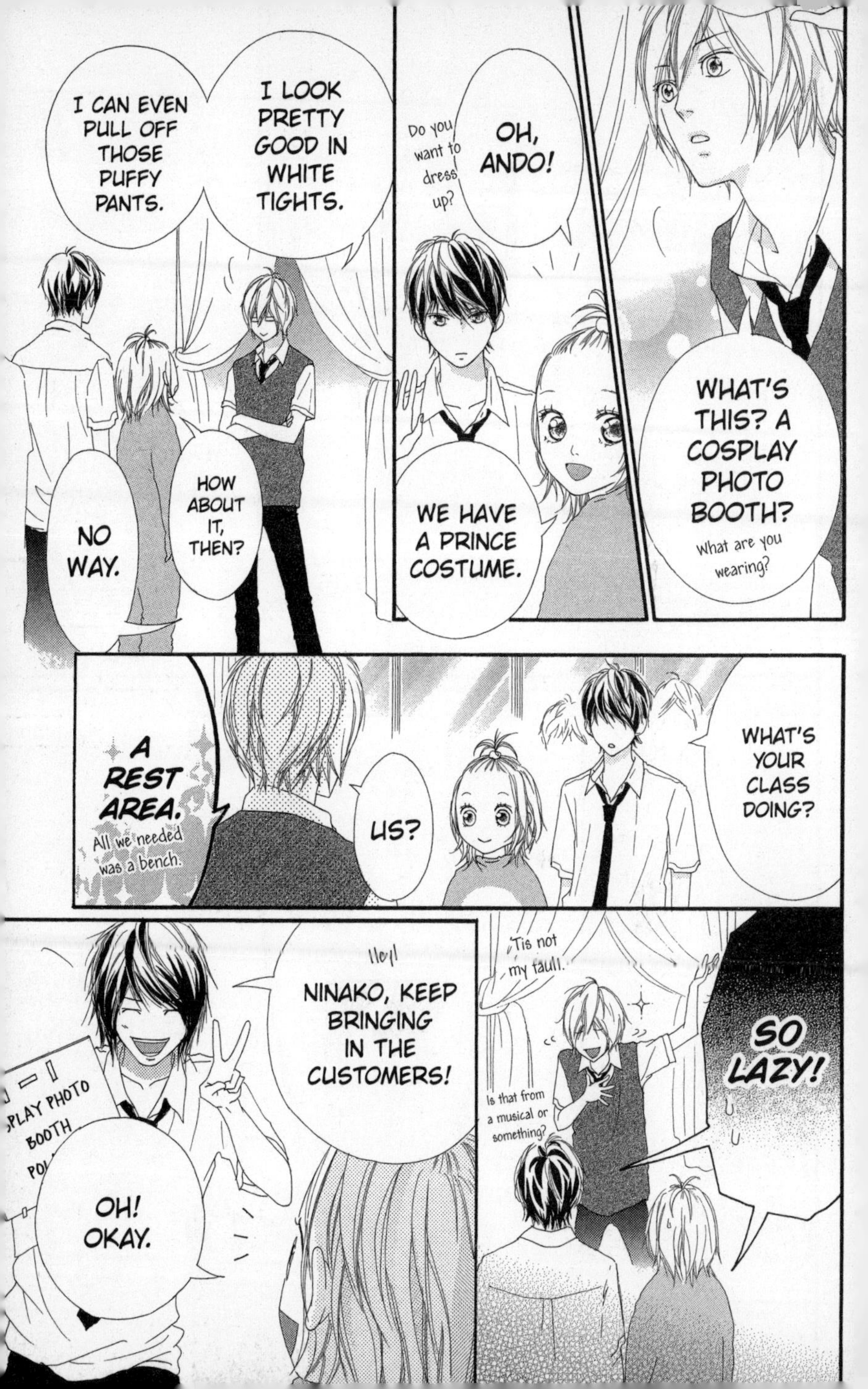
WHAT'S THIS? A COSPLAY PHOTO BOOTH?
What are you wearing?
OH, ANDO!
Do you want to dress up?
WE HAVE A PRINCE COSTUME.
I LOOK PRETTY GOOD IN WHITE TIGHTS.
I CAN EVEN PULL OFF THOSE PUFFY PANTS.
HOW ABOUT IT, THEN?
NO WAY.
WHAT'S YOUR CLASS DOING?
US?
A REST AREA.
All we needed was a bench.
'Tis not my fault.
SO LAZY!
Is that from a musical or something?
Hey!
NINAKO, KEEP BRINGING IN THE CUSTOMERS!
OH! OKAY.

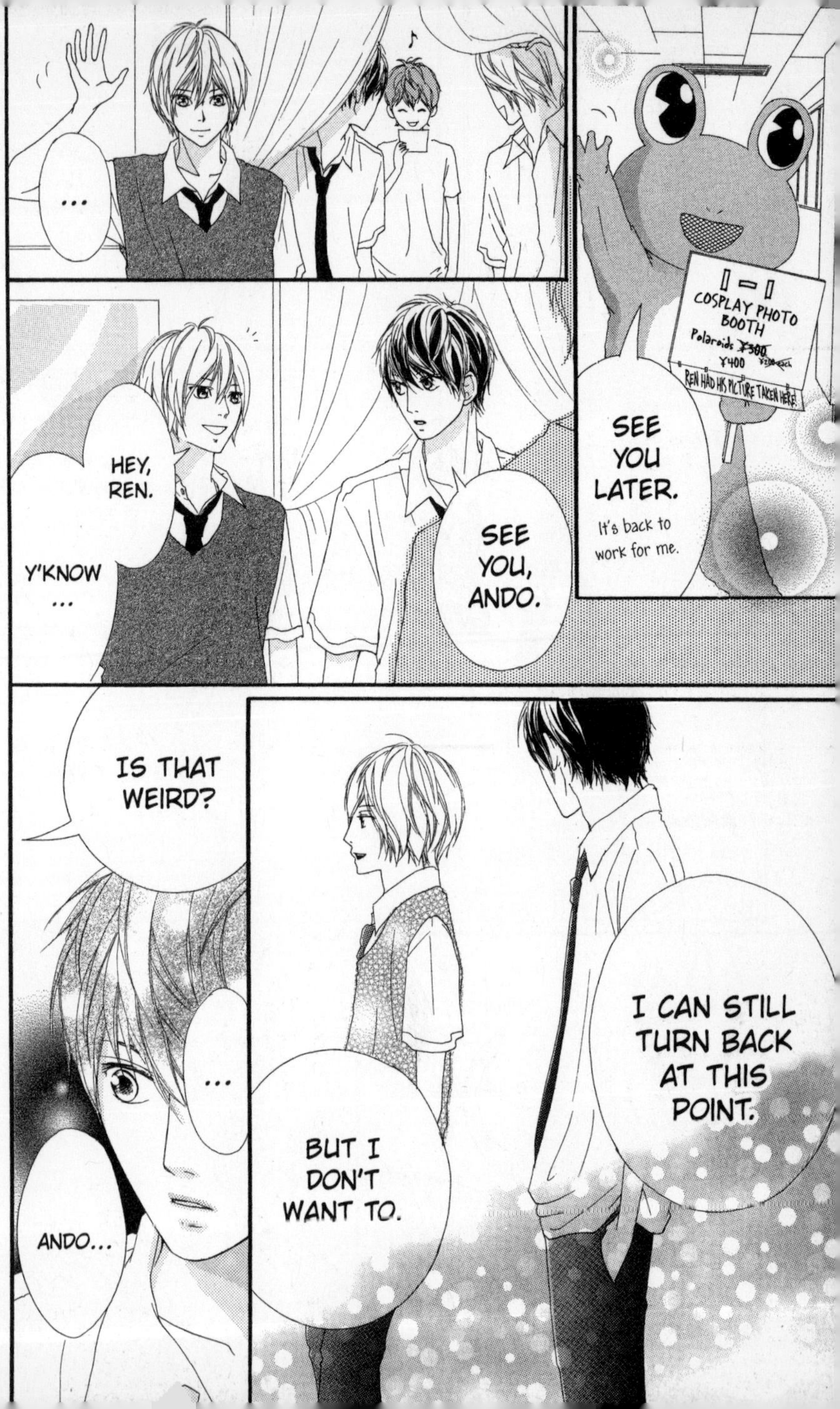
COSPLAY PHOTO BOOTH
Polaroids ¥300 ¥400 ¥200 each
REN HAD HIS PICTURE TAKEN HERE!
SEE YOU LATER.
It's back to work for me.
...
SEE YOU, ANDO.
HEY, REN.
Y'KNOW ...
I CAN STILL TURN BACK AT THIS POINT.
BUT I DON'T WANT TO.
IS THAT WEIRD?
...
ANDO...

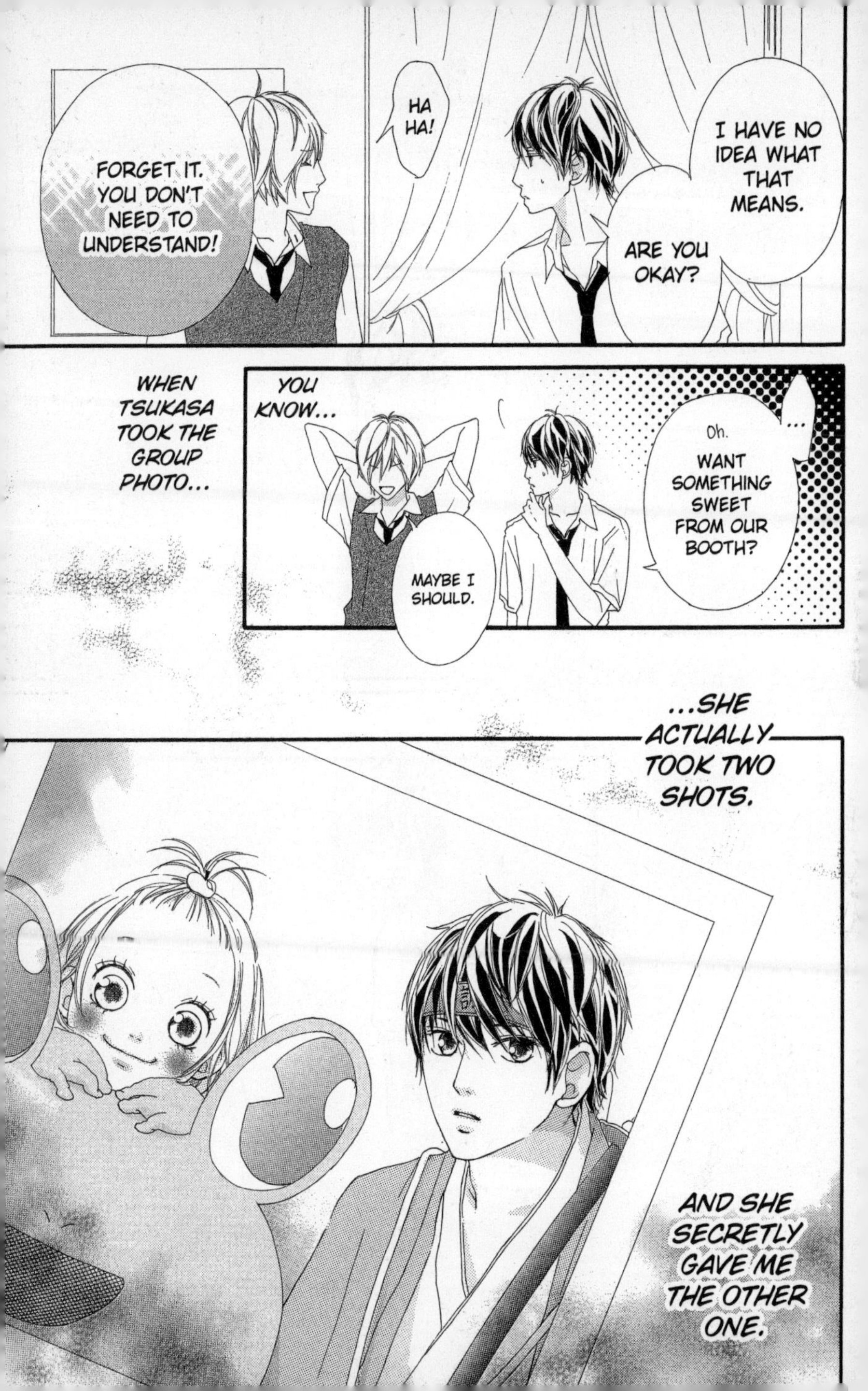
I HAVE NO IDEA WHAT THAT MEANS.
ARE YOU OKAY?
HA HA!
FORGET IT. YOU DON'T NEED TO UNDERSTAND!
...
Oh.
WANT SOMETHING SWEET FROM OUR BOOTH?
MAYBE I SHOULD.
YOU KNOW...
WHEN TSUKASA TOOK THE GROUP PHOTO...
...SHE ACTUALLY TOOK TWO SHOTS.
AND SHE SECRETLY GAVE ME THE OTHER ONE.

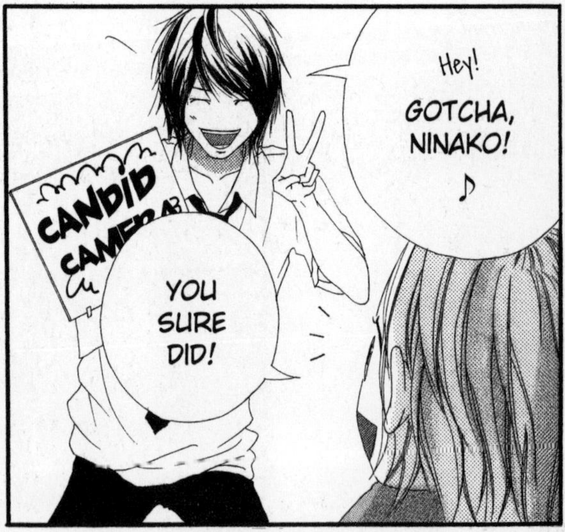
Hey!
GOTCHA, NINAKO! ♪
CANDID
YOU SURE DID!

★ Technopolice Sakisaka ★

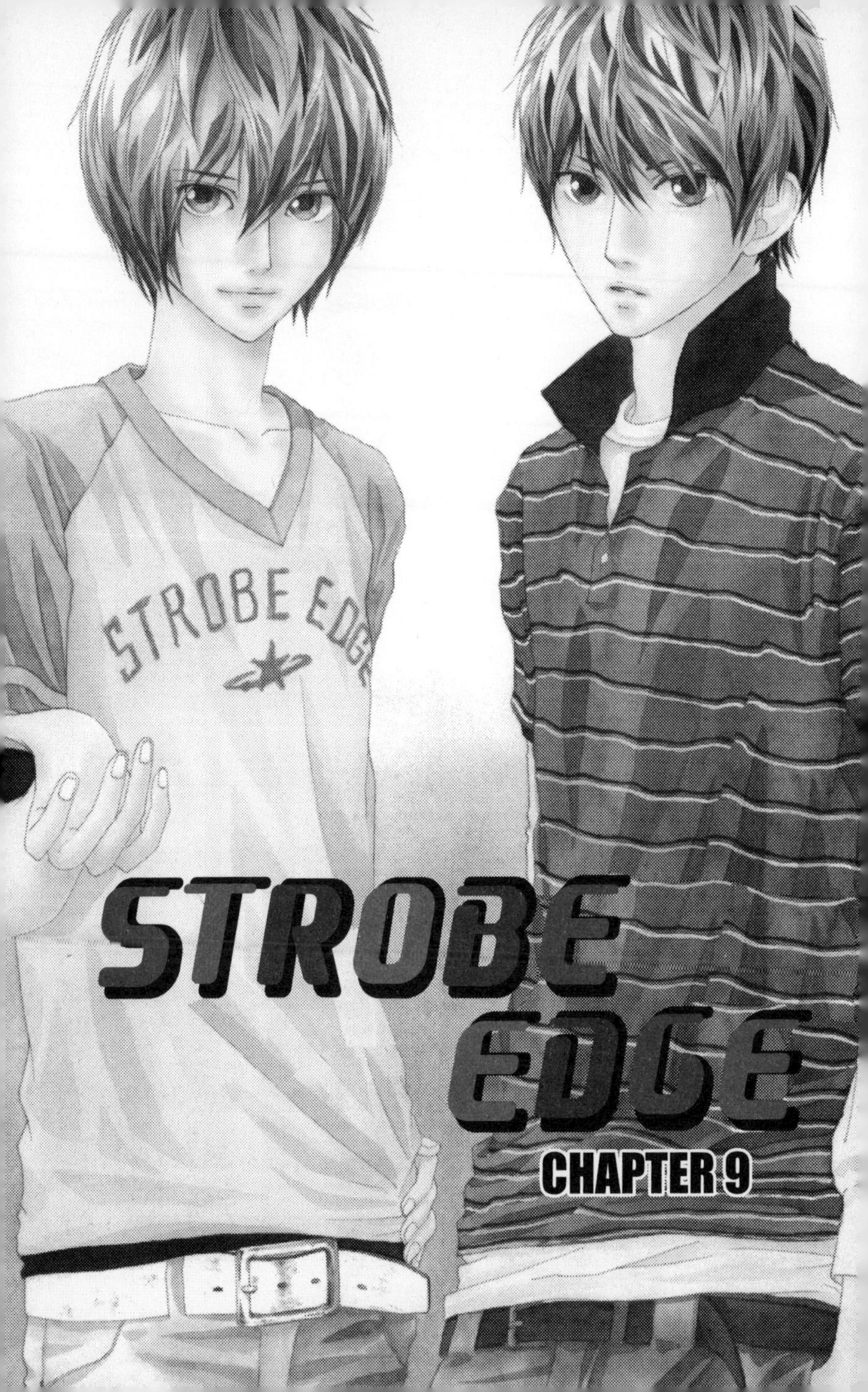
STROBE EDGE
STROBE
EDGE
CHAPTER 9

While I'm drawing, I have a mirror propped up on my desk. I like using it to check the movement of my hands or the wrinkles in my clothes.

Once, I had to draw a picture of feet in a squatting position, so I perched on my chair to see my feet in the mirror.

Here's where my knees would be. So I should draw them higher. *1

※1 My legs are shorter than average, so I have to draw the legs much longer. But I refuse to cry!

As I shifted around to catch my reflection in the tiny mirror, I fell off the chair and landed right on my butt!

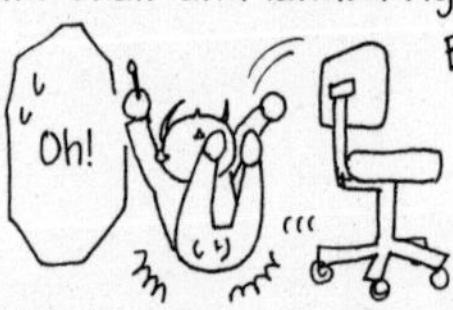

Oh!

Bam! In the middle of the night. Bam!

The house shook. My brain rattled. It hurt so much I couldn't breathe. And that moment of falling on my butt made me feel an overwhelming sense of defeat. The pain faded quickly, but I couldn't find the energy to get back up. I just lay there for about five minutes, too dazed to budge.

I learned that falling on your butt is scary, because it immediately drains all your energy. So I've learned an important lesson: you should never fall on your butt while working, especially when you're on deadline. It should be forbidden.

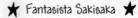

...

I-I want to go home... *2

※2 But I am home...

An aura of disappointment

★ Fantasista Sakisaka ★

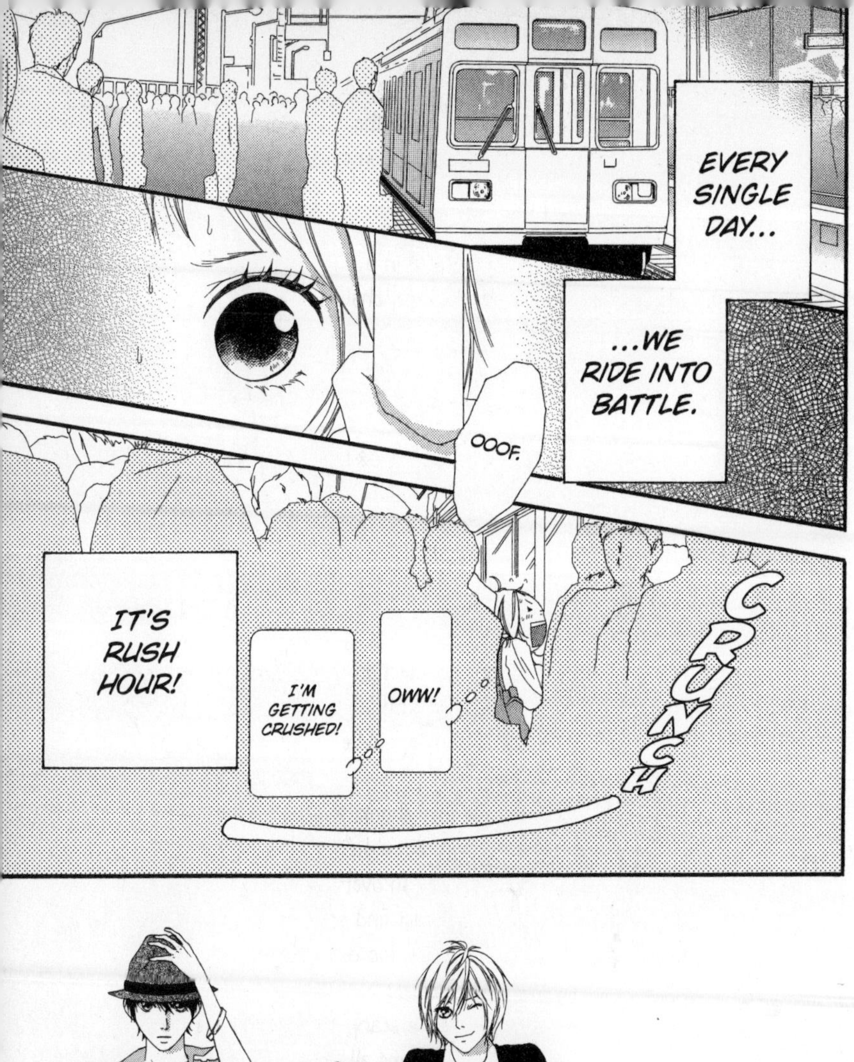
EVERY SINGLE DAY...
...WE RIDE INTO BATTLE.
OOOF.
CRUNCH
OWW!
I'M GETTING CRUSHED!
IT'S RUSH HOUR!

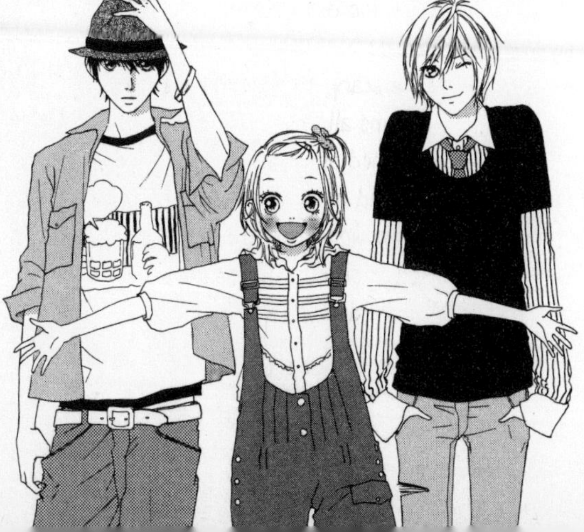

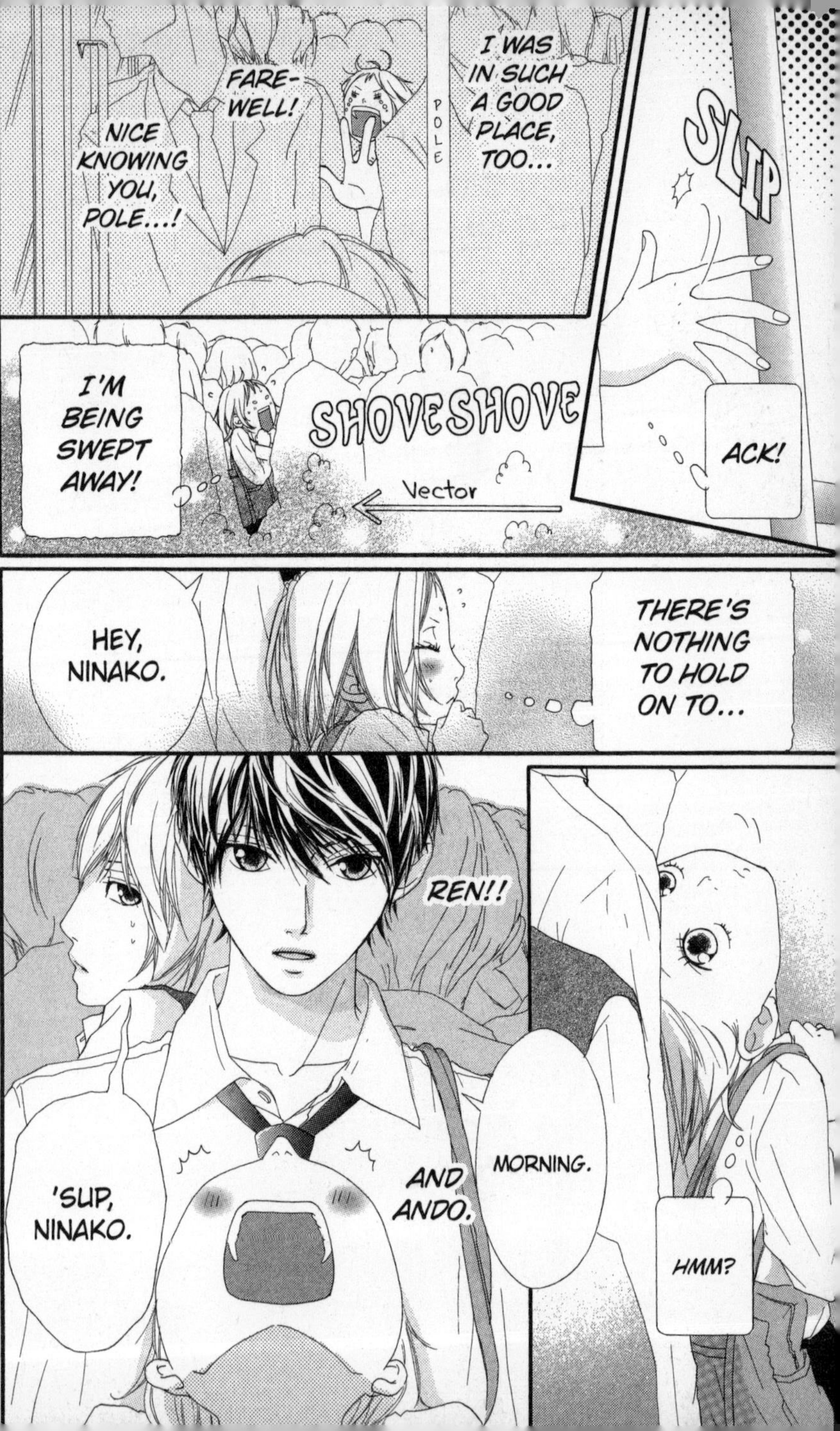
SLIP
ACK!
I WAS IN SUCH A GOOD PLACE, TOO...
POLE
FARE-WELL!
NICE KNOWING YOU, POLE...!
SHOVESHOVE
Vector
I'M BEING SWEPT AWAY!
THERE'S NOTHING TO HOLD ON TO...
HEY, NINAKO.
HMM?
REN!!
MORNING.
AND ANDO.
'SUP, NINAKO.

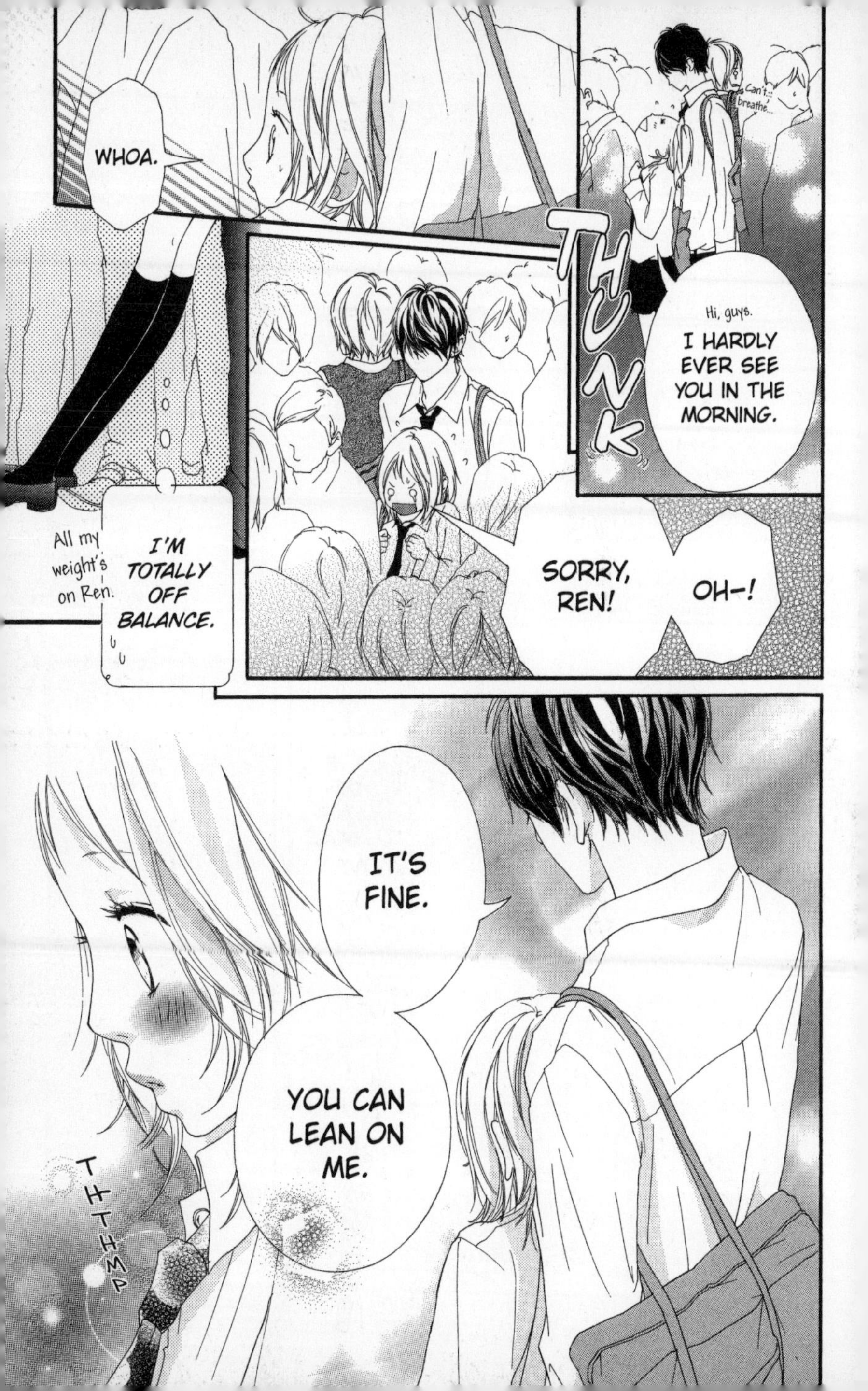
Can't... breathe...
THUNK
Hi, guys.
I HARDLY EVER SEE YOU IN THE MORNING.
WHOA.
OH-!
SORRY, REN!
I'M TOTALLY OFF BALANCE.
All my weight's on Ren.
IT'S FINE.
YOU CAN LEAN ON ME.
THTHMP

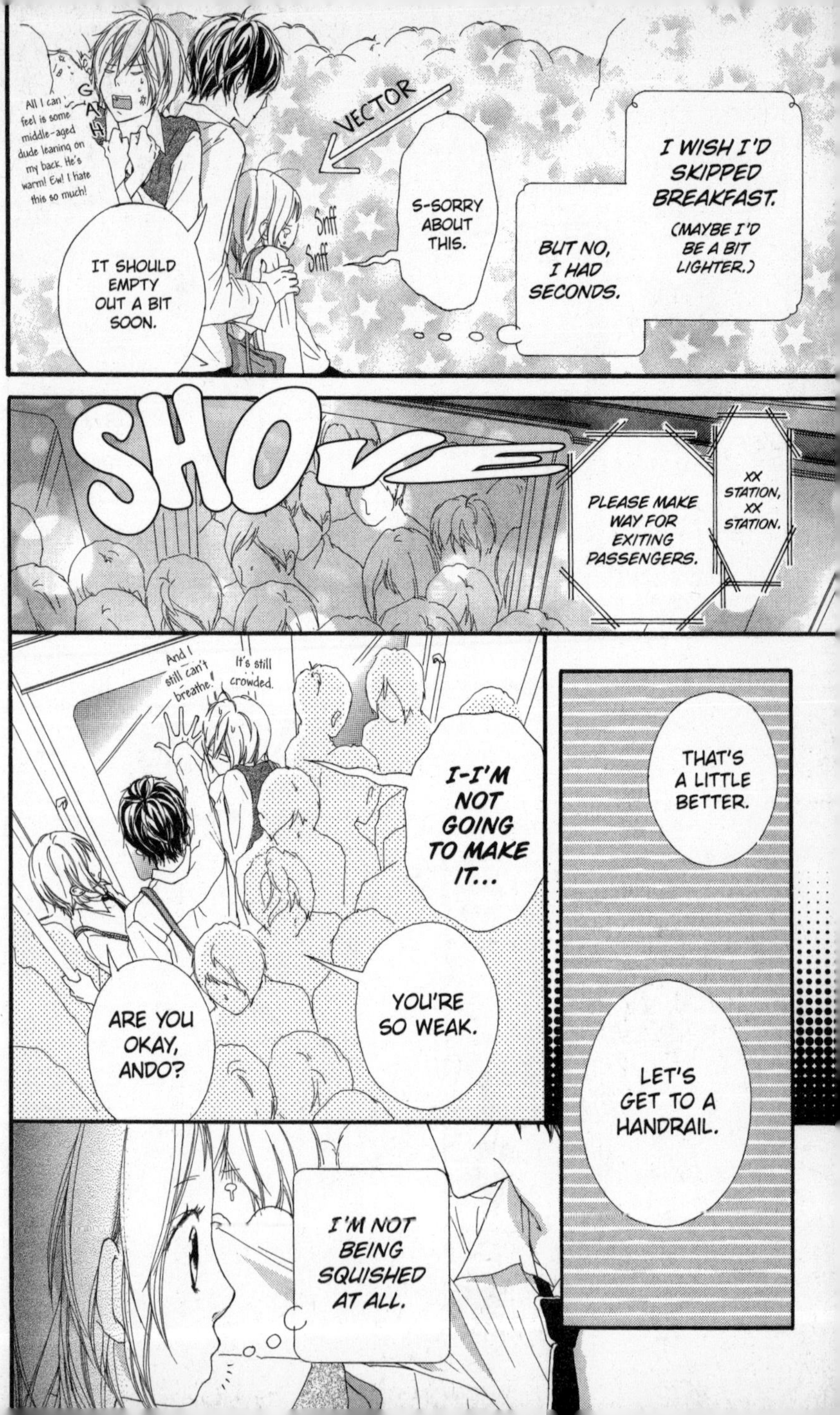
I WISH I'D SKIPPED BREAKFAST.
(MAYBE I'D BE A BIT LIGHTER.)
BUT NO, I HAD SECONDS.
S-SORRY ABOUT THIS.
VECTOR
Snff Snff
GAAH
All I can feel is some middle-aged dude leaning on my back. He's warm! Ew! I hate this so much!
IT SHOULD EMPTY OUT A BIT SOON.
XX STATION, XX STATION.
PLEASE MAKE WAY FOR EXITING PASSENGERS.
SHOVE
THAT'S A LITTLE BETTER.
LET'S GET TO A HANDRAIL.
I-I'M NOT GOING TO MAKE IT...
It's still crowded.
And I still can't breathe!
YOU'RE SO WEAK.
ARE YOU OKAY, ANDO?
I'M NOT BEING SQUISHED AT ALL.

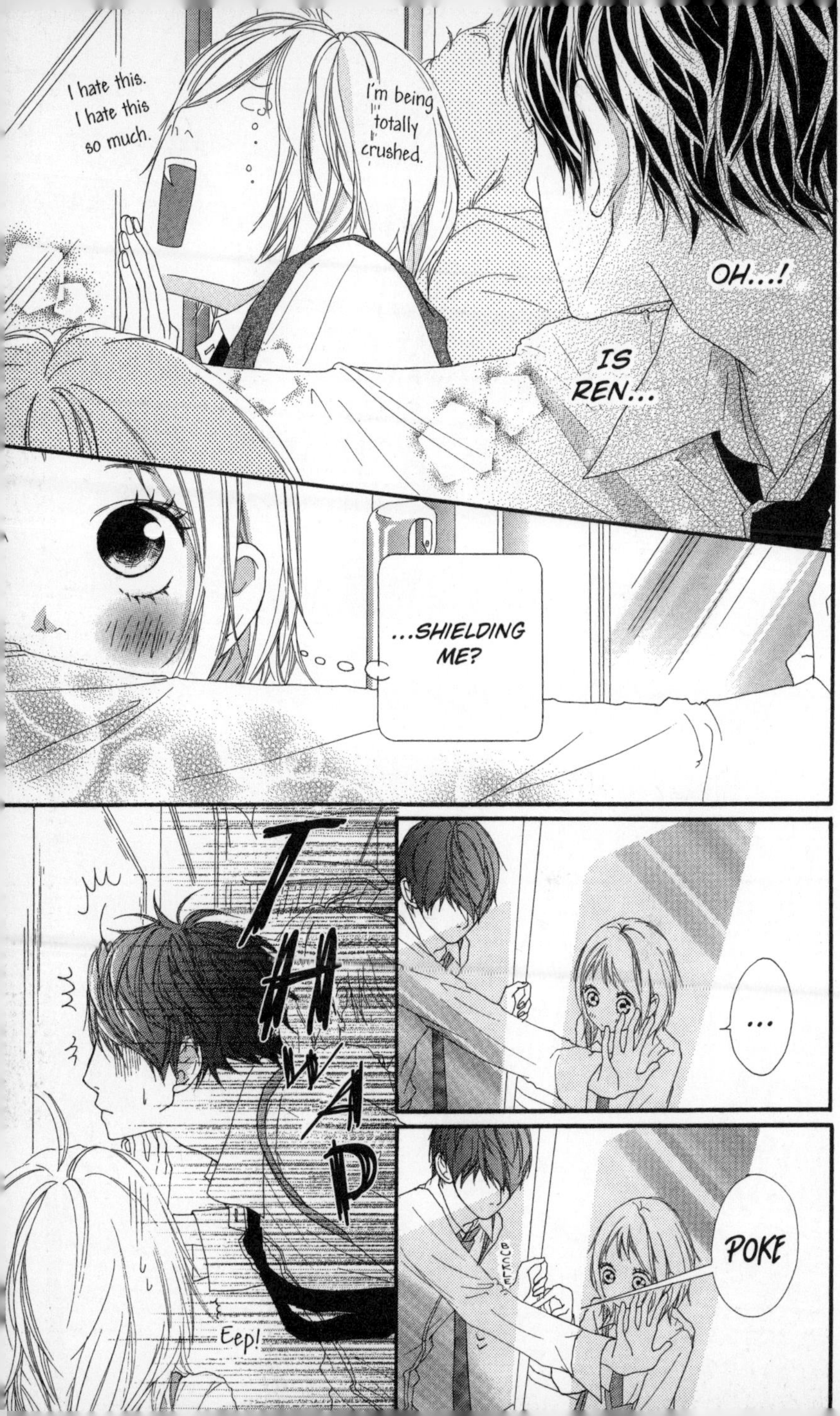

I'm being totally crushed.
I hate this. I hate this so much.
OH...!
IS REN...
...SHIELDING ME?
...
BUCKLE
POKE
THWAP
Eep!

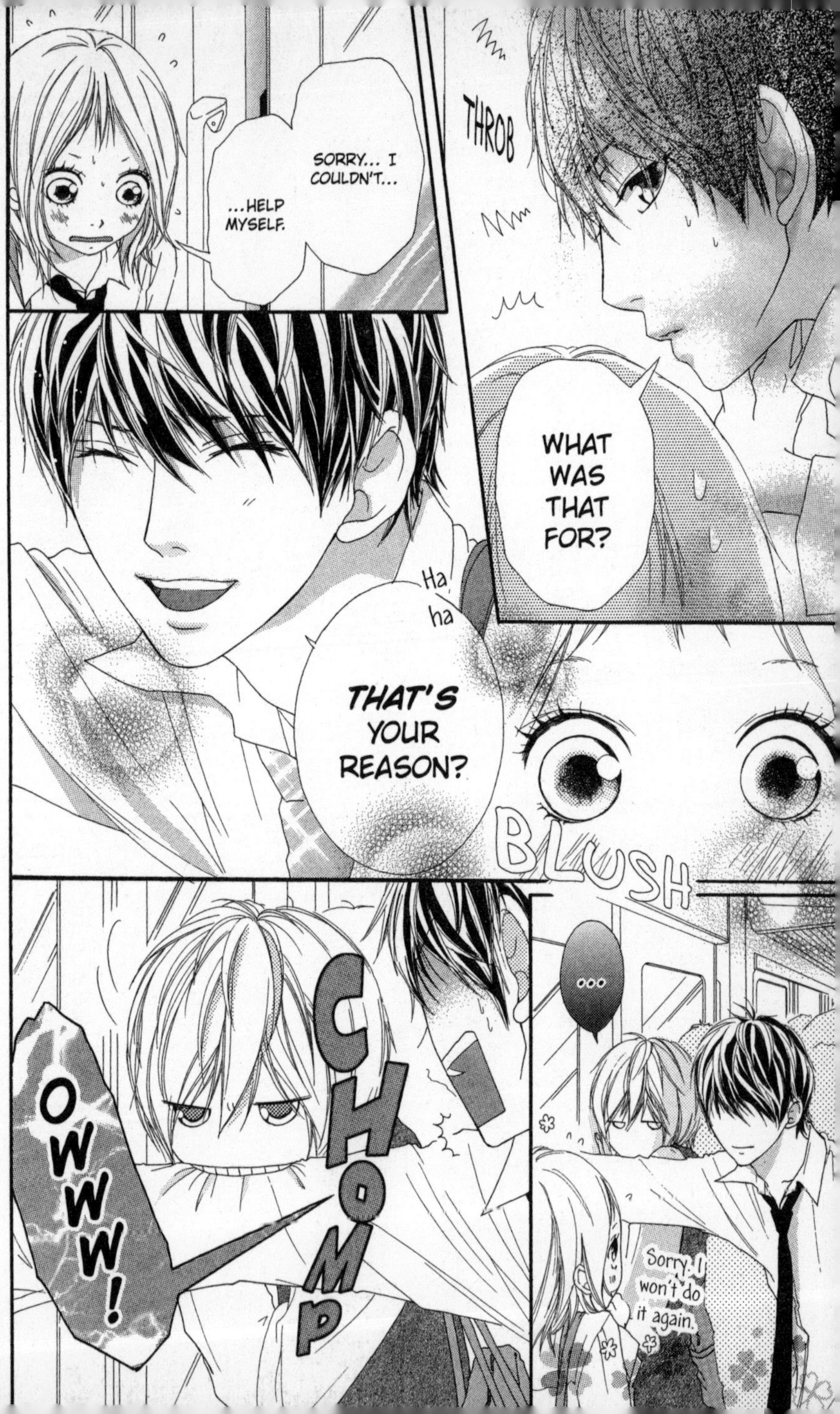
THROB
WHAT WAS THAT FOR?
SORRY... I COULDN'T...
...HELP MYSELF.
Ha ha
THAT'S YOUR REASON?
BLUSH
...
Sorry. I won't do it again.
CHOMP
OWWW!

WORKFLOW

~My Particular Method~

④ DRAFT OF A DRAFT
I tend to draw quickly so I can nail down the tempo of the story. But then I end up with very rough sketches that only I can understand.

⑤ ACTUAL DRAFT
In this phase, I draw so that others can see what's going on, but without faces or hair. Even in intense scenes, the characters are bald, which scales the intensity way down.

Example:

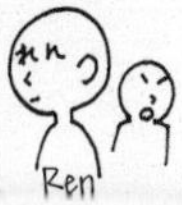
Ren

⑥ ROUGH SKETCH
I'm dreadfully slow. I trace over sketchy lines to make them solid. I wish I could ink right over sketches like a pro, but I wouldn't know where the actual lines go, so I have to draw fairly neatly in the rough sketch stage.

← To be continued

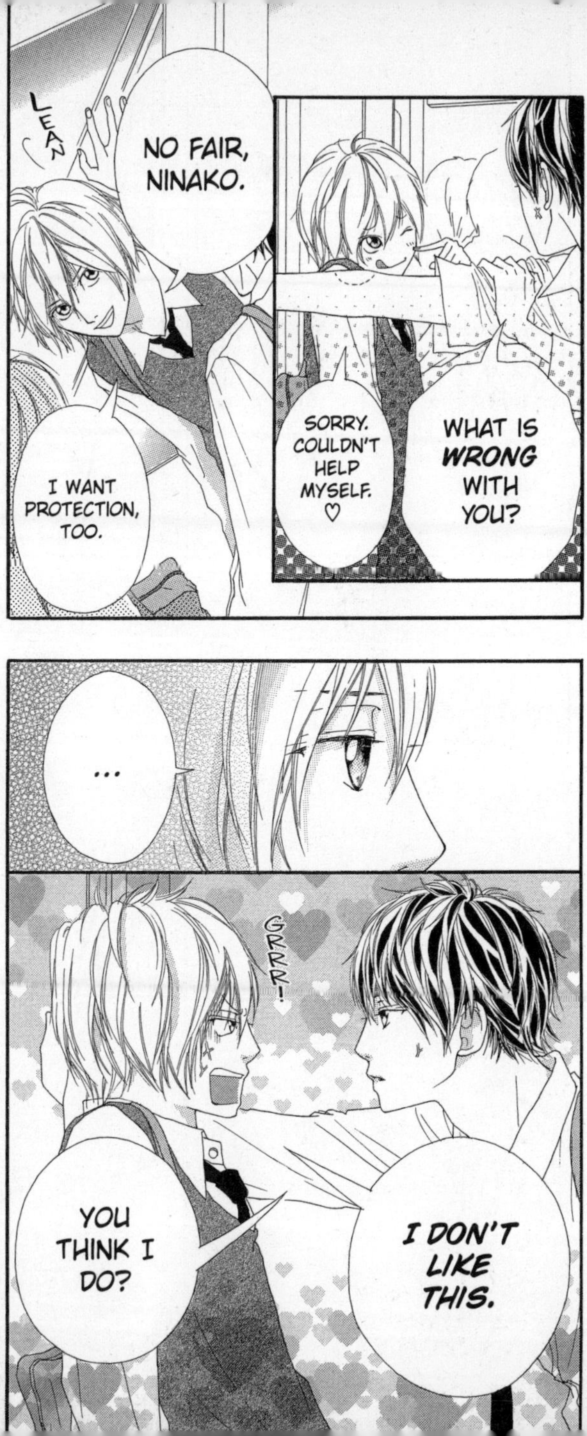
WHAT IS *WRONG* WITH YOU?
SORRY. COULDN'T HELP MYSELF. ♡
LEAN
NO FAIR, NINAKO.
I WANT PROTECTION, TOO.
...
GRRR!
I DON'T LIKE THIS.
YOU THINK I DO?

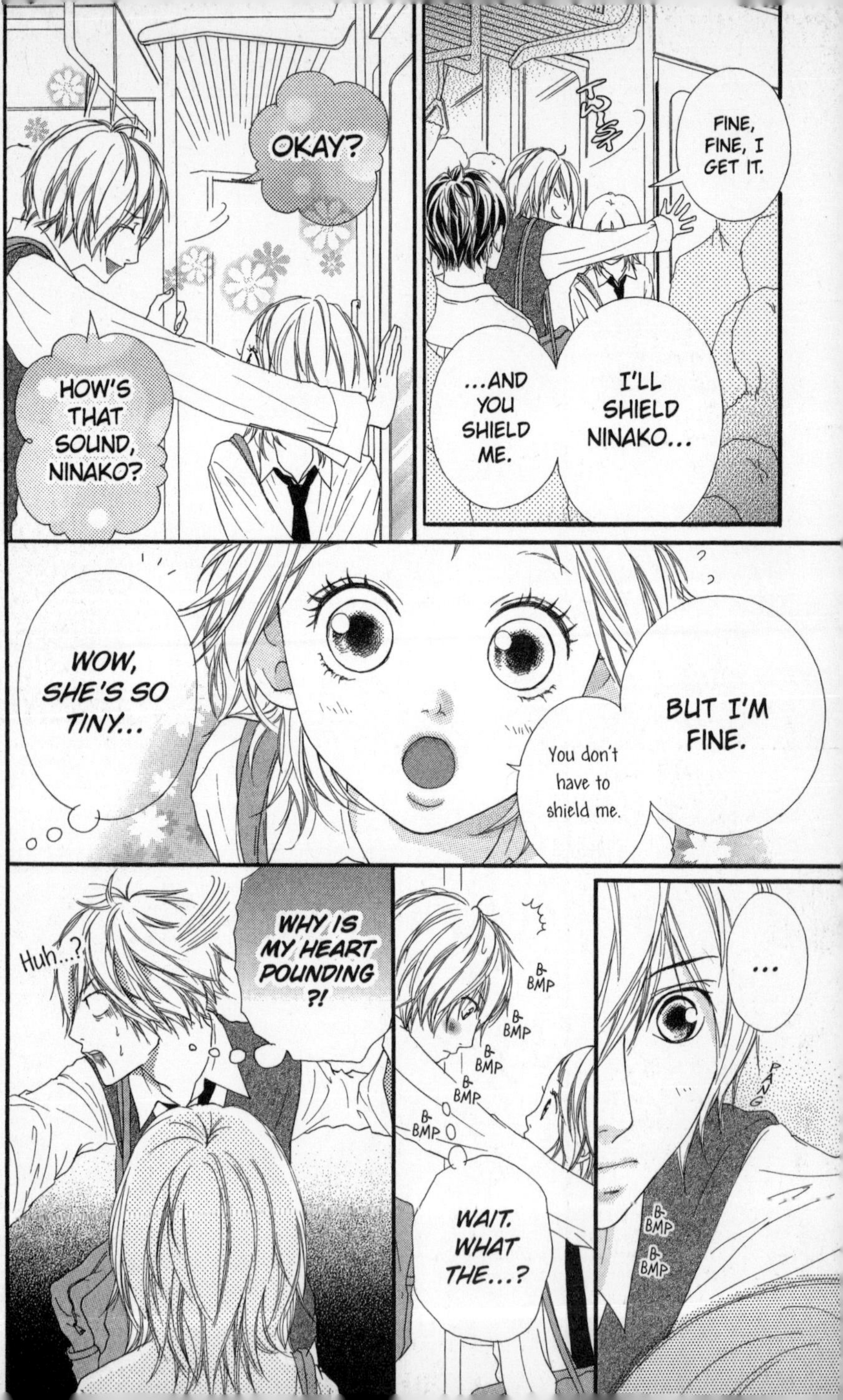
FINE, FINE, I GET IT.
I'LL SHIELD NINAKO...
...AND YOU SHIELD ME.
OKAY?
HOW'S THAT SOUND, NINAKO?
BUT I'M FINE.
You don't have to shield me.
WOW, SHE'S SO TINY...
...
PANG
B-BMP
B-BMP
B-BMP
B-BMP
B-BMP
B-BMP
B-BMP
WAIT. WHAT THE...?
WHY IS MY HEART POUNDING?!
Huh...?

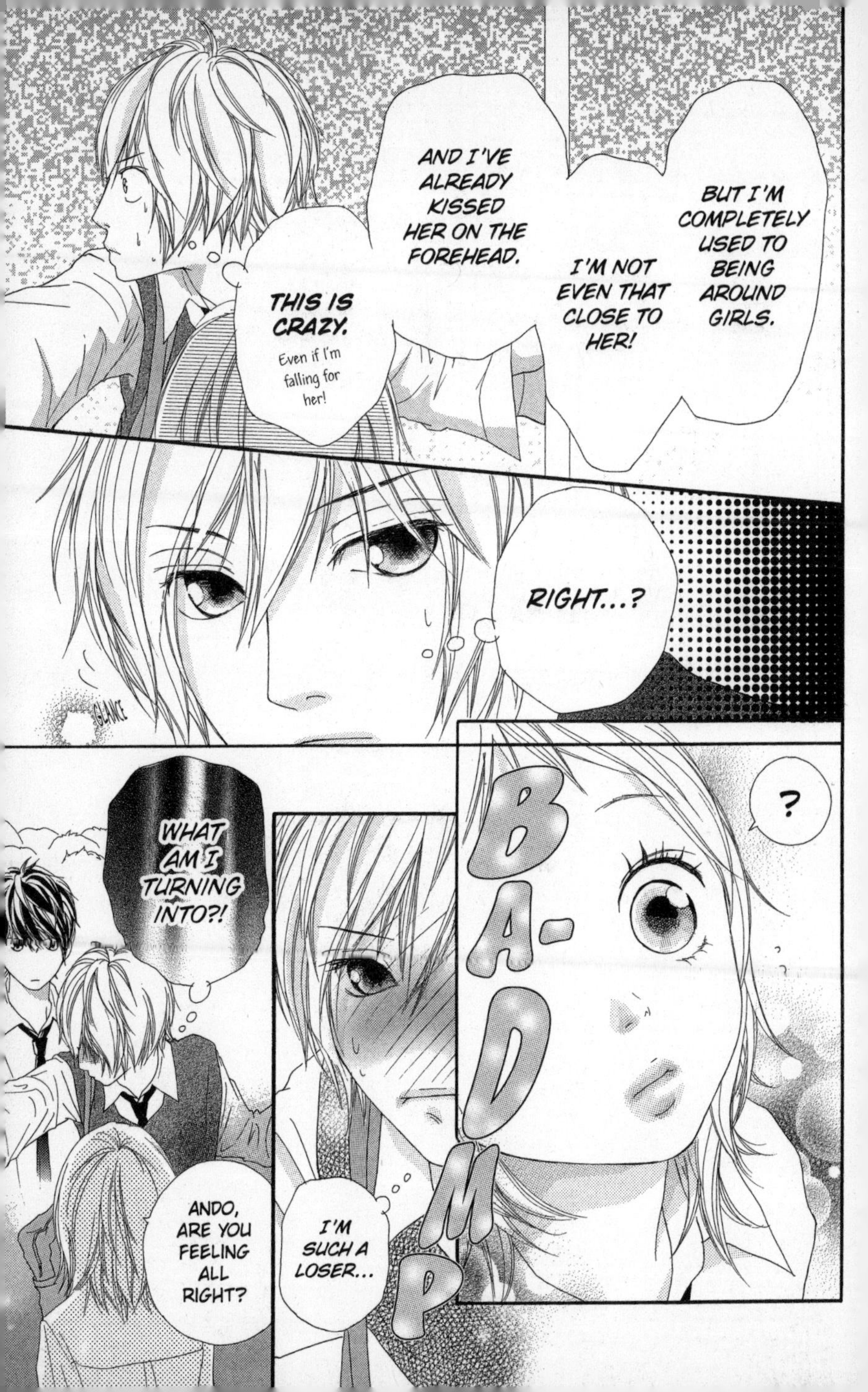
BUT I'M COMPLETELY USED TO BEING AROUND GIRLS.
I'M NOT EVEN THAT CLOSE TO HER!
AND I'VE ALREADY KISSED HER ON THE FOREHEAD.
THIS IS CRAZY.
Even if I'm falling for her!
RIGHT...?
GLANCE
?
BA-DUMP
I'M SUCH A LOSER...
WHAT AM I TURNING INTO?!
ANDO, ARE YOU FEELING ALL RIGHT?

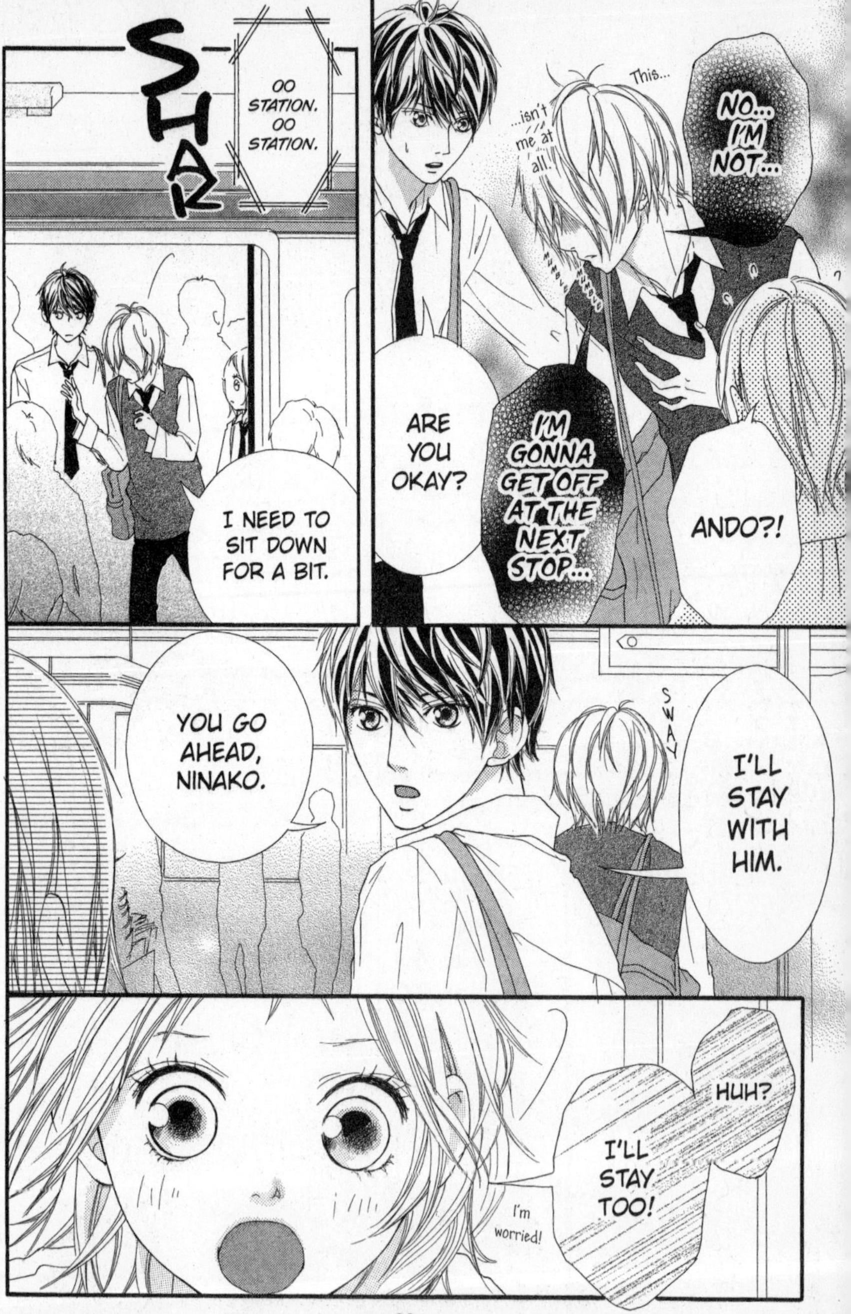
This...
NO... I'M NOT...
...isn't me at all!
MUMBLE MUMBLE
ANDO?!
I'M GONNA GET OFF AT THE NEXT STOP...
ARE YOU OKAY?
SHAR
OO STATION. OO STATION.
I NEED TO SIT DOWN FOR A BIT.
I'LL STAY WITH HIM.
SWAY
YOU GO AHEAD, NINAKO.
HUH?
I'LL STAY TOO!
I'm worried!

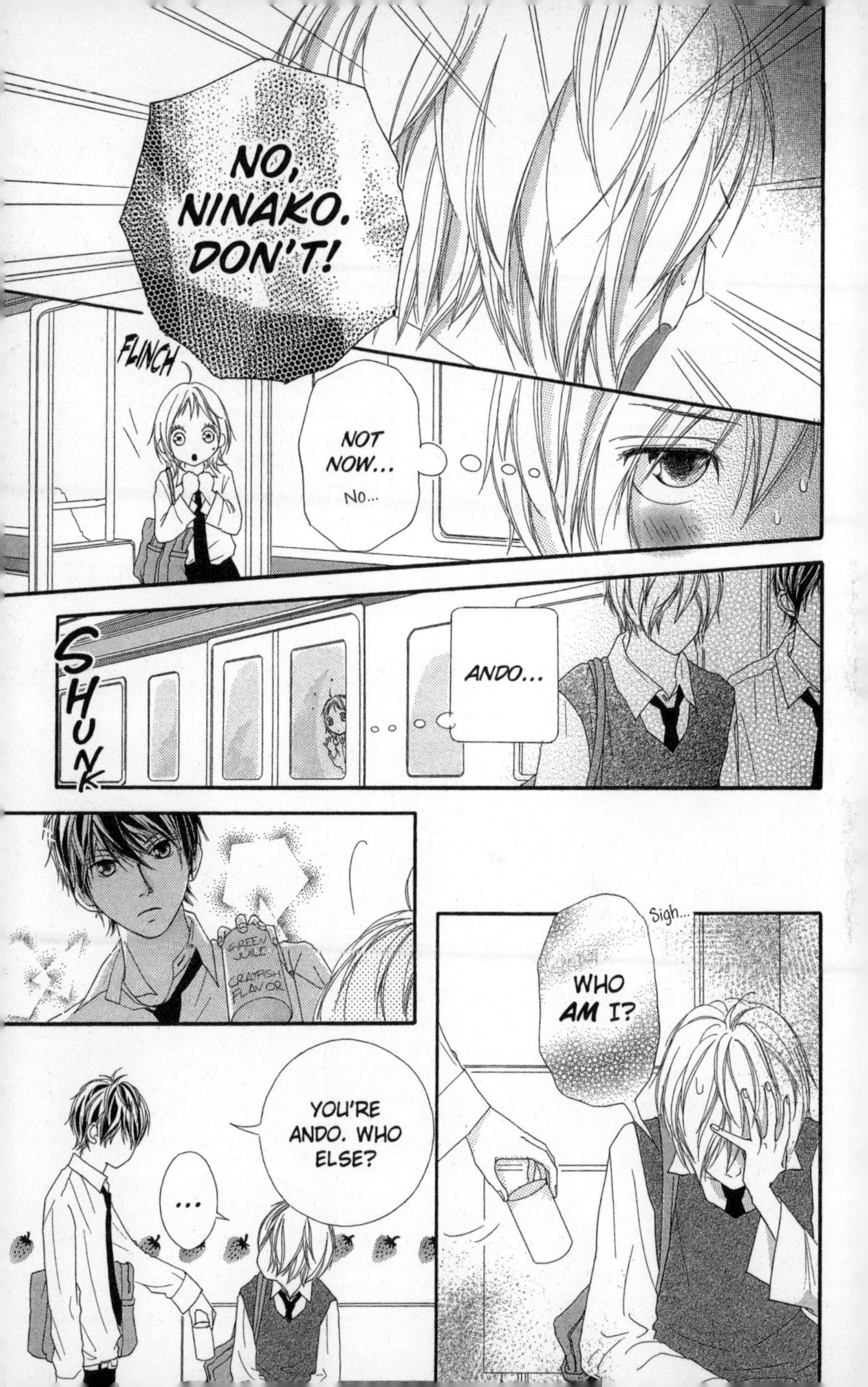
NO, NINAKO. DON'T!
NOT NOW...
No...
FLINCH
ANDO...
SHUNK
Sigh...
WHO AM I?
CRAYFISH FLAVOR
YOU'RE ANDO. WHO ELSE?
...

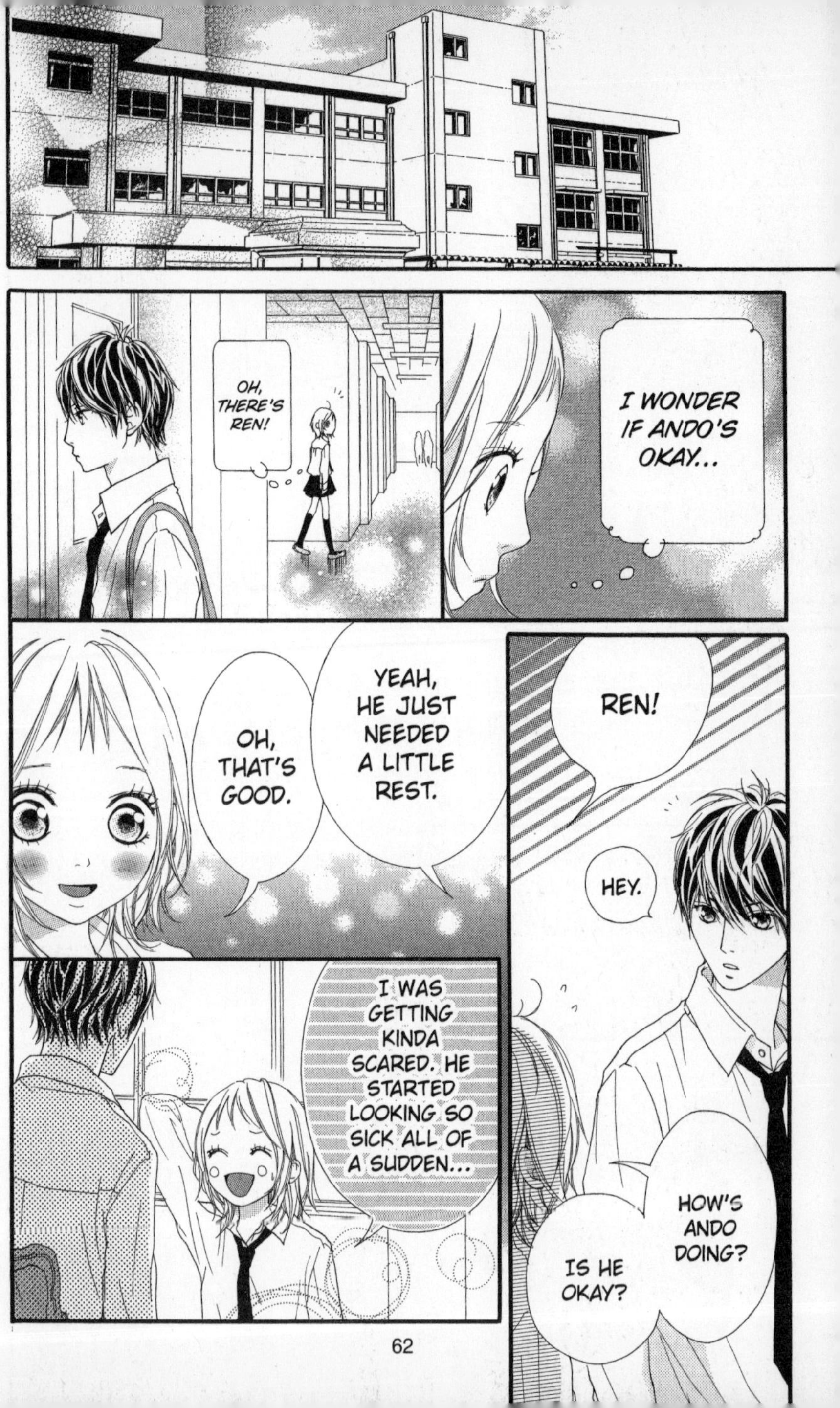
I WONDER IF ANDO'S OKAY...
OH, THERE'S REN!
REN!
HEY.
HOW'S ANDO DOING?
IS HE OKAY?
YEAH, HE JUST NEEDED A LITTLE REST.
OH, THAT'S GOOD.
I WAS GETTING KINDA SCARED. HE STARTED LOOKING SO SICK ALL OF A SUDDEN...

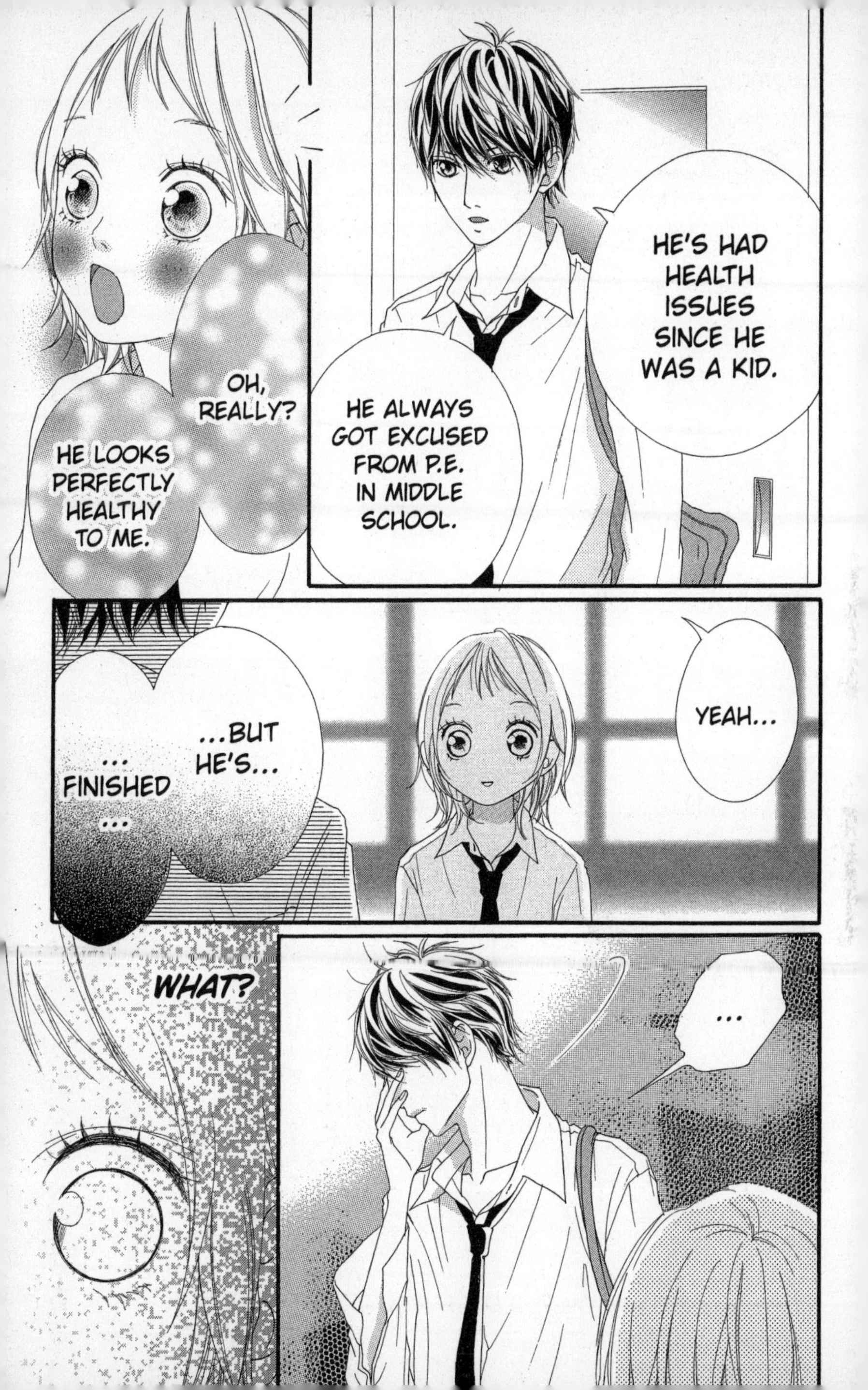
HE'S HAD HEALTH ISSUES SINCE HE WAS A KID.
HE ALWAYS GOT EXCUSED FROM P.E. IN MIDDLE SCHOOL.
OH, REALLY?
HE LOOKS PERFECTLY HEALTHY TO ME.
YEAH...
...BUT HE'S...
... FINISHED ...
...
WHAT?

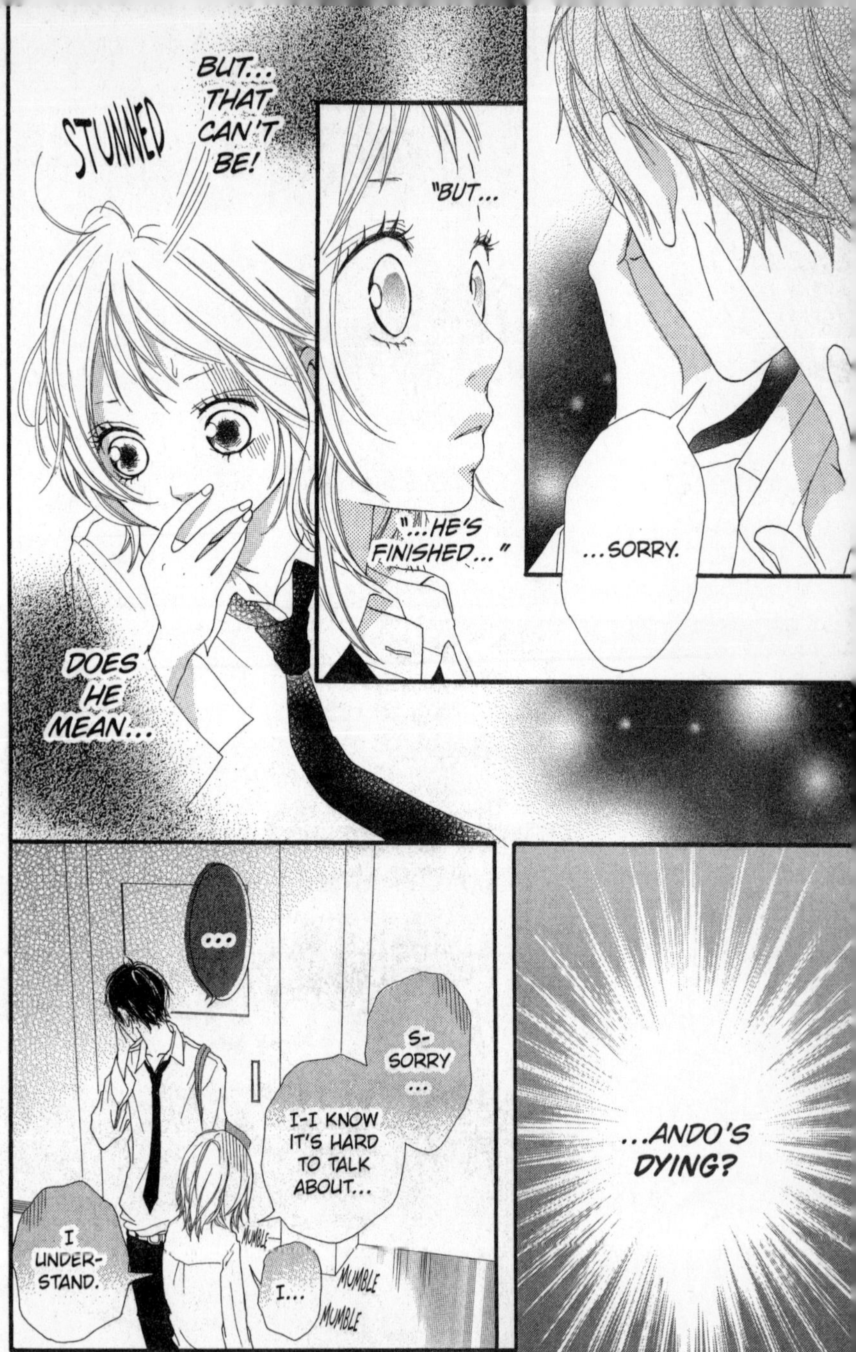
...SORRY.
"BUT...
"...HE'S FINISHED..."
BUT... THAT CAN'T BE!
STUNNED
DOES HE MEAN...
...ANDO'S DYING?
...
S-SORRY...
I-I KNOW IT'S HARD TO TALK ABOUT...
I UNDERSTAND.
MUMBLE
I...
MUMBLE
MUMBLE

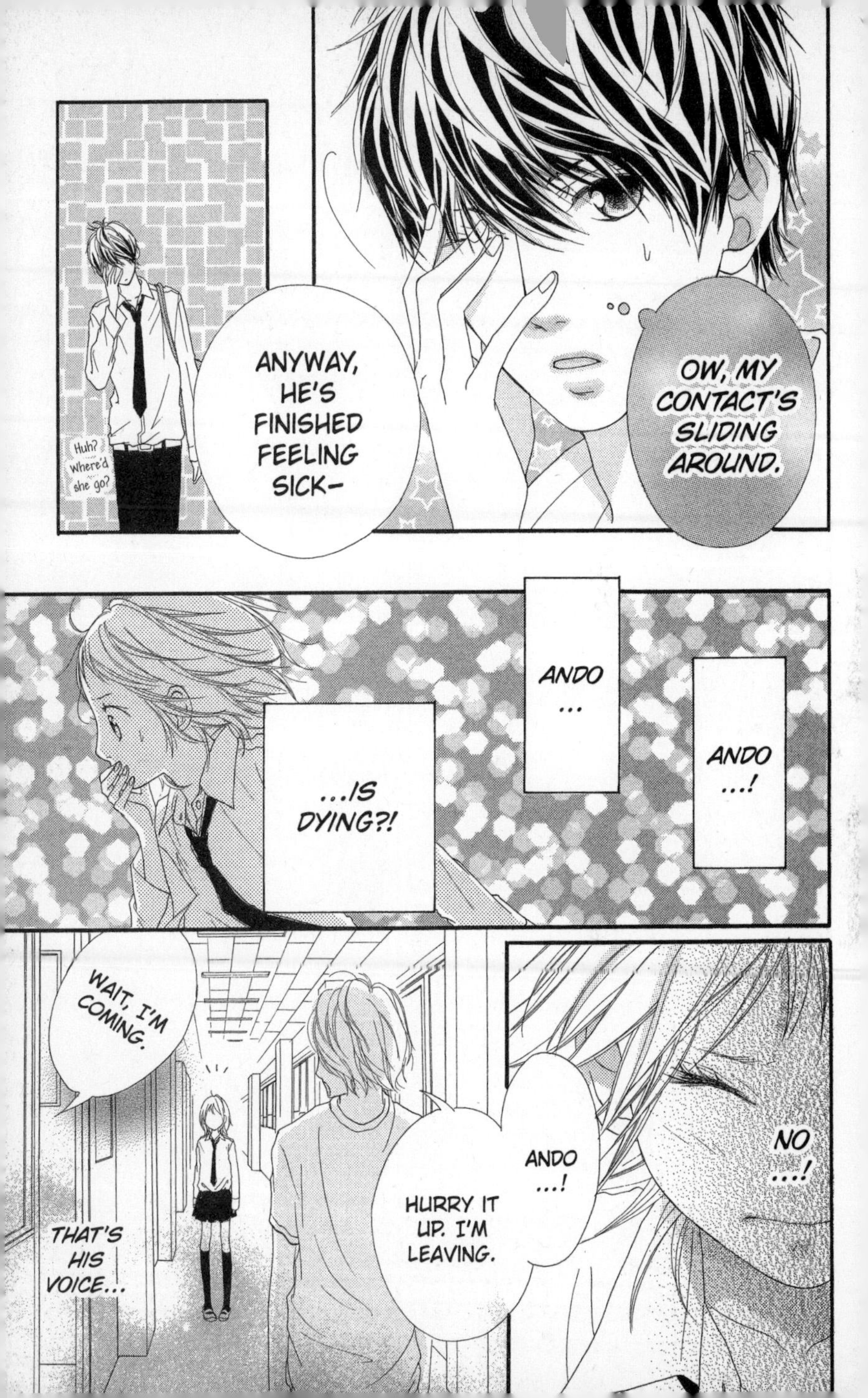
OW, MY CONTACT'S SLIDING AROUND.
ANYWAY, HE'S FINISHED FEELING SICK–
Huh? Where'd she go?
ANDO ...!
ANDO ...
...IS DYING?!
NO ...!
ANDO ...!
HURRY IT UP. I'M LEAVING.
WAIT, I'M COMING.
THAT'S HIS VOICE...

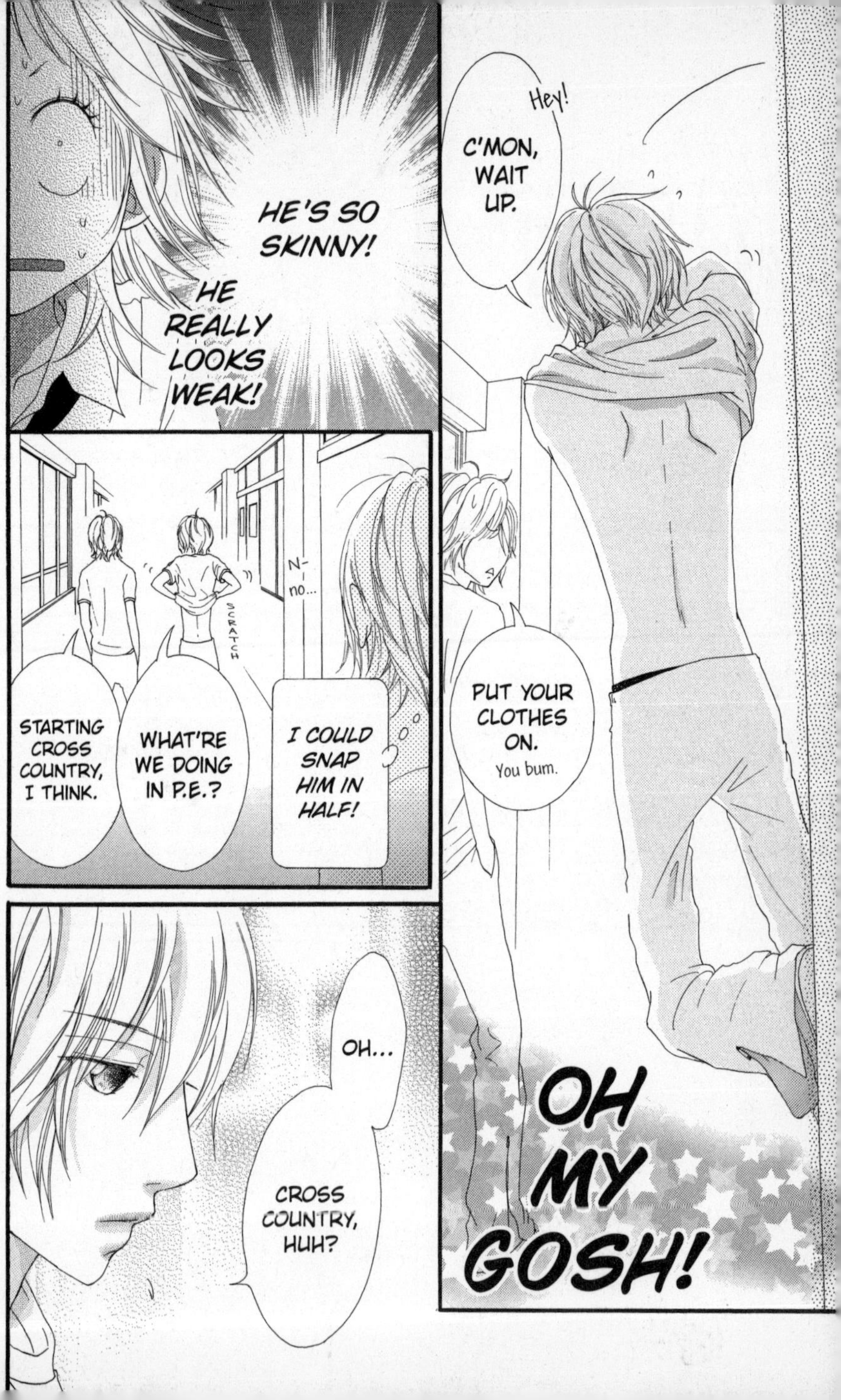
Hey!
C'MON, WAIT UP.
PUT YOUR CLOTHES ON.
You bum.
OH MY GOSH!
HE'S SO SKINNY!
HE REALLY LOOKS WEAK!
N-no...
I COULD SNAP HIM IN HALF!
SCRATCH
WHAT'RE WE DOING IN P.E.?
STARTING CROSS COUNTRY, I THINK.
OH...
CROSS COUNTRY, HUH?

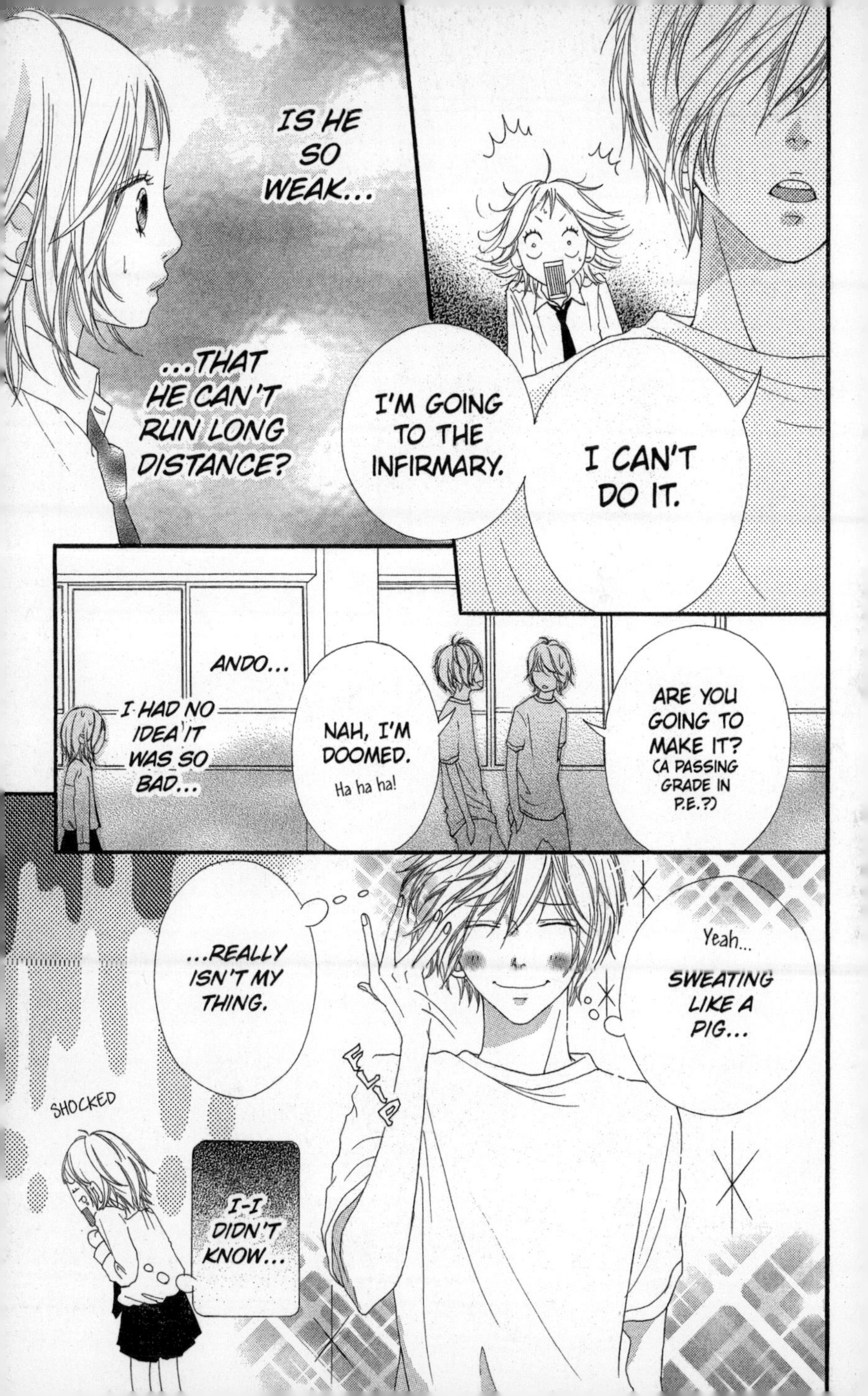
I CAN'T DO IT.
I'M GOING TO THE INFIRMARY.
IS HE SO WEAK...
...THAT HE CAN'T RUN LONG DISTANCE?
ARE YOU GOING TO MAKE IT? (A PASSING GRADE IN P.E.?)
NAH, I'M DOOMED.
Ha ha ha!
ANDO...
I HAD NO IDEA IT WAS SO BAD...
Yeah... SWEATING LIKE A PIG...
...REALLY ISN'T MY THING.
SHOCKED
I-I DIDN'T KNOW...

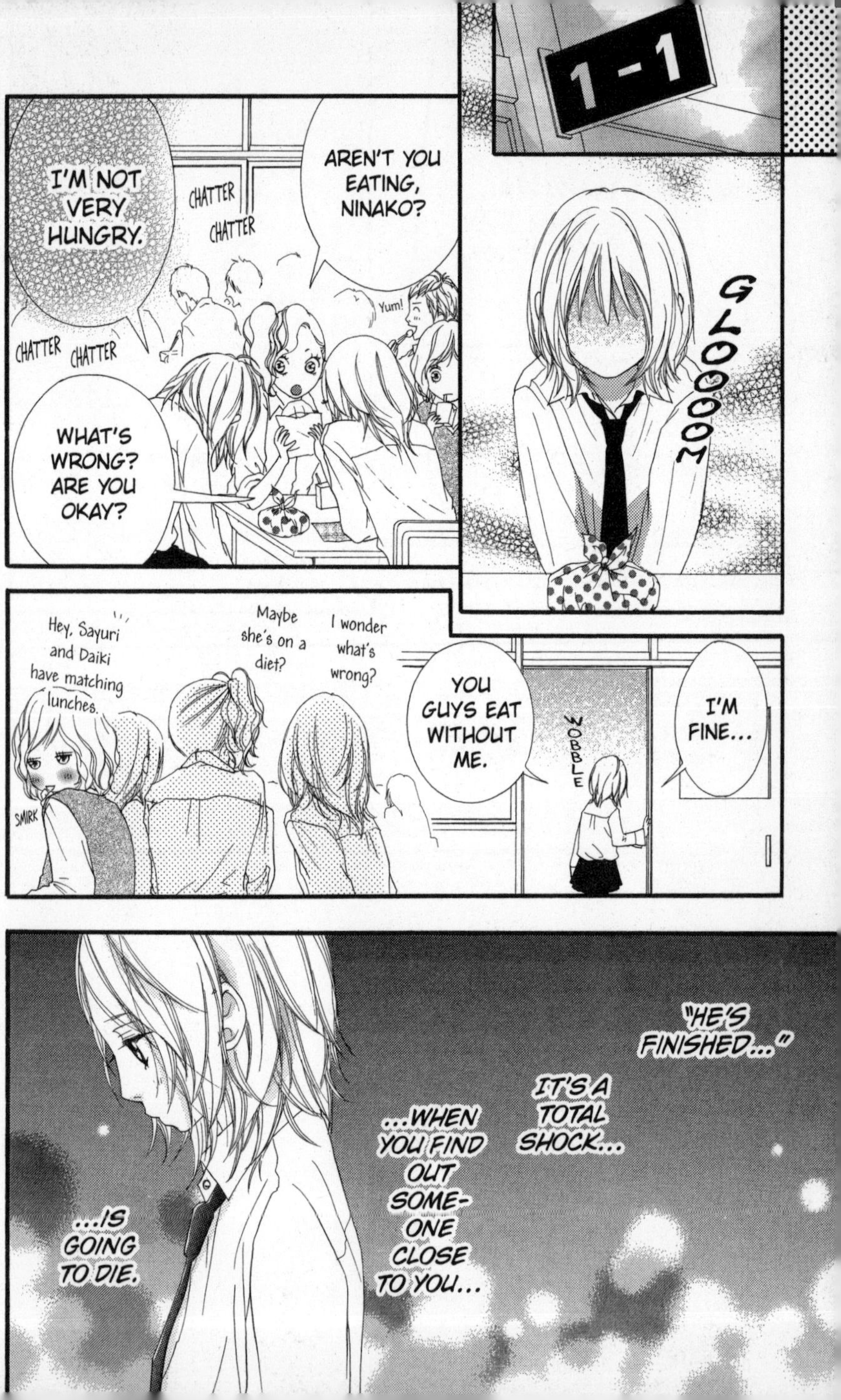
1-1
GLOOOOOM
AREN'T YOU EATING, NINAKO?
I'M NOT VERY HUNGRY.
CHATTER CHATTER
Yum!
CHATTER CHATTER
WHAT'S WRONG? ARE YOU OKAY?
I'M FINE...
YOU GUYS EAT WITHOUT ME.
WOBBLE
I wonder what's wrong?
Maybe she's on a diet?
Hey, Sayuri and Daiki have matching lunches.
SMIRK
"HE'S FINISHED..."
IT'S A TOTAL SHOCK...
...WHEN YOU FIND OUT SOME-ONE CLOSE TO YOU...
...IS GOING TO DIE.

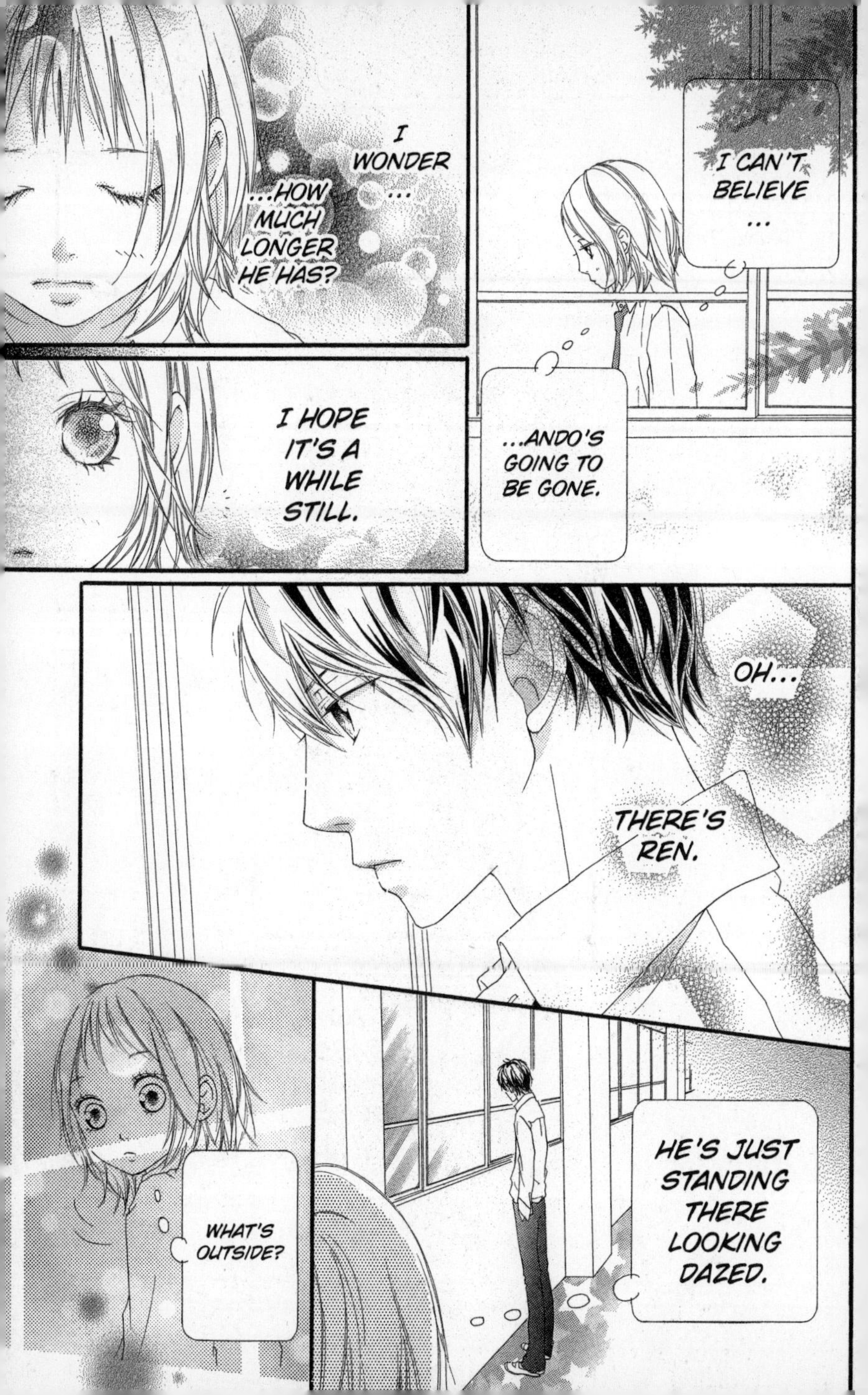
I CAN'T BELIEVE ...
...ANDO'S GOING TO BE GONE.
I WONDER ...
...HOW MUCH LONGER HE HAS?
I HOPE IT'S A WHILE STILL.
OH...
THERE'S REN.
HE'S JUST STANDING THERE LOOKING DAZED.
WHAT'S OUTSIDE?

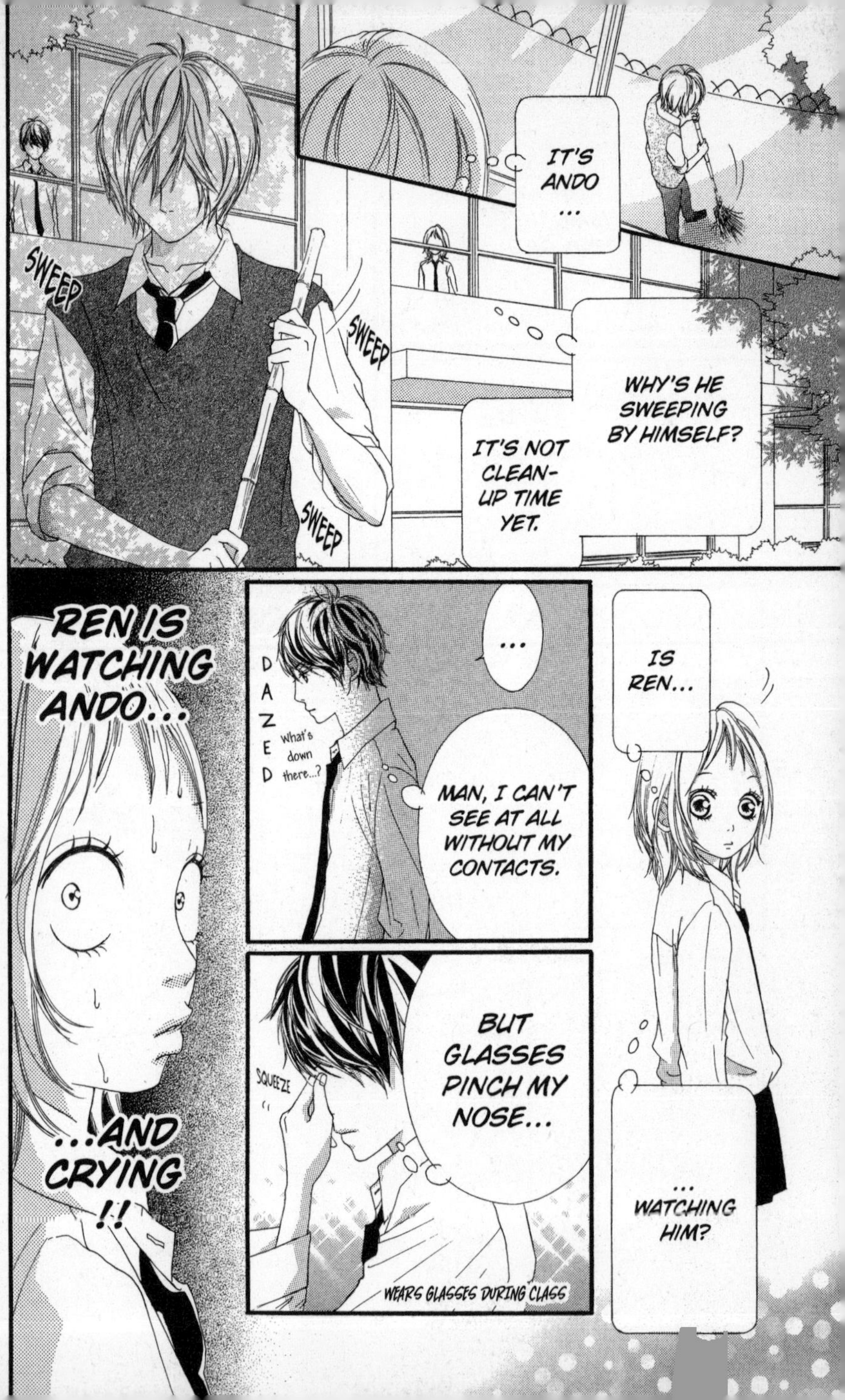
IT'S ANDO...
WHY'S HE SWEEPING BY HIMSELF?
IT'S NOT CLEAN-UP TIME YET.
SWEEP
SWEEP
SWEEP
IS REN...
...WATCHING HIM?
...
DAZED
What's down there...?
MAN, I CAN'T SEE AT ALL WITHOUT MY CONTACTS.
BUT GLASSES PINCH MY NOSE...
SQUEEZE
WEARS GLASSES DURING CLASS
REN IS WATCHING ANDO...
...AND CRYING !!

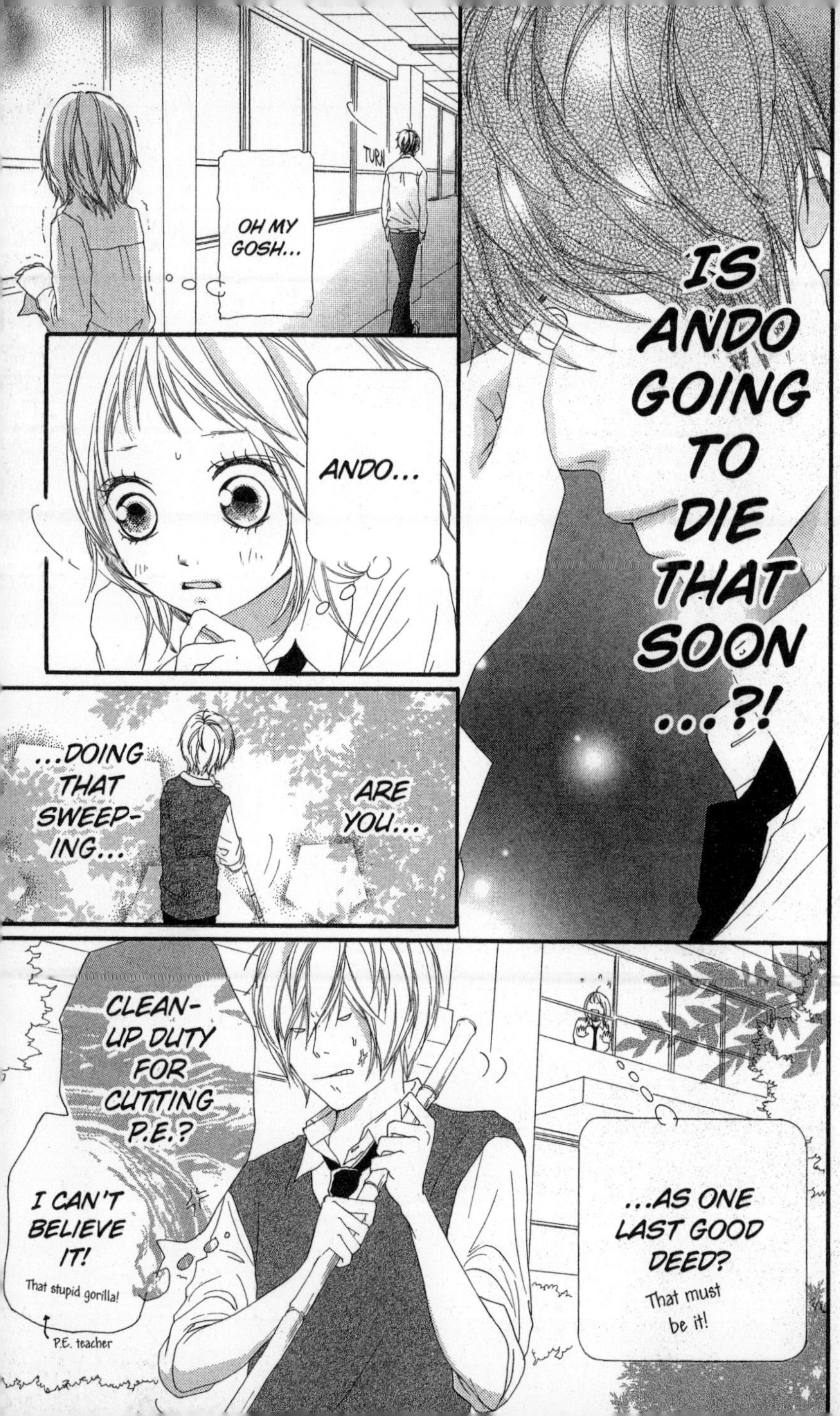
IS ANDO GOING TO DIE THAT SOON...?!
TURN
OH MY GOSH...
ANDO...
ARE YOU...
...DOING THAT SWEEPING...
...AS ONE LAST GOOD DEED?
That must be it!
CLEAN-UP DUTY FOR CUTTING P.E.?
I CAN'T BELIEVE IT!
That stupid gorilla!
P.E. teacher

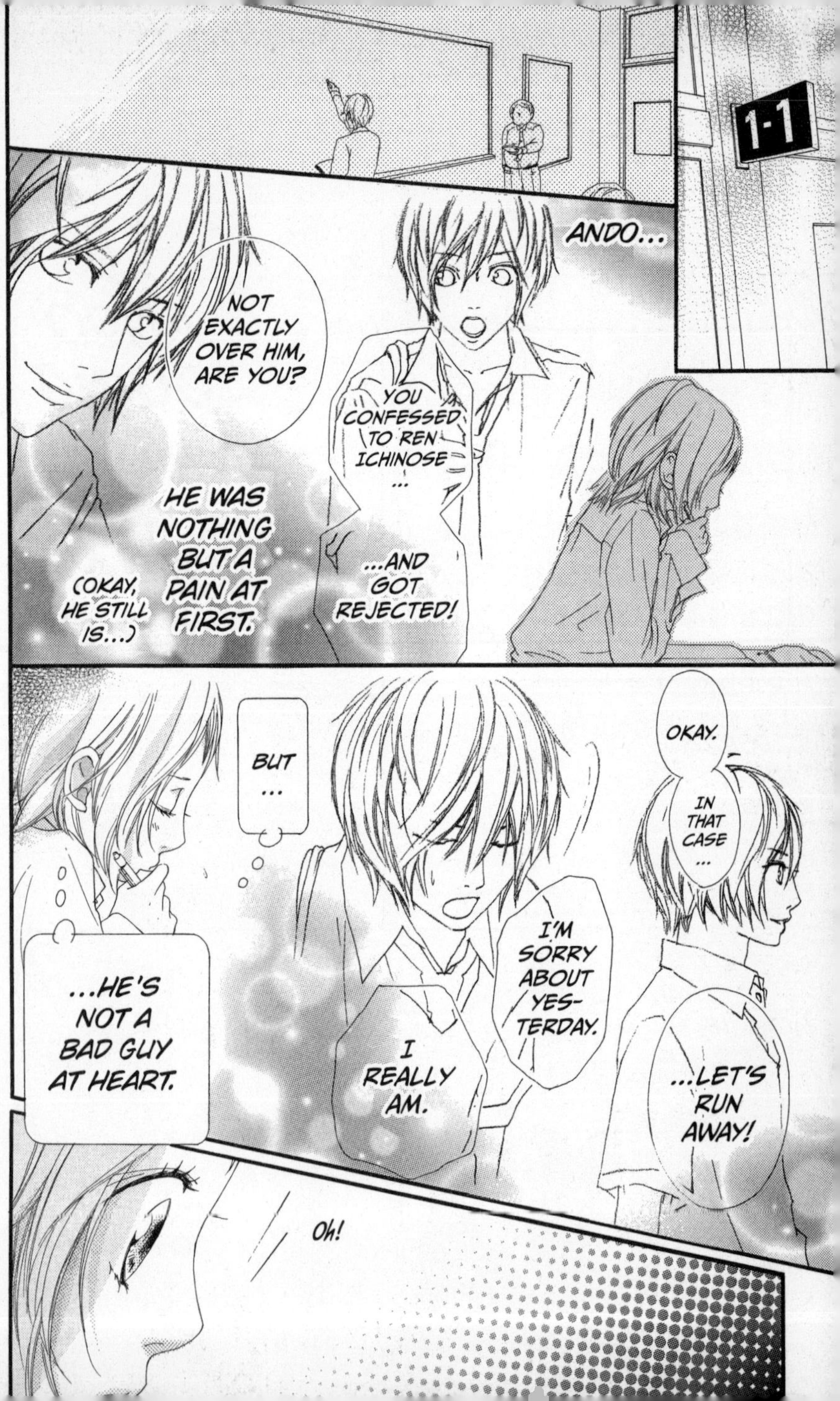

1-1
ANDO...
YOU CONFESSED TO REN ICHINOSE...
...AND GOT REJECTED!
NOT EXACTLY OVER HIM, ARE YOU?
HE WAS NOTHING BUT A PAIN AT FIRST.
(OKAY, HE STILL IS...)
OKAY.
IN THAT CASE...
...LET'S RUN AWAY!
I'M SORRY ABOUT YES-TERDAY.
I REALLY AM.
BUT...
...HE'S NOT A BAD GUY AT HEART.
Oh!

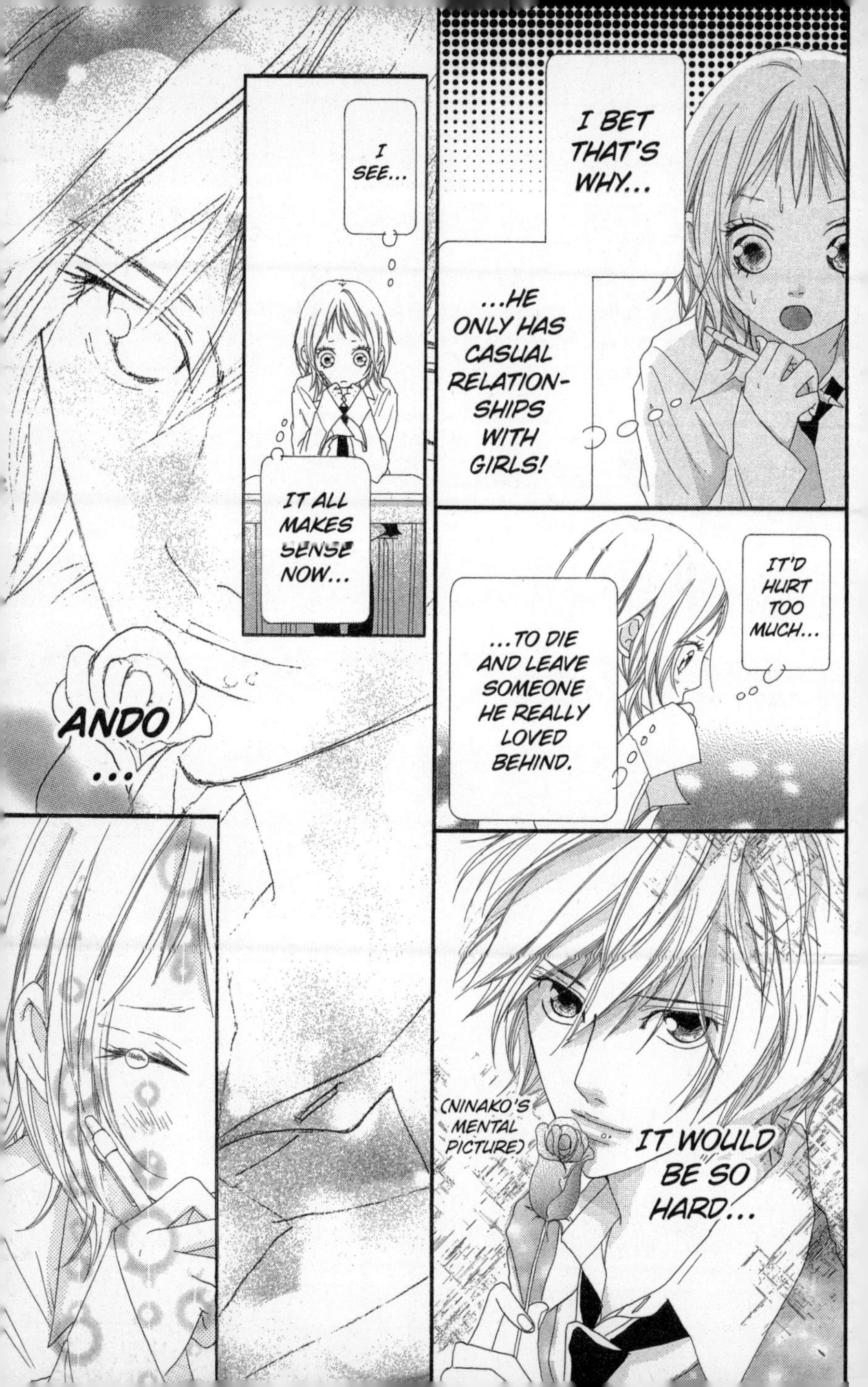
I BET THAT'S WHY...
...HE ONLY HAS CASUAL RELATION-SHIPS WITH GIRLS!
I SEE...
IT ALL MAKES SENSE NOW...
IT'D HURT TOO MUCH...
...TO DIE AND LEAVE SOMEONE HE REALLY LOVED BEHIND.
ANDO...
(NINAKO'S MENTAL PICTURE)
IT WOULD BE SO HARD...

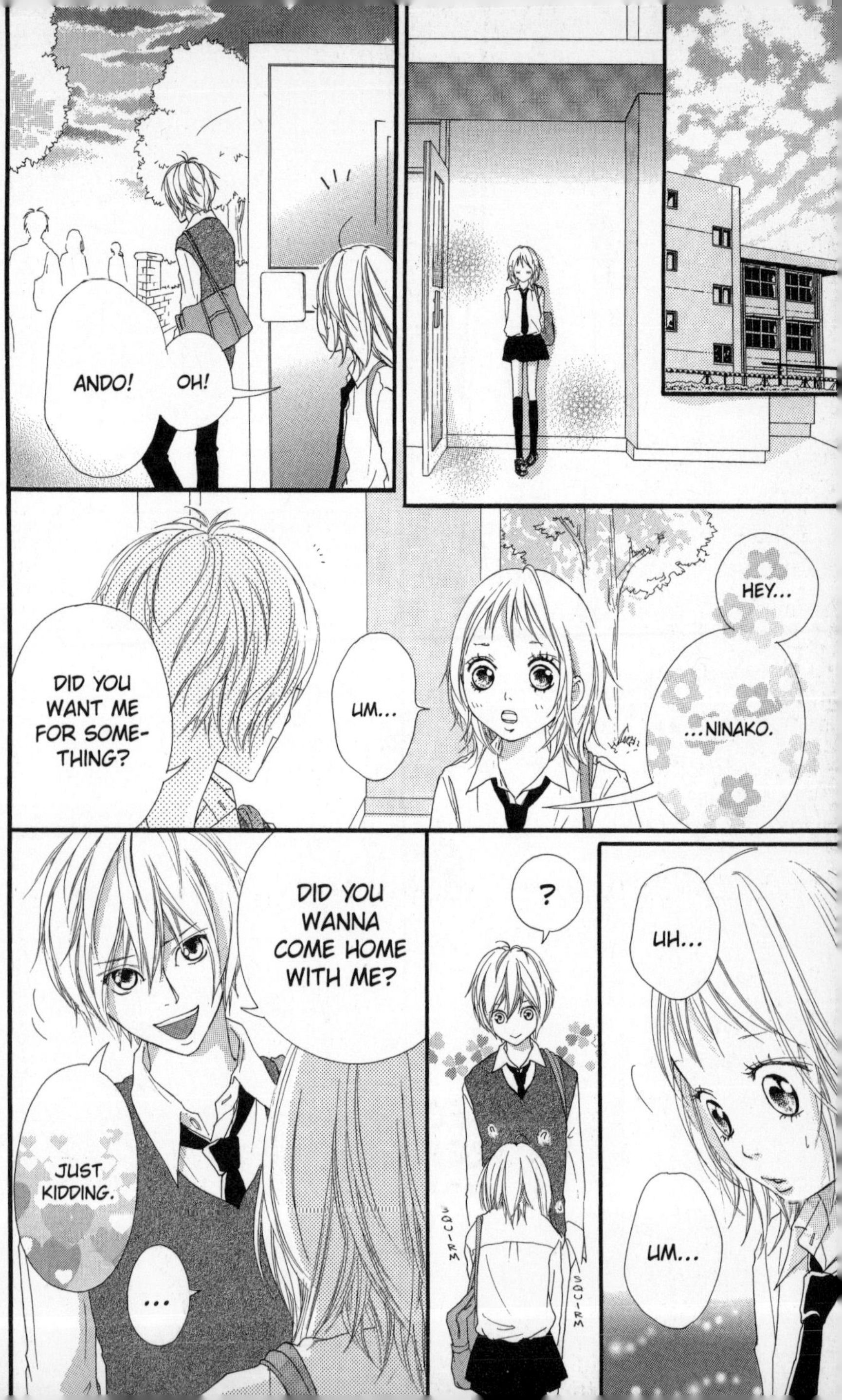
ANDO! OH!
HEY...
...NINAKO.
UM...
DID YOU WANT ME FOR SOME-THING?
UH...
UM...
?
SQUIRM
SQUIRM
DID YOU WANNA COME HOME WITH ME?
JUST KIDDING.
...

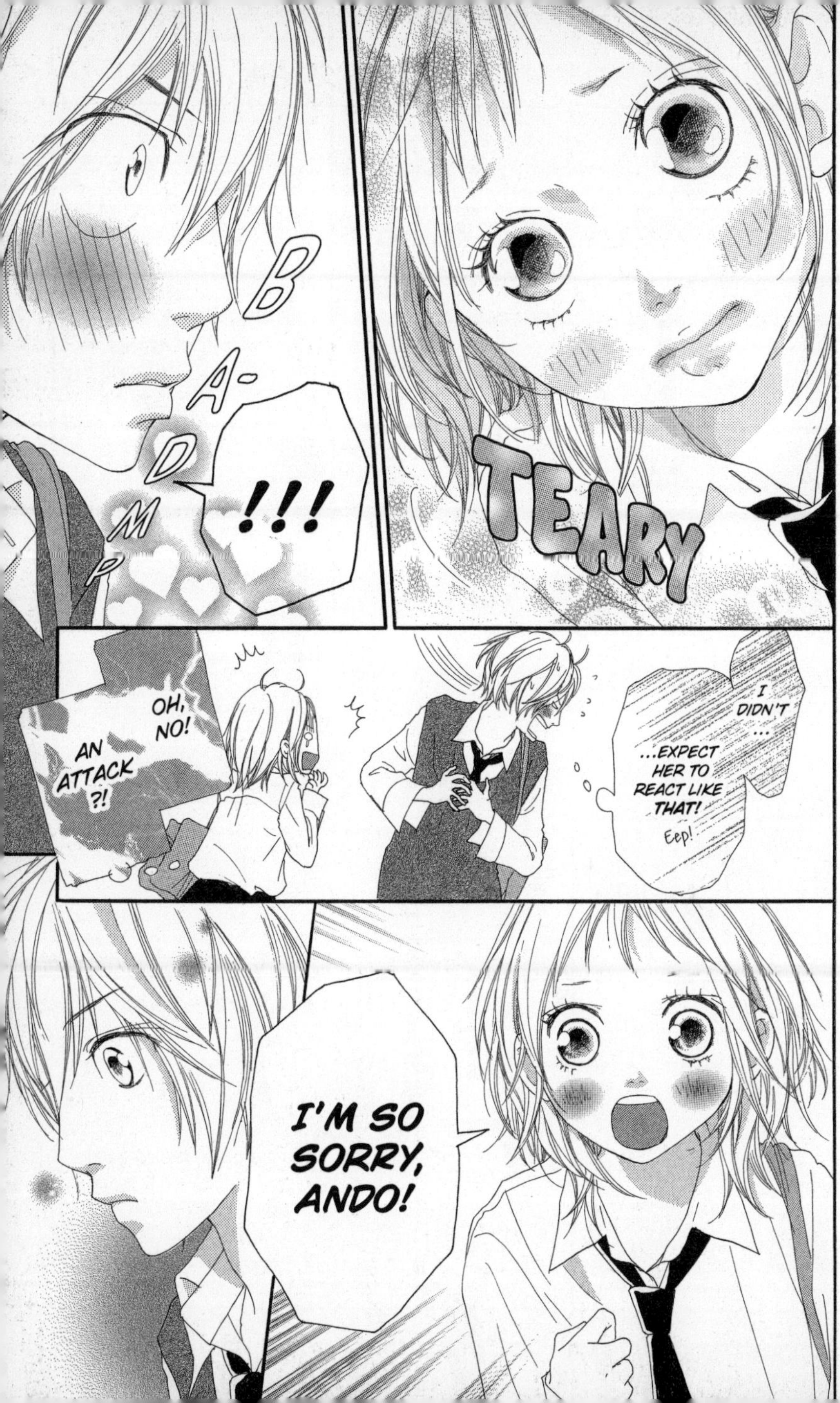
TEARY
!!!
BA-DUMP
I DIDN'T ...
...EXPECT HER TO REACT LIKE THAT!
Eep!
OH, NO!
AN ATTACK ?!
I'M SO SORRY, ANDO!

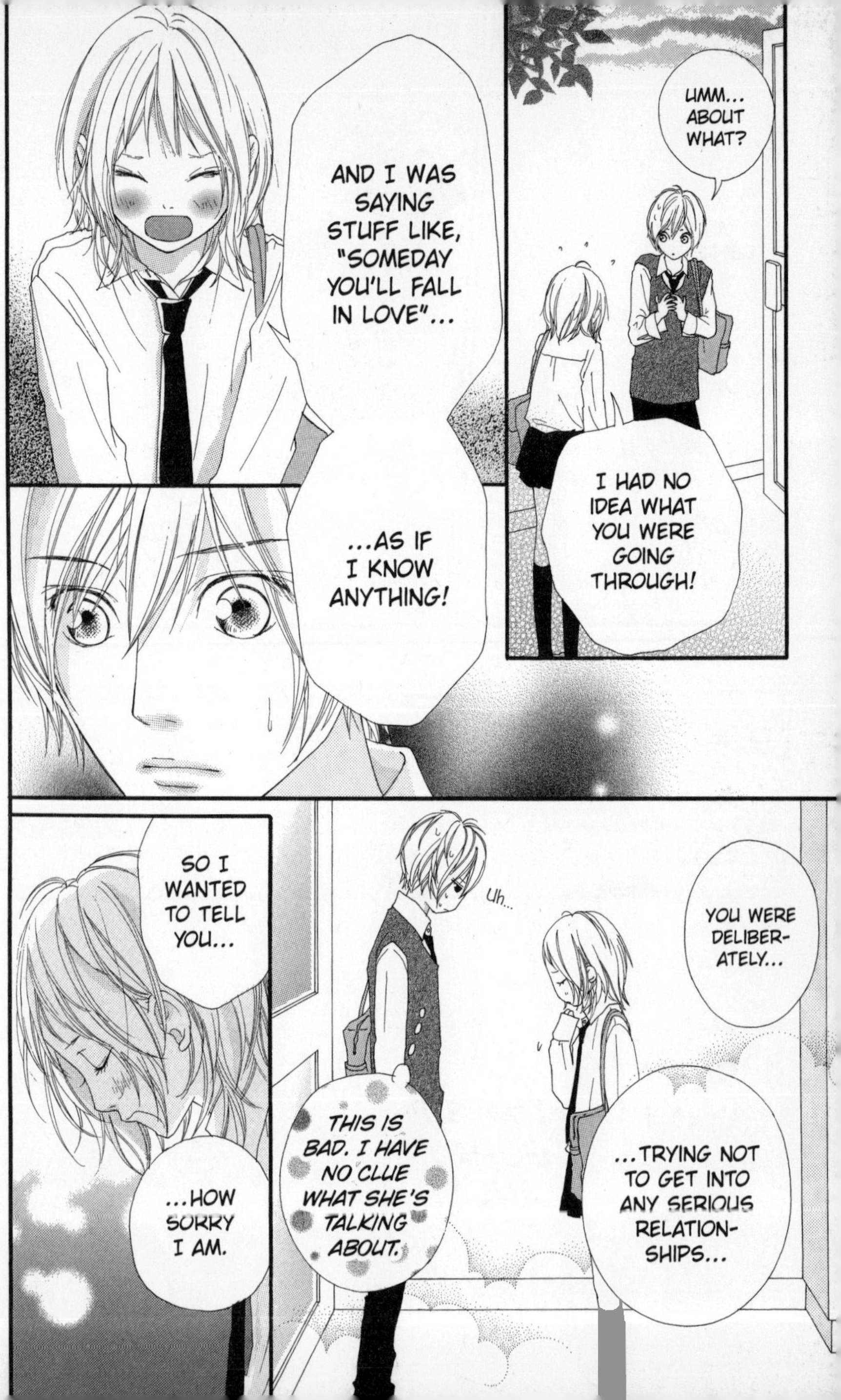
UMM... ABOUT WHAT?
I HAD NO IDEA WHAT YOU WERE GOING THROUGH!
AND I WAS SAYING STUFF LIKE, "SOMEDAY YOU'LL FALL IN LOVE"...
...AS IF I KNOW ANYTHING!
YOU WERE DELIBERATELY...
...TRYING NOT TO GET INTO ANY SERIOUS RELATIONSHIPS...
Uh...
THIS IS BAD. I HAVE NO CLUE WHAT SHE'S TALKING ABOUT.
SO I WANTED TO TELL YOU...
...HOW SORRY I AM.

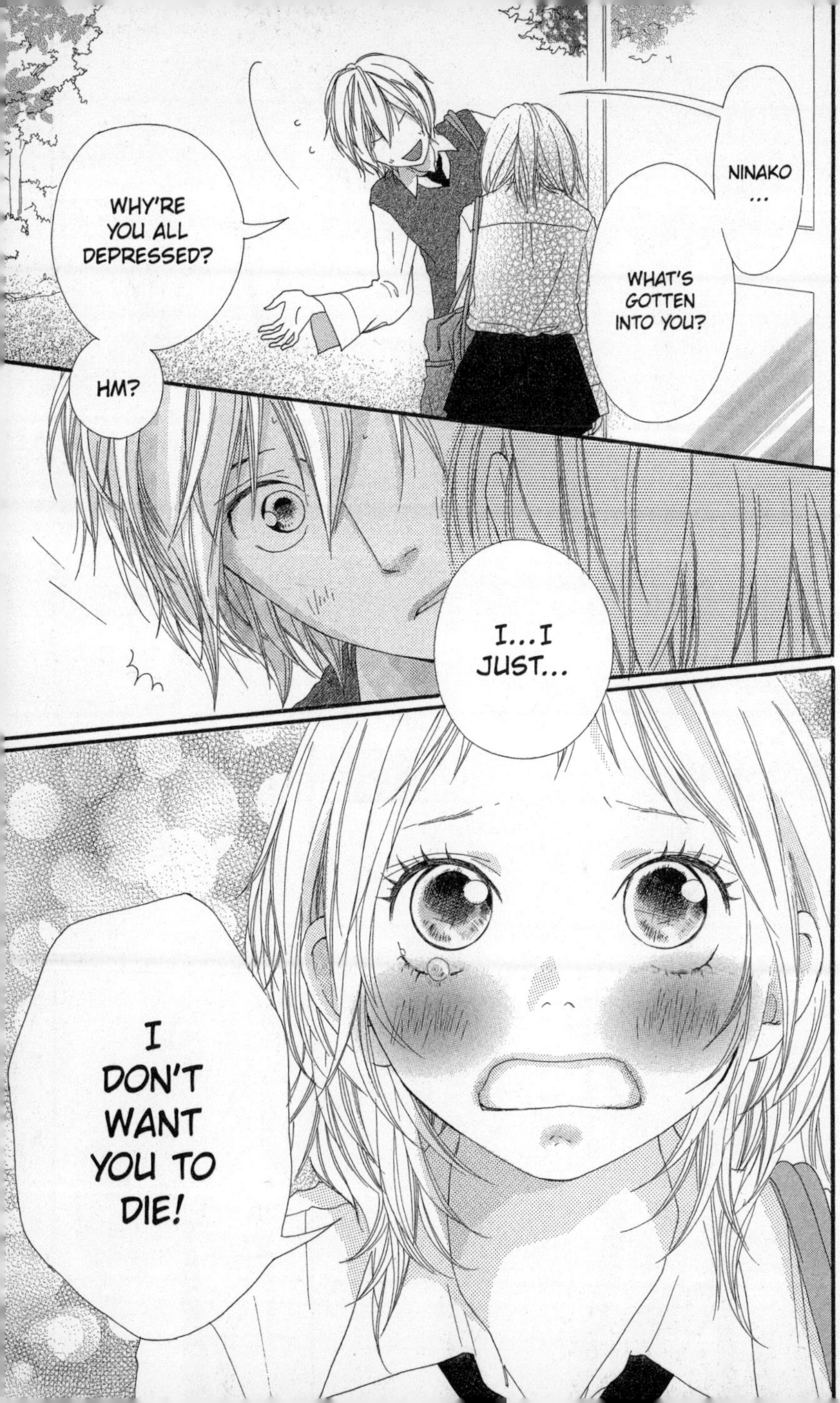
NINAKO ...
WHAT'S GOTTEN INTO YOU?
WHY'RE YOU ALL DEPRESSED?
HM?
I...I JUST...
I DON'T WANT YOU TO DIE!

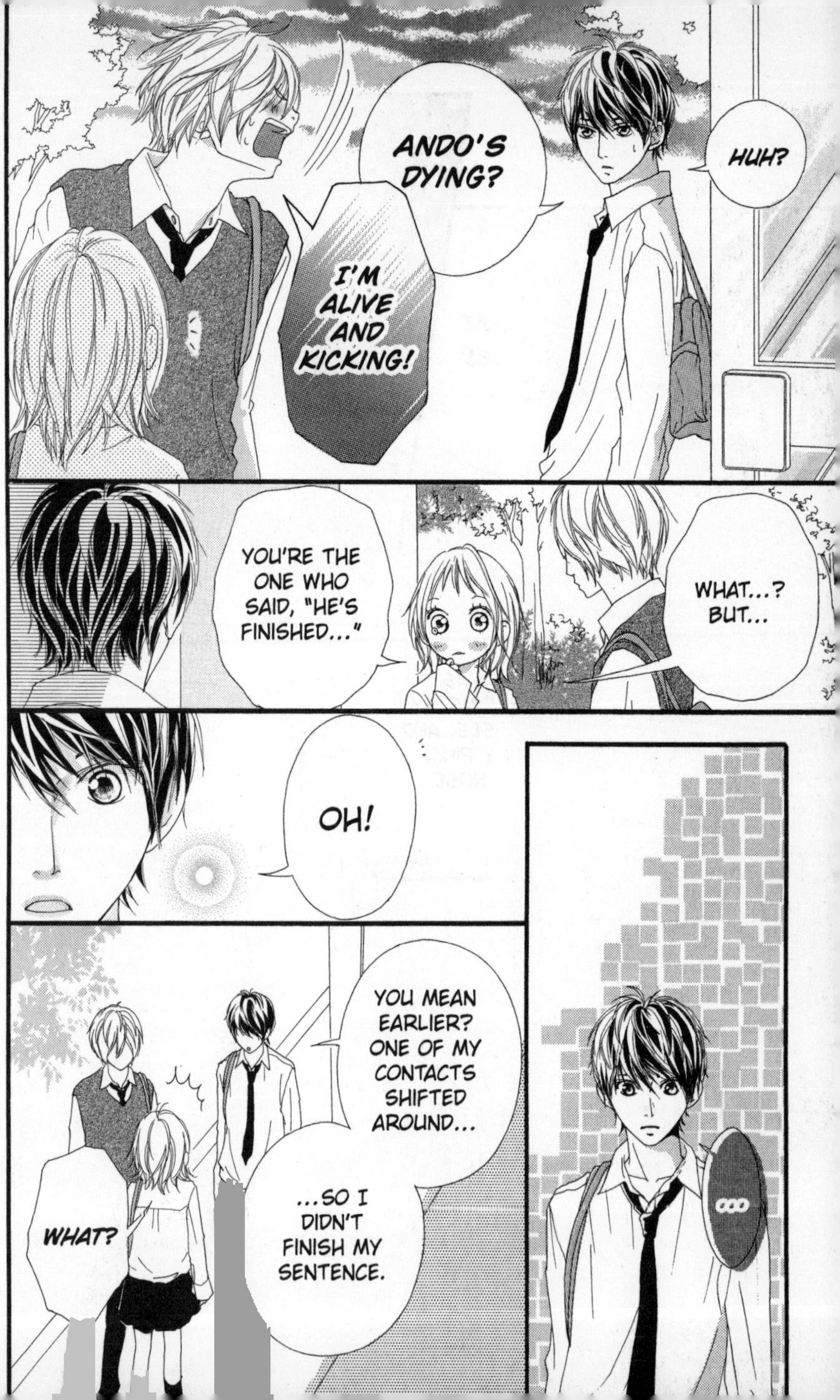
HUH?
ANDO'S DYING?
I'M ALIVE AND KICKING!
WHAT...? BUT...
YOU'RE THE ONE WHO SAID, "HE'S FINISHED..."
OH!
YOU MEAN EARLIER? ONE OF MY CONTACTS SHIFTED AROUND...
...SO I DIDN'T FINISH MY SENTENCE.
WHAT?

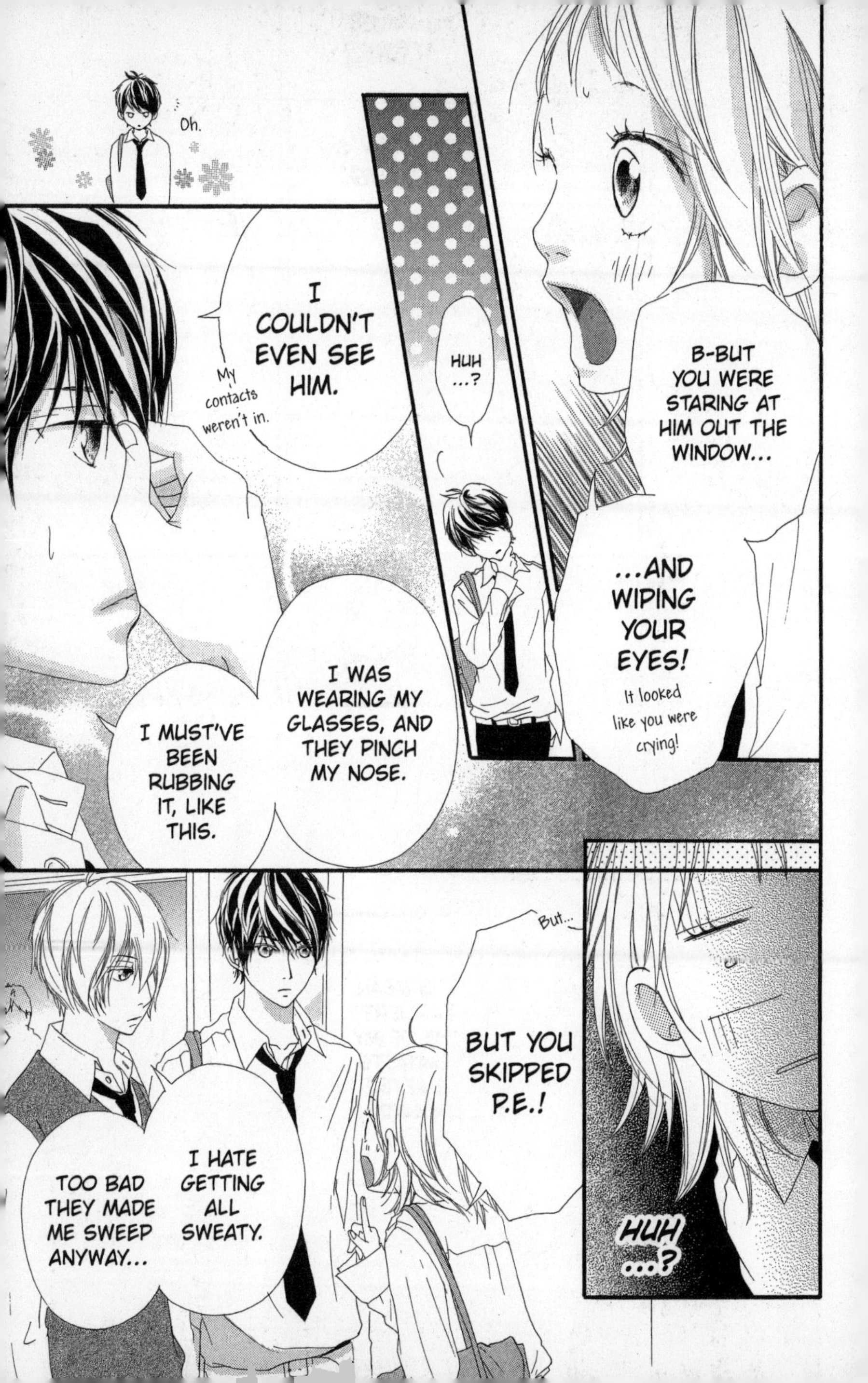
B-BUT YOU WERE STARING AT HIM OUT THE WINDOW...
...AND WIPING YOUR EYES!
It looked like you were crying!
HUH ...?
Oh.
I COULDN'T EVEN SEE HIM.
My contacts weren't in.
I WAS WEARING MY GLASSES, AND THEY PINCH MY NOSE.
I MUST'VE BEEN RUBBING IT, LIKE THIS.
HUH ...?
But...
BUT YOU SKIPPED P.E.!
I HATE GETTING ALL SWEATY.
TOO BAD THEY MADE ME SWEEP ANYWAY...

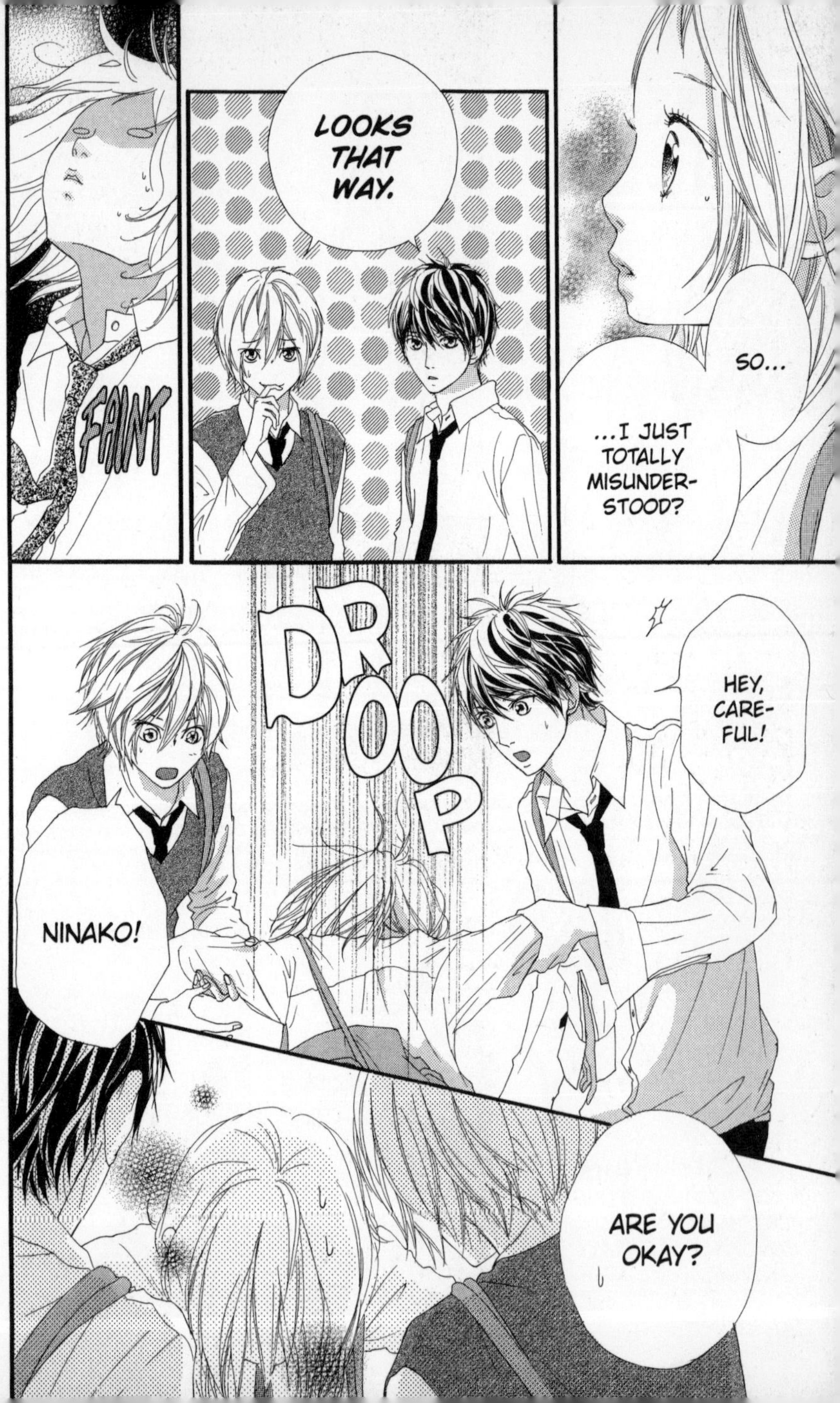
SO...
...I JUST TOTALLY MISUNDER-STOOD?
LOOKS THAT WAY.
FAINT
HEY, CARE-FUL!
DROOP
NINAKO!
ARE YOU OKAY?

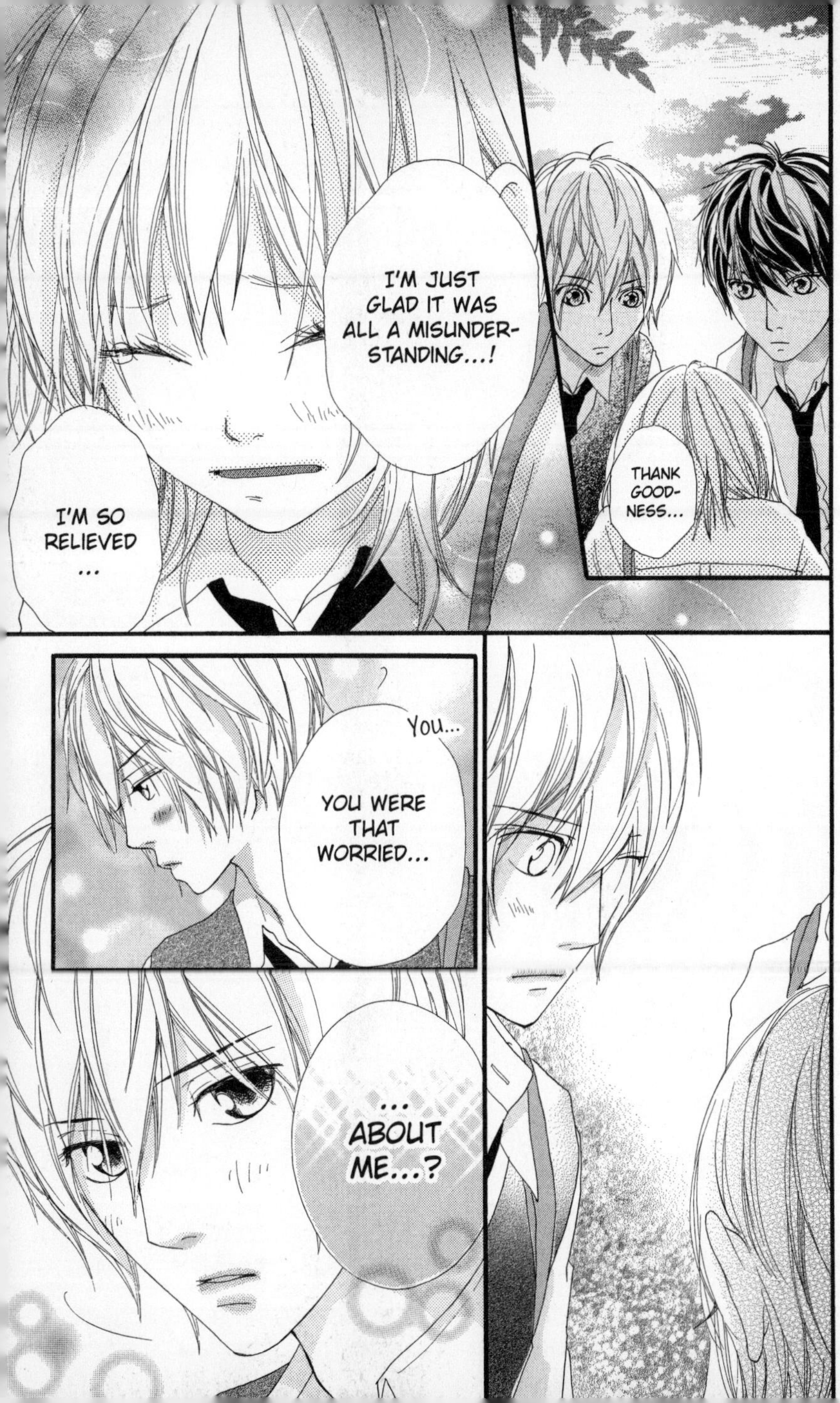
THANK GOODNESS...
I'M JUST GLAD IT WAS ALL A MISUNDERSTANDING...!
I'M SO RELIEVED...
You...
YOU WERE THAT WORRIED...
... ABOUT ME...?

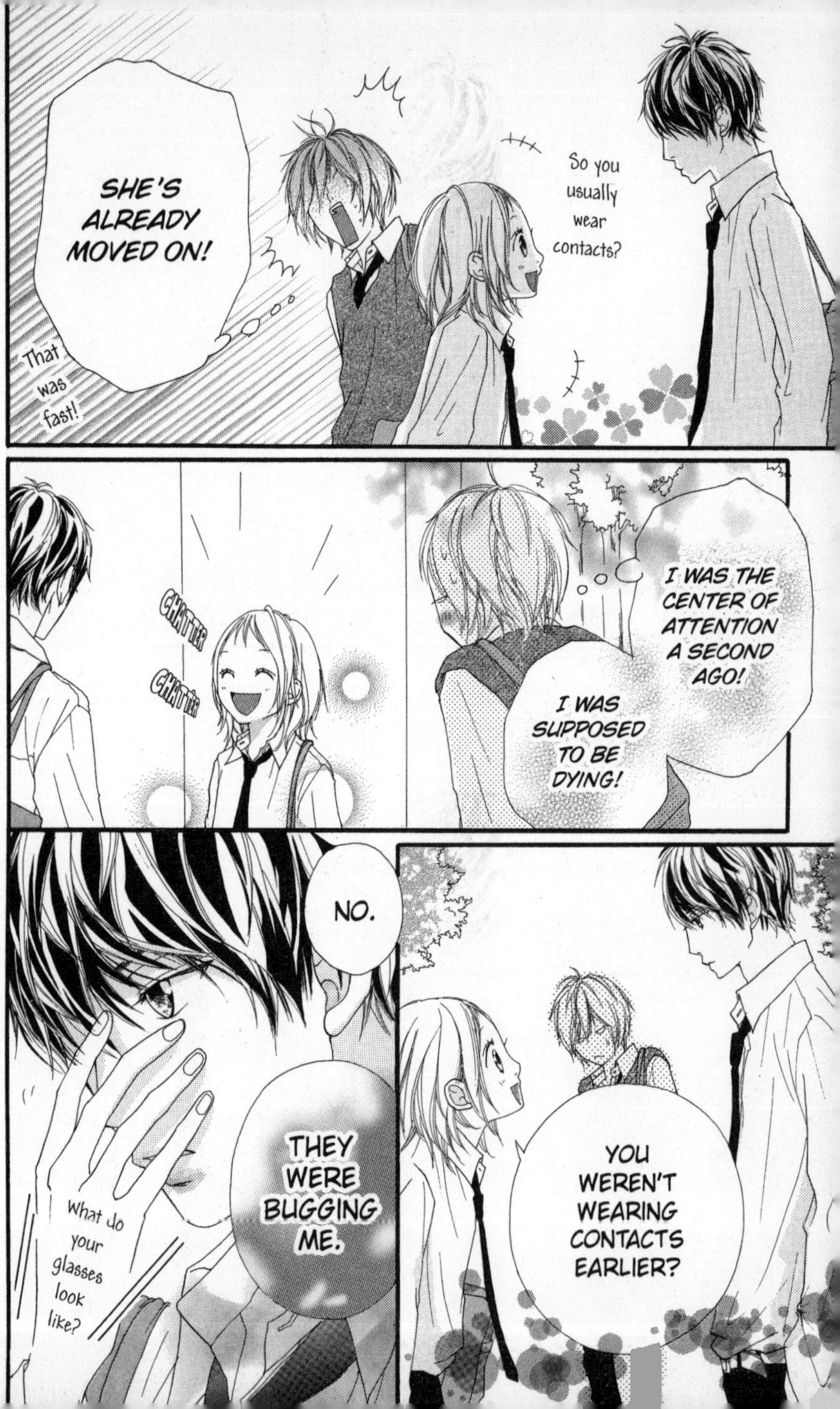
So you usually wear contacts?
SHE'S ALREADY MOVED ON!
That was fast!
I WAS THE CENTER OF ATTENTION A SECOND AGO!
I WAS SUPPOSED TO BE DYING!
CHATTER
CHATTER
YOU WEREN'T WEARING CONTACTS EARLIER?
NO.
THEY WERE BUGGING ME.
What do your glasses look like?

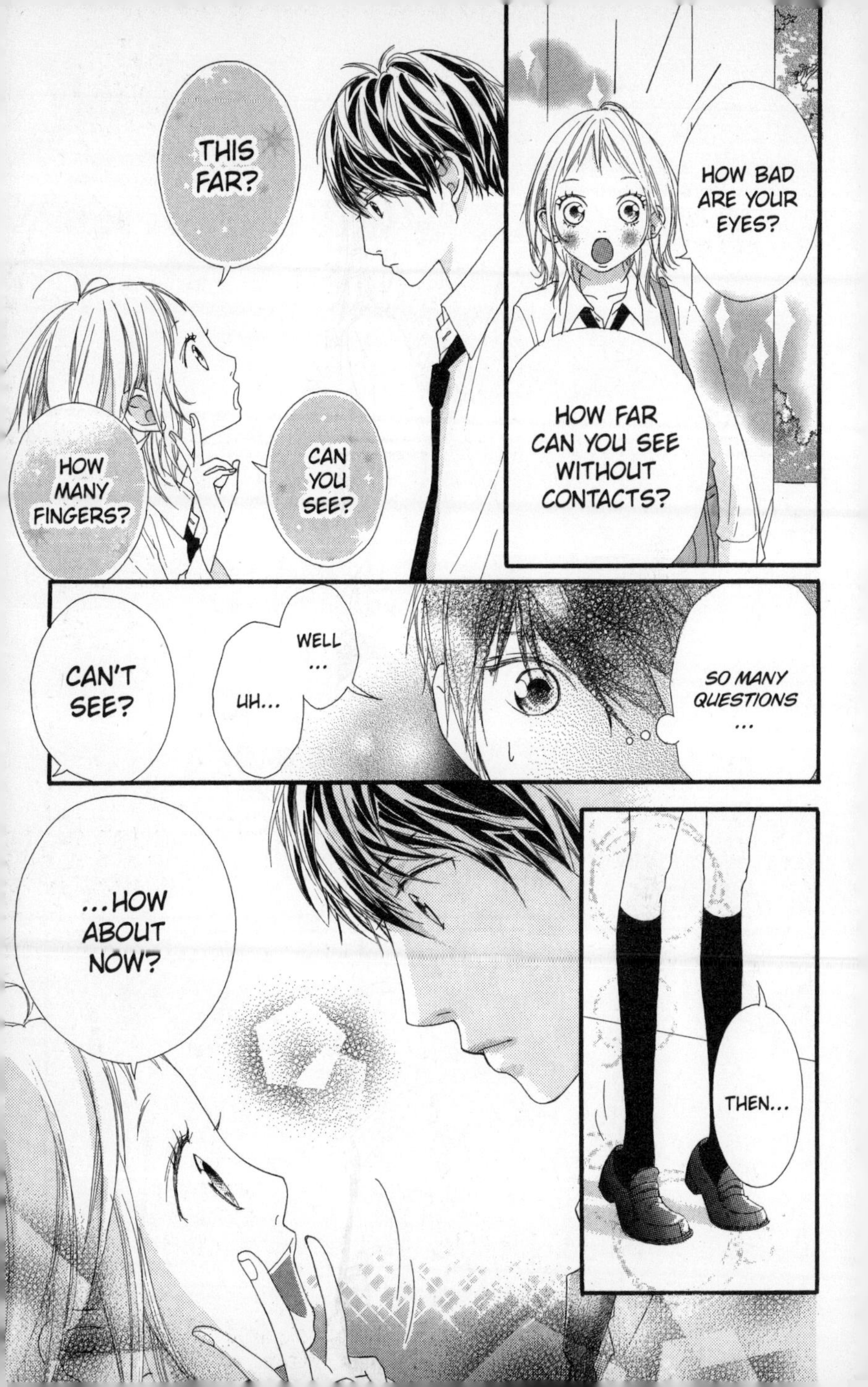
HOW BAD ARE YOUR EYES?
HOW FAR CAN YOU SEE WITHOUT CONTACTS?
THIS FAR?
CAN YOU SEE?
HOW MANY FINGERS?
SO MANY QUESTIONS ...
WELL ...
UH...
CAN'T SEE?
THEN...
...HOW ABOUT NOW?

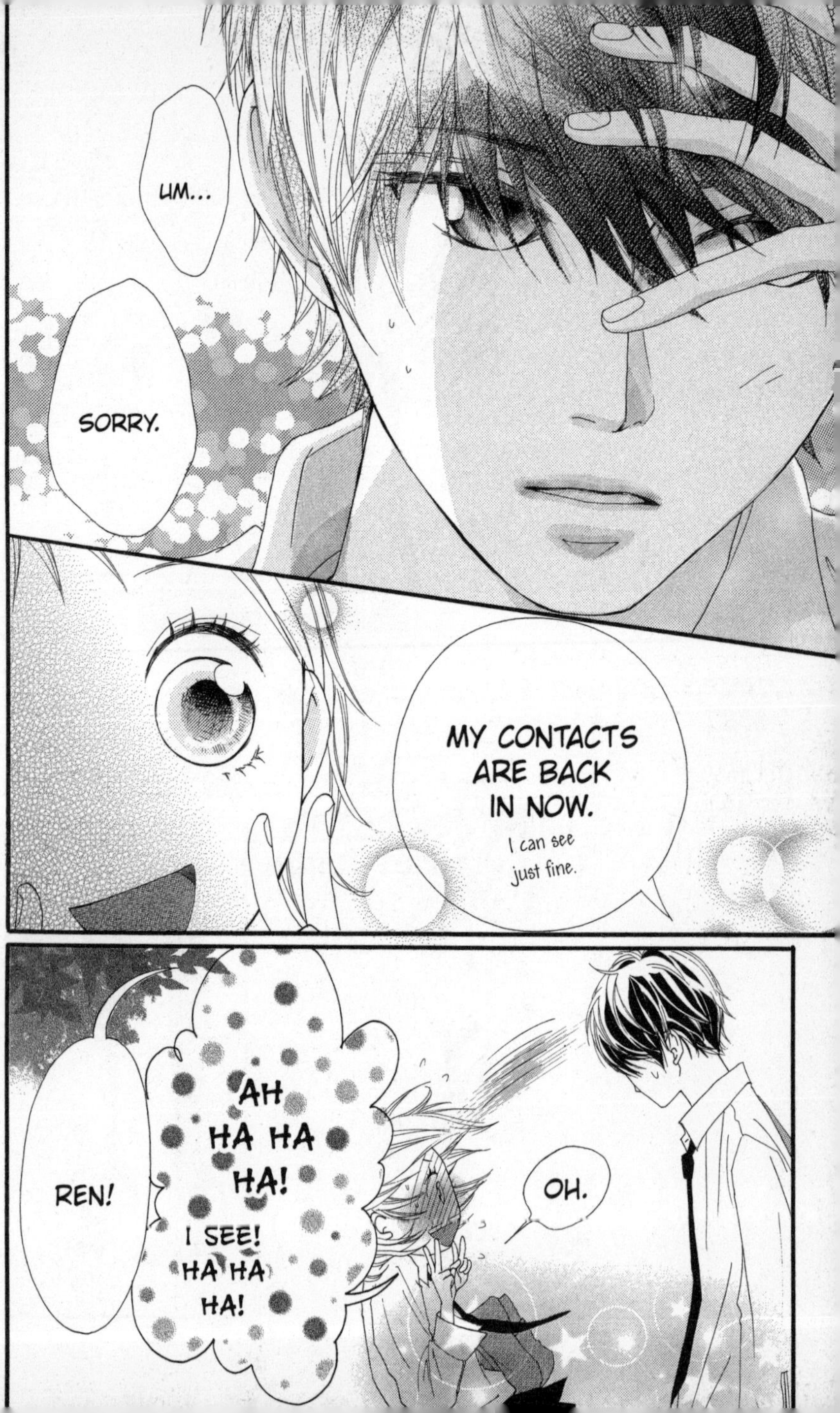
UM...
SORRY.
MY CONTACTS ARE BACK IN NOW.
I can see just fine.
OH.
AH HA HA HA!
I SEE! HA HA HA!
REN!

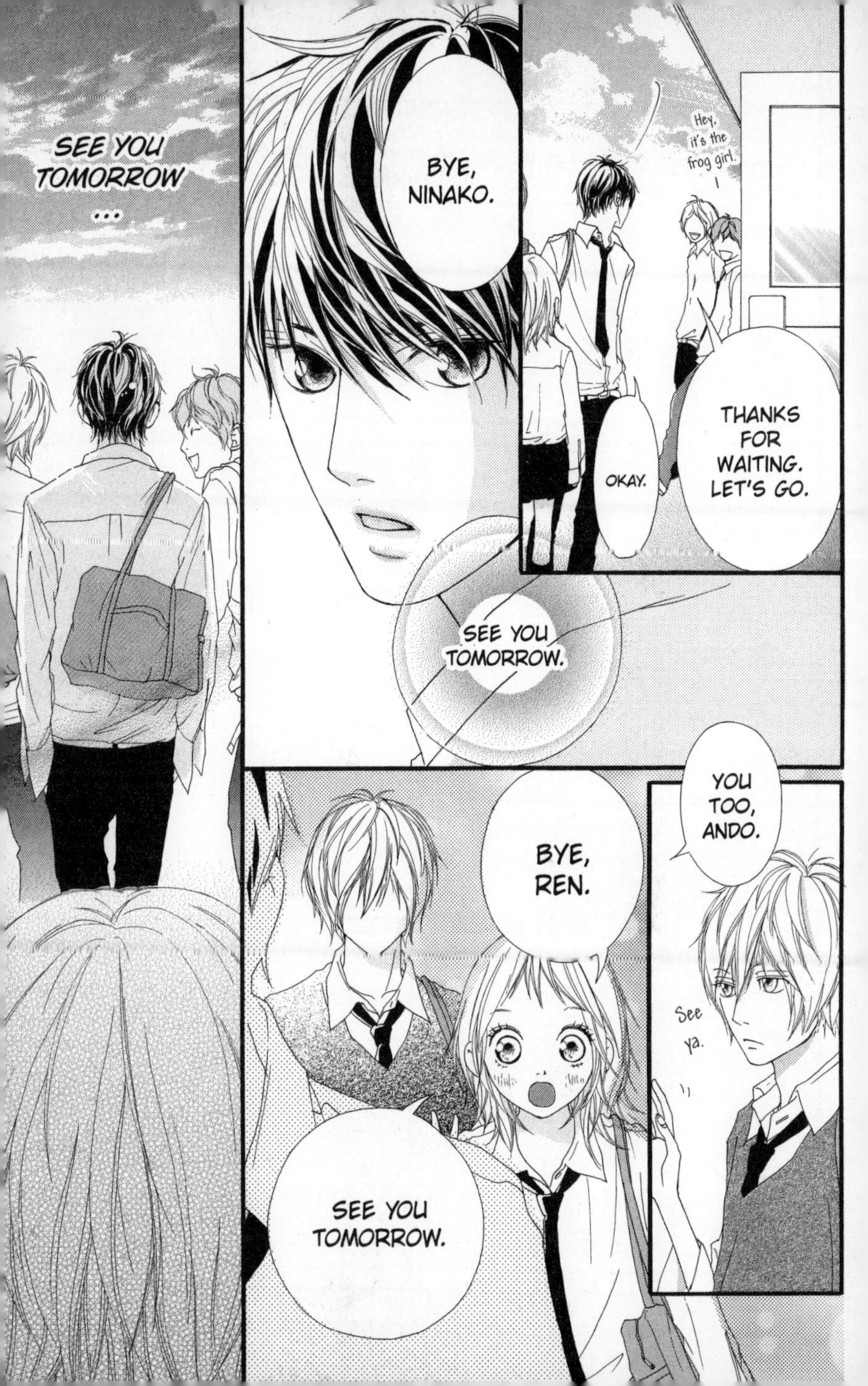
Hey, it's the frog girl.
THANKS FOR WAITING. LET'S GO.
OKAY.
BYE, NINAKO.
SEE YOU TOMORROW.
BYE, REN.
SEE YOU TOMORROW.
YOU TOO, ANDO.
See ya.
SEE YOU TOMORROW...

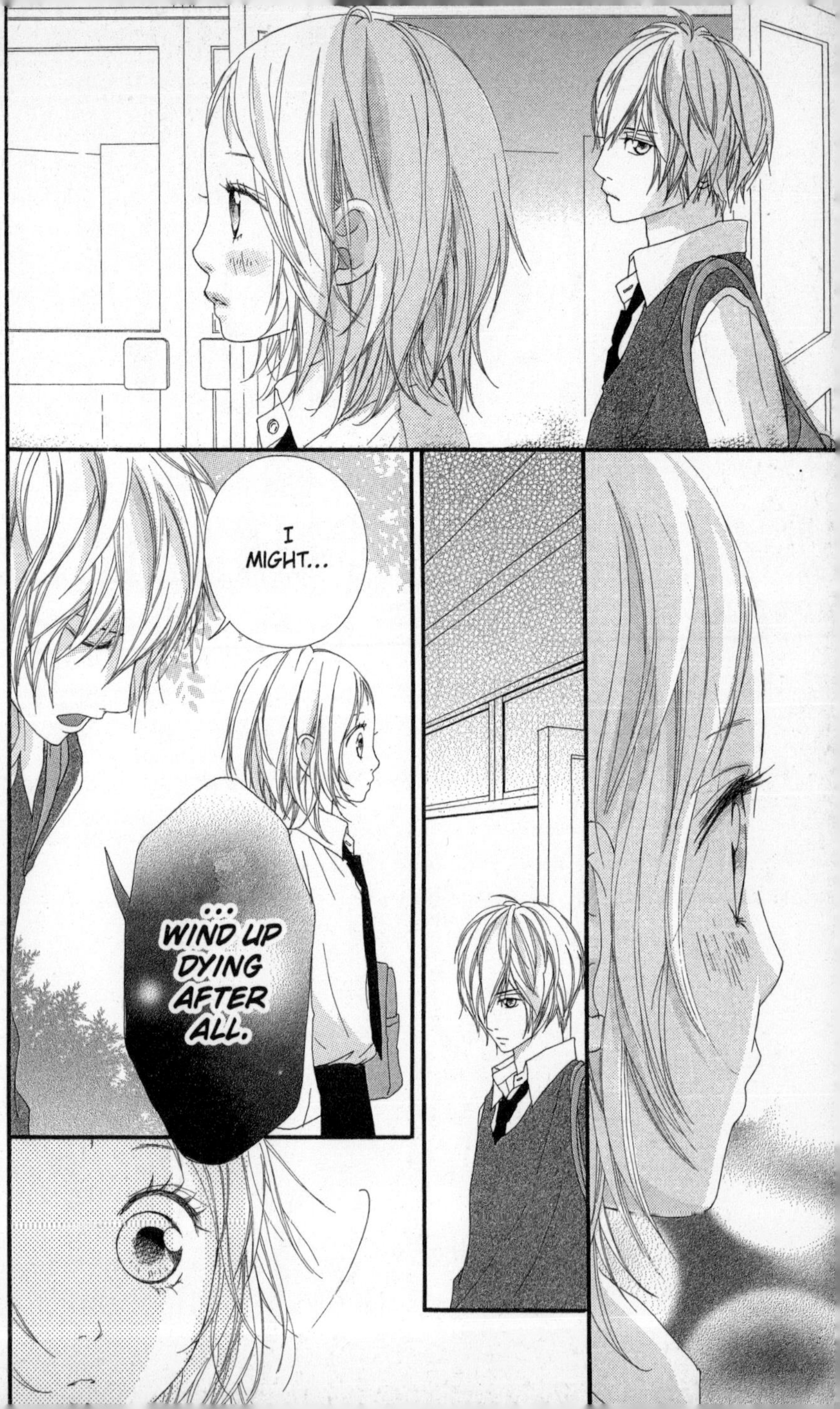
I MIGHT...
...WIND UP DYING AFTER ALL.

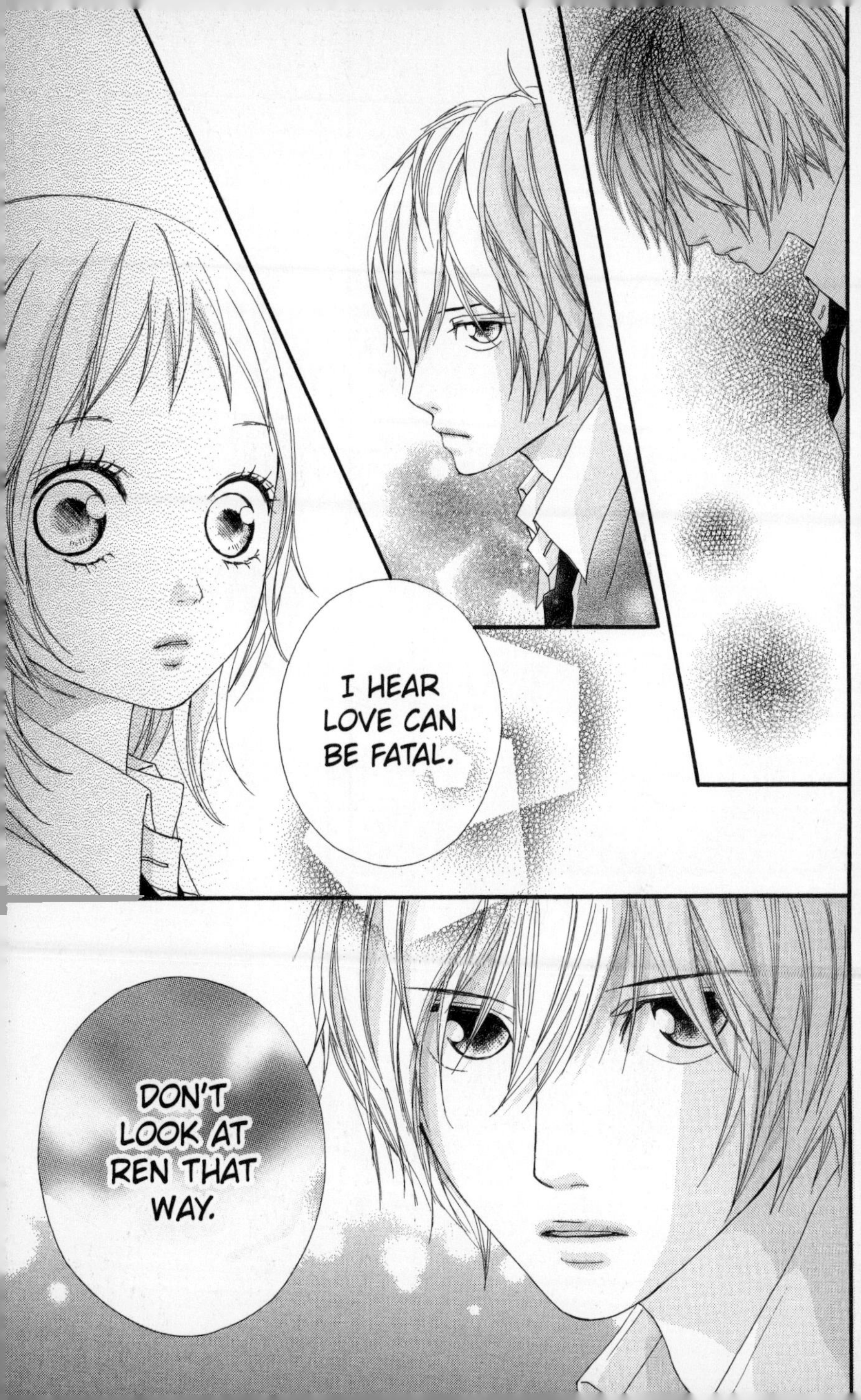
I HEAR LOVE CAN BE FATAL.
DON'T LOOK AT REN THAT WAY.

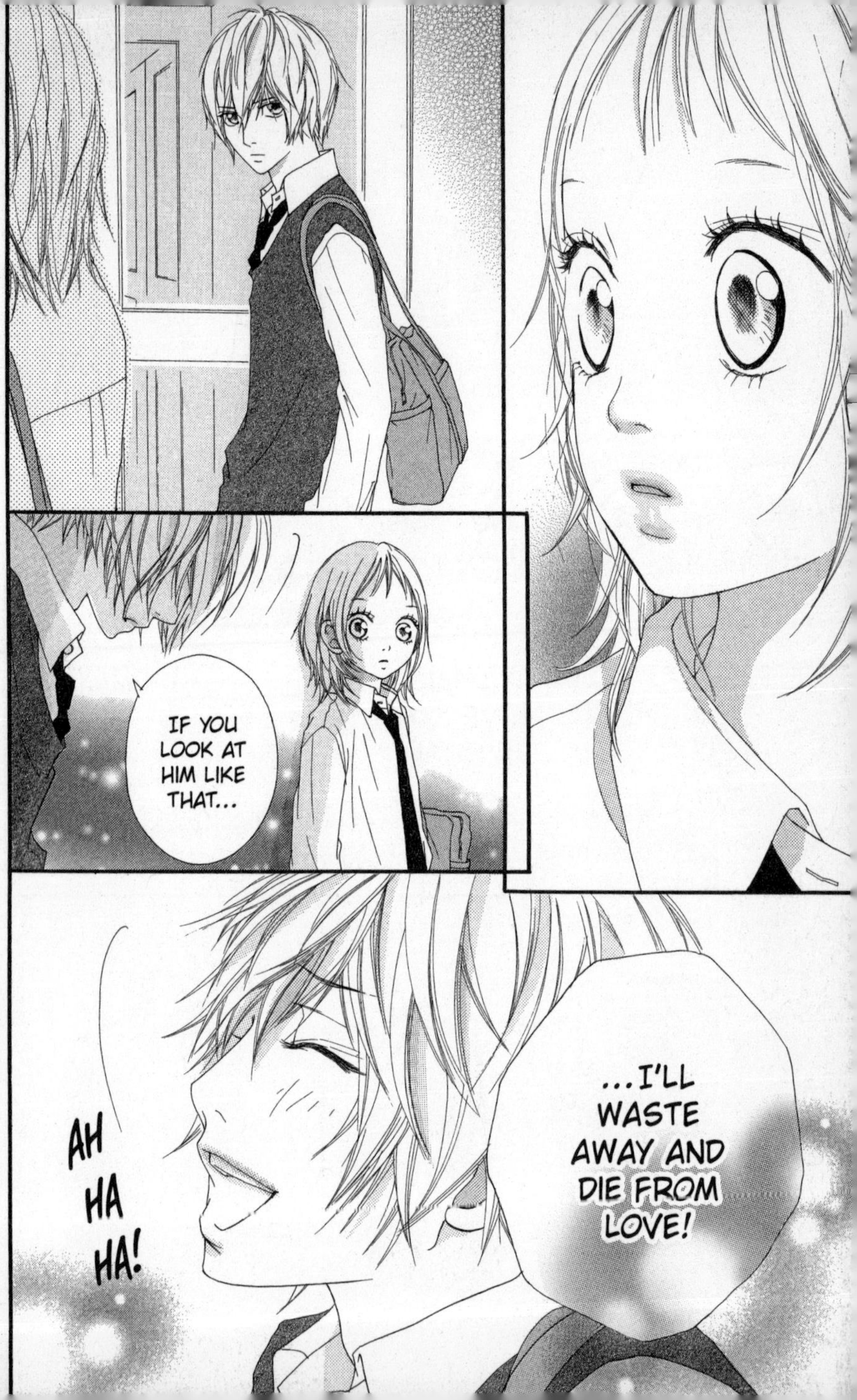
IF YOU LOOK AT HIM LIKE THAT...
...I'LL WASTE AWAY AND DIE FROM LOVE!
AH HA HA!

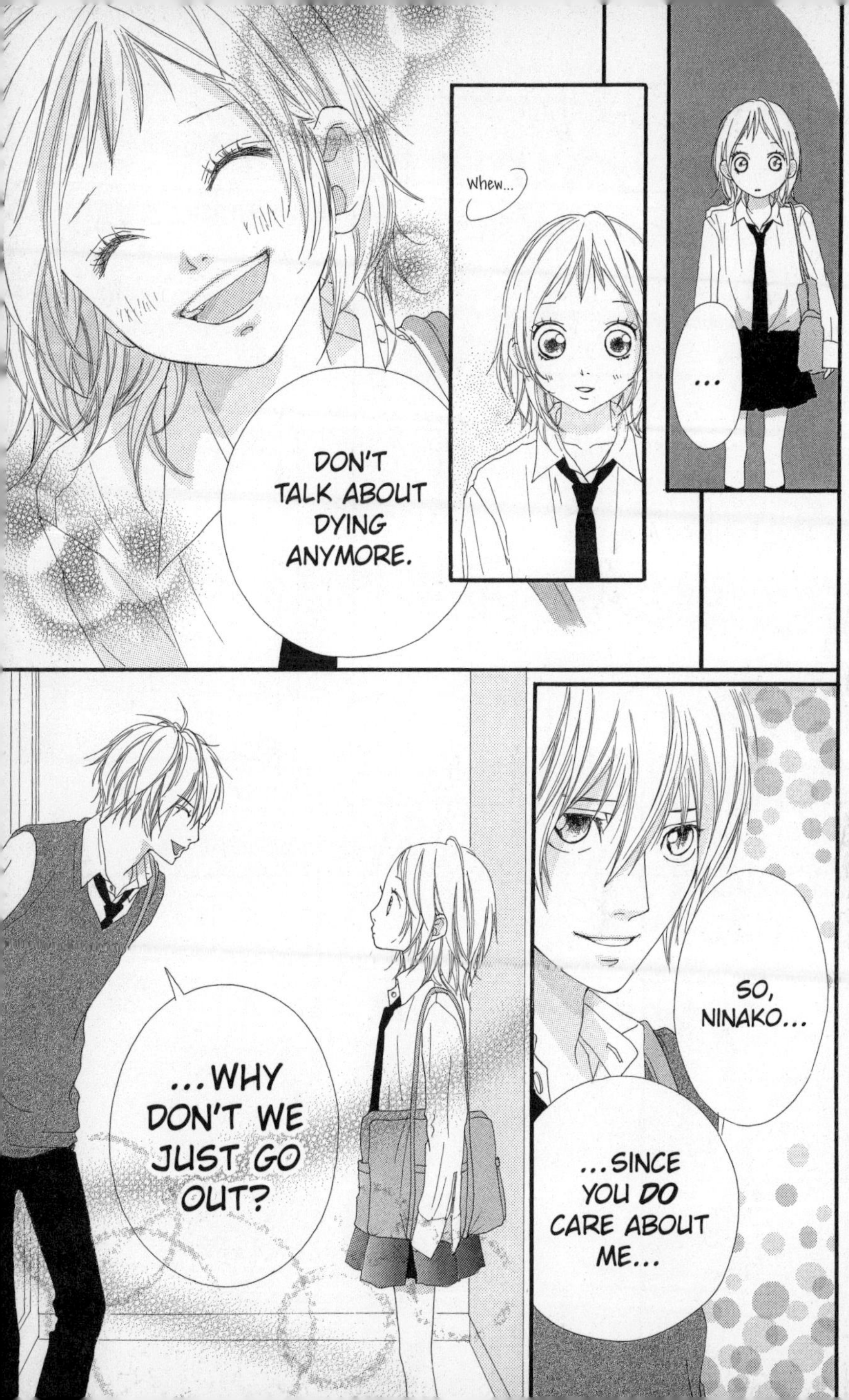
...
Whew...
DON'T TALK ABOUT DYING ANYMORE.
SO, NINAKO...
...SINCE YOU *DO* CARE ABOUT ME...
...WHY DON'T WE JUST GO OUT?

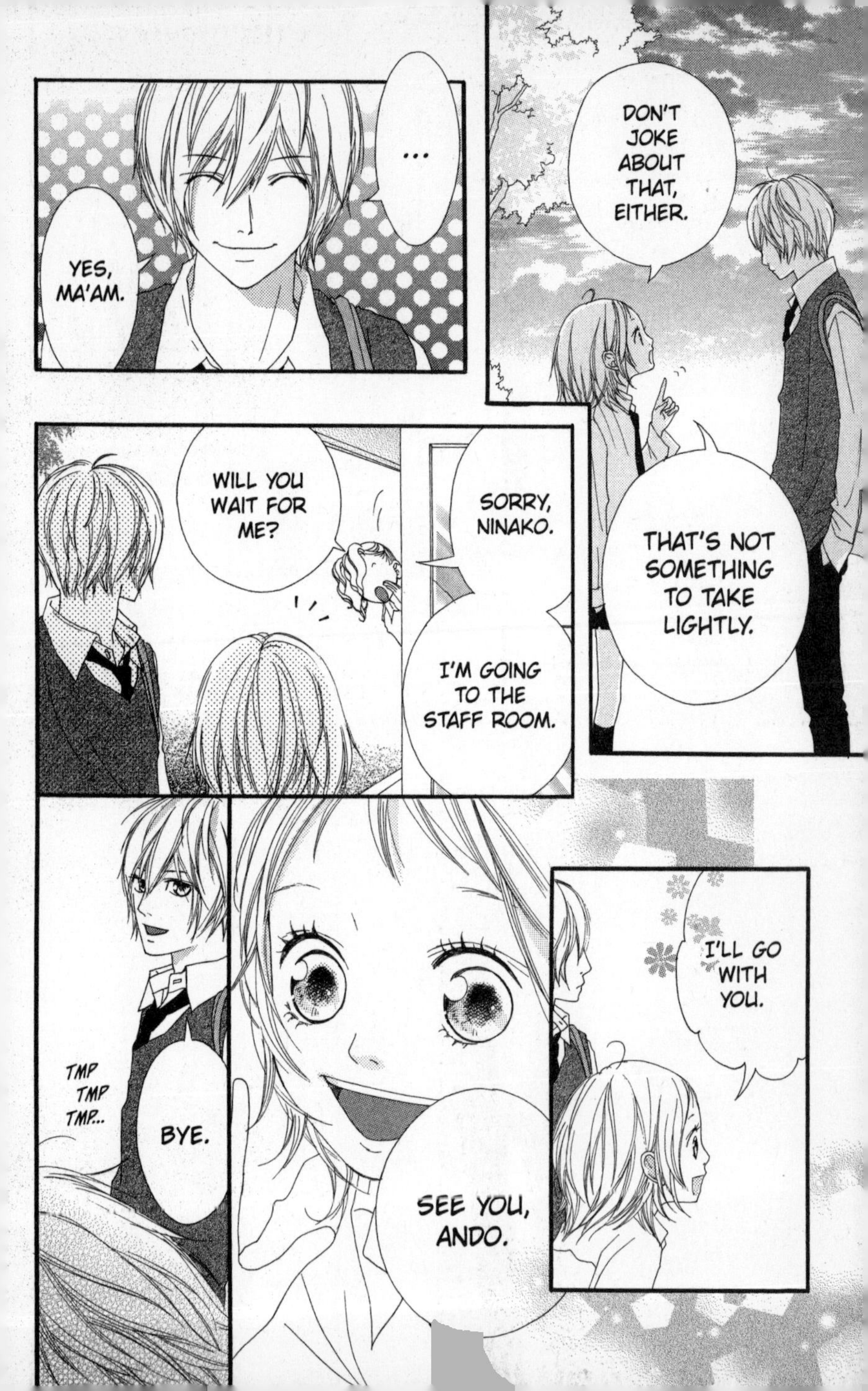
DON'T JOKE ABOUT THAT, EITHER.
THAT'S NOT SOMETHING TO TAKE LIGHTLY.
...
YES, MA'AM.
SORRY, NINAKO.
I'M GOING TO THE STAFF ROOM.
WILL YOU WAIT FOR ME?
I'LL GO WITH YOU.
SEE YOU, ANDO.
BYE.
TMP TMP TMP...

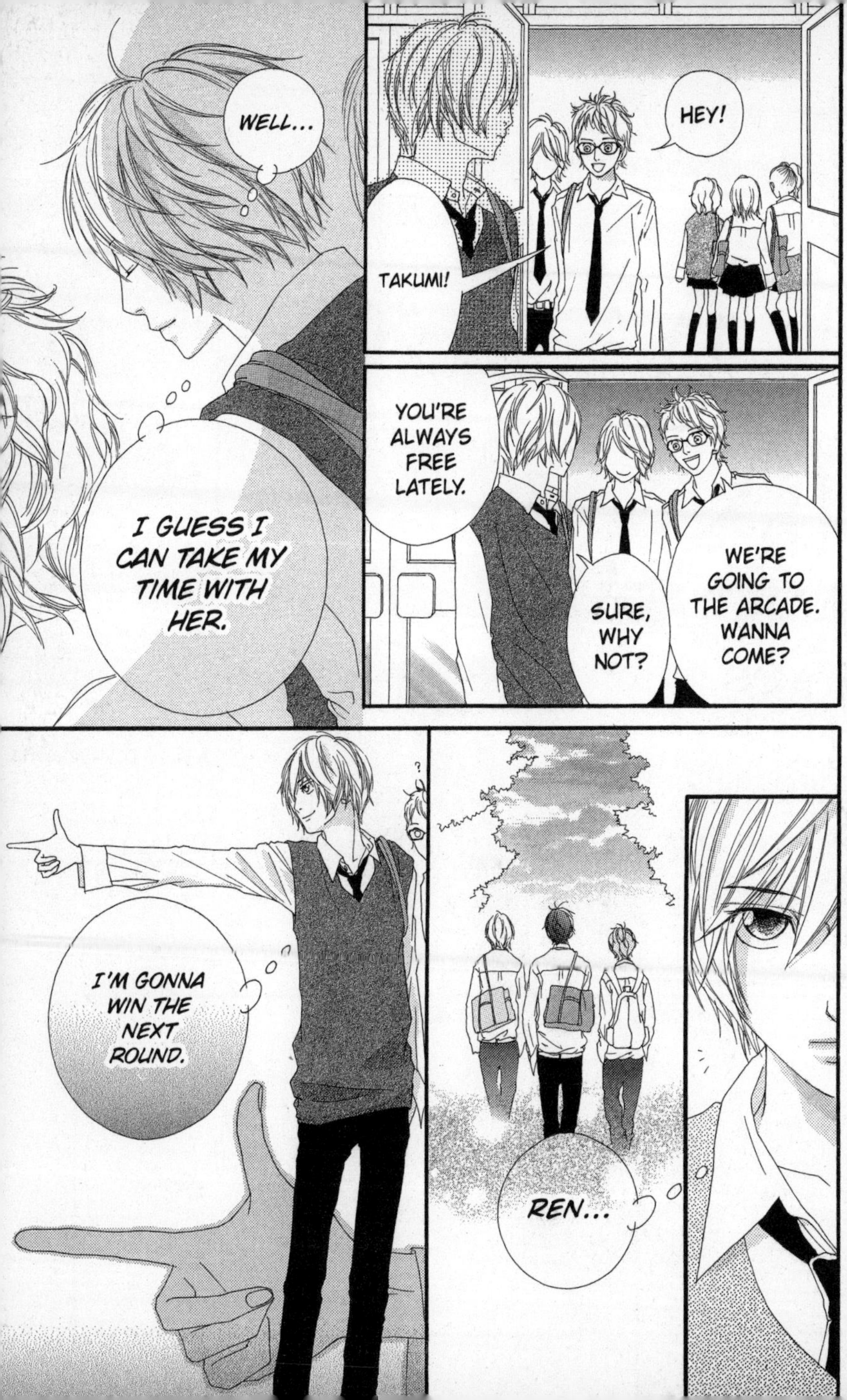
HEY!
TAKUMI!
YOU'RE ALWAYS FREE LATELY.
WE'RE GOING TO THE ARCADE. WANNA COME?
SURE, WHY NOT?
WELL...
I GUESS I CAN TAKE MY TIME WITH HER.
REN...
I'M GONNA WIN THE NEXT ROUND.

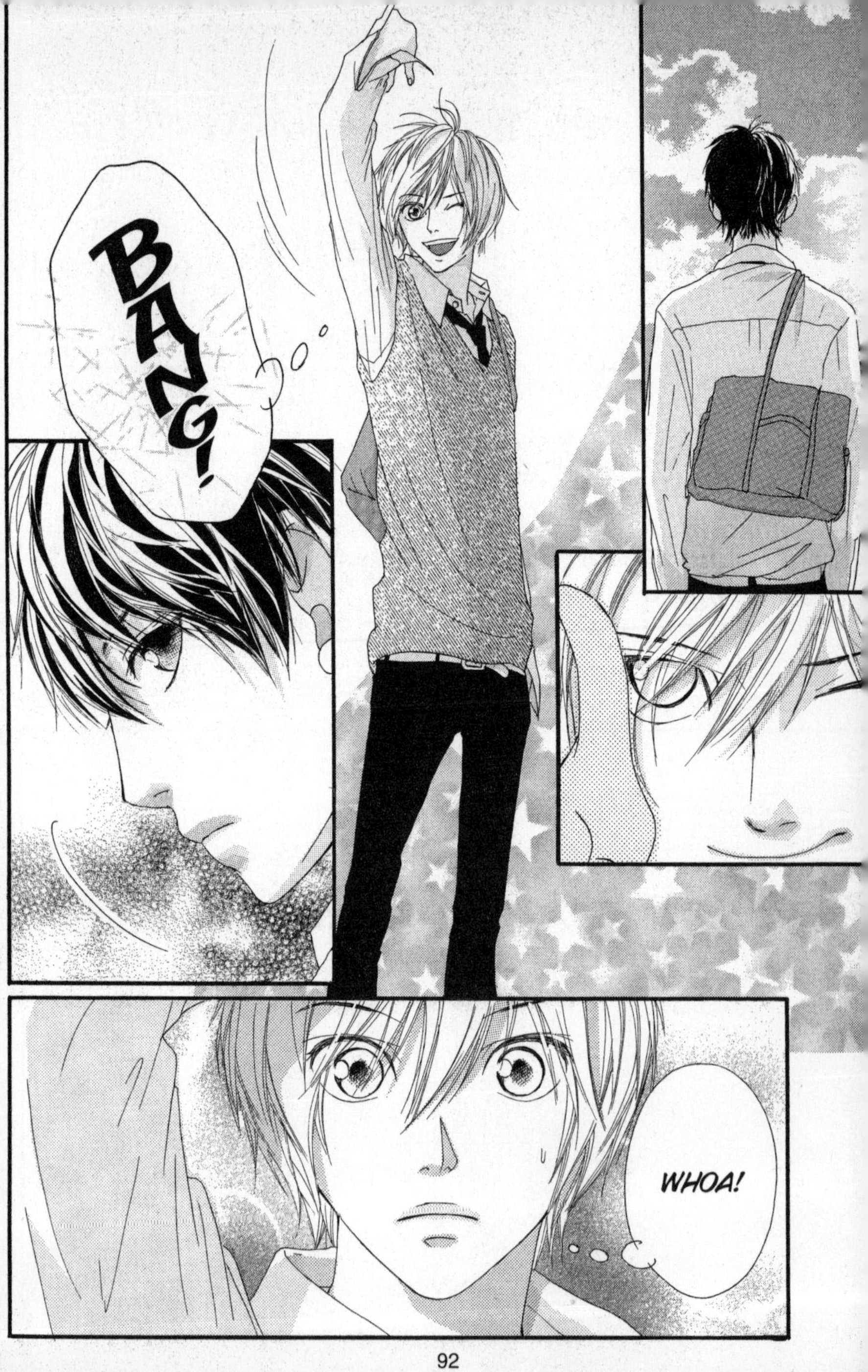
BANG!
WHOA!

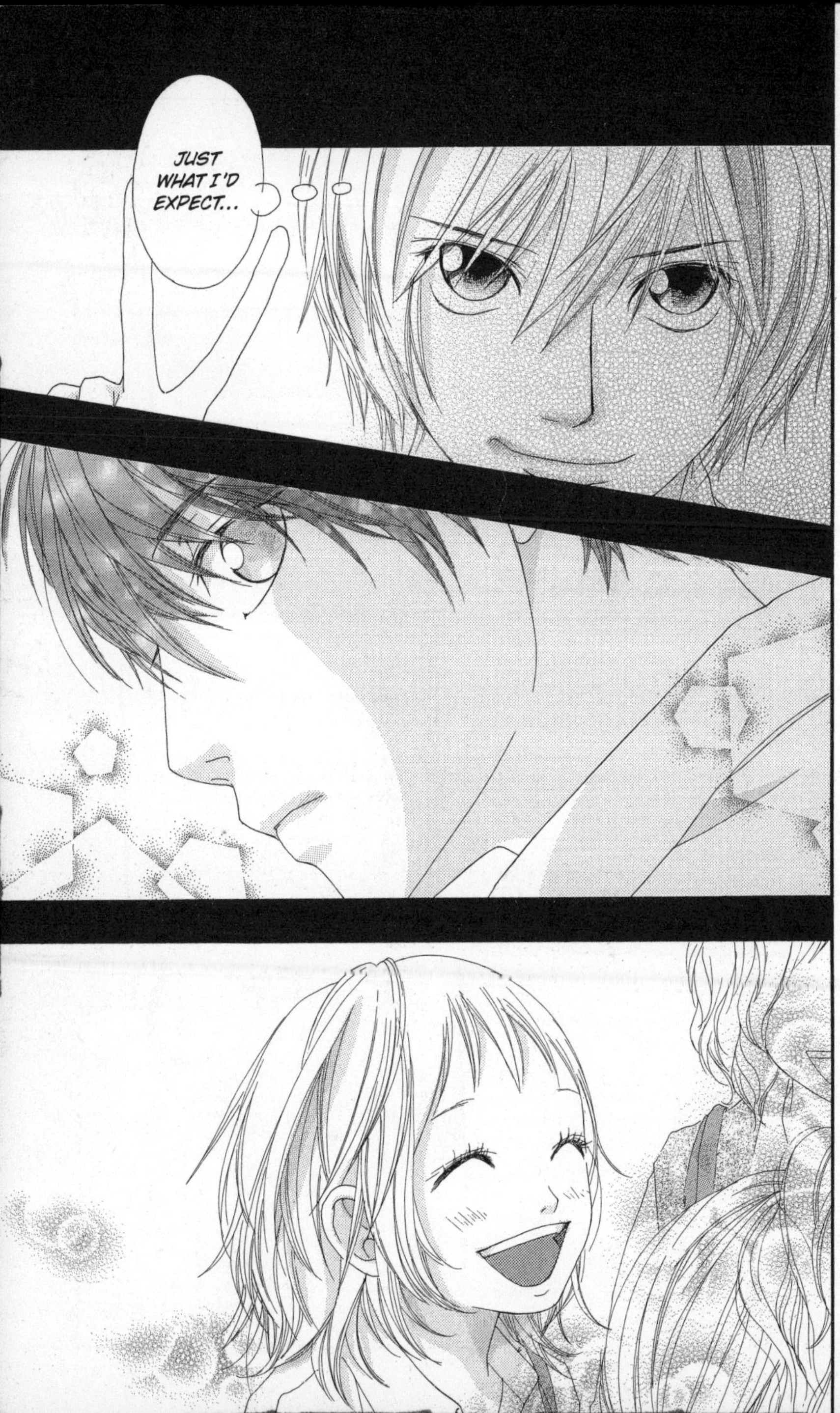
JUST WHAT I'D EXPECT...

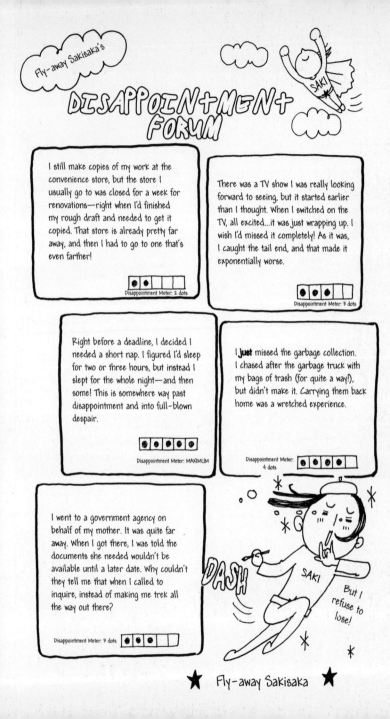

Fly-away Sakisaka's

DISAPPOINTMENT FORUM

SAKI

I still make copies of my work at the convenience store, but the store I usually go to was closed for a week for renovations—right when I'd finished my rough draft and needed to get it copied. That store is already pretty far away, and then I had to go to one that's even farther!

Disappointment Meter: 2 dots

There was a TV show I was really looking forward to seeing, but it started earlier than I thought. When I switched on the TV, all excited...it was just wrapping up. I wish I'd missed it completely! As it was, I caught the tail end, and that made it exponentially worse.

Disappointment Meter: 3 dots

Right before a deadline, I decided I needed a short nap. I figured I'd sleep for two or three hours, but instead I slept for the whole night—and then some! This is somewhere way past disappointment and into full-blown despair.

Disappointment Meter: MAXIMUM

I **just** missed the garbage collection. I chased after the garbage truck with my bags of trash (for quite a way!), but didn't make it. Carrying them back home was a wretched experience.

Disappointment Meter: 4 dots

I went to a government agency on behalf of my mother. It was quite far away. When I got there, I was told the documents she needed wouldn't be available until a later date. Why couldn't they tell me that when I called to inquire, instead of making me trek all the way out there?

Disappointment Meter: 3 dots

DASH

SAKI

But I refuse to lose!

★ Fly-away Sakisaka ★

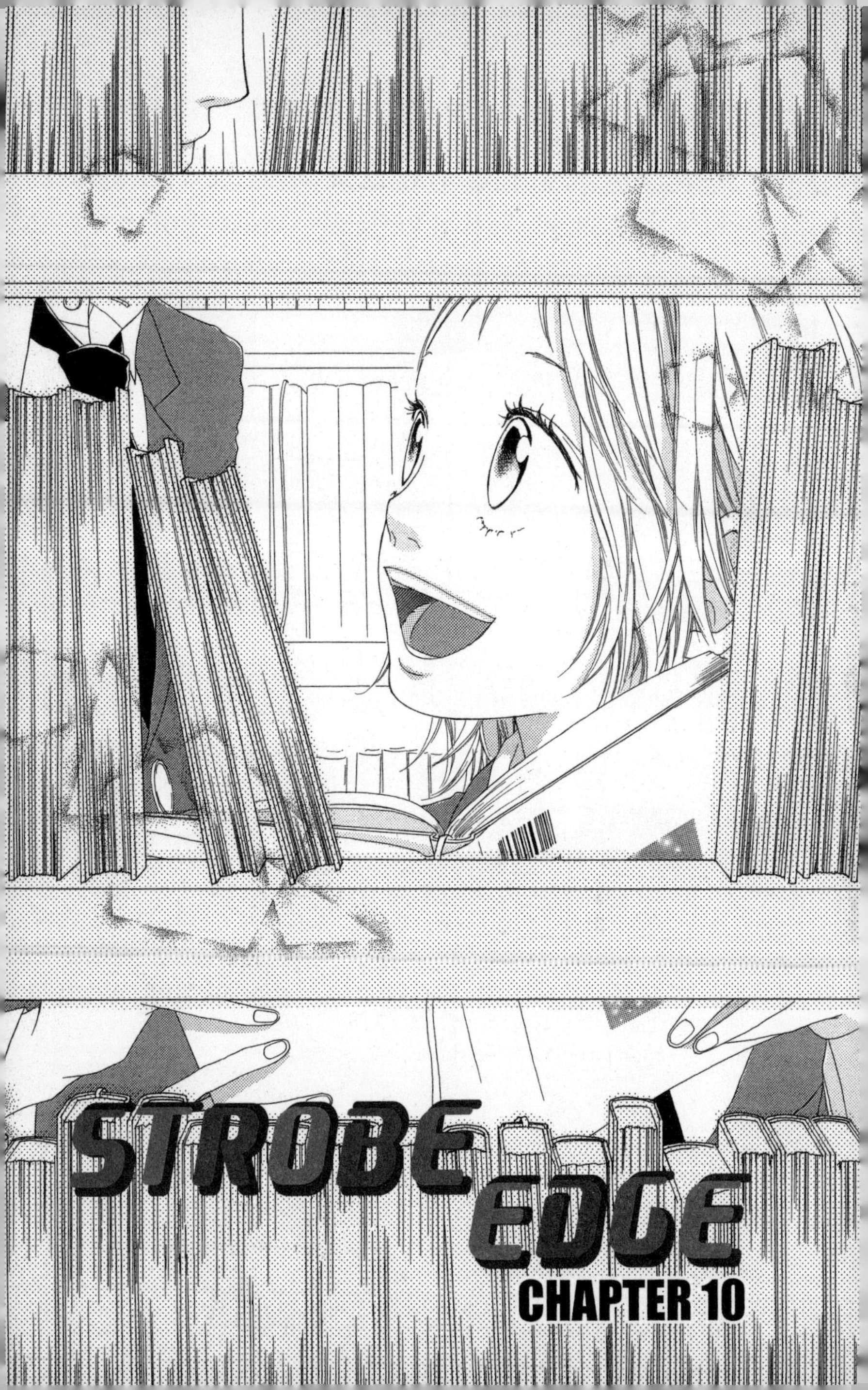
STROBE EDGE
CHAPTER 10

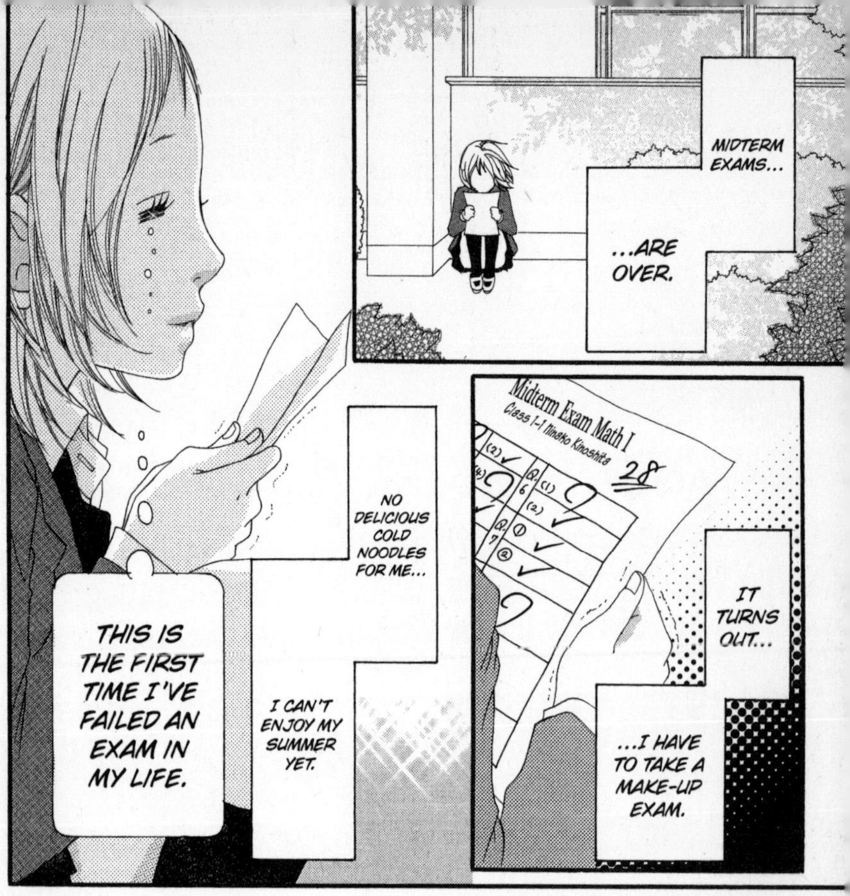
MIDTERM EXAMS...
...ARE OVER.
Midterm Exam Math I
Class 1-1 Ninako Kinoshita
28
IT TURNS OUT...
...I HAVE TO TAKE A MAKE-UP EXAM.
NO DELICIOUS COLD NOODLES FOR ME...
I CAN'T ENJOY MY SUMMER YET.
THIS IS THE FIRST TIME I'VE FAILED AN EXAM IN MY LIFE.

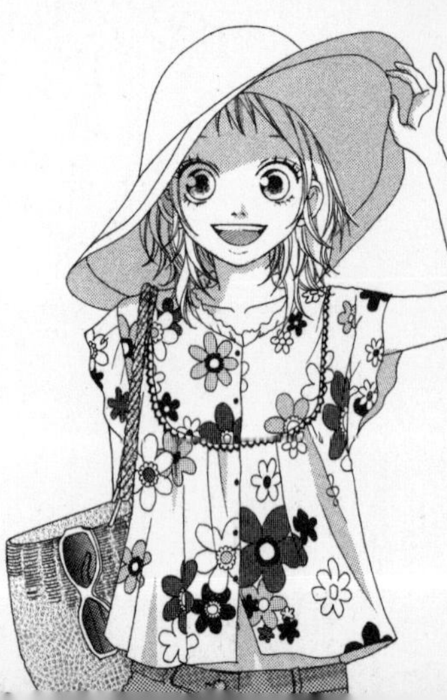

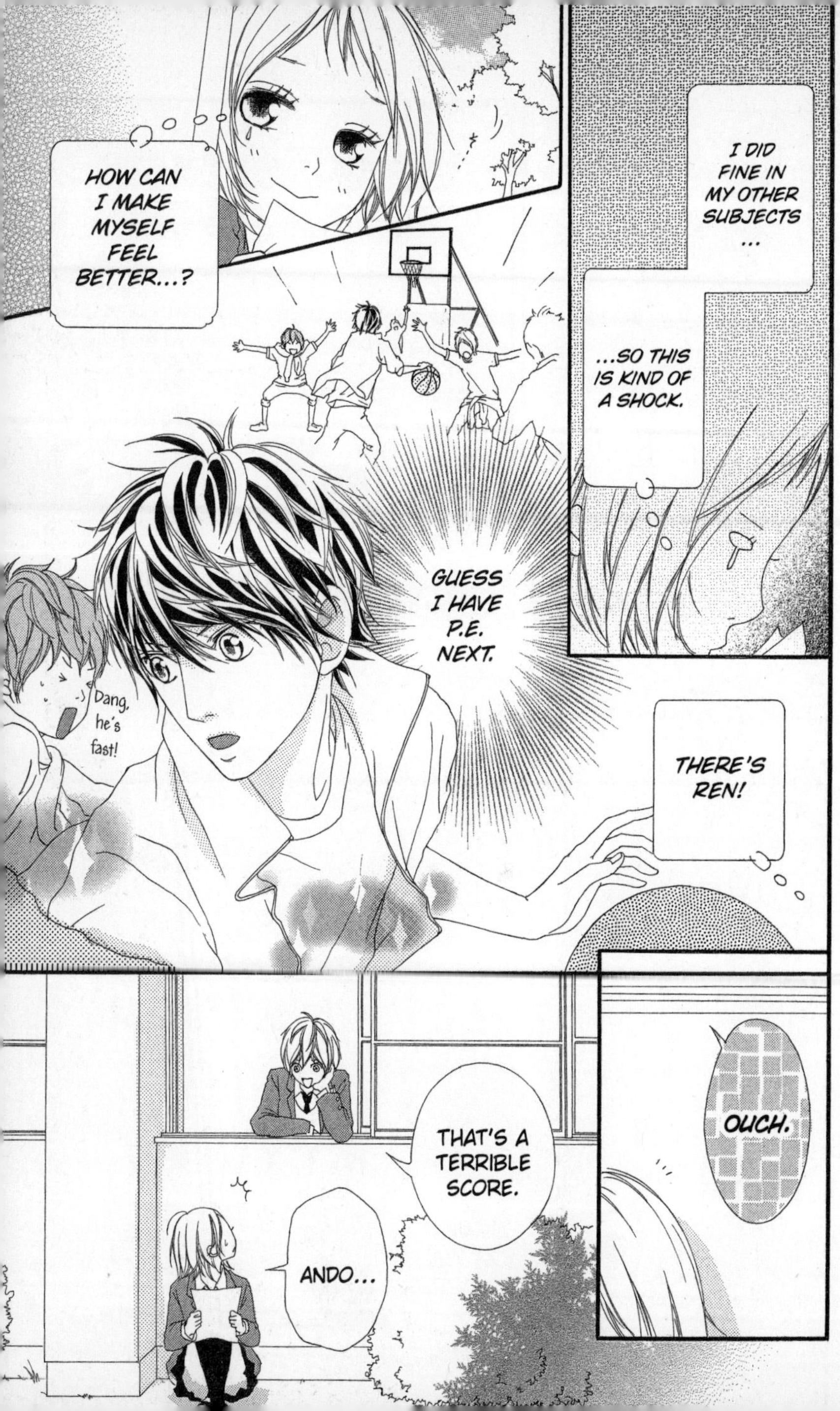
I DID FINE IN MY OTHER SUBJECTS...
...SO THIS IS KIND OF A SHOCK.
HOW CAN I MAKE MYSELF FEEL BETTER...?
GUESS I HAVE P.E. NEXT.
THERE'S REN!
Dang, he's fast!
OUCH.
...
THAT'S A TERRIBLE SCORE.
ANDO...

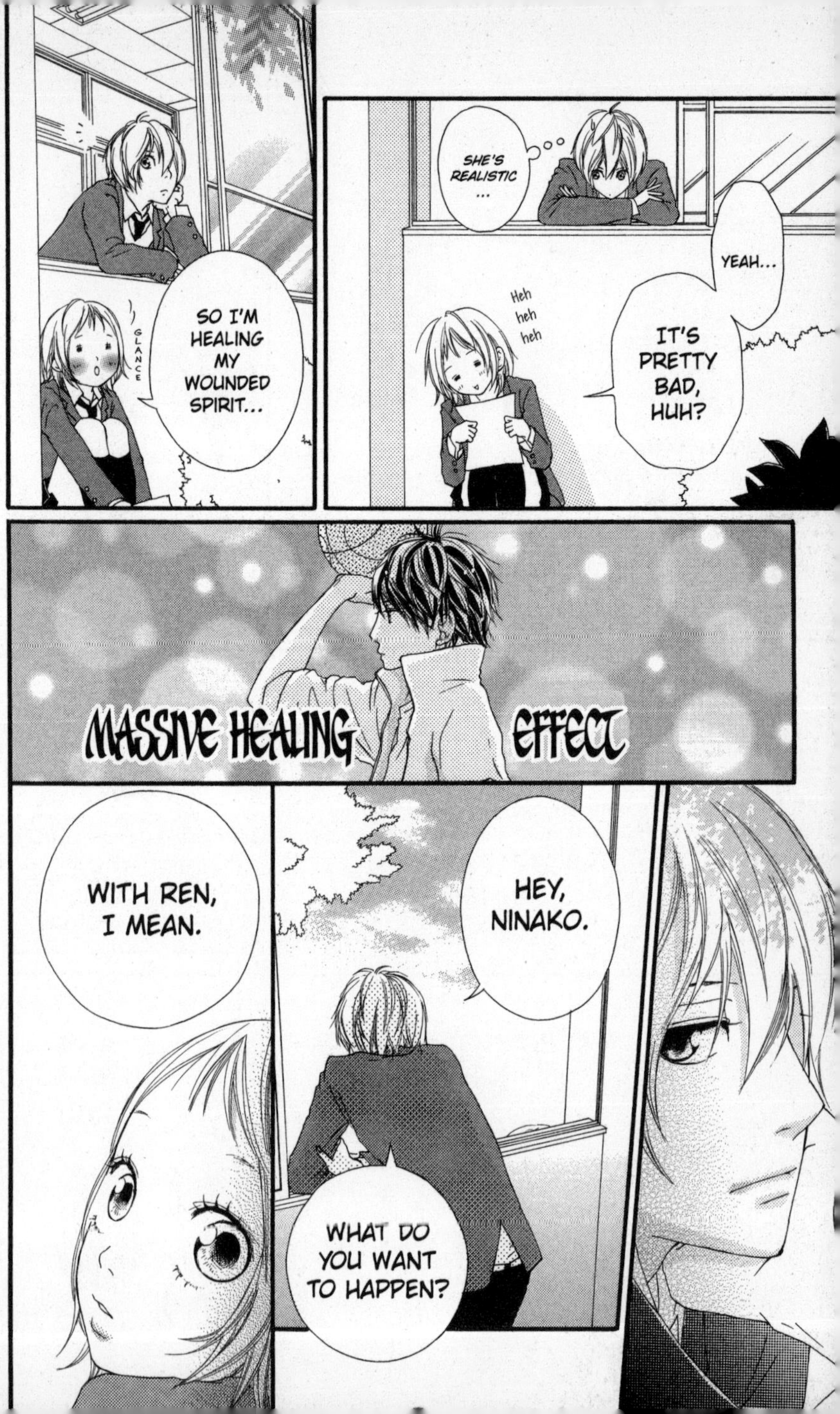
SHE'S REALISTIC...
YEAH...
IT'S PRETTY BAD, HUH?
Heh heh heh
GLANCE
SO I'M HEALING MY WOUNDED SPIRIT...
MASSIVE HEALING EFFECT
HEY, NINAKO.
WHAT DO YOU WANT TO HAPPEN?
WITH REN, I MEAN.

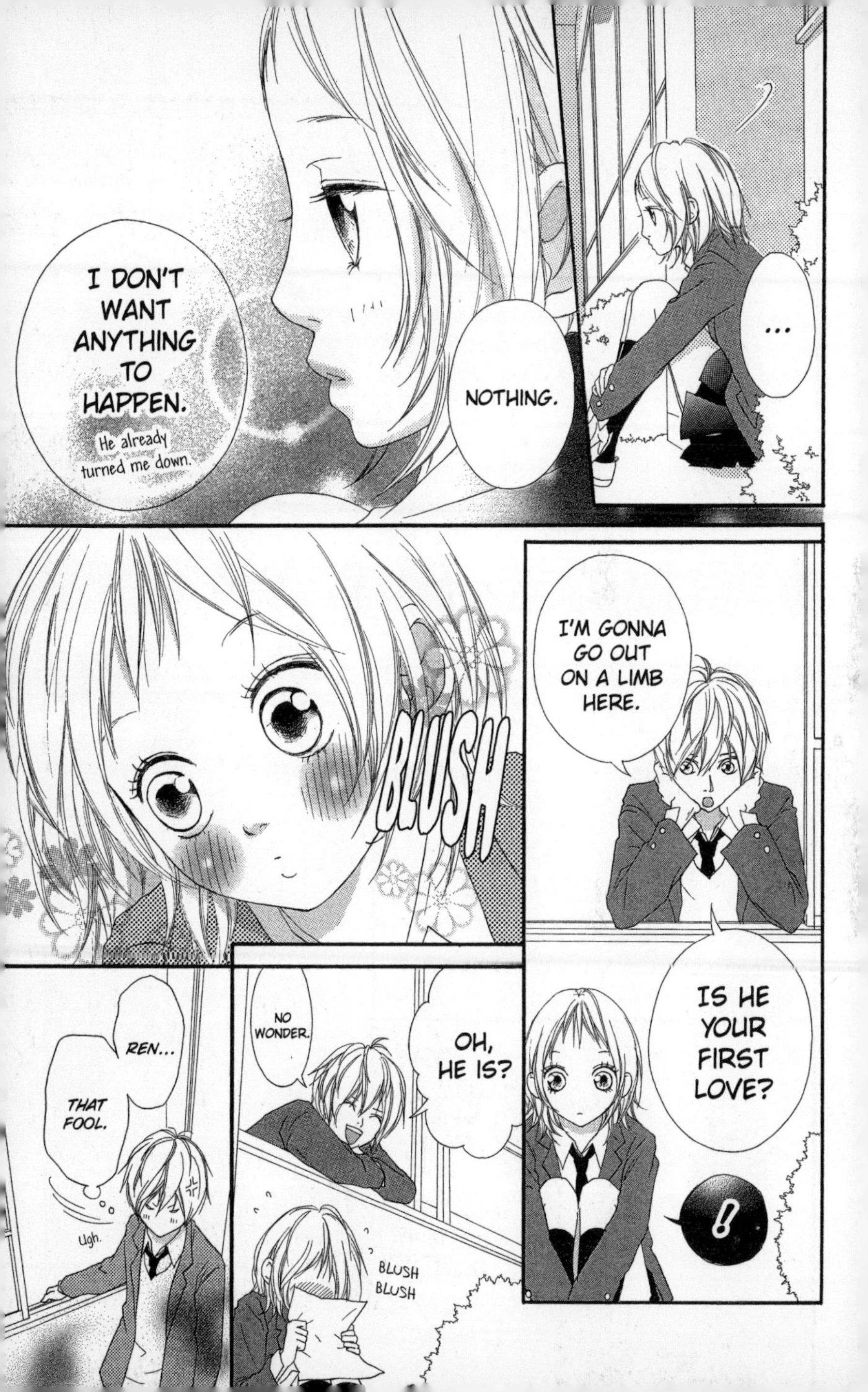
...
NOTHING.
I DON'T WANT ANYTHING TO HAPPEN.
He already turned me down.
I'M GONNA GO OUT ON A LIMB HERE.
BLUSH
IS HE YOUR FIRST LOVE?
!
OH, HE IS?
NO WONDER.
BLUSH BLUSH
REN...
THAT FOOL.
Ugh.

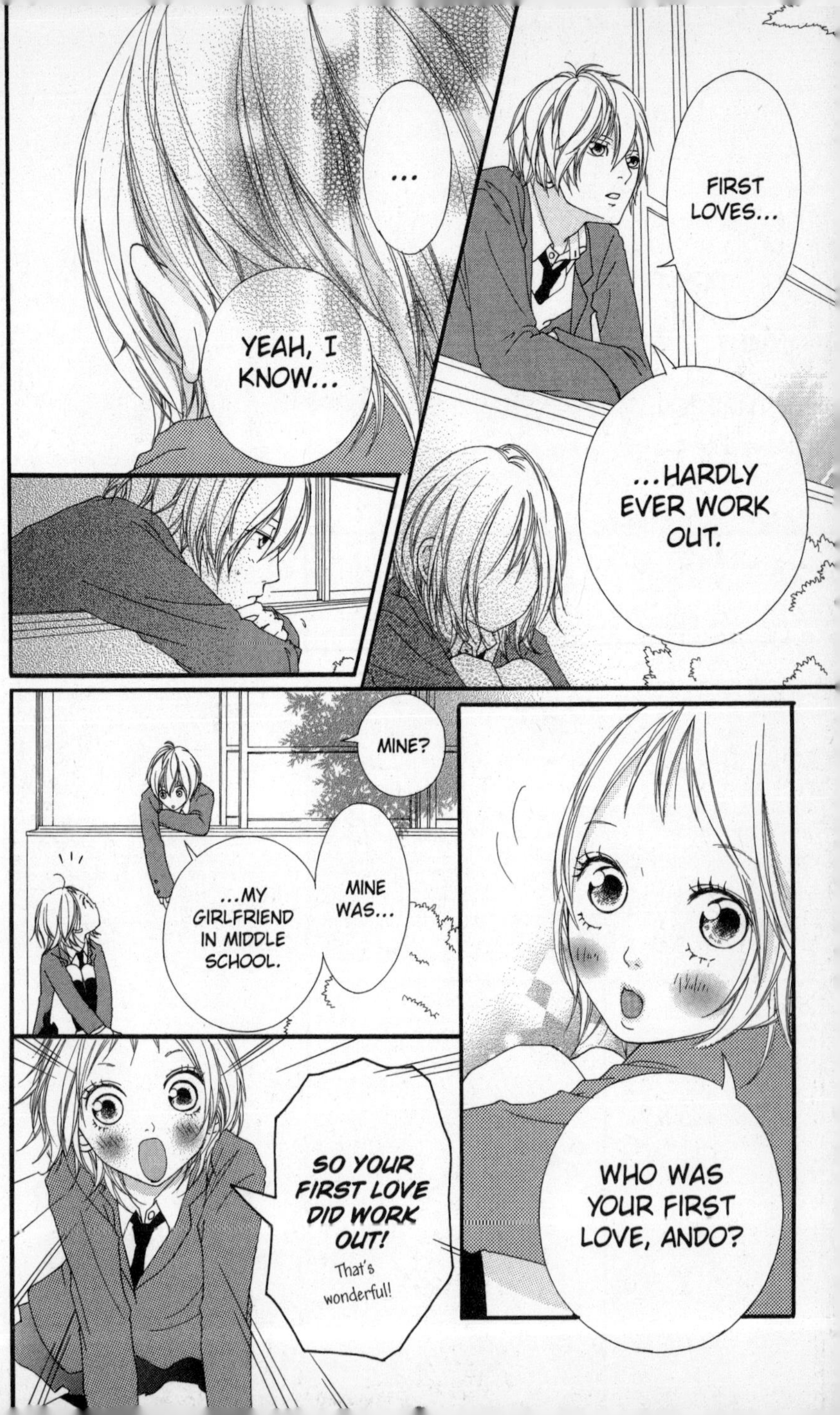
FIRST LOVES...
...HARDLY EVER WORK OUT.
...
YEAH, I KNOW...
WHO WAS YOUR FIRST LOVE, ANDO?
MINE?
MINE WAS...
...MY GIRLFRIEND IN MIDDLE SCHOOL.
SO YOUR FIRST LOVE DID WORK OUT!
That's wonderful!

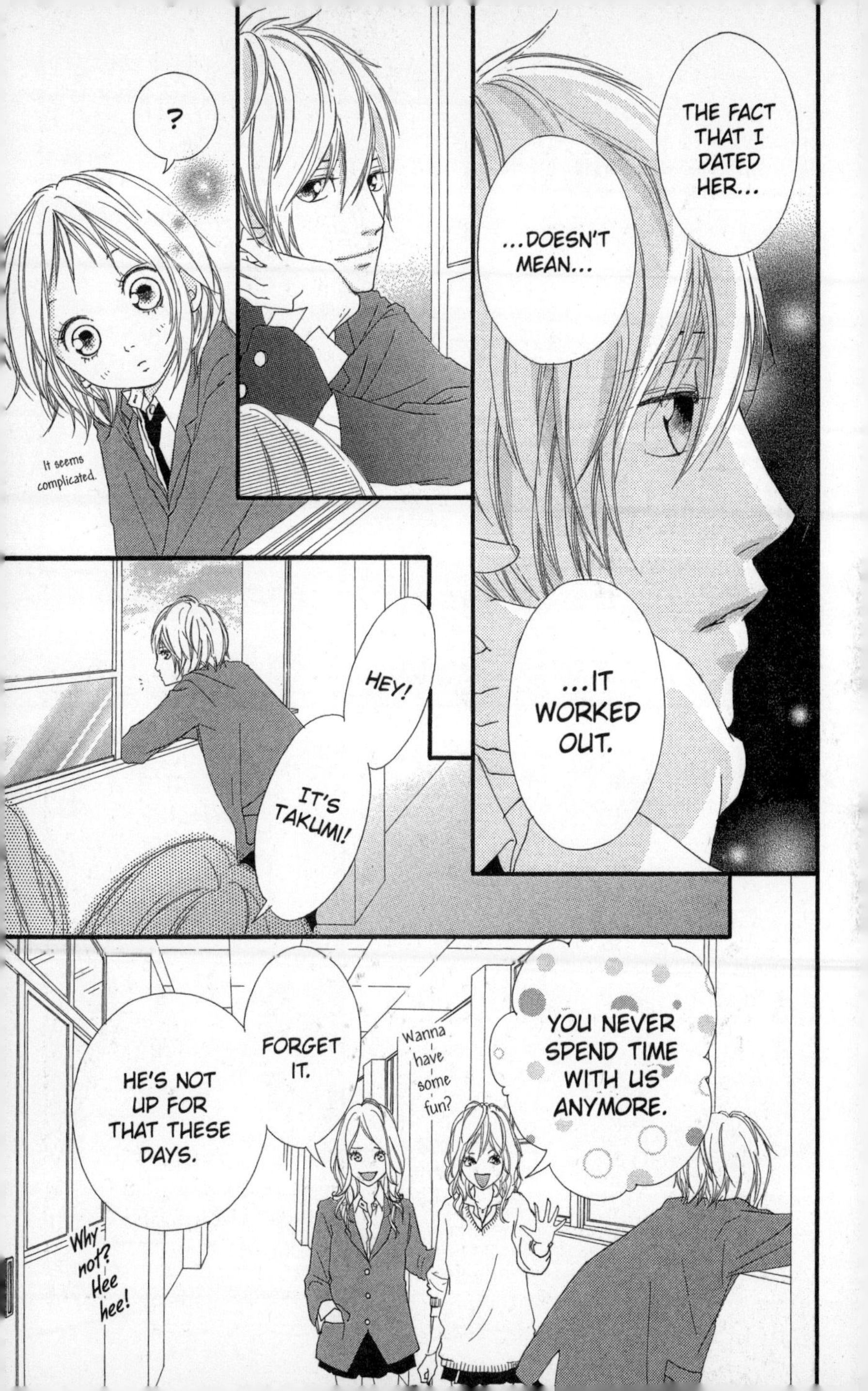
THE FACT THAT I DATED HER...
...DOESN'T MEAN...
...IT WORKED OUT.
?
It seems complicated.
HEY!
IT'S TAKUMI!
YOU NEVER SPEND TIME WITH US ANYMORE.
Wanna have some fun?
FORGET IT.
HE'S NOT UP FOR THAT THESE DAYS.
Why not? Hee hee!

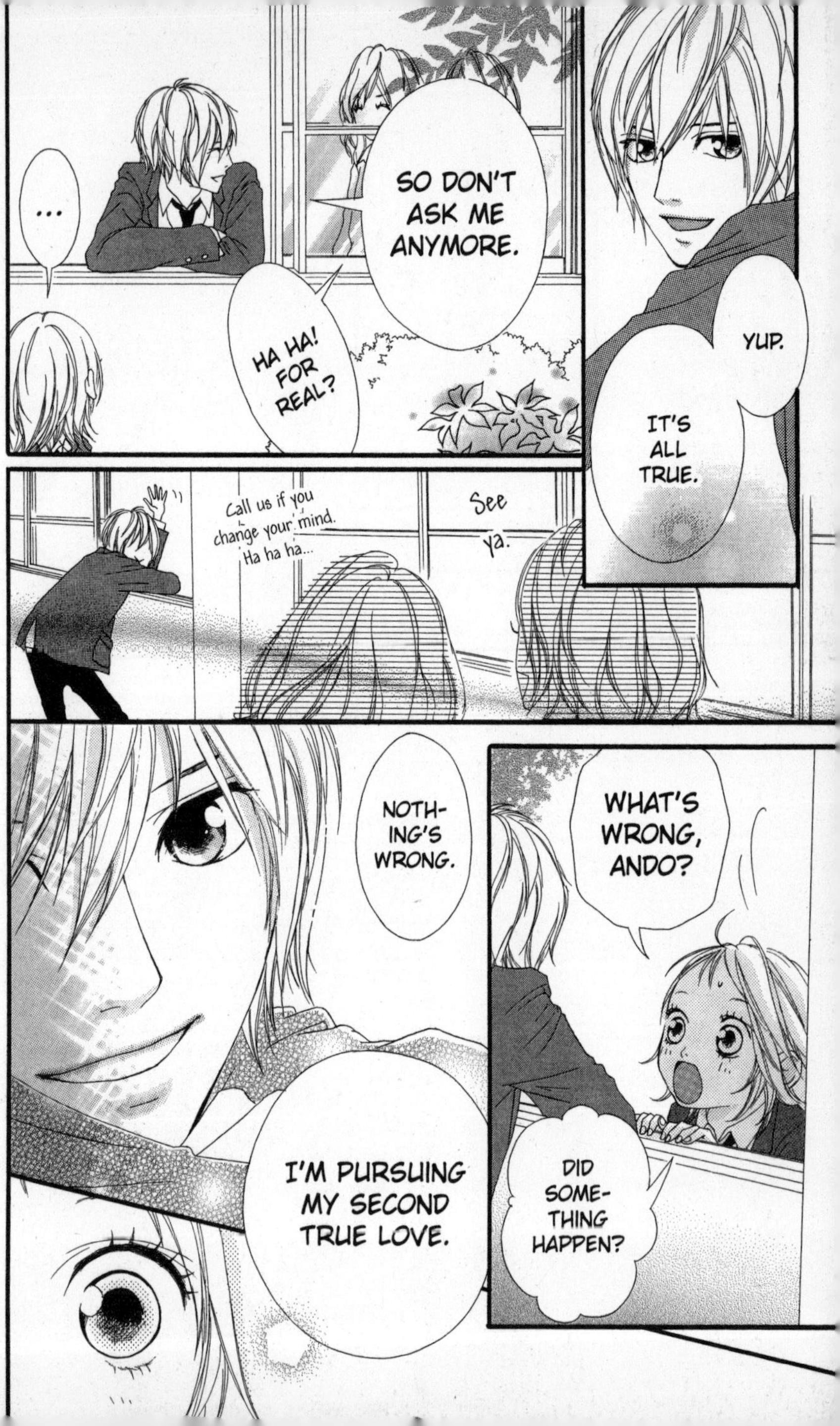
YUP.
IT'S ALL TRUE.
SO DON'T ASK ME ANYMORE.
HA HA! FOR REAL?
...
See ya.
Call us if you change your mind. Ha ha ha...
WHAT'S WRONG, ANDO?
DID SOME-THING HAPPEN?
NOTH-ING'S WRONG.
I'M PURSUING MY SECOND TRUE LOVE.

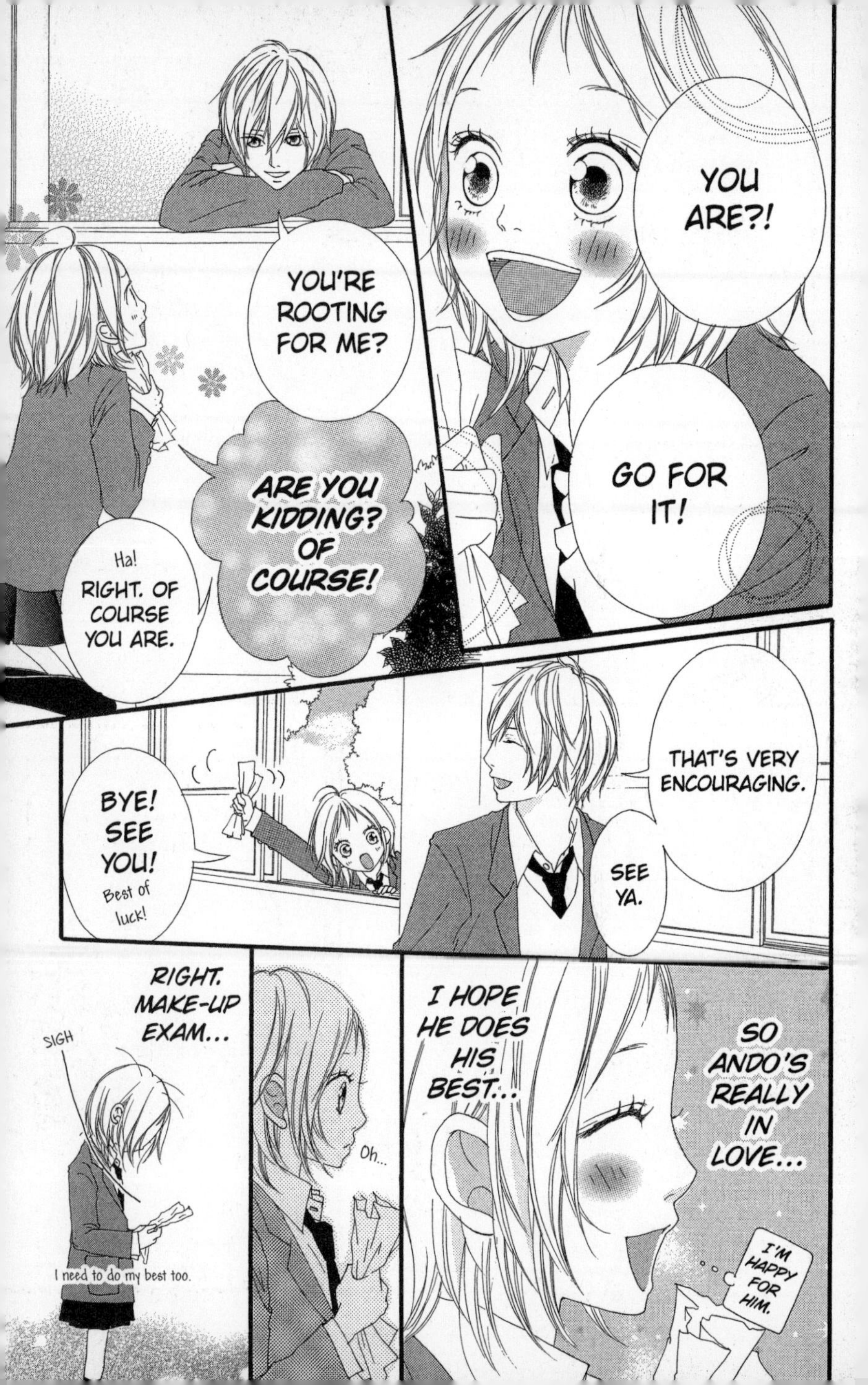
YOU ARE?!
GO FOR IT!
YOU'RE ROOTING FOR ME?
ARE YOU KIDDING? OF COURSE!
Ha! RIGHT. OF COURSE YOU ARE.
THAT'S VERY ENCOURAGING.
SEE YA.
BYE! SEE YOU! Best of luck!
SO ANDO'S REALLY IN LOVE...
I'M HAPPY FOR HIM.
I HOPE HE DOES HIS BEST...
Oh...
RIGHT. MAKE-UP EXAM...
SIGH
I need to do my best too.

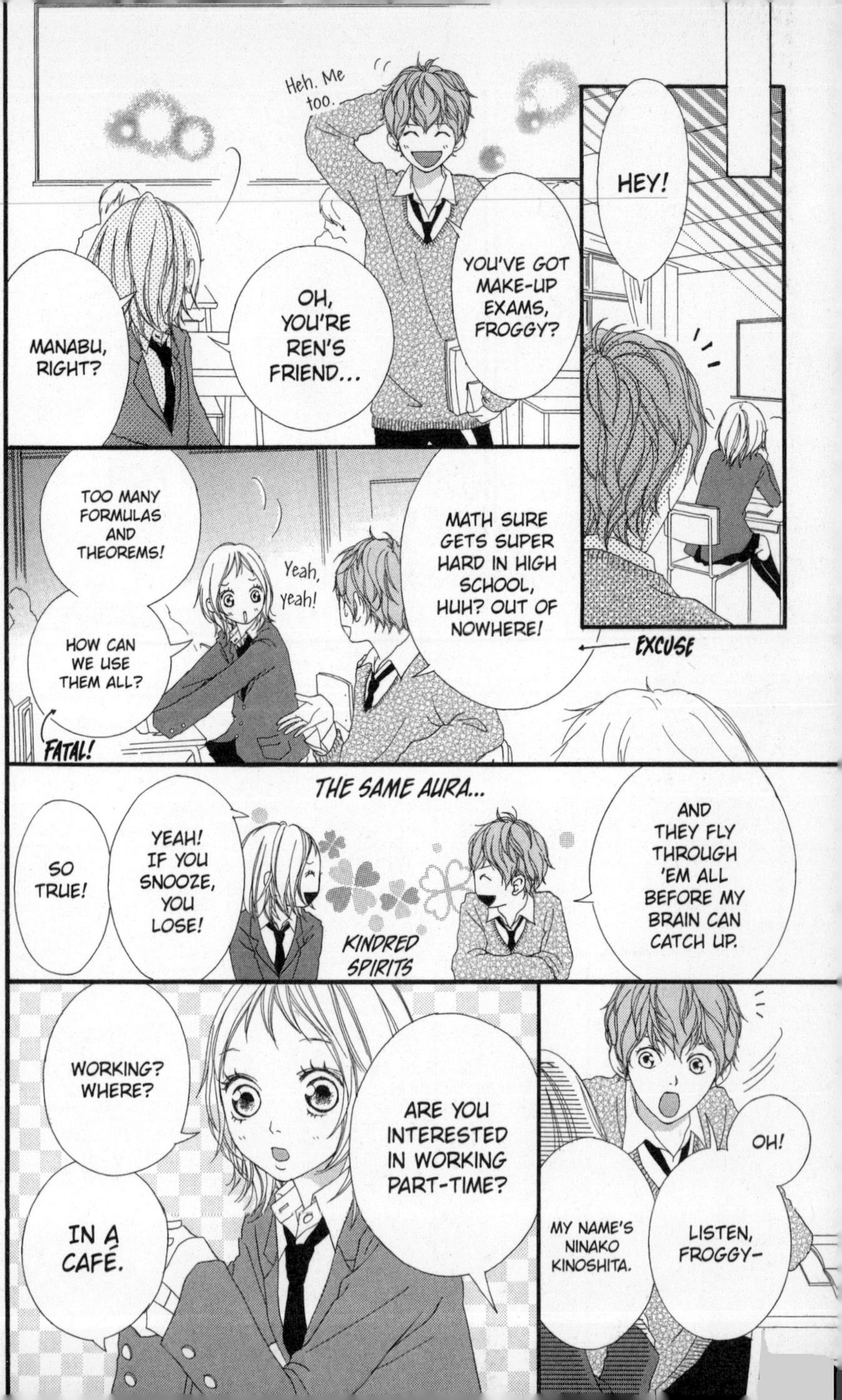
HEY!
YOU'VE GOT MAKE-UP EXAMS, FROGGY?
Heh. Me too.
OH, YOU'RE REN'S FRIEND...
MANABU, RIGHT?
MATH SURE GETS SUPER HARD IN HIGH SCHOOL, HUH? OUT OF NOWHERE!
EXCUSE
Yeah, yeah!
TOO MANY FORMULAS AND THEOREMS!
HOW CAN WE USE THEM ALL?
FATAL!
THE SAME AURA...
AND THEY FLY THROUGH 'EM ALL BEFORE MY BRAIN CAN CATCH UP.
KINDRED SPIRITS
YEAH! IF YOU SNOOZE, YOU LOSE!
SO TRUE!
OH!
LISTEN, FROGGY-
MY NAME'S NINAKO KINOSHITA.
ARE YOU INTERESTED IN WORKING PART-TIME?
WORKING? WHERE?
IN A CAFÉ.

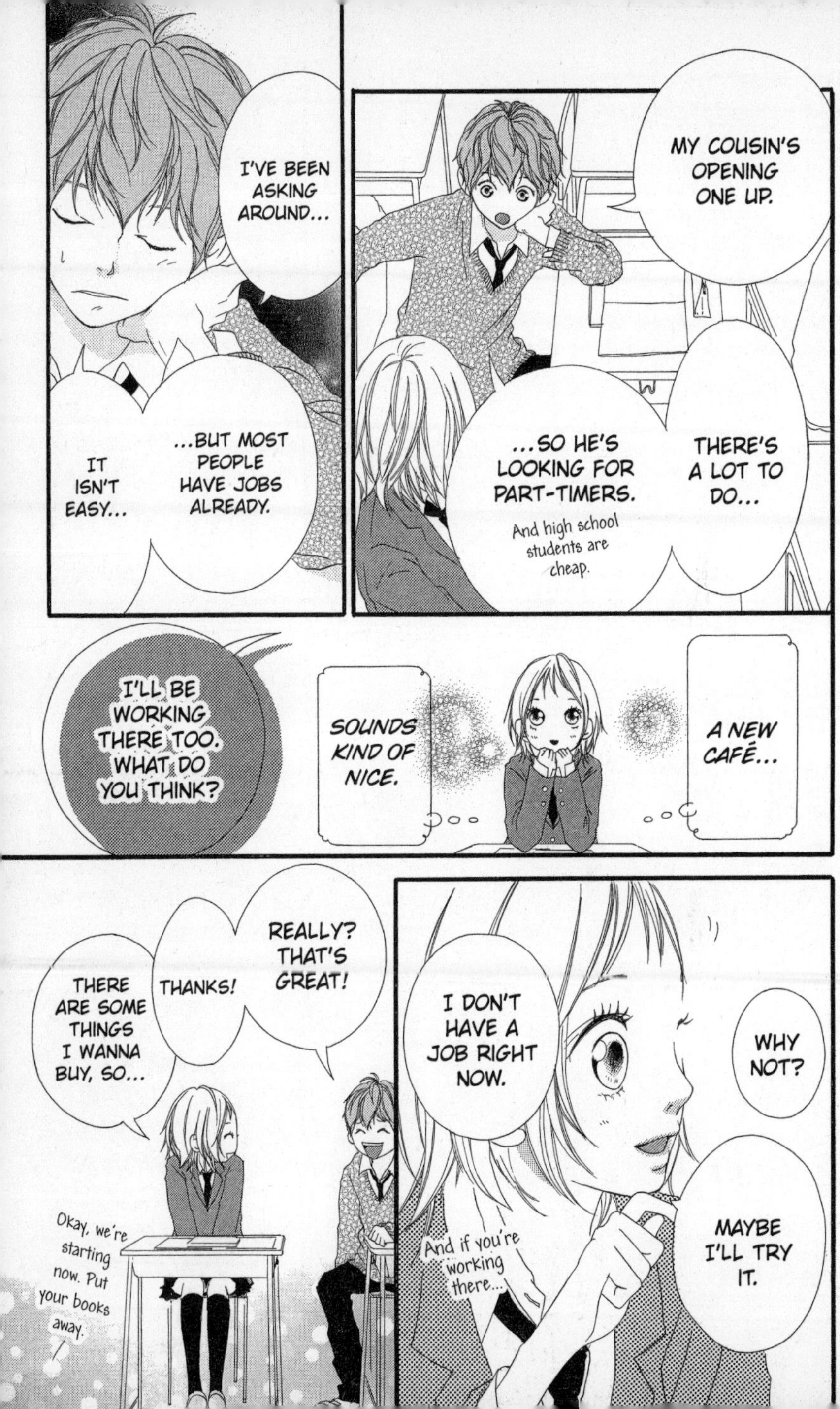
MY COUSIN'S OPENING ONE UP.
THERE'S A LOT TO DO...
...SO HE'S LOOKING FOR PART-TIMERS.
And high school students are cheap.
I'VE BEEN ASKING AROUND...
...BUT MOST PEOPLE HAVE JOBS ALREADY.
IT ISN'T EASY...
A NEW CAFÉ...
SOUNDS KIND OF NICE.
I'LL BE WORKING THERE TOO. WHAT DO YOU THINK?
WHY NOT?
I DON'T HAVE A JOB RIGHT NOW.
MAYBE I'LL TRY IT.
And if you're working there...
REALLY? THAT'S GREAT!
THANKS!
THERE ARE SOME THINGS I WANNA BUY, SO...
Okay, we're starting now. Put your books away.

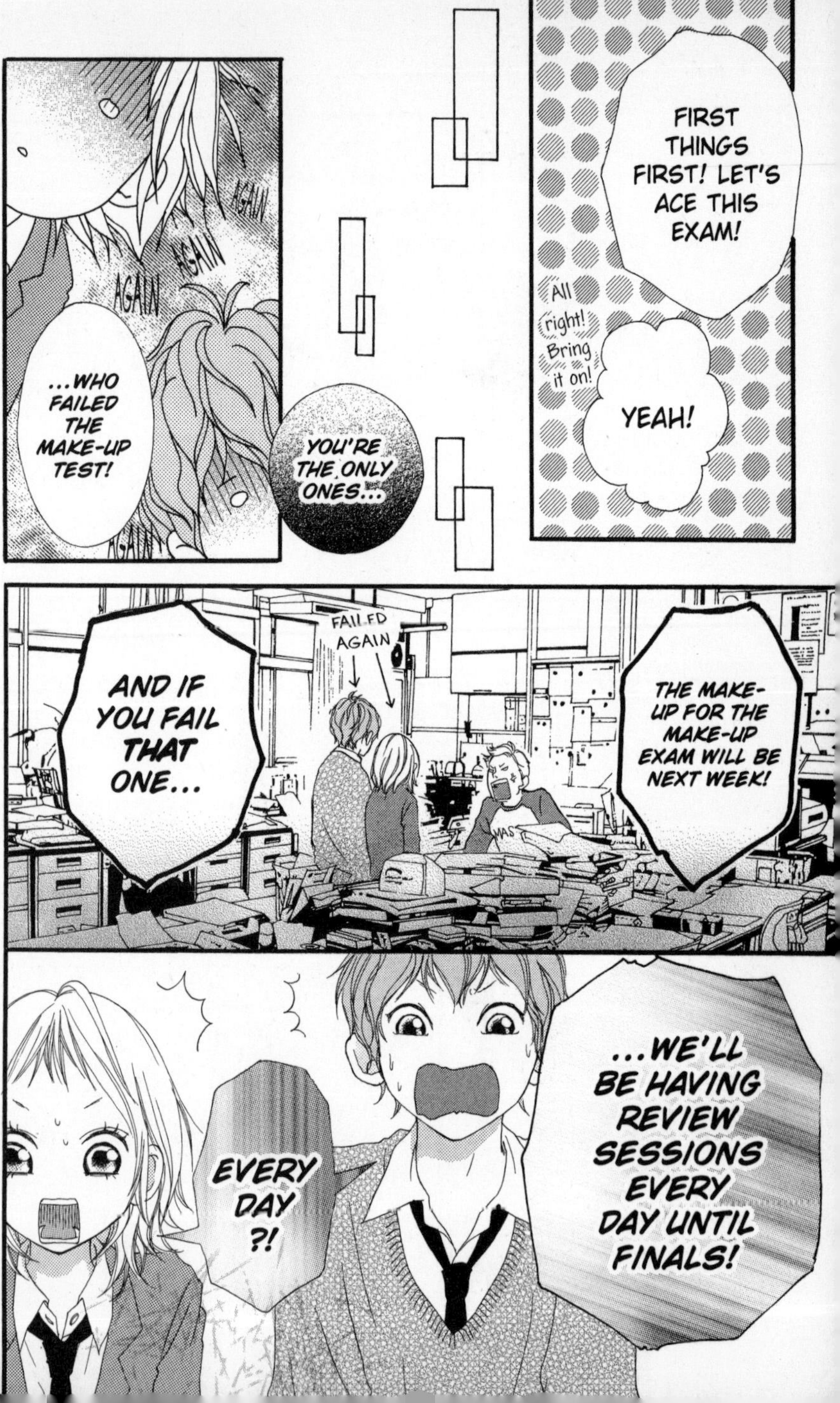
FIRST THINGS FIRST! LET'S ACE THIS EXAM!
All right! Bring it on!
YEAH!
AGAIN AGAIN AGAIN AGAIN
YOU'RE THE ONLY ONES...
...WHO FAILED THE MAKE-UP TEST!
THE MAKE-UP FOR THE MAKE-UP EXAM WILL BE NEXT WEEK!
FAILED AGAIN
AND IF YOU FAIL THAT ONE...
...WE'LL BE HAVING REVIEW SESSIONS EVERY DAY UNTIL FINALS!
EVERY DAY ?!

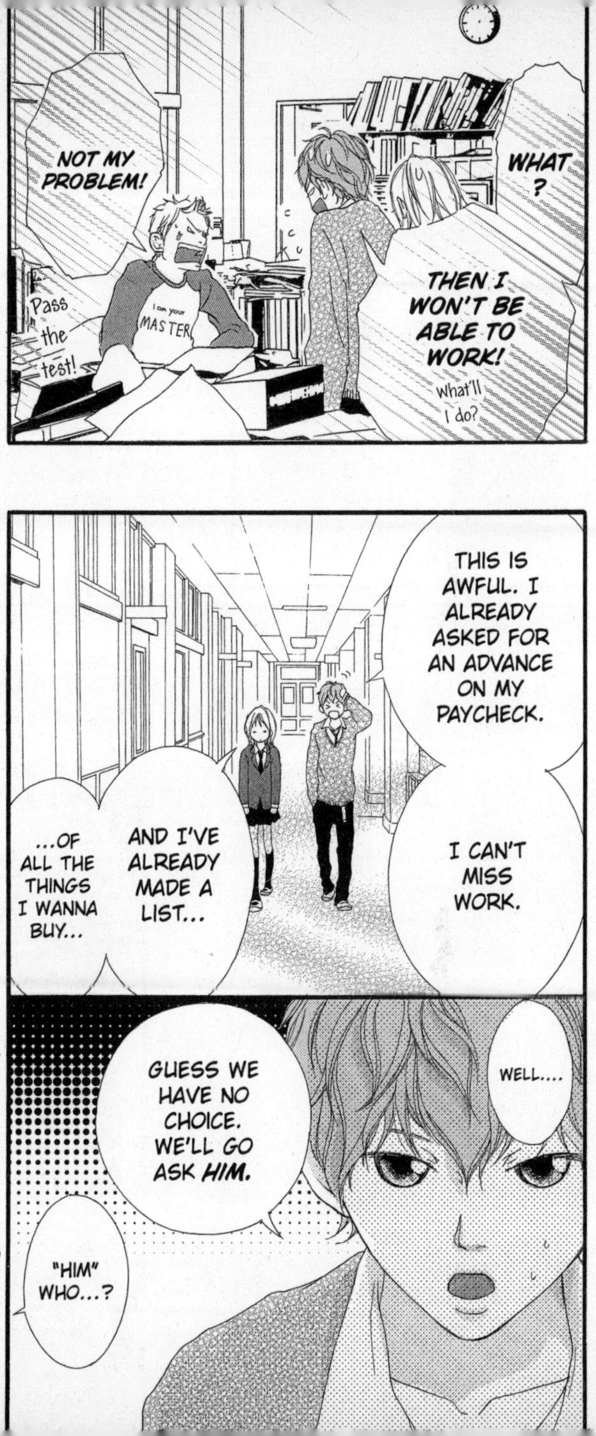
WHAT?
THEN I WON'T BE ABLE TO WORK!
What'll I do?
NOT MY PROBLEM!
I am your MASTER
Pass the test!
THIS IS AWFUL. I ALREADY ASKED FOR AN ADVANCE ON MY PAYCHECK.
I CAN'T MISS WORK.
AND I'VE ALREADY MADE A LIST...
...OF ALL THE THINGS I WANNA BUY...
WELL....
GUESS WE HAVE NO CHOICE. WE'LL GO ASK *HIM*.
"HIM" WHO...?

WORKFLOW

~My Particular Method~

⑦ INKING

If I draw at my own speed and pressure, the ink doesn't take. So I have to take my time and press harder, which is why I'm so slow. But even then, when I use the eraser, my lines look weak. It makes me want to cry.

⑧ FILLING IN BLACKS

This is a surprisingly intensive process. For Ren, I focus on his tufts of hair and making them look shiny. I let the others do the rest.

⑨ SCREENTONING

I use screentones in this order: basic tones (for uniforms, bags, anything repetitive), shadow tones, and then emotion tones. This is the one process that I can do pretty quickly. I like to think so, anyway...

← To be continued

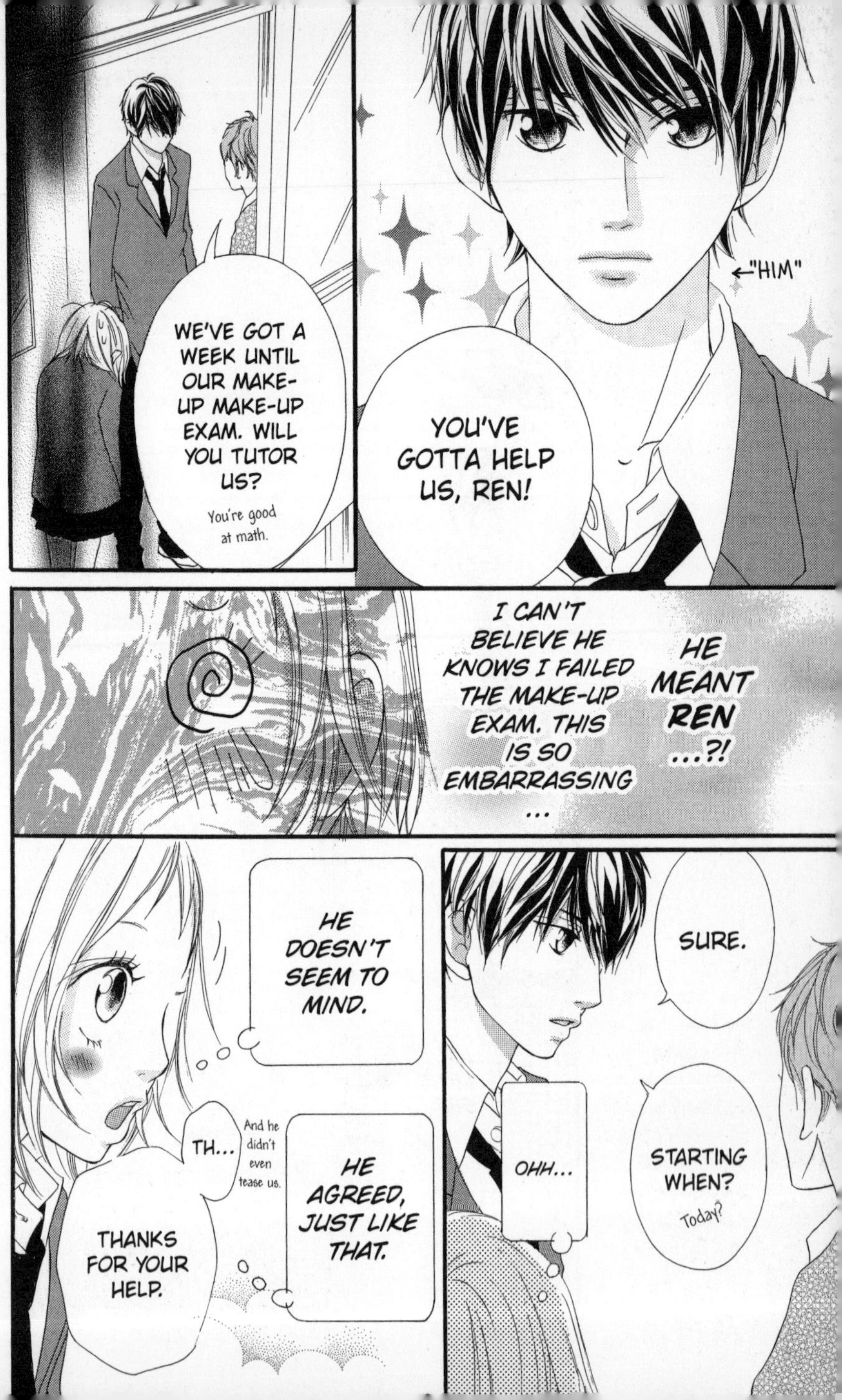

←"HIM"
YOU'VE GOTTA HELP US, REN!
WE'VE GOT A WEEK UNTIL OUR MAKE-UP MAKE-UP EXAM. WILL YOU TUTOR US?
You're good at math.
HE MEANT REN ...?!
I CAN'T BELIEVE HE KNOWS I FAILED THE MAKE-UP EXAM. THIS IS SO EMBARRASSING ...
SURE.
STARTING WHEN?
Today?
OHH...
HE DOESN'T SEEM TO MIND.
HE AGREED, JUST LIKE THAT.
And he didn't even tease us.
TH...
THANKS FOR YOUR HELP.

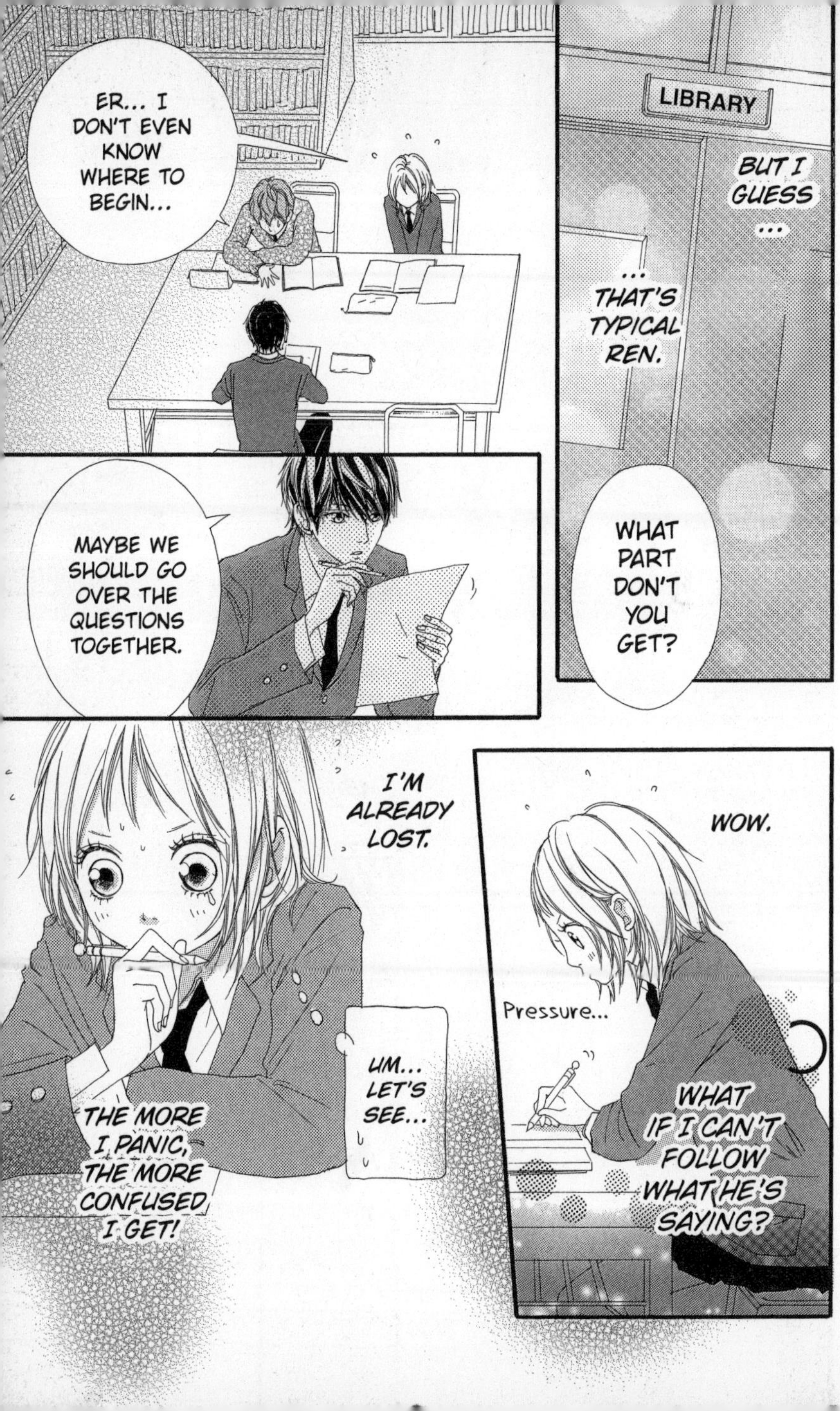

LIBRARY
BUT I GUESS...
... THAT'S TYPICAL REN.
WHAT PART DON'T YOU GET?
ER... I DON'T EVEN KNOW WHERE TO BEGIN...
MAYBE WE SHOULD GO OVER THE QUESTIONS TOGETHER.
WOW.
Pressure...
WHAT IF I CAN'T FOLLOW WHAT HE'S SAYING?
I'M ALREADY LOST.
UM... LET'S SEE...
THE MORE I PANIC, THE MORE CONFUSED I GET!

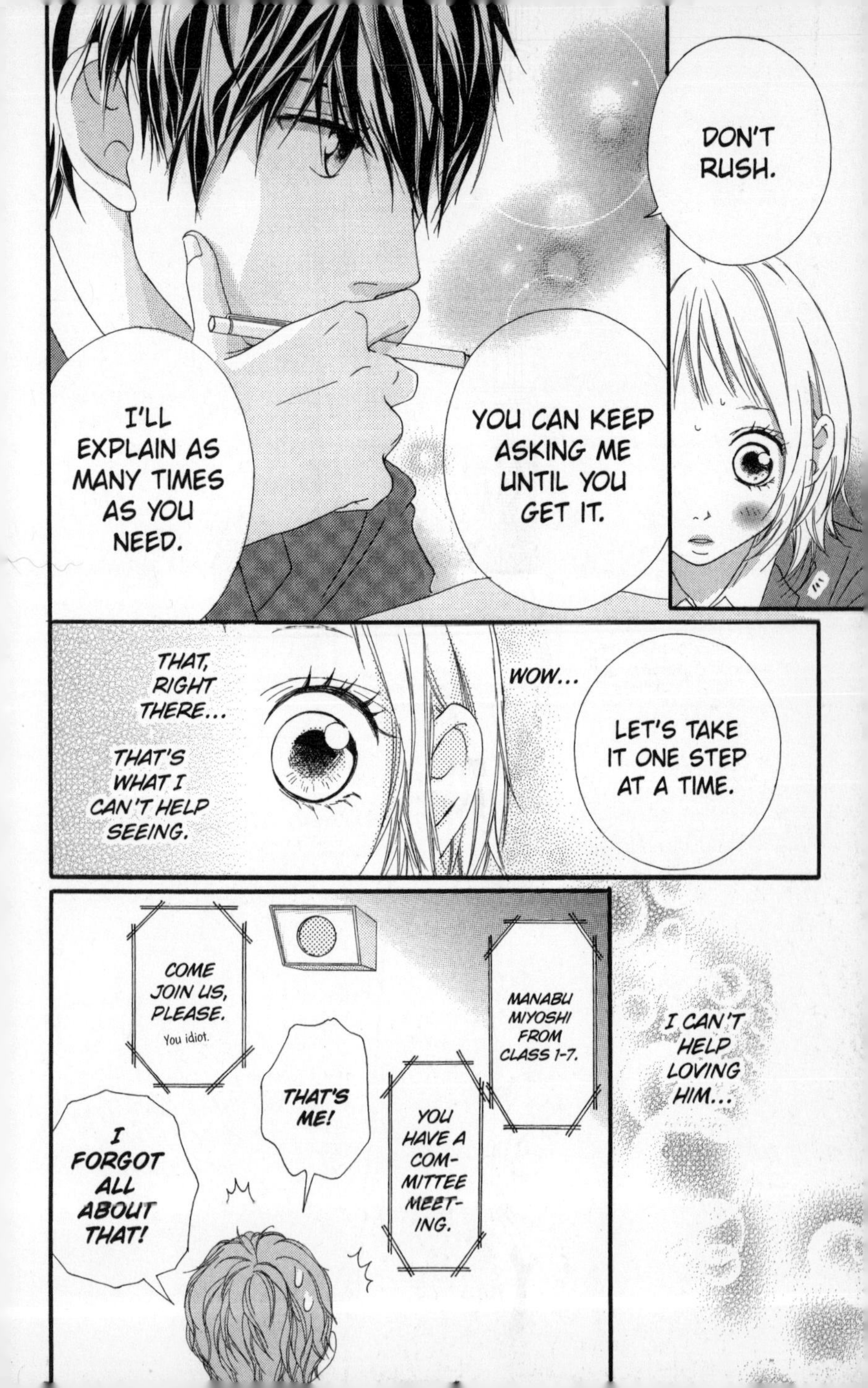
DON'T RUSH.
YOU CAN KEEP ASKING ME UNTIL YOU GET IT.
I'LL EXPLAIN AS MANY TIMES AS YOU NEED.
LET'S TAKE IT ONE STEP AT A TIME.
WOW...
THAT, RIGHT THERE...
THAT'S WHAT I CAN'T HELP SEEING.
I CAN'T HELP LOVING HIM...
MANABU MIYOSHI FROM CLASS 1-7.
COME JOIN US, PLEASE.
You idiot.
YOU HAVE A COM-MITTEE MEET-ING.
THAT'S ME!
I FORGOT ALL ABOUT THAT!

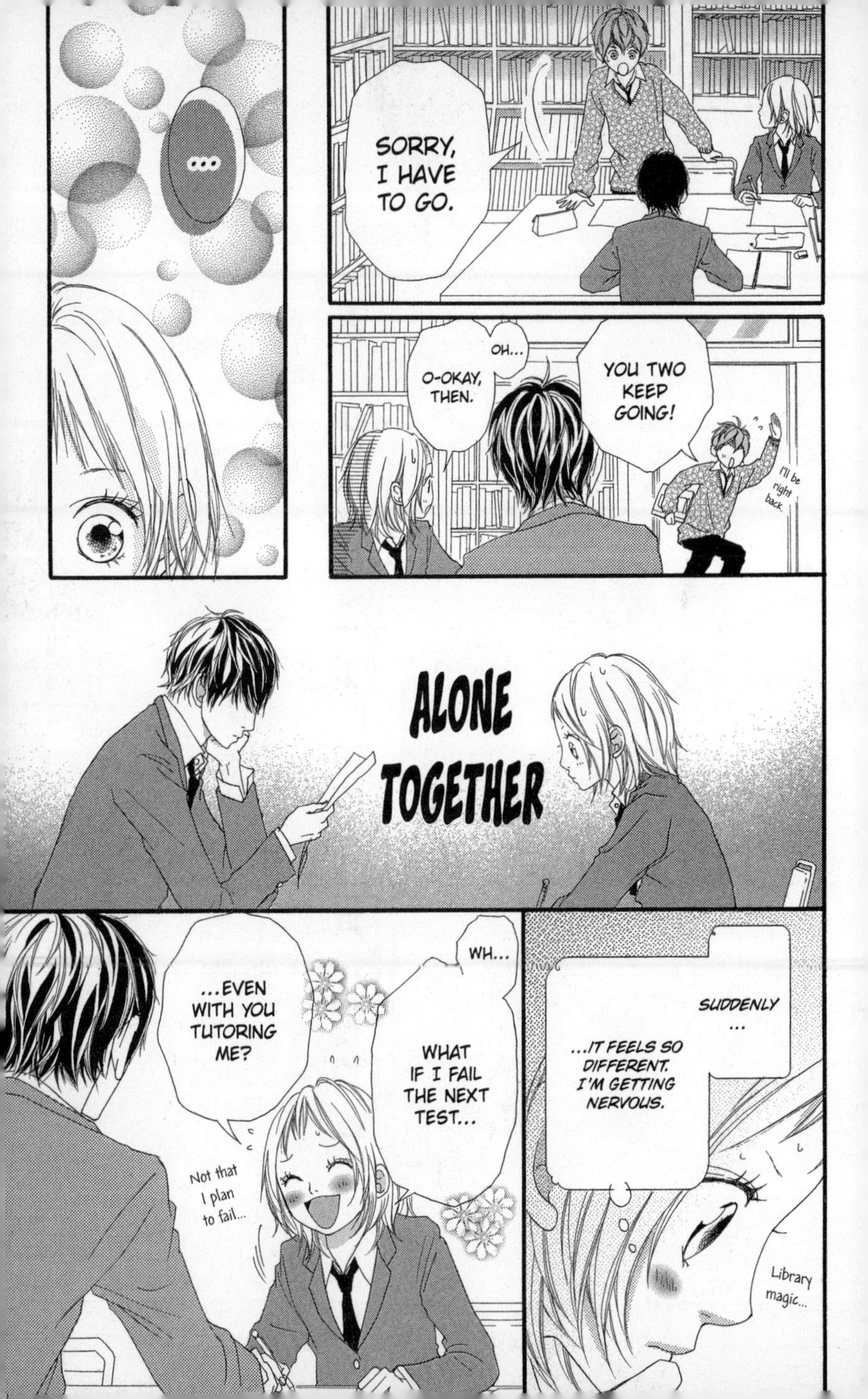
SORRY, I HAVE TO GO.
YOU TWO KEEP GOING!
I'll be right back.
OH...
O-OKAY, THEN.
...
ALONE TOGETHER
SUDDENLY...
...IT FEELS SO DIFFERENT. I'M GETTING NERVOUS.
Library magic...
WH...
WHAT IF I FAIL THE NEXT TEST...
...EVEN WITH YOU TUTORING ME?
Not that I plan to fail...

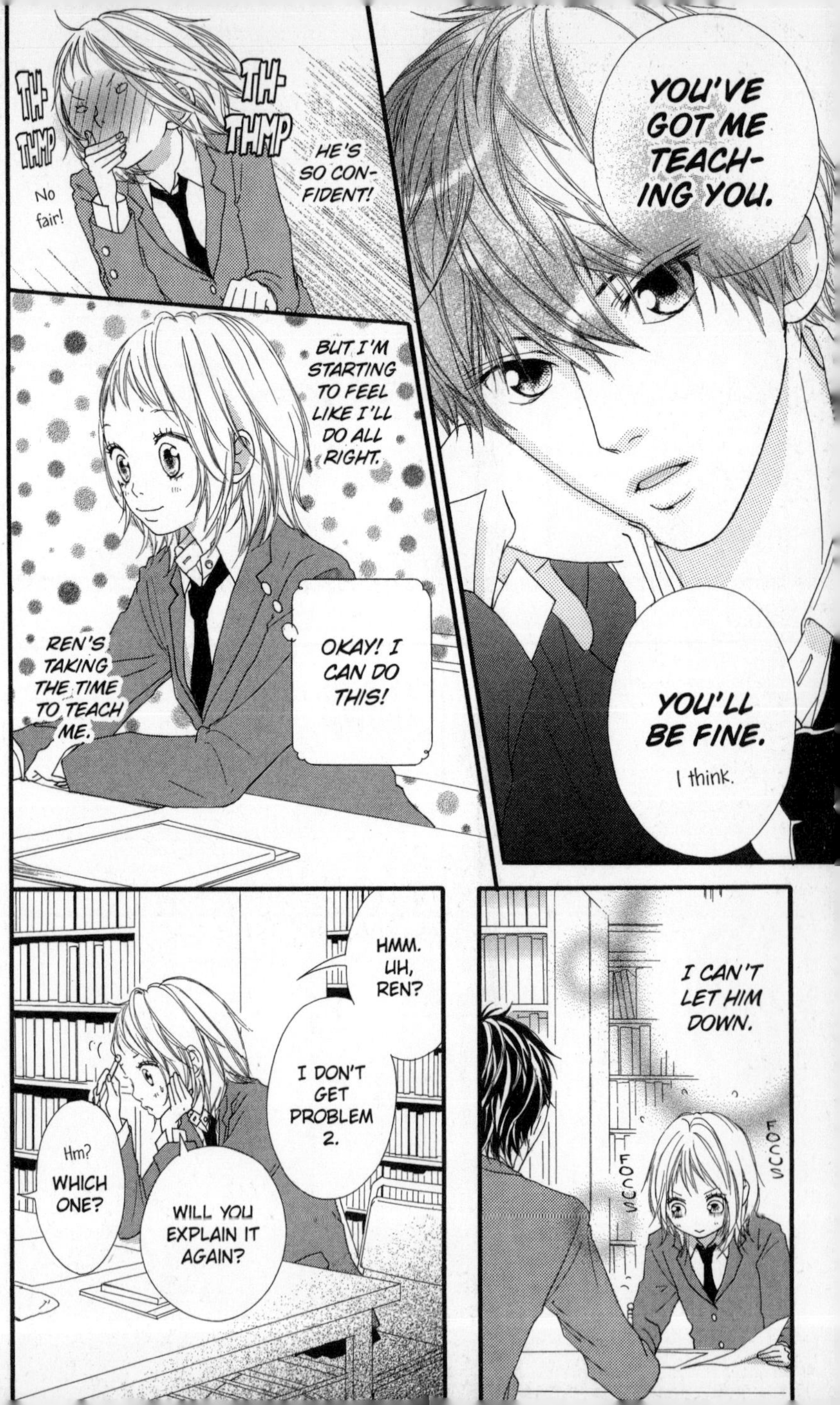
YOU'VE GOT ME TEACHING YOU.
YOU'LL BE FINE.
I think.
TH-THMP
HE'S SO CONFIDENT!
TH-THMP
No fair!
BUT I'M STARTING TO FEEL LIKE I'LL DO ALL RIGHT.
OKAY! I CAN DO THIS!
REN'S TAKING THE TIME TO TEACH ME.
I CAN'T LET HIM DOWN.
FOCUS
FOCUS
HMM. UH, REN?
I DON'T GET PROBLEM 2.
WILL YOU EXPLAIN IT AGAIN?
Hm? WHICH ONE?

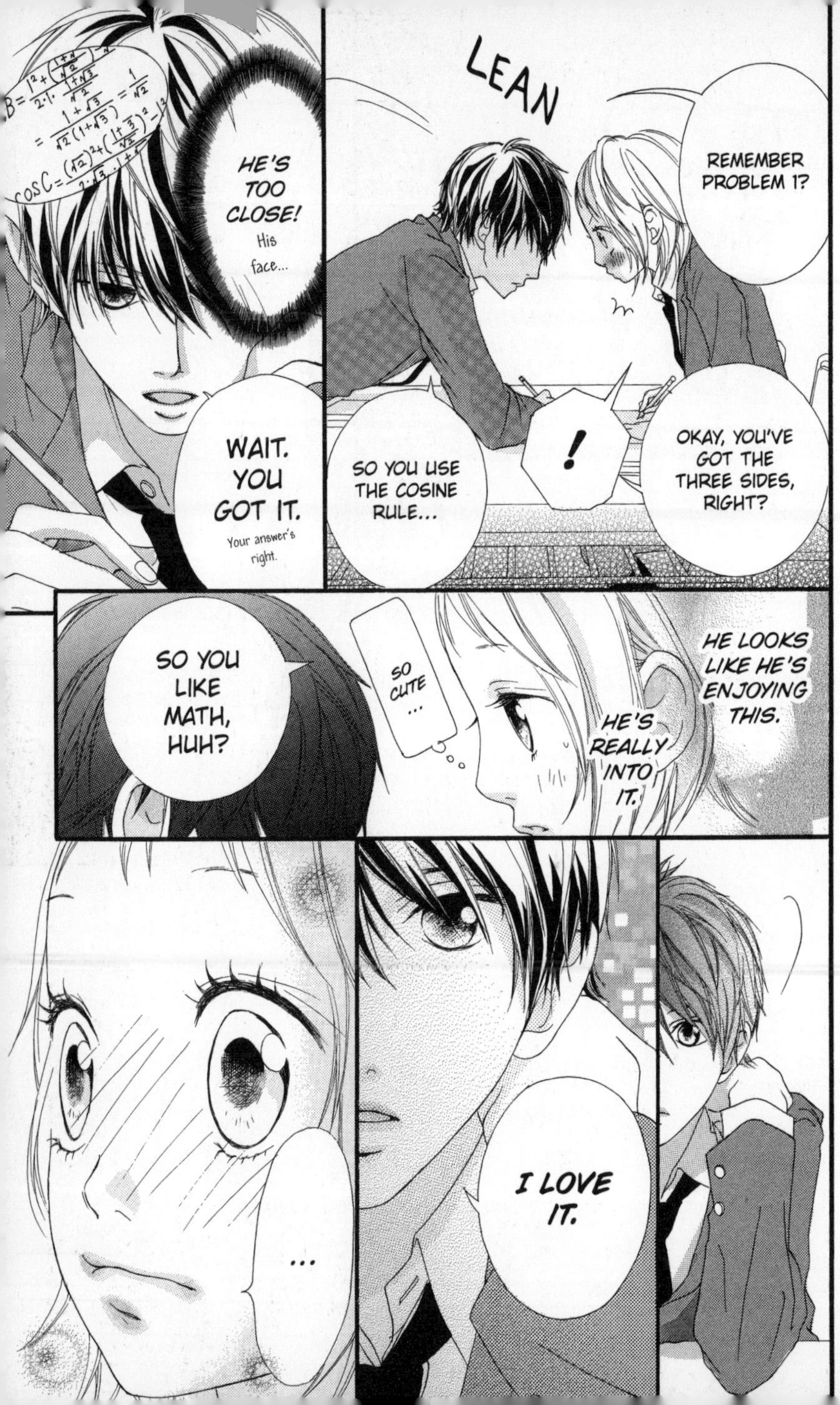
LEAN
REMEMBER PROBLEM 1?
OKAY, YOU'VE GOT THE THREE SIDES, RIGHT?
!
SO YOU USE THE COSINE RULE...
HE'S TOO CLOSE! His face...
WAIT. YOU GOT IT. Your answer's right.
HE LOOKS LIKE HE'S ENJOYING THIS.
HE'S REALLY INTO IT.
SO CUTE...
SO YOU LIKE MATH, HUH?
I LOVE IT.
...

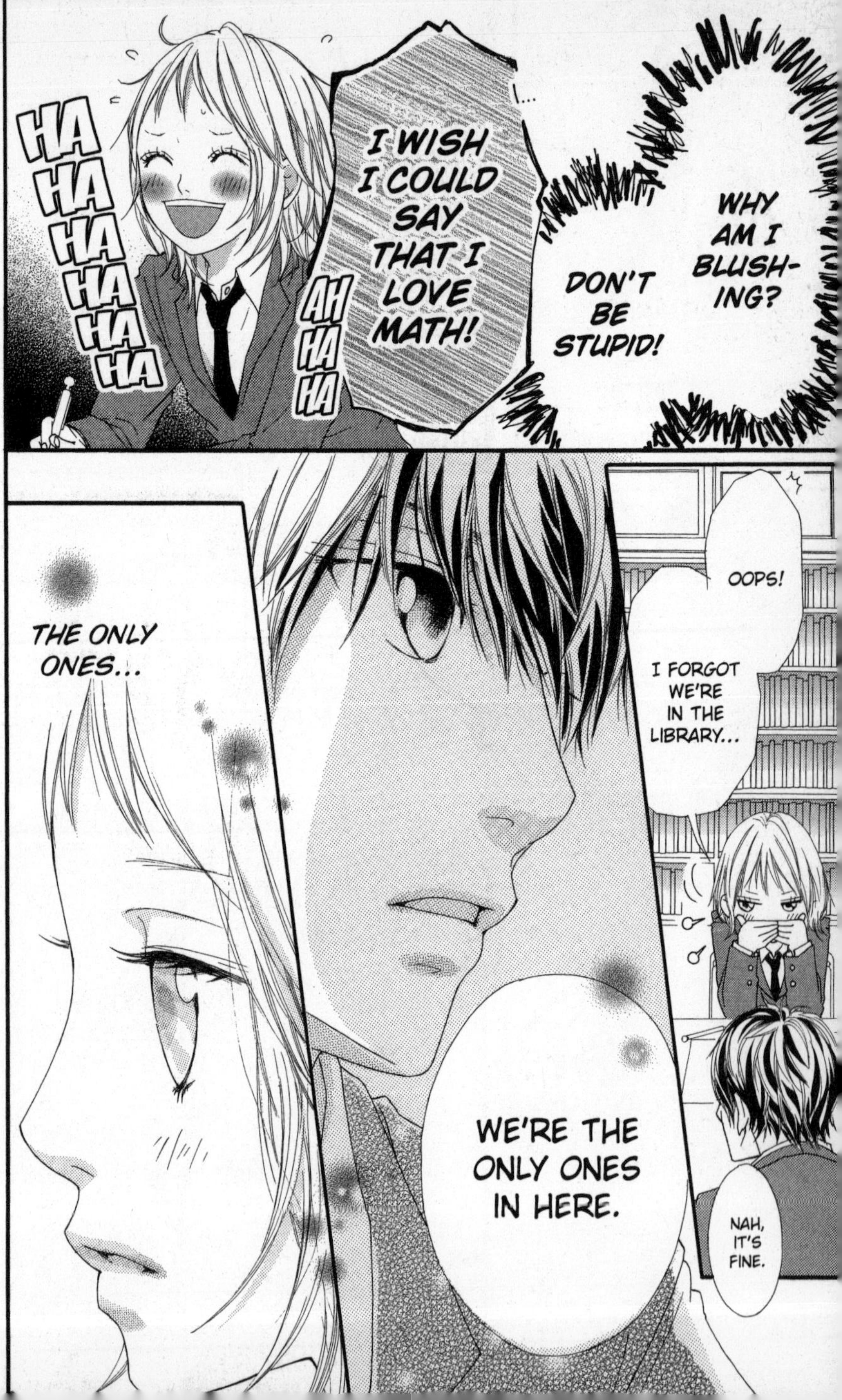
WHY AM I BLUSHING?
DON'T BE STUPID!
I...
I WISH I COULD SAY THAT I LOVE MATH!
AH HA HA HA
HA HA HA HA HA HA
OOPS!
I FORGOT WE'RE IN THE LIBRARY...
NAH, IT'S FINE.
WE'RE THE ONLY ONES IN HERE.
THE ONLY ONES...

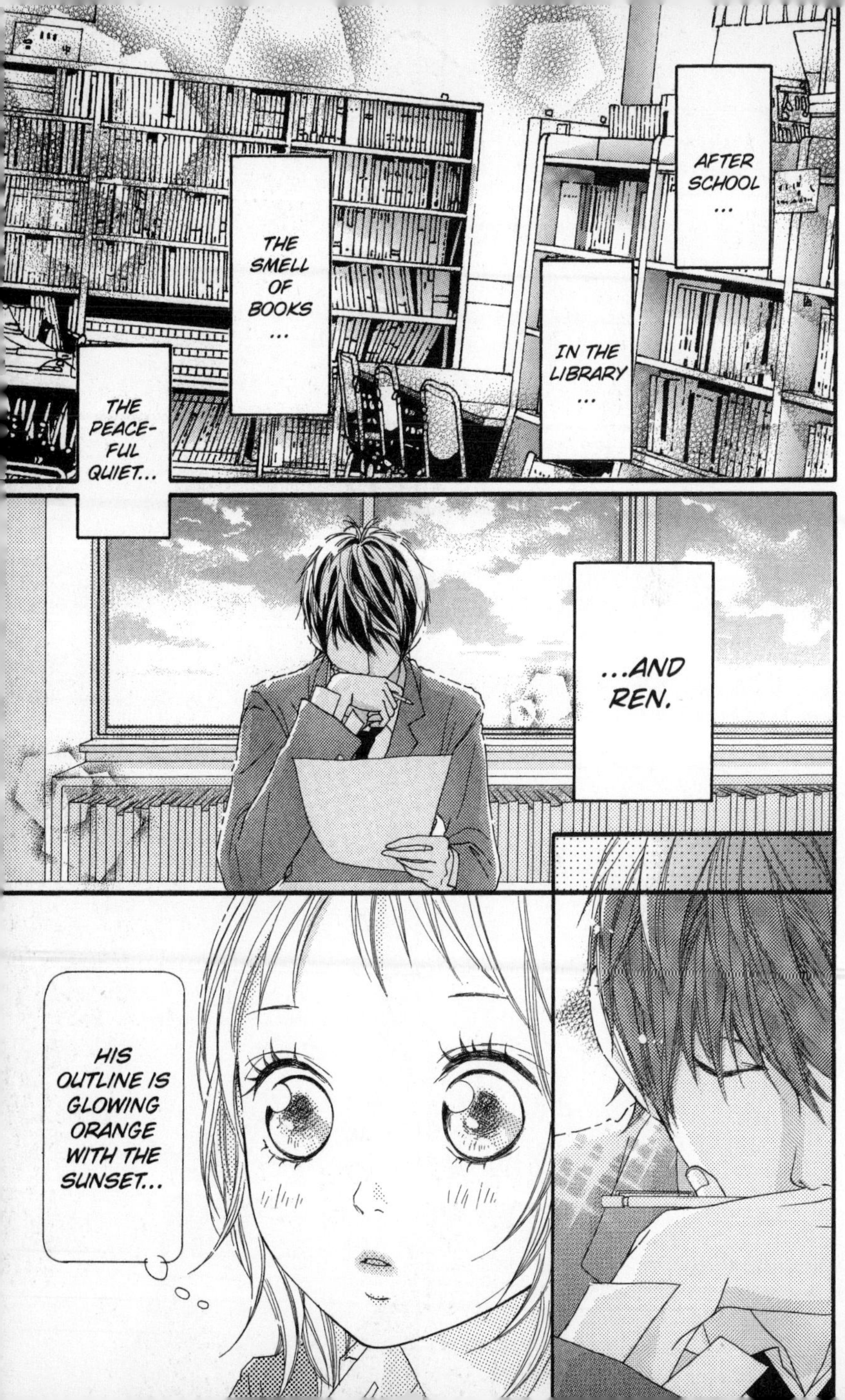
AFTER SCHOOL ...
IN THE LIBRARY ...
THE SMELL OF BOOKS ...
THE PEACE-FUL QUIET...
...AND REN.
HIS OUTLINE IS GLOWING ORANGE WITH THE SUNSET...

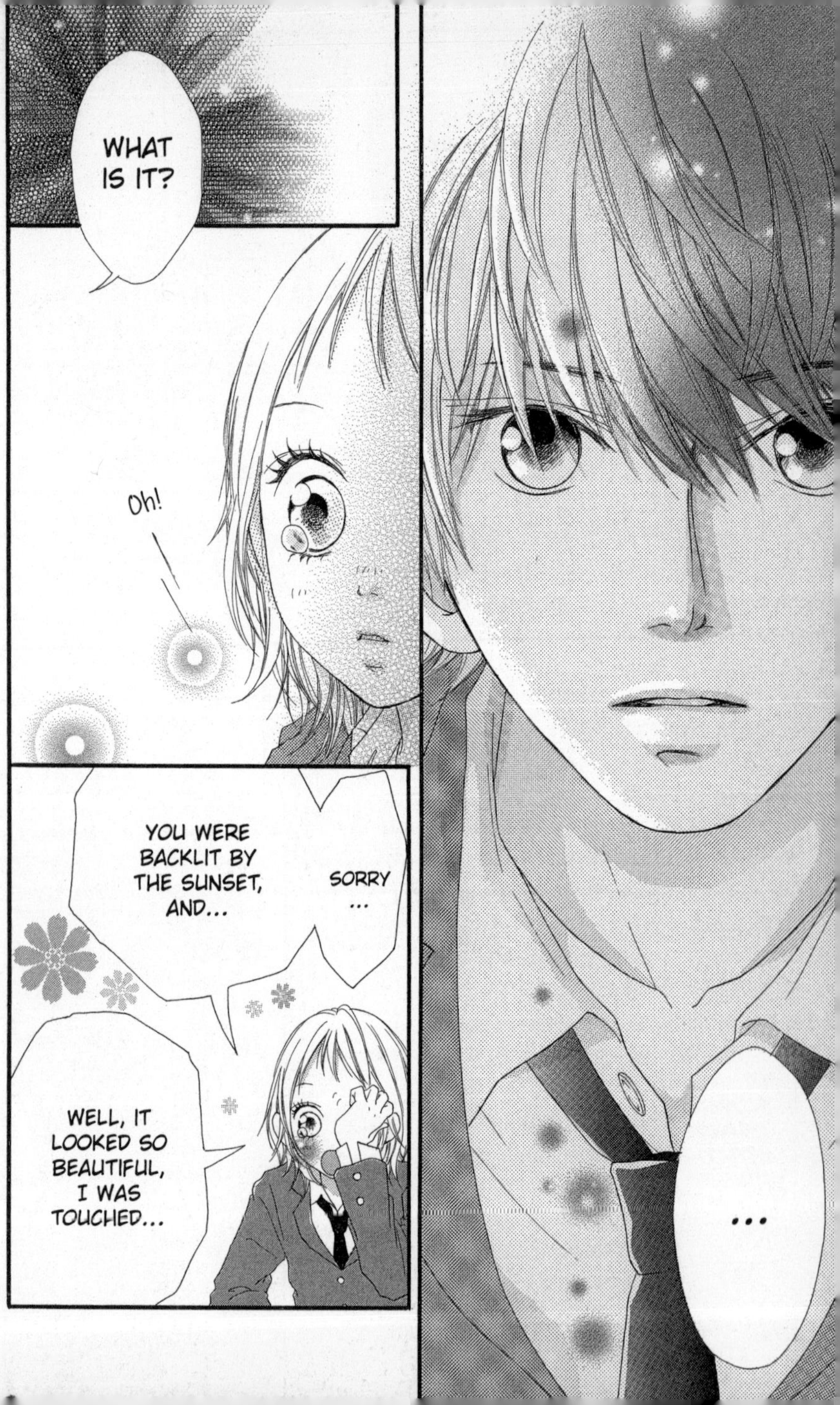
...
WHAT IS IT?
Oh!
SORRY...
YOU WERE BACKLIT BY THE SUNSET, AND...
WELL, IT LOOKED SO BEAUTIFUL, I WAS TOUCHED...

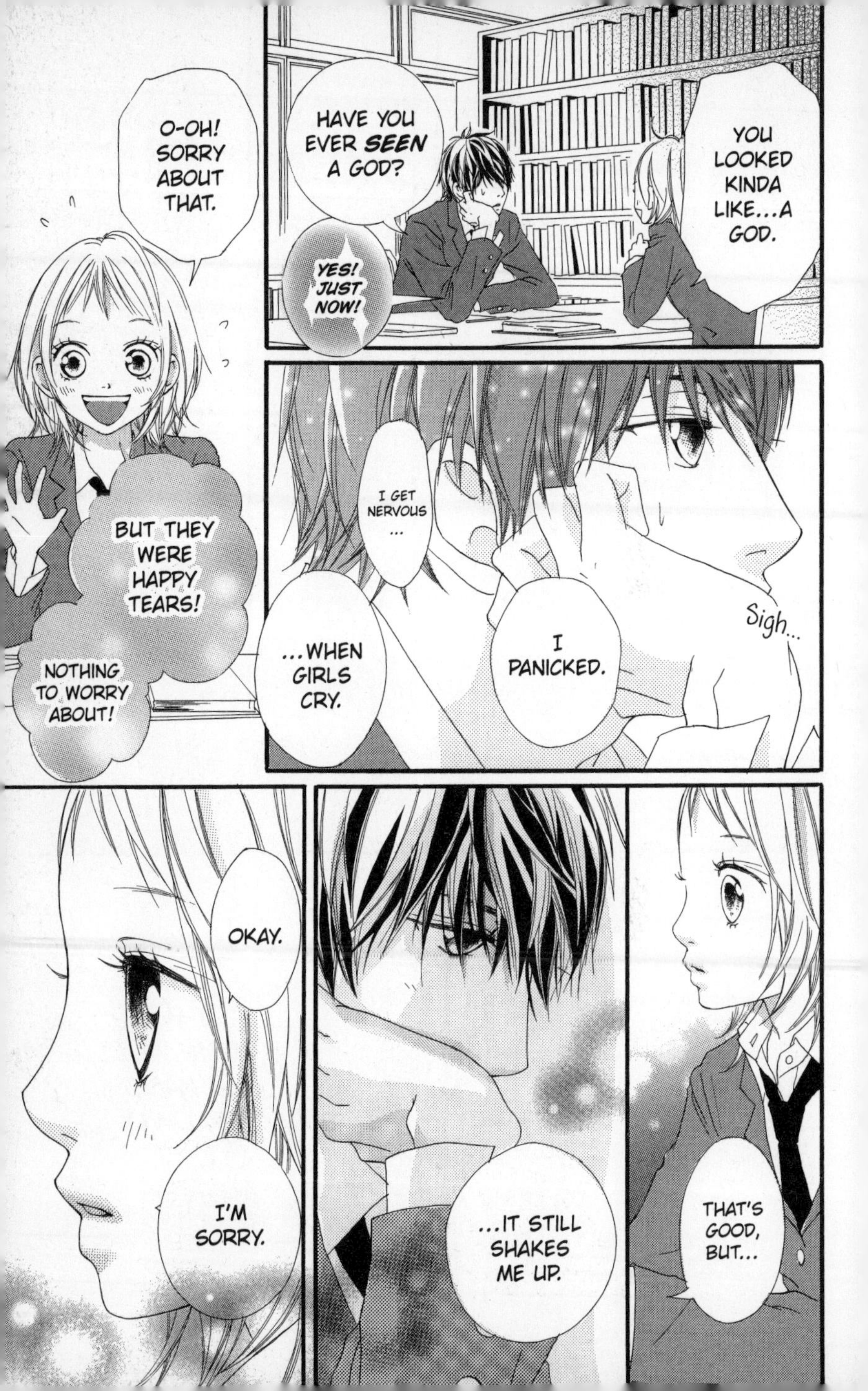
YOU LOOKED KINDA LIKE...A GOD.
HAVE YOU EVER SEEN A GOD?
YES! JUST NOW!
Sigh...
I PANICKED.
I GET NERVOUS...
...WHEN GIRLS CRY.
O-OH! SORRY ABOUT THAT.
BUT THEY WERE HAPPY TEARS!
NOTHING TO WORRY ABOUT!
THAT'S GOOD, BUT...
...IT STILL SHAKES ME UP.
OKAY.
I'M SORRY.

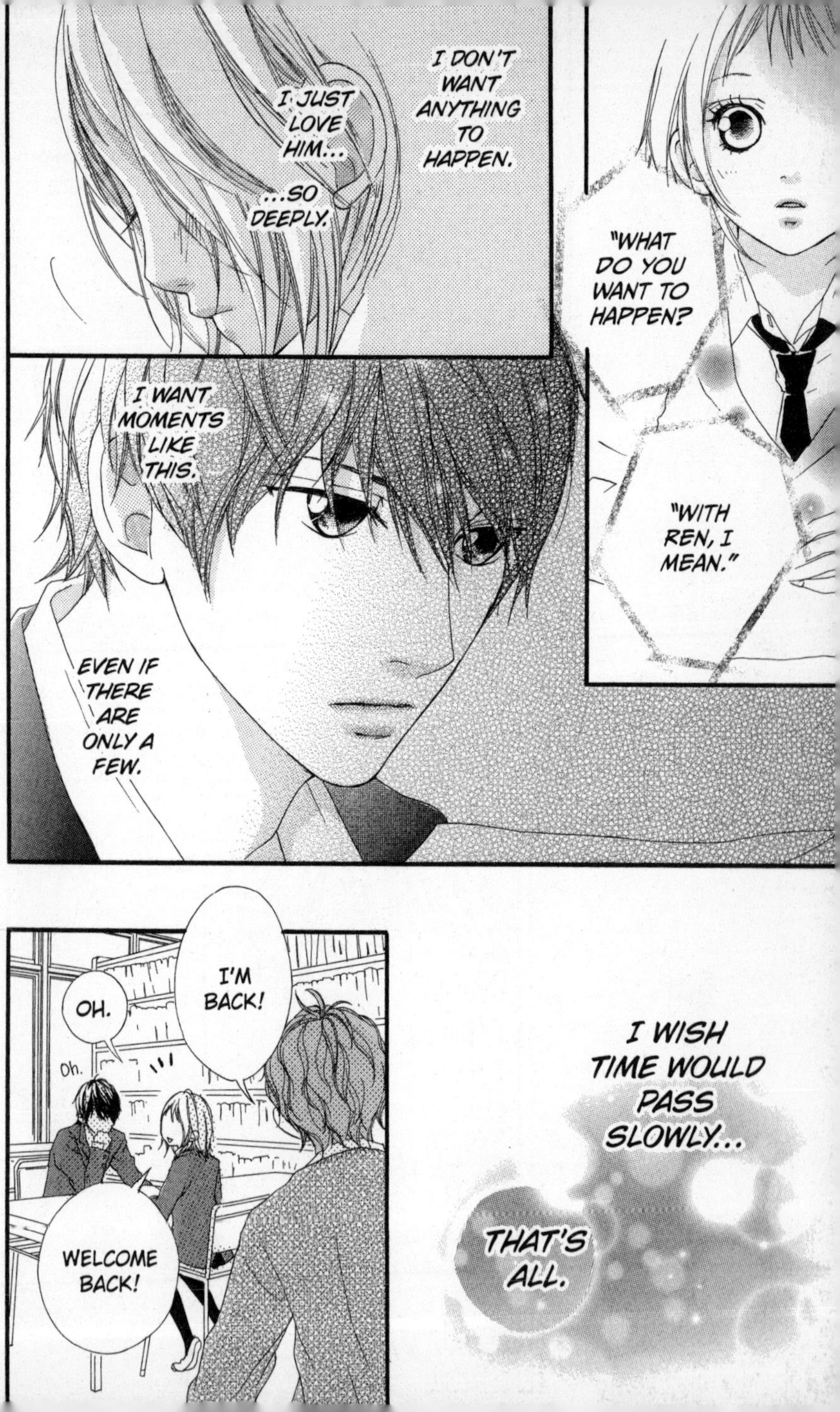
"WHAT DO YOU WANT TO HAPPEN?
"WITH REN, I MEAN."
I DON'T WANT ANYTHING TO HAPPEN.
I JUST LOVE HIM...
...SO DEEPLY.
I WANT MOMENTS LIKE THIS.
EVEN IF THERE ARE ONLY A FEW.
I WISH TIME WOULD PASS SLOWLY...
THAT'S ALL.
I'M BACK!
OH.
Oh.
WELCOME BACK!

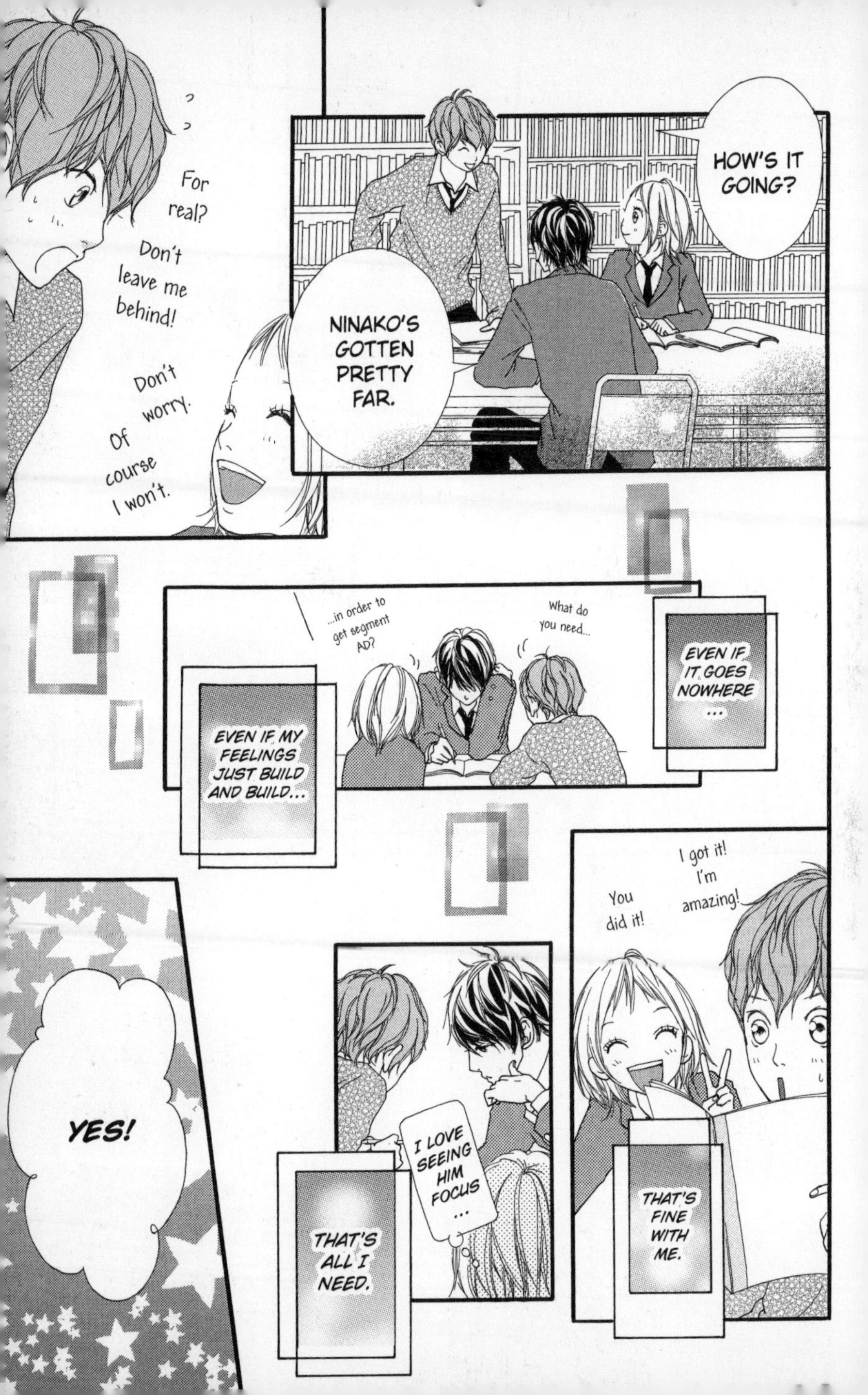
HOW'S IT GOING?
NINAKO'S GOTTEN PRETTY FAR.
For real? Don't leave me behind!
Don't worry. Of course I won't.
EVEN IF IT GOES NOWHERE...
What do you need...
...in order to get segment AD?
EVEN IF MY FEELINGS JUST BUILD AND BUILD...
I got it! I'm amazing!
You did it!
THAT'S FINE WITH ME.
I LOVE SEEING HIM FOCUS...
THAT'S ALL I NEED.
YES!

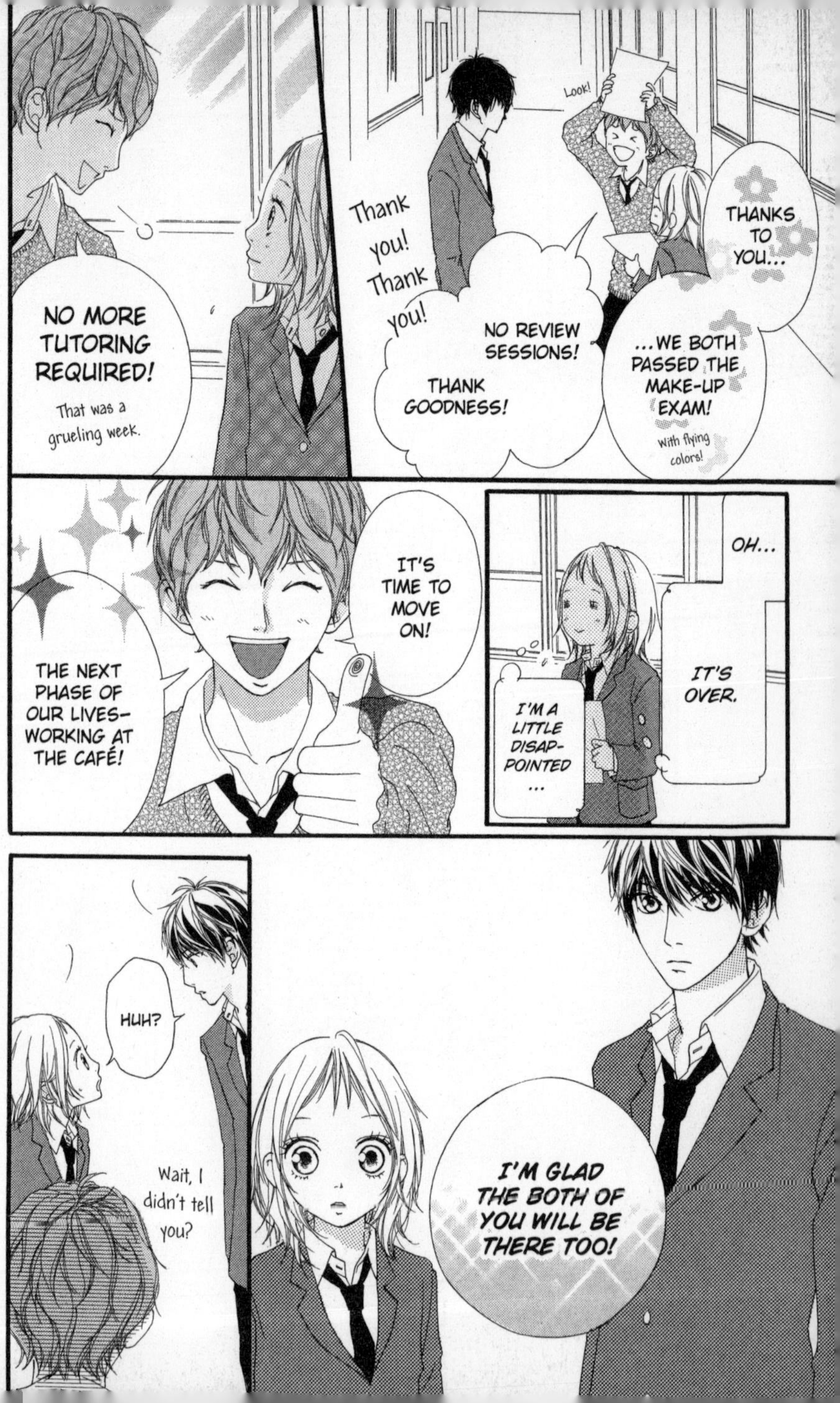
LOOK!
THANKS TO YOU...
...WE BOTH PASSED THE MAKE-UP EXAM!
With flying colors!
Thank you! Thank you!
NO REVIEW SESSIONS!
THANK GOODNESS!
NO MORE TUTORING REQUIRED!
That was a grueling week.
OH...
IT'S OVER.
I'M A LITTLE DISAP-POINTED ...
IT'S TIME TO MOVE ON!
THE NEXT PHASE OF OUR LIVES-WORKING AT THE CAFÉ!
I'M GLAD THE BOTH OF YOU WILL BE THERE TOO!
HUH?
Wait, I didn't tell you?

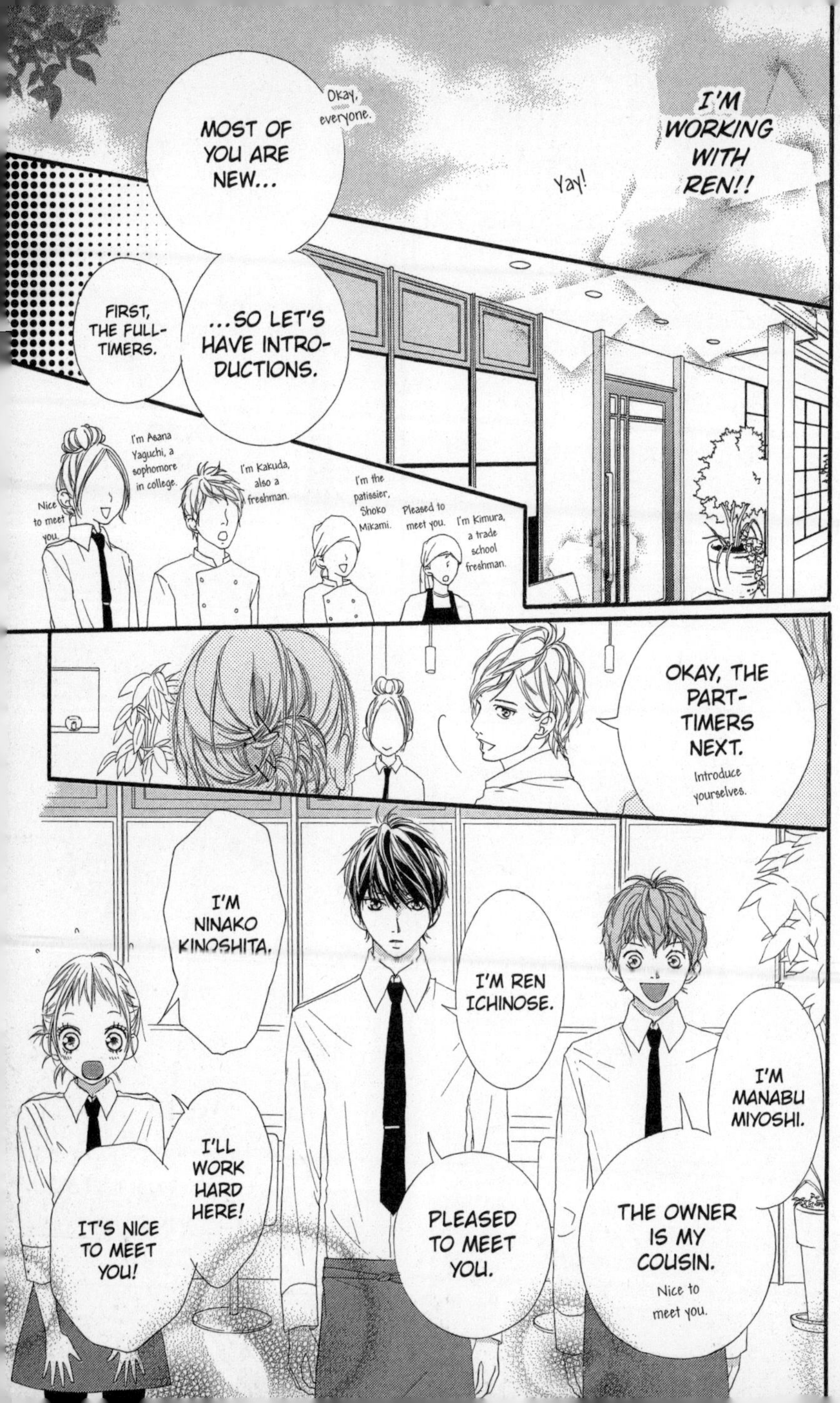
I'M WORKING WITH REN!!
Yay!
Okay, everyone.
MOST OF YOU ARE NEW...
...SO LET'S HAVE INTRODUCTIONS.
FIRST, THE FULL-TIMERS.
I'm Kimura, a trade school freshman.
Pleased to meet you.
I'm the patissier, Shoko Mikami.
I'm Kakuda, also a freshman.
I'm Asana Yaguchi, a sophomore in college.
Nice to meet you.
OKAY, THE PART-TIMERS NEXT.
Introduce yourselves.
I'M MANABU MIYOSHI.
THE OWNER IS MY COUSIN.
Nice to meet you.
I'M REN ICHINOSE.
PLEASED TO MEET YOU.
I'M NINAKO KINOSHITA.
I'LL WORK HARD HERE!
IT'S NICE TO MEET YOU!

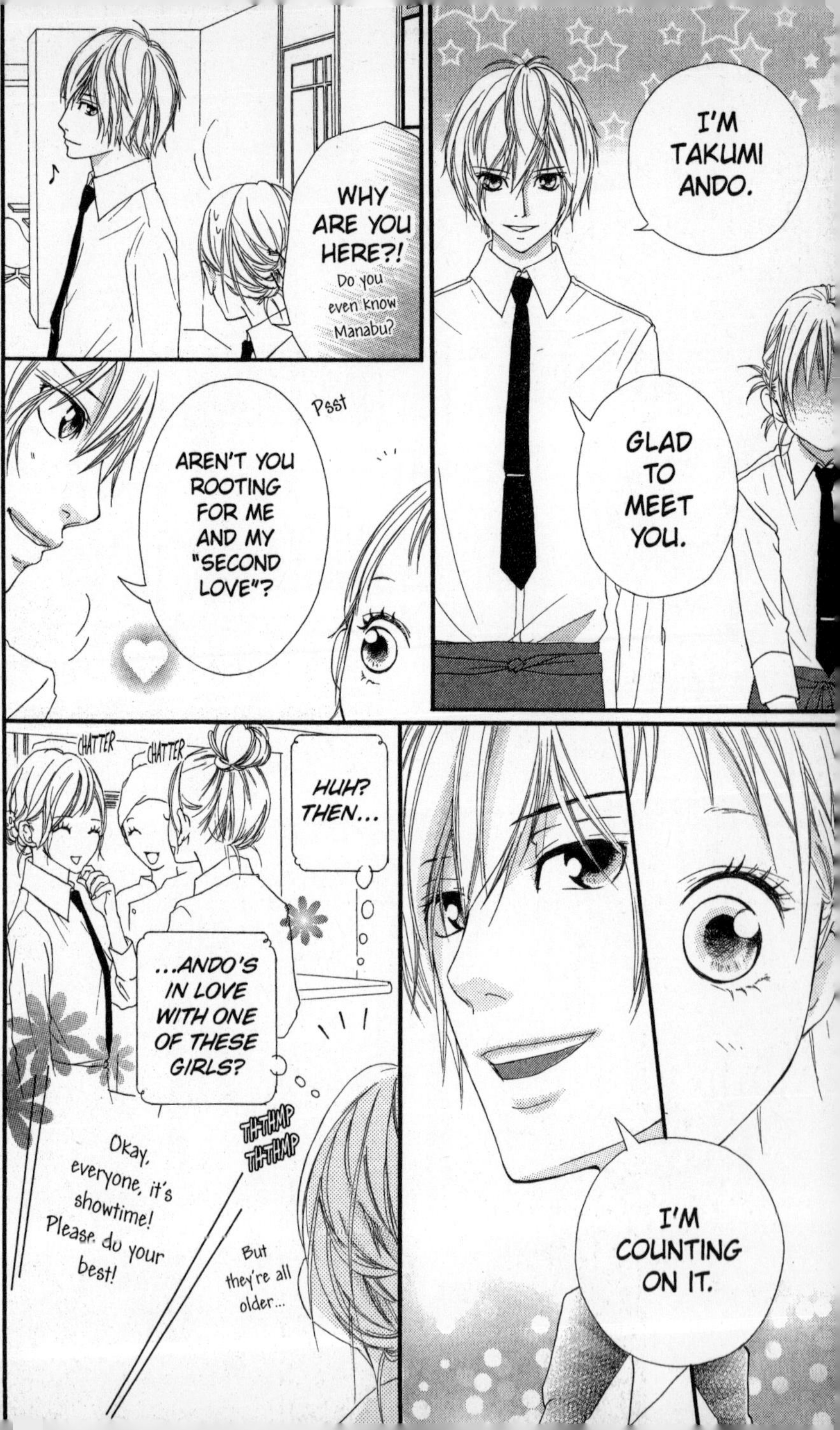
I'M TAKUMI ANDO.
GLAD TO MEET YOU.
WHY ARE YOU HERE?!
Do you even know Manabu?
Psst
AREN'T YOU ROOTING FOR ME AND MY "SECOND LOVE"?
I'M COUNTING ON IT.
CHATTER
CHATTER
HUH? THEN...
...ANDO'S IN LOVE WITH ONE OF THESE GIRLS?
THTHMP THTHMP
Okay, everyone, it's showtime! Please do your best!
But they're all older...

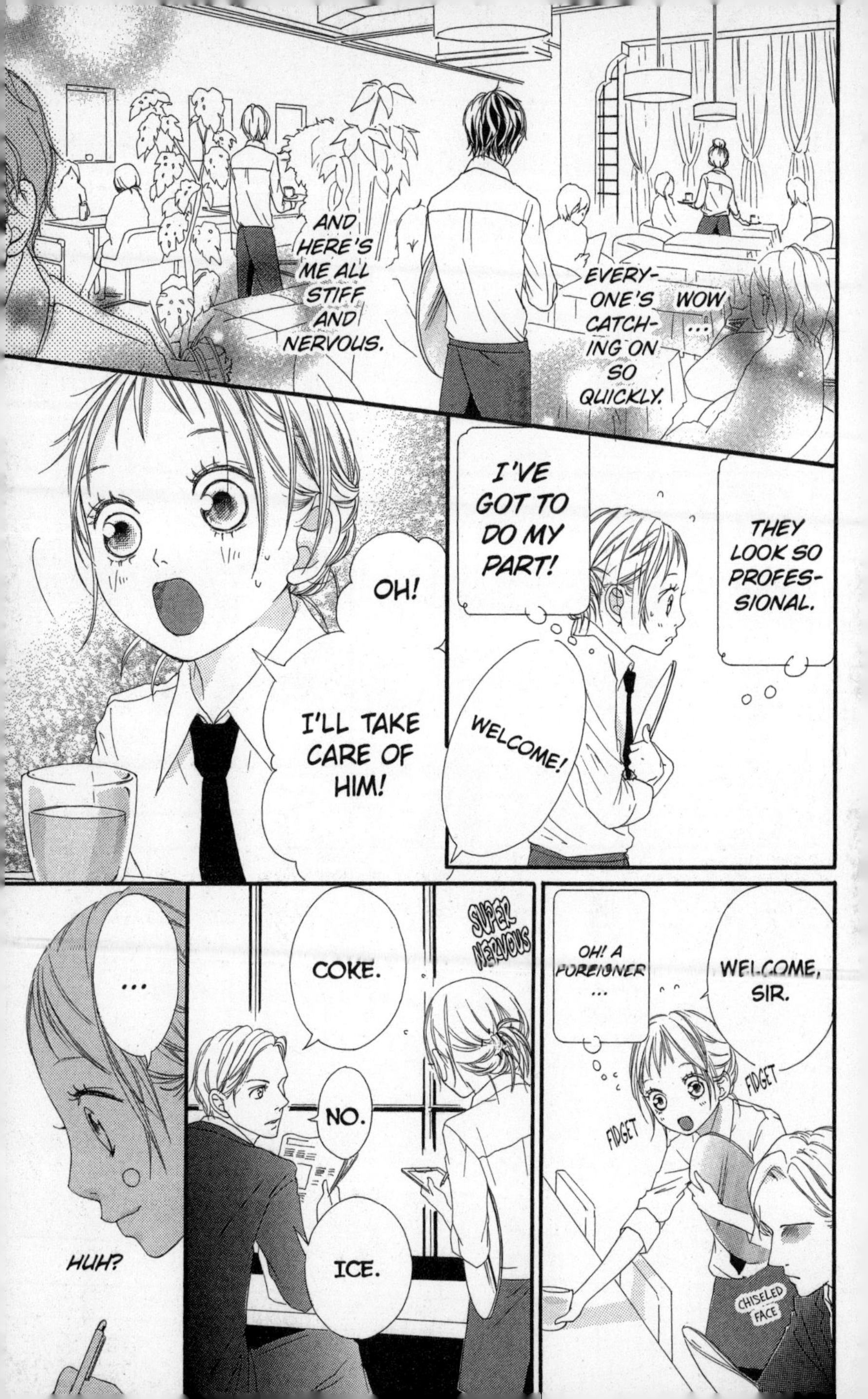
WOW ...
EVERYONE'S CATCHING ON SO QUICKLY.
AND HERE'S ME ALL STIFF AND NERVOUS.
THEY LOOK SO PROFESSIONAL.
I'VE GOT TO DO MY PART!
WELCOME!
OH!
I'LL TAKE CARE OF HIM!
WELCOME, SIR.
OH! A FOREIGNER ...
FIDGET
FIDGET
CHISELED FACE
SUPER NERVOUS
COKE.
NO.
ICE.
...
HUH?

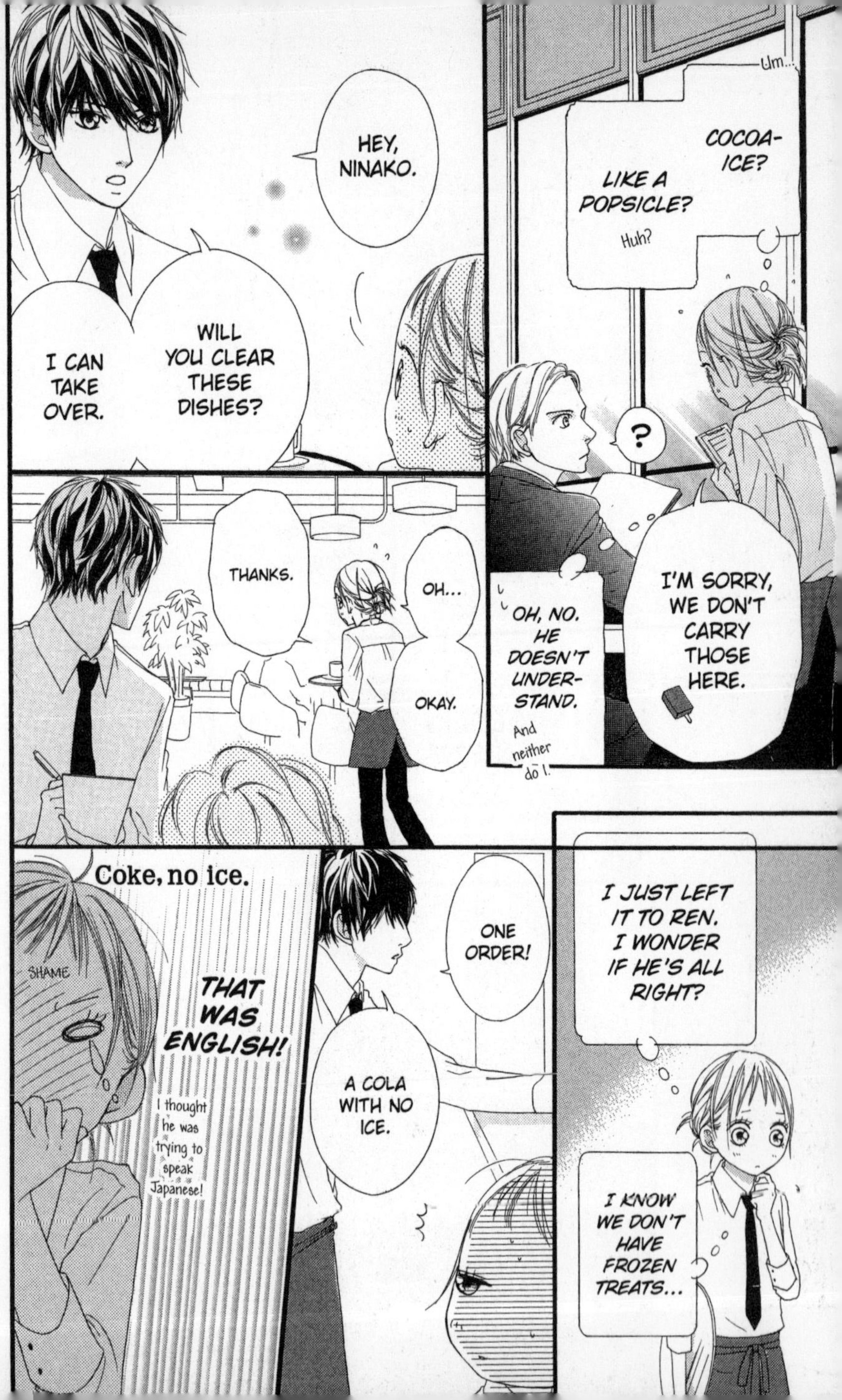
Um...
COCOA-ICE?
LIKE A POPSICLE?
Huh?
?
I'M SORRY, WE DON'T CARRY THOSE HERE.
OH, NO. HE DOESN'T UNDERSTAND.
And neither do I.
HEY, NINAKO.
WILL YOU CLEAR THESE DISHES?
I CAN TAKE OVER.
OH...
OKAY.
THANKS.
I JUST LEFT IT TO REN. I WONDER IF HE'S ALL RIGHT?
I KNOW WE DON'T HAVE FROZEN TREATS...
ONE ORDER!
A COLA WITH NO ICE.
Coke, no ice.
THAT WAS ENGLISH!
SHAME
I thought he was trying to speak Japanese!

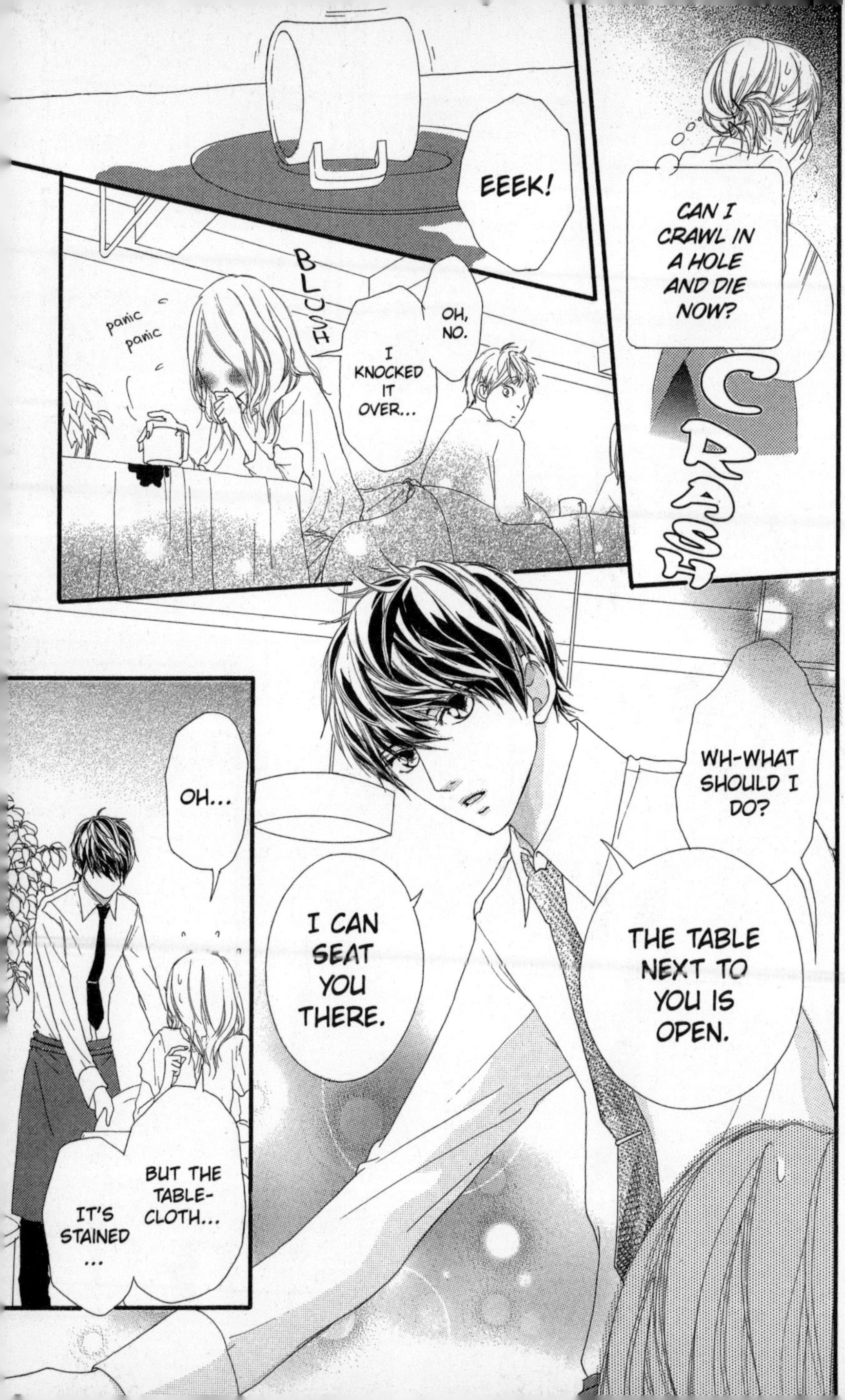
CAN I CRAWL IN A HOLE AND DIE NOW?
CRASH
EEEK!
BLUSH
panic panic
OH, NO.
I KNOCKED IT OVER...
WH-WHAT SHOULD I DO?
THE TABLE NEXT TO YOU IS OPEN.
I CAN SEAT YOU THERE.
OH...
BUT THE TABLE-CLOTH...
IT'S STAINED...

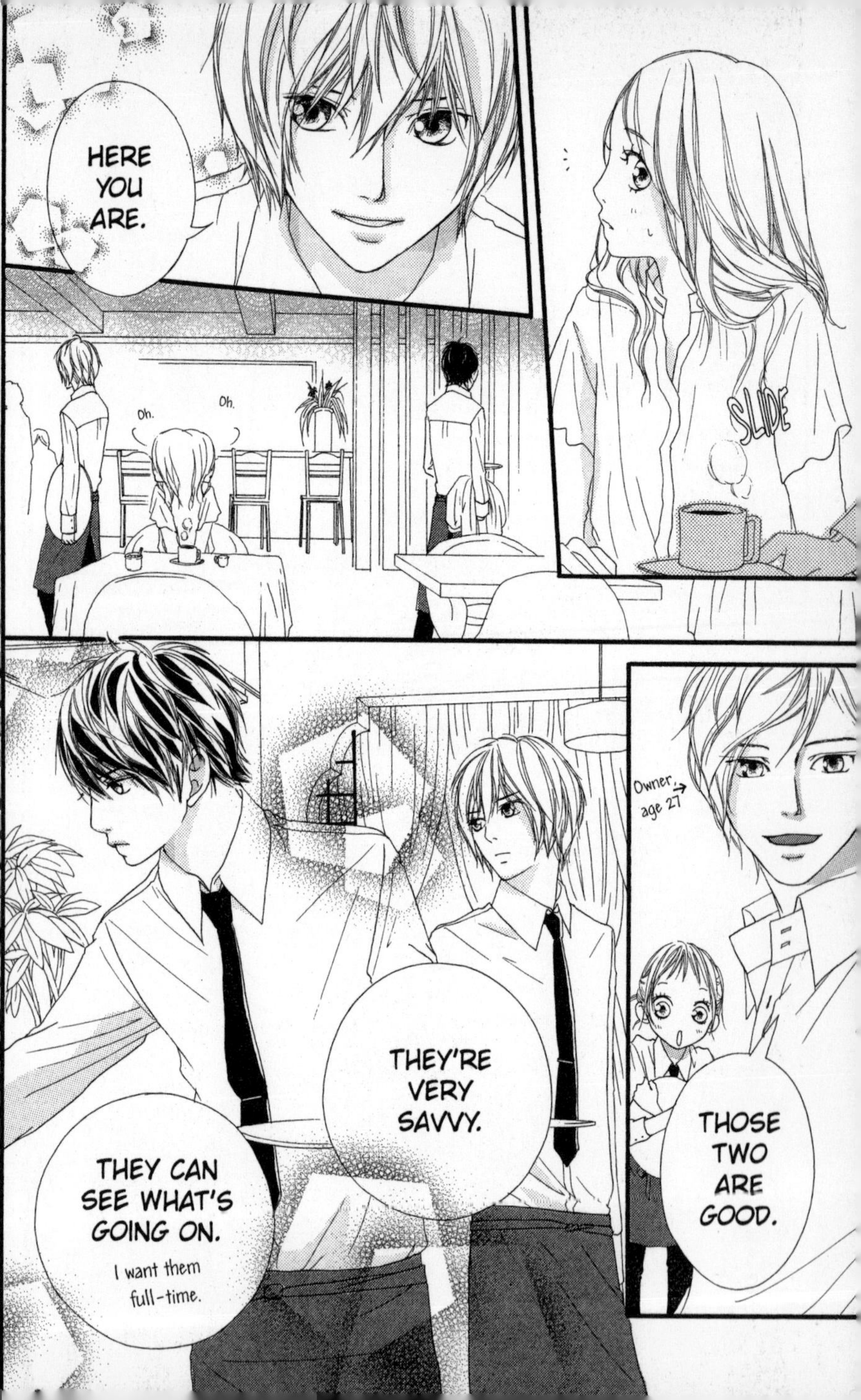
HERE YOU ARE.
Oh.
Oh.
SLIDE
Owner, age 27
THOSE TWO ARE GOOD.
THEY'RE VERY SAVVY.
THEY CAN SEE WHAT'S GOING ON.
I want them full-time.

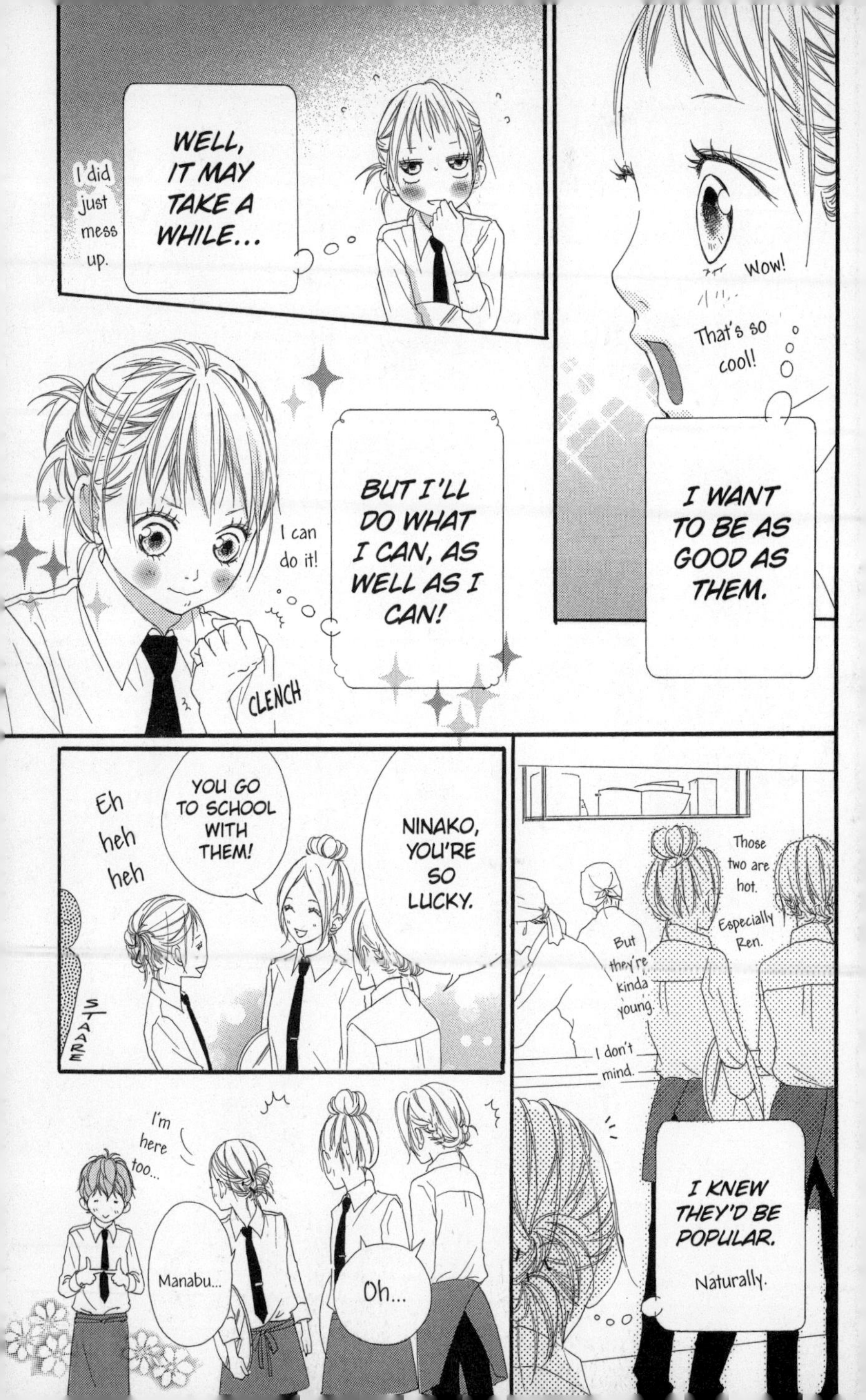

Wow!
That's so cool!
I WANT TO BE AS GOOD AS THEM.
WELL, IT MAY TAKE A WHILE...
I did just mess up.
BUT I'LL DO WHAT I CAN, AS WELL AS I CAN!
I can do it!
CLENCH
Those two are hot.
Especially Ren.
But they're kinda young.
I don't mind.
I KNEW THEY'D BE POPULAR.
Naturally.
NINAKO, YOU'RE SO LUCKY.
YOU GO TO SCHOOL WITH THEM!
Eh heh heh
STAARE
Oh...
Manabu...
I'm here too...

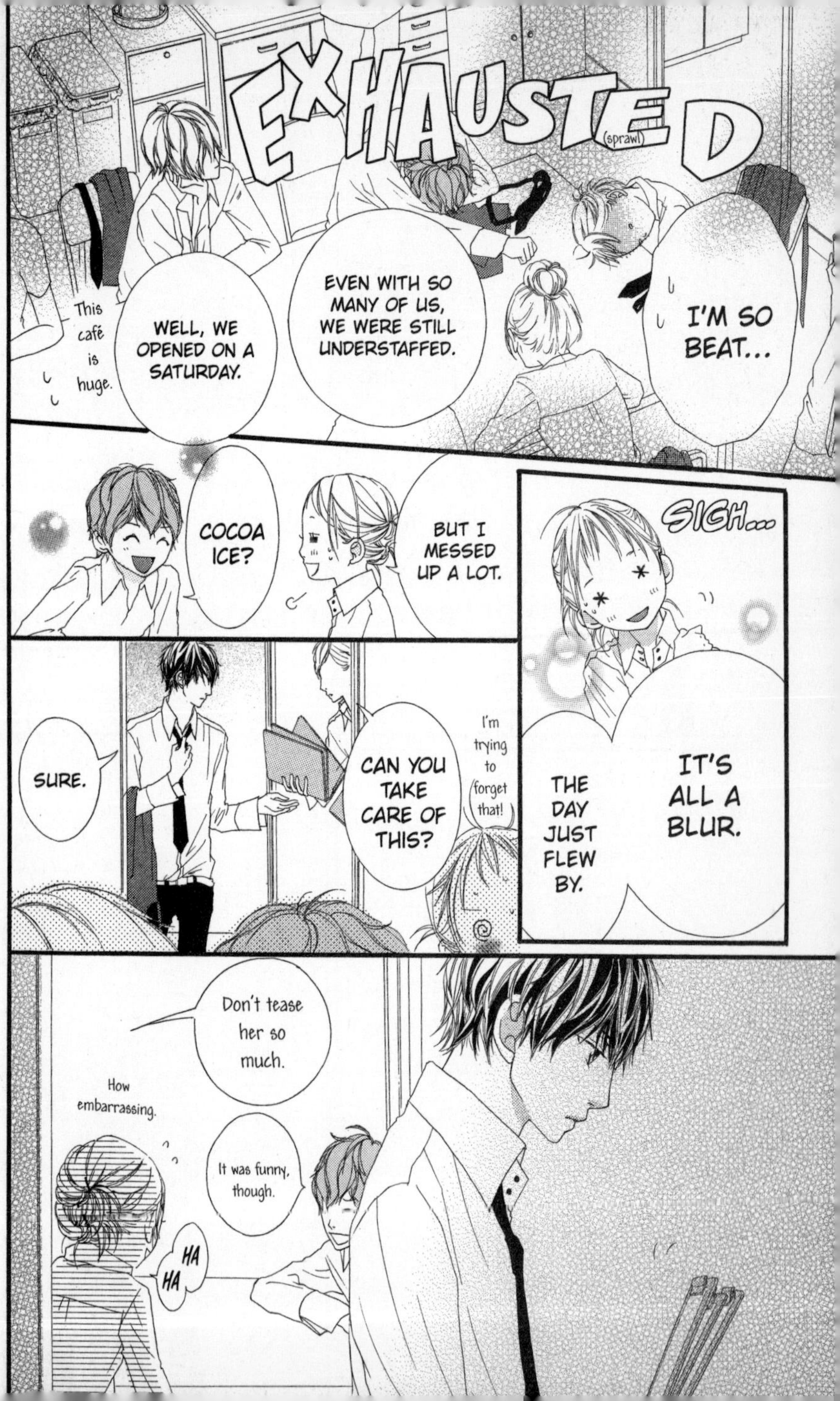
EXHAUSTED
(sprawl)
I'M SO BEAT...
EVEN WITH SO MANY OF US, WE WERE STILL UNDERSTAFFED.
WELL, WE OPENED ON A SATURDAY.
This café is huge.
SIGH...
IT'S ALL A BLUR.
THE DAY JUST FLEW BY.
BUT I MESSED UP A LOT.
COCOA ICE?
I'm trying to forget that!
CAN YOU TAKE CARE OF THIS?
SURE.
Don't tease her so much.
How embarrassing.
It was funny, though.
HA
HA

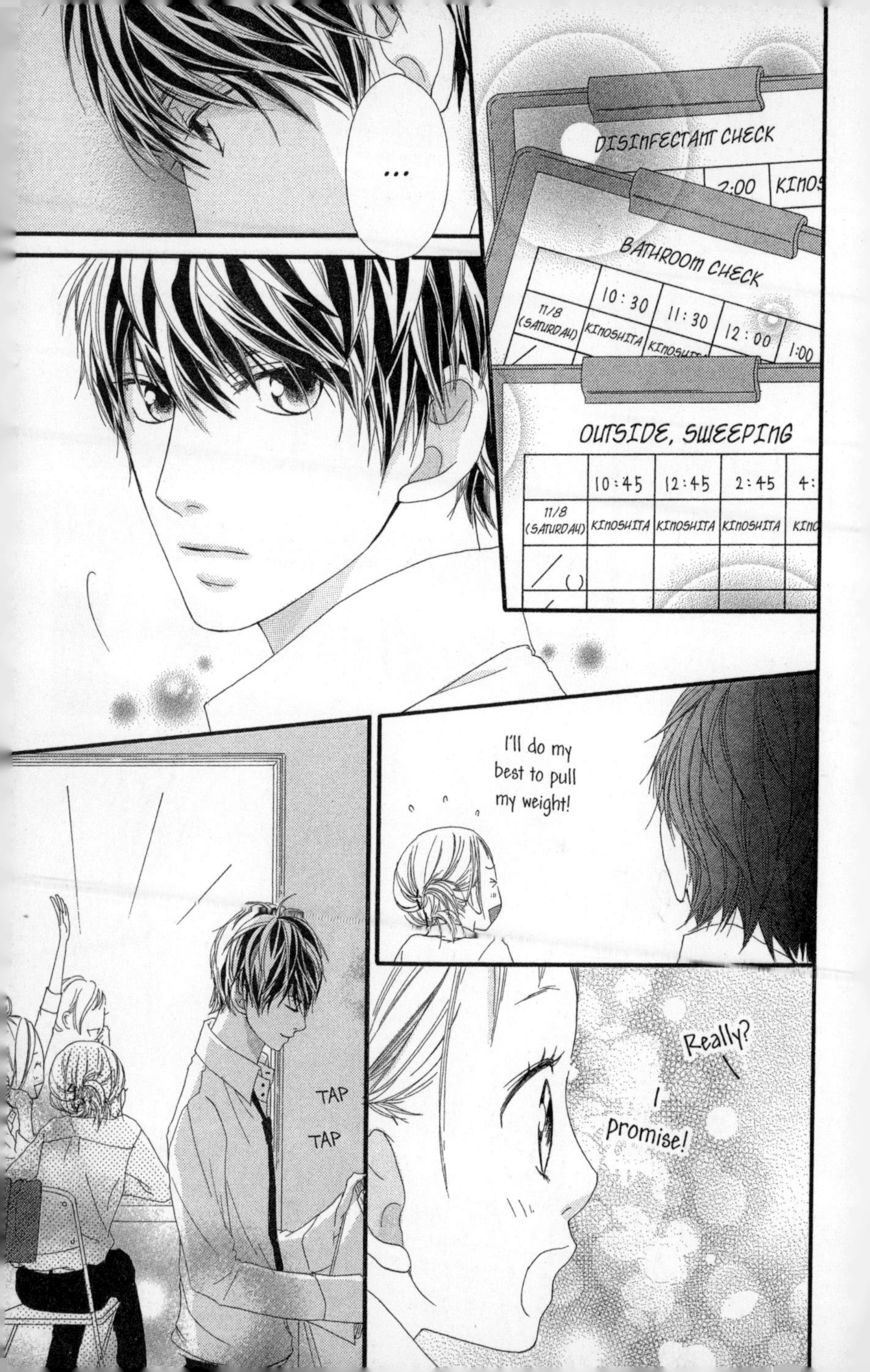
DISINFECTANT CHECK
2:00
BATHROOM CHECK
10:30
11:30
12:00
1:00
11/8 (SATURDAY)
KINOSHITA
OUTSIDE, SWEEPING
10:45
12:45
2:45
11/8 (SATURDAY)
KINOSHITA
KINOSHITA
KINOSHITA
...
I'll do my best to pull my weight!
Really?
I promise!
TAP
TAP

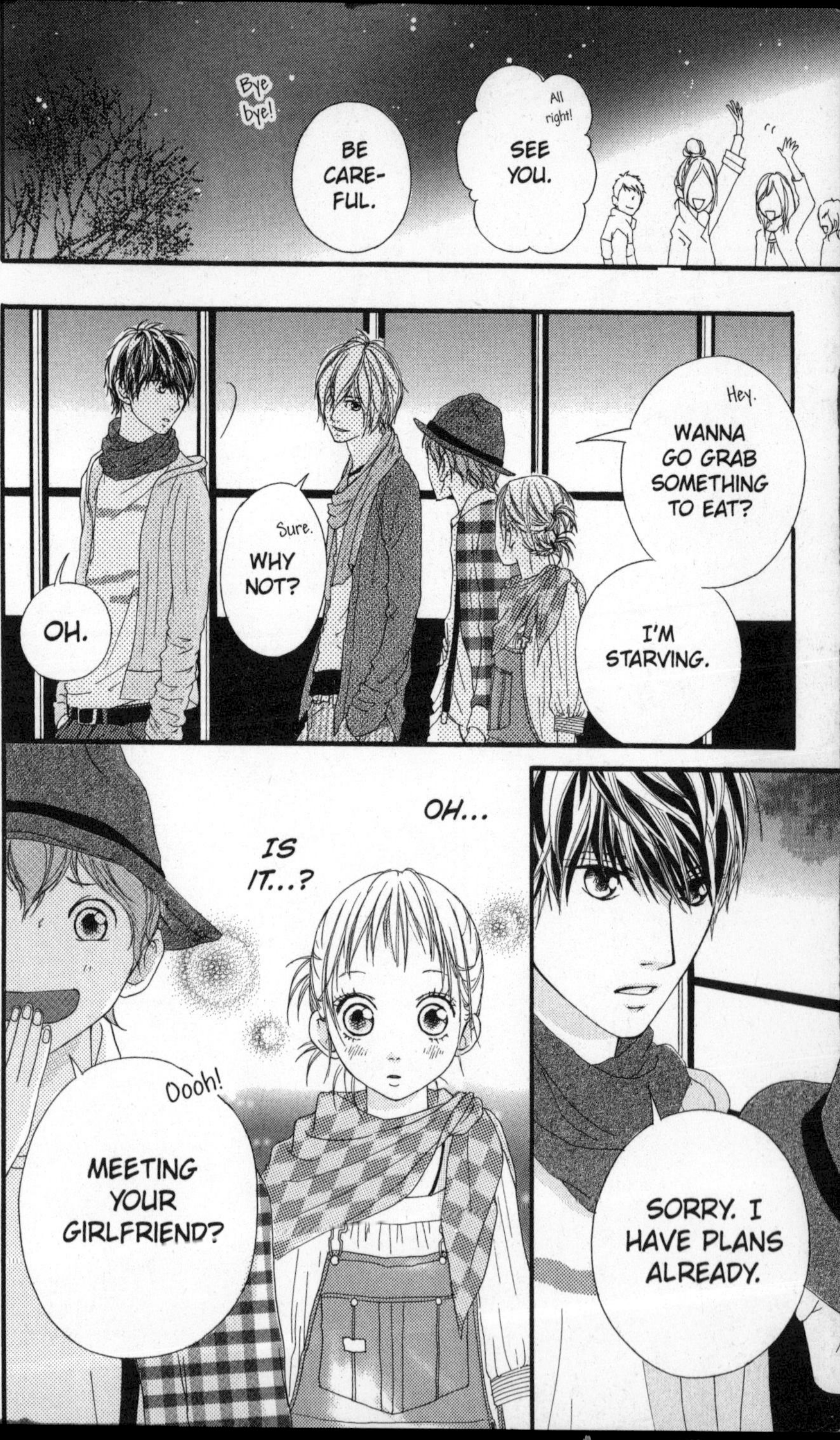
All right!
SEE YOU.
BE CAREFUL.
Bye bye!
Hey.
WANNA GO GRAB SOMETHING TO EAT?
I'M STARVING.
Sure.
WHY NOT?
OH.
SORRY. I HAVE PLANS ALREADY.
OH...
IS IT...?
Oooh!
MEETING YOUR GIRLFRIEND?

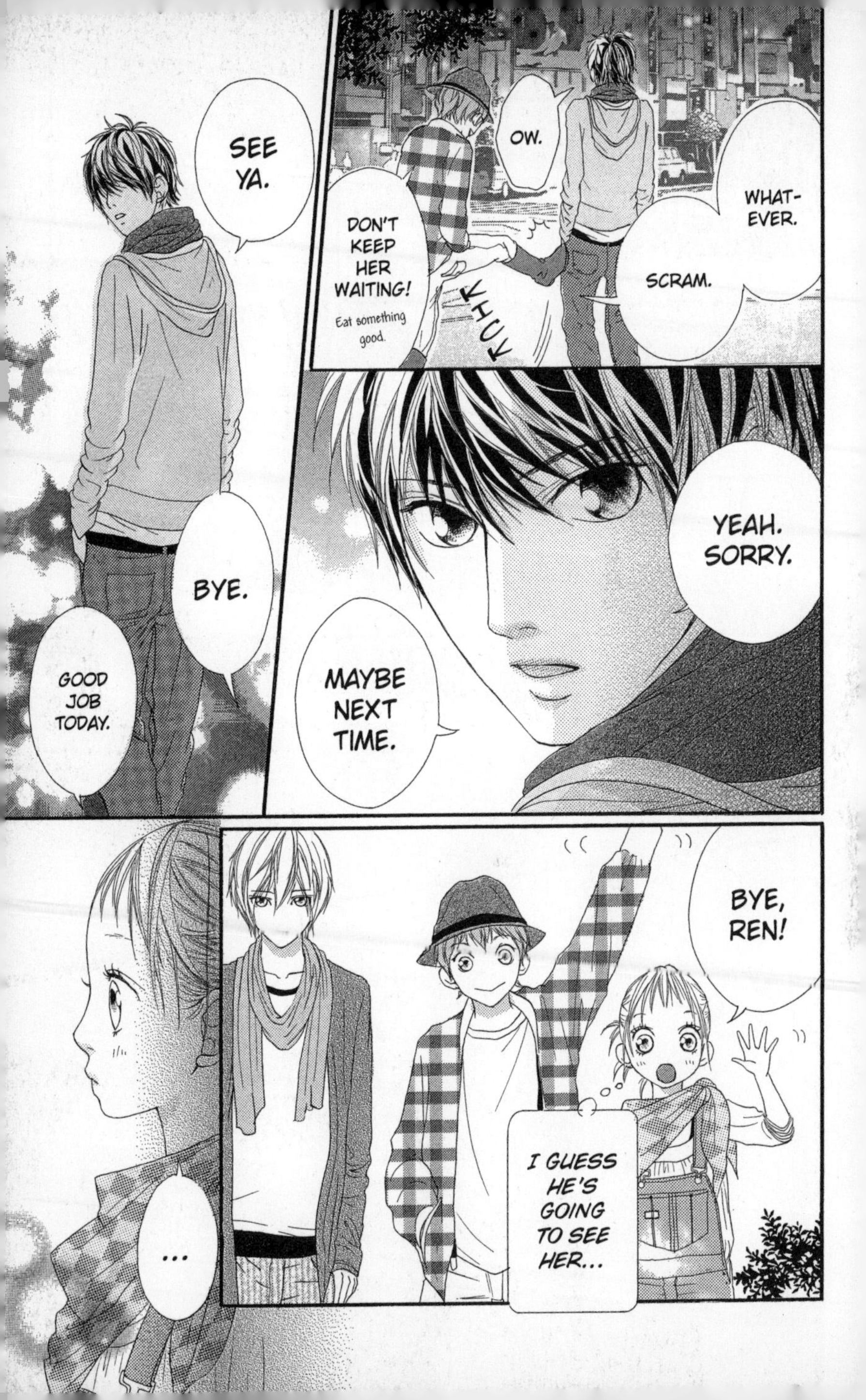
WHAT-
EVER.
SCRAM.
OW.
DON'T KEEP HER WAITING!
Eat something good.
KHUK
YEAH. SORRY.
MAYBE NEXT TIME.
SEE YA.
BYE.
GOOD JOB TODAY.
BYE, REN!
I GUESS HE'S GOING TO SEE HER...
...

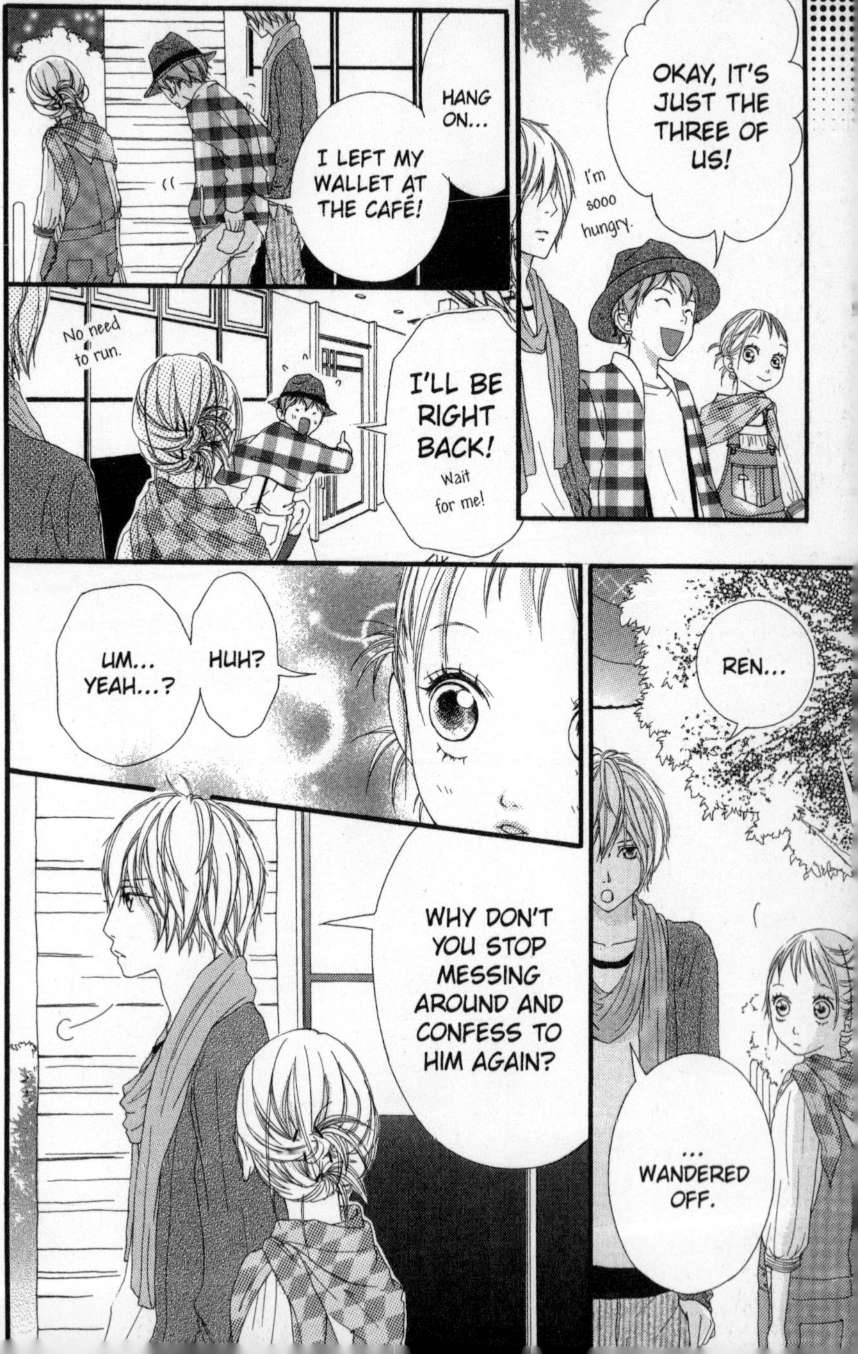
OKAY, IT'S JUST THE THREE OF US!
I'm sooo hungry.
HANG ON...
I LEFT MY WALLET AT THE CAFÉ!
I'LL BE RIGHT BACK!
Wait for me!
No need to run.
REN...
... WANDERED OFF.
HUH?
UM... YEAH...?
WHY DON'T YOU STOP MESSING AROUND AND CONFESS TO HIM AGAIN?

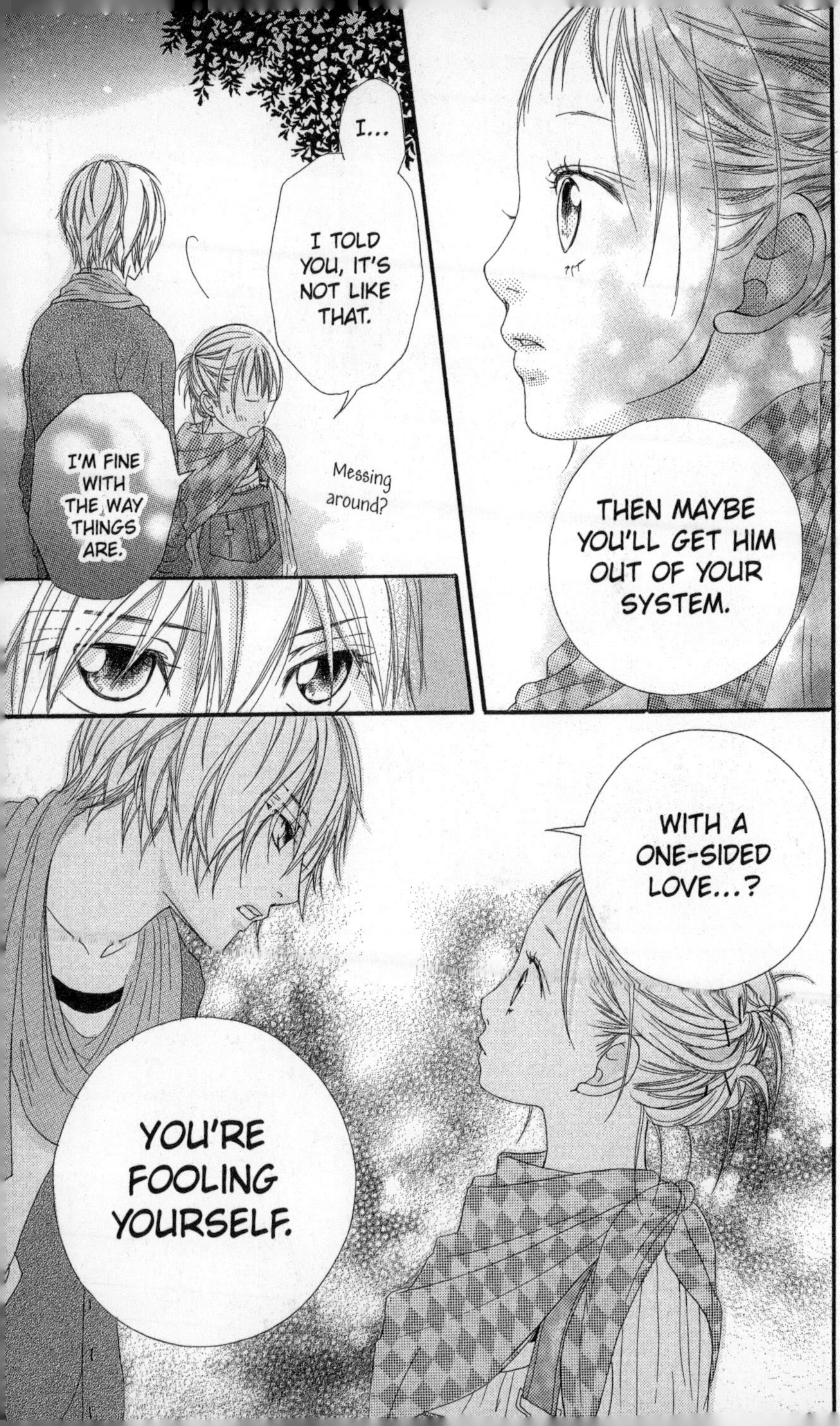
THEN MAYBE YOU'LL GET HIM OUT OF YOUR SYSTEM.
I...
I TOLD YOU, IT'S NOT LIKE THAT.
Messing around?
I'M FINE WITH THE WAY THINGS ARE.
WITH A ONE-SIDED LOVE...?
YOU'RE FOOLING YOURSELF.

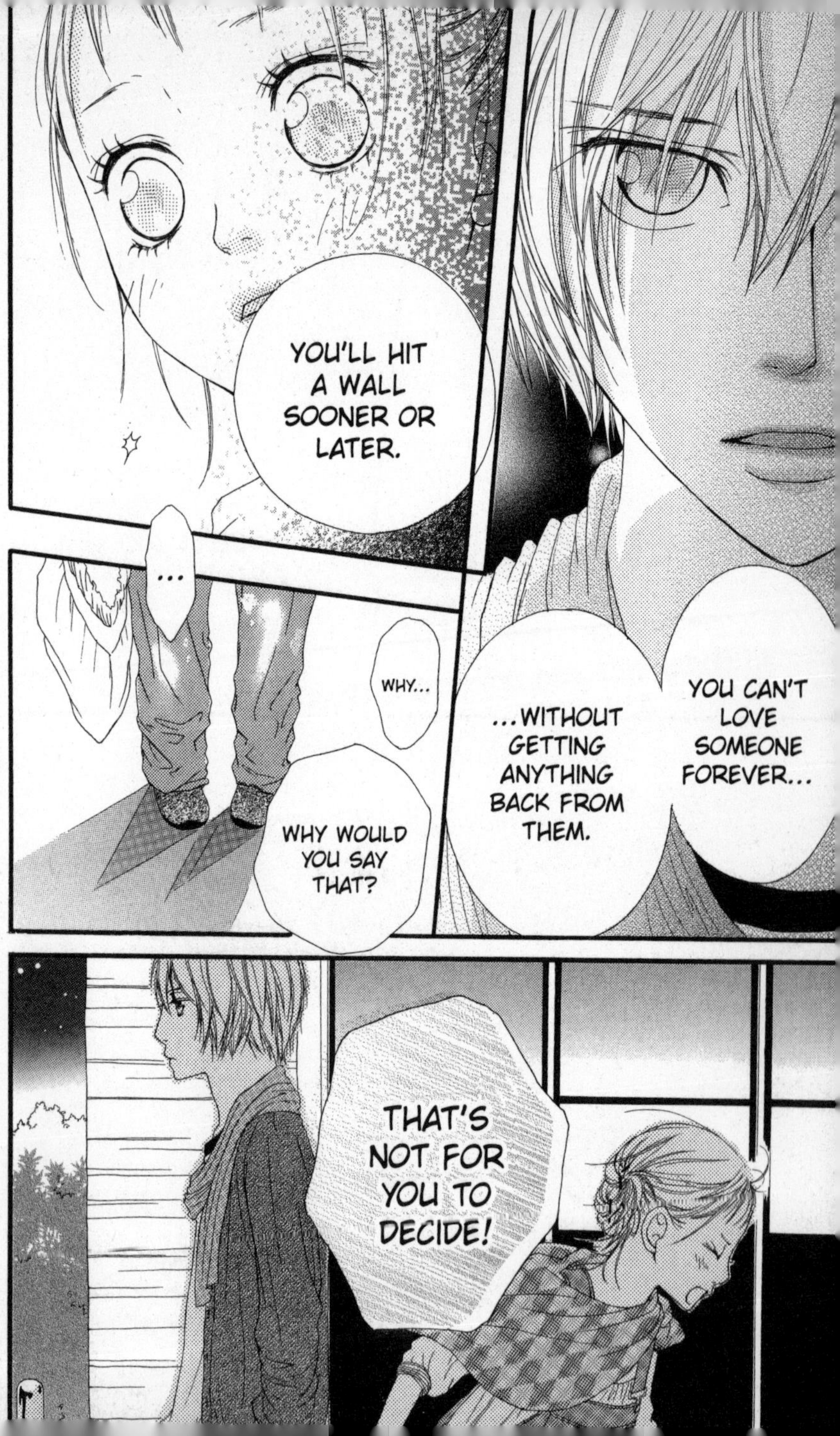
YOU CAN'T LOVE SOMEONE FOREVER...
...WITHOUT GETTING ANYTHING BACK FROM THEM.
YOU'LL HIT A WALL SOONER OR LATER.
...
WHY...
WHY WOULD YOU SAY THAT?
THAT'S NOT FOR YOU TO DECIDE!

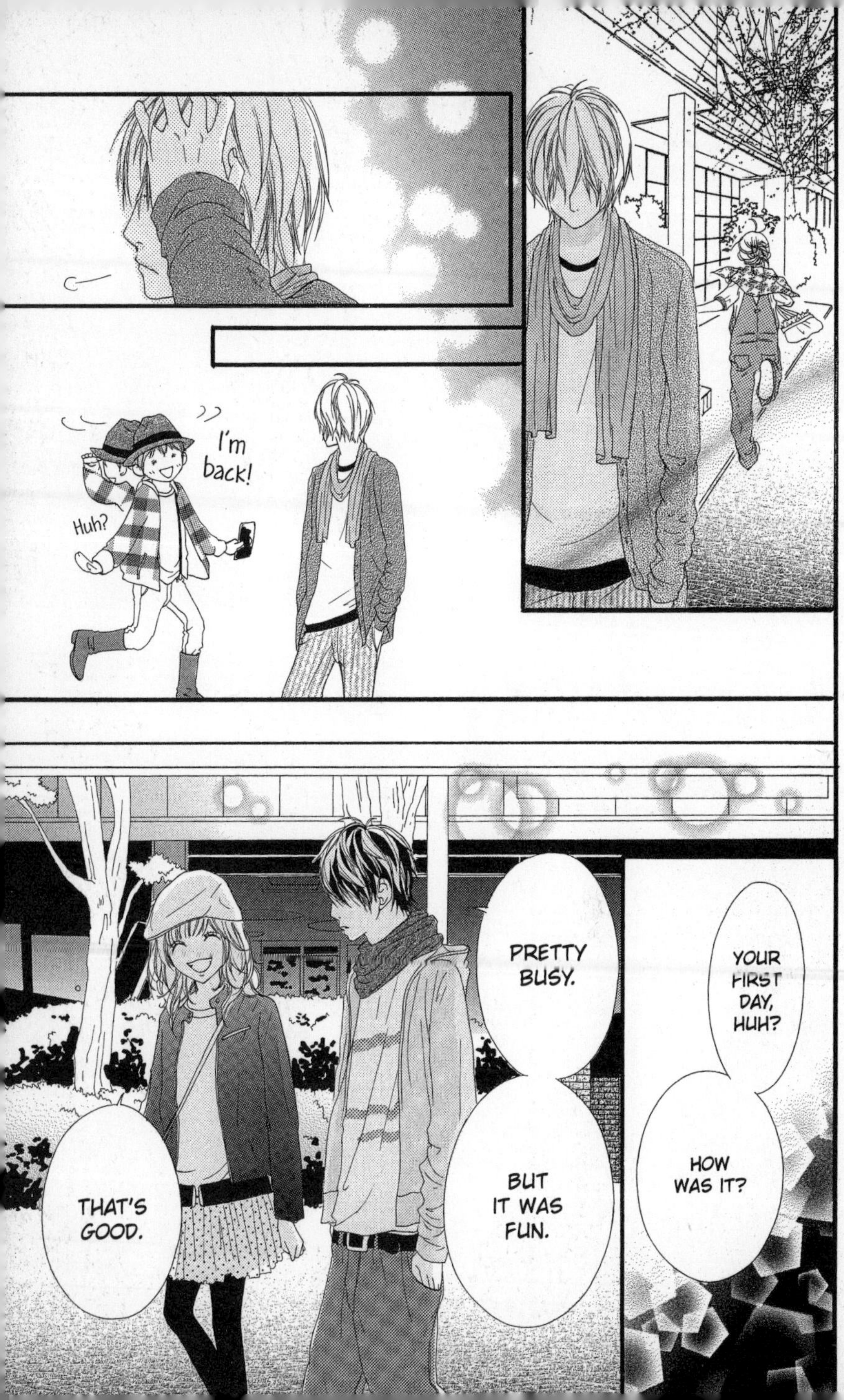
I'm back!
Huh?
YOUR FIRST DAY, HUH?
HOW WAS IT?
PRETTY BUSY.
BUT IT WAS FUN.
THAT'S GOOD.

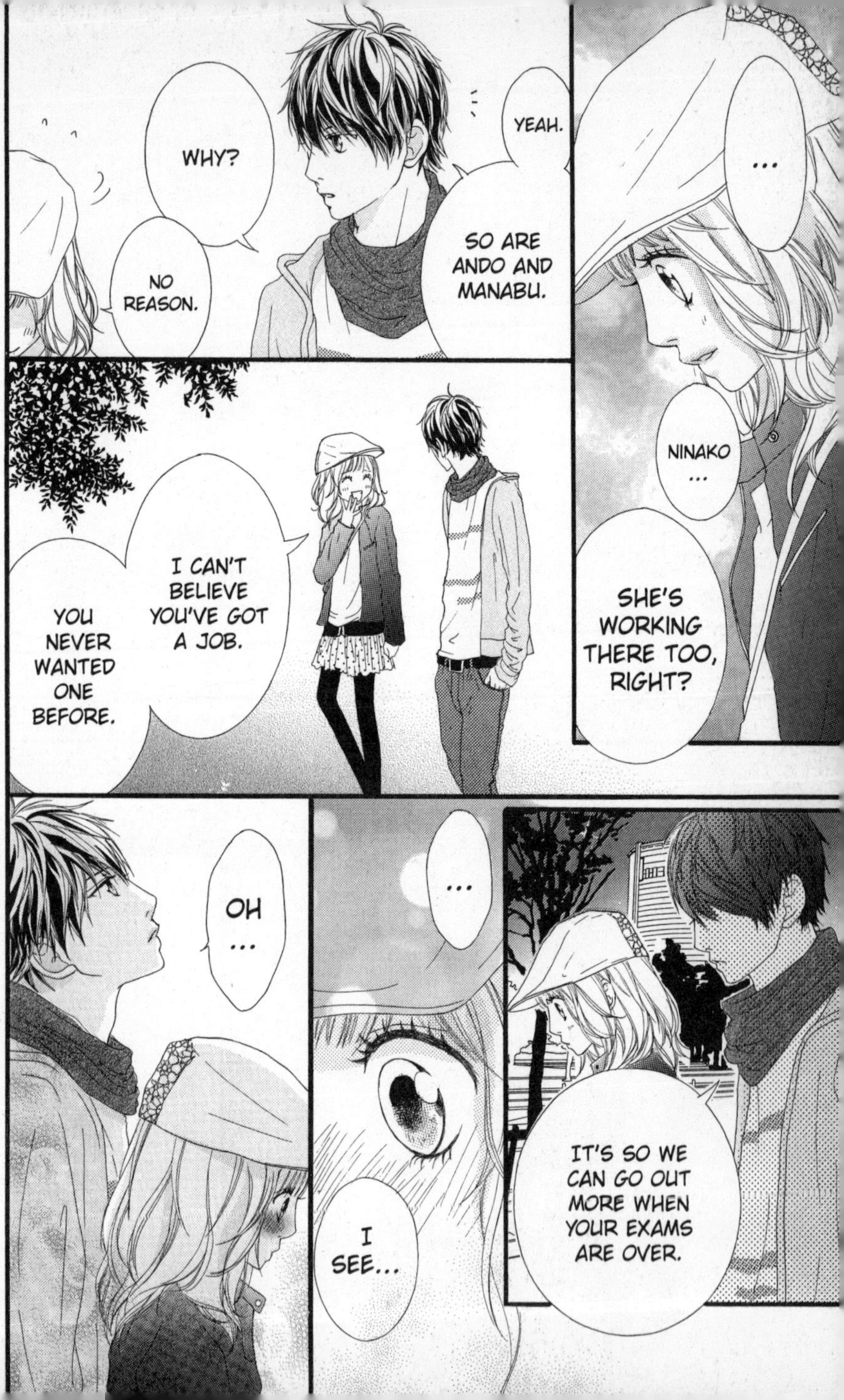
...
NINAKO ...
SHE'S WORKING THERE TOO, RIGHT?
YEAH.
SO ARE ANDO AND MANABU.
WHY?
NO REASON.
I CAN'T BELIEVE YOU'VE GOT A JOB.
YOU NEVER WANTED ONE BEFORE.
IT'S SO WE CAN GO OUT MORE WHEN YOUR EXAMS ARE OVER.
...
I SEE...
OH ...

← Continued

But maybe all that fantasizing is what allows me to be a manga artist. It contributes hugely to my plot development. So I'm not crazy! It's totally justifiable! (And I'm totally making excuses here.)

That said, what I'm doing doesn't hurt anyone or cause problems. It's all in my head, so it doesn't use up any natural resources. It's a very environmentally friendly way to live! And financially, it costs nothing.

So who wants to join the Fantasy Club? New members are always welcome.

*Towel Blanket Club members (see volume 2) are also welcome! Let's wrap ourselves in kindness. By the way, a few people have already joined my Towel Blanket Club.

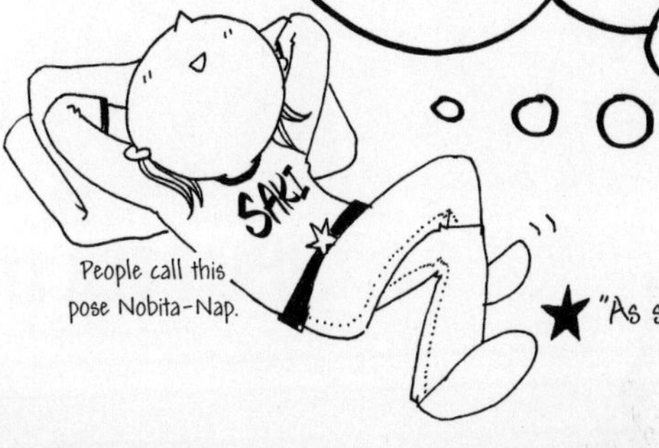
SAKI
People call this pose Nobita-Nap.

★ "As soon as" Sakisaka ★

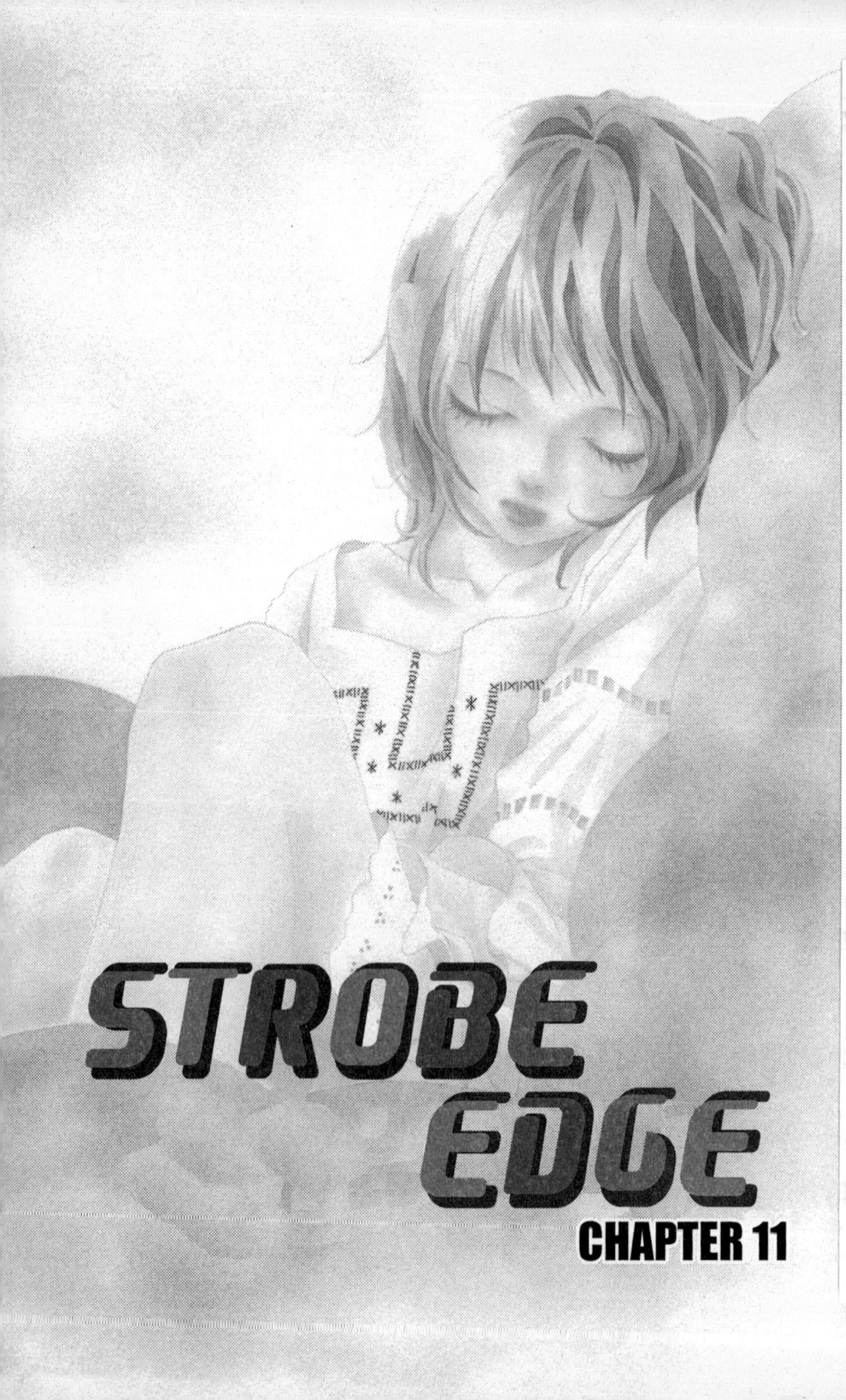
STROBE EDGE
CHAPTER 11

MY PRIVATE AMUSEMENT

I'm always daydreaming—or maybe I should say I'm always happily lost in thought. That may sound like I'm very intelligent, but nothing could be further from the truth. About 90 percent of my thoughts are utterly useless. Sometimes I'll be looking back on a funny thing that happened and laughing to myself. Other times I'm thinking, "I should have done that!" and rewriting history to fix things I did badly. Sometimes I'm listening to music and making videos in my head. They're more like fantasies or delusions than thought.

Wait. Is that dark? No way...

Anyway, I find myself daydreaming without even noticing it. In practice, that means I often get lost without noticing too! Like, sometimes I miss my stop when I'm on the train. Or worse, I get on the wrong train and it's ages before I notice it's going the wrong way. Sometimes I'm so immersed in my fantasies that I can't remember what I was doing or what was happening around me, even though I was awake.

Does that sound crazy...? No way.

← To be continued

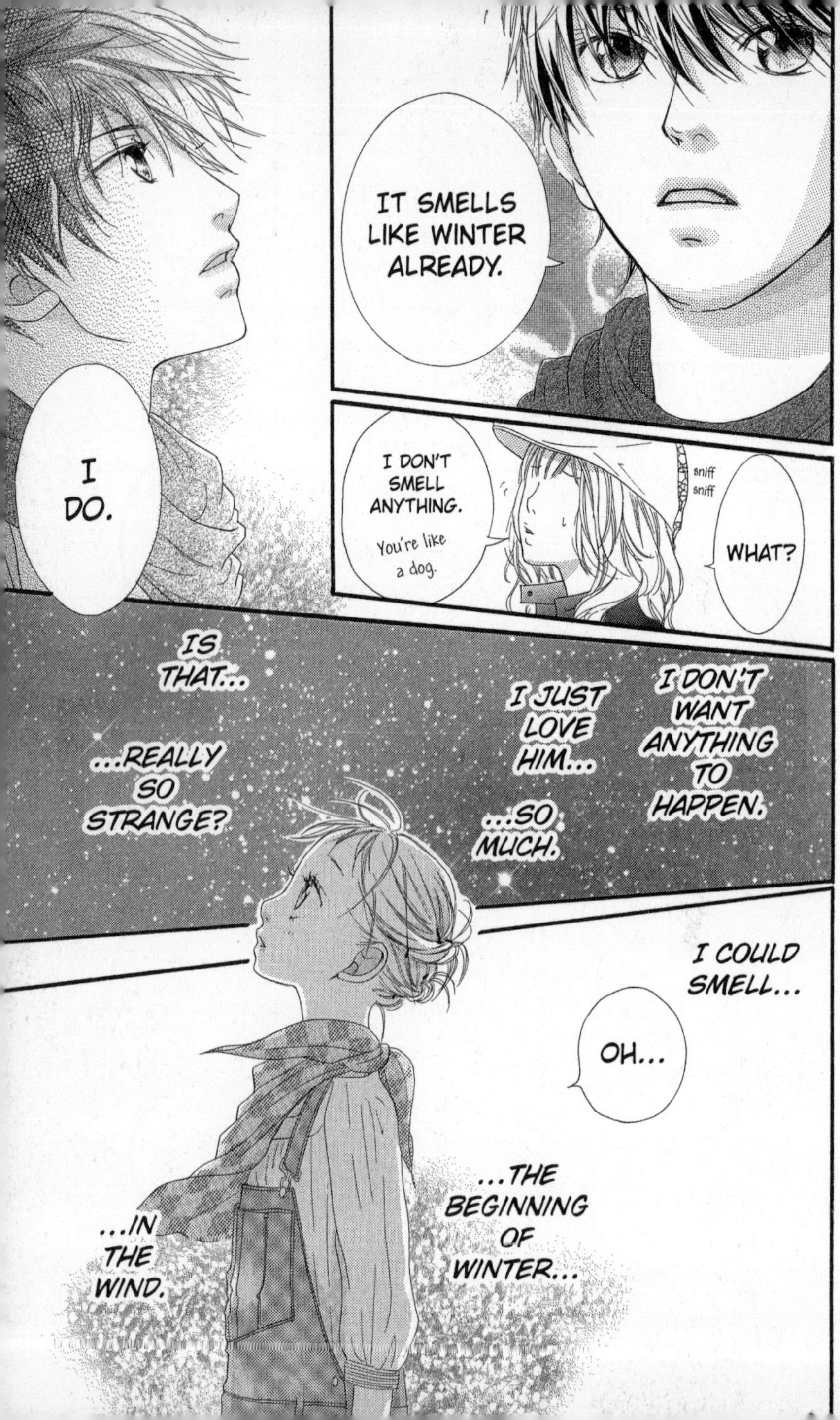
IT SMELLS LIKE WINTER ALREADY.
WHAT?
sniff sniff
I DON'T SMELL ANYTHING.
You're like a dog.
I DO.
I DON'T WANT ANYTHING TO HAPPEN.
I JUST LOVE HIM...
...SO MUCH.
IS THAT...
...REALLY SO STRANGE?
I COULD SMELL...
OH...
...THE BEGINNING OF WINTER...
...IN THE WIND.

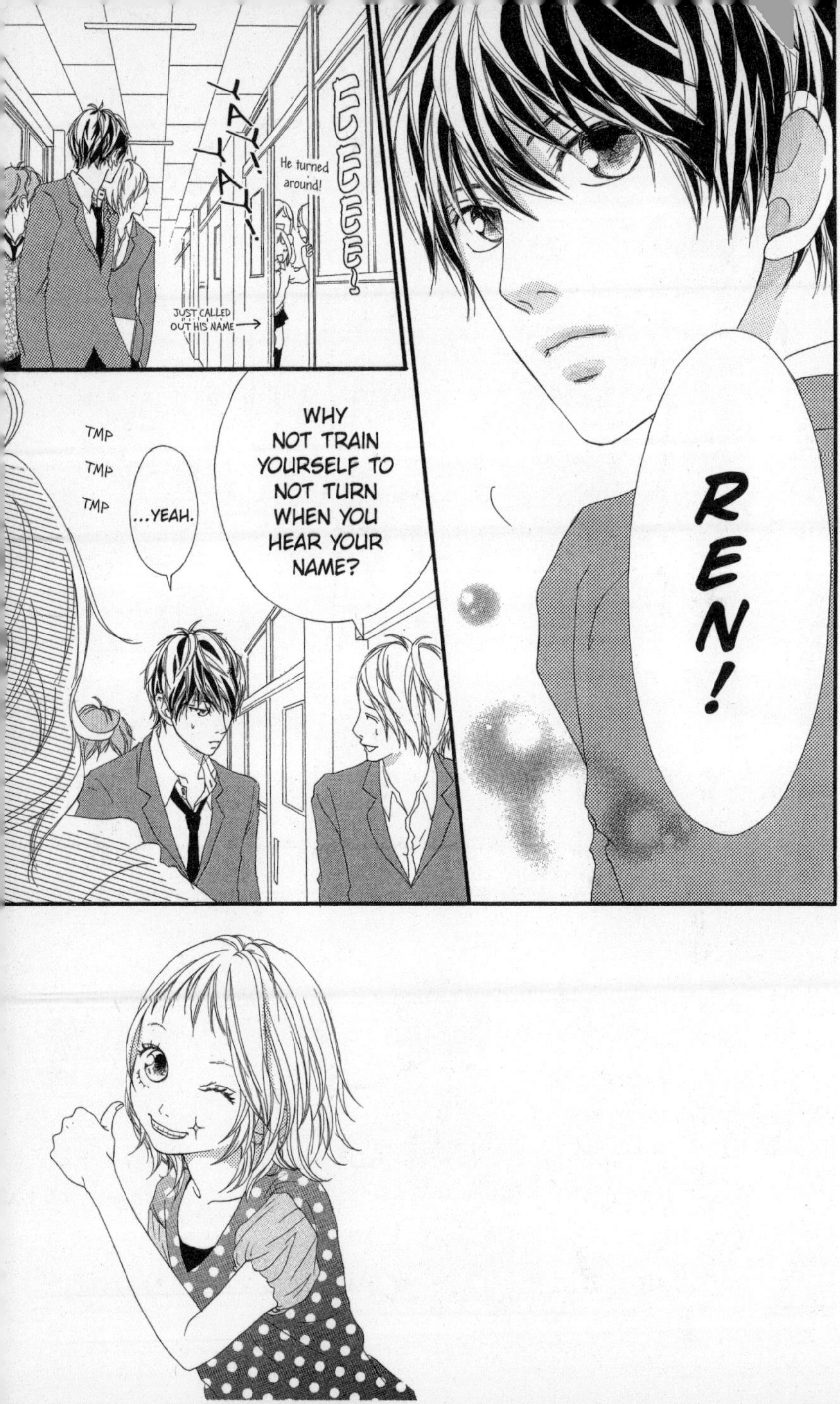
REN!
EEEEE!
He turned around!
YAY! YAY!
JUST CALLED OUT HIS NAME
WHY NOT TRAIN YOURSELF TO NOT TURN WHEN YOU HEAR YOUR NAME?
...YEAH.
TMP TMP TMP

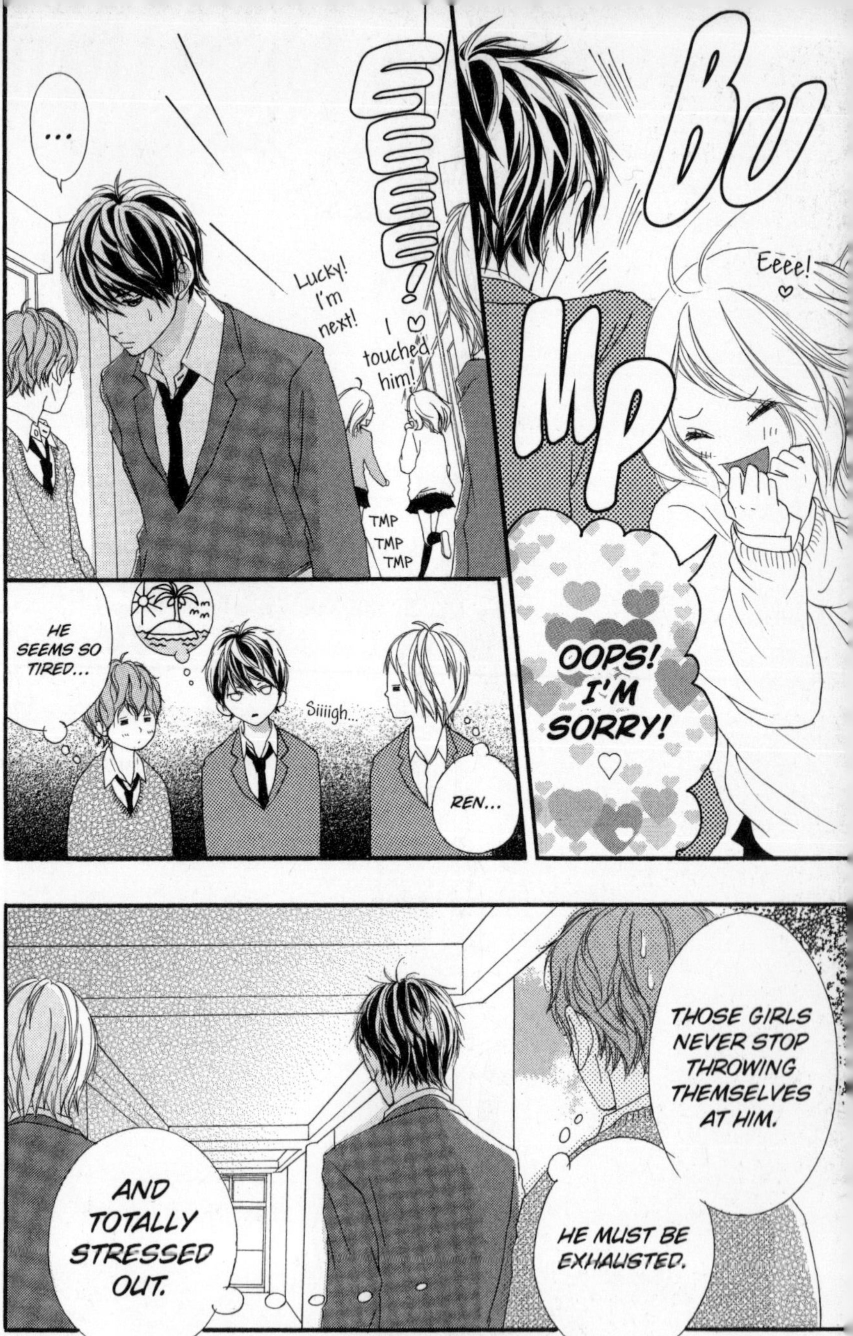

BUMP
Eeee! ♡
OOPS! I'M SORRY! ♡
EEEEE!
I ♡ touched him!
Lucky! I'm next!
TMP TMP TMP
...
REN...
Siiiigh...
HE SEEMS SO TIRED...
THOSE GIRLS NEVER STOP THROWING THEMSELVES AT HIM.
HE MUST BE EXHAUSTED.
AND TOTALLY STRESSED OUT.

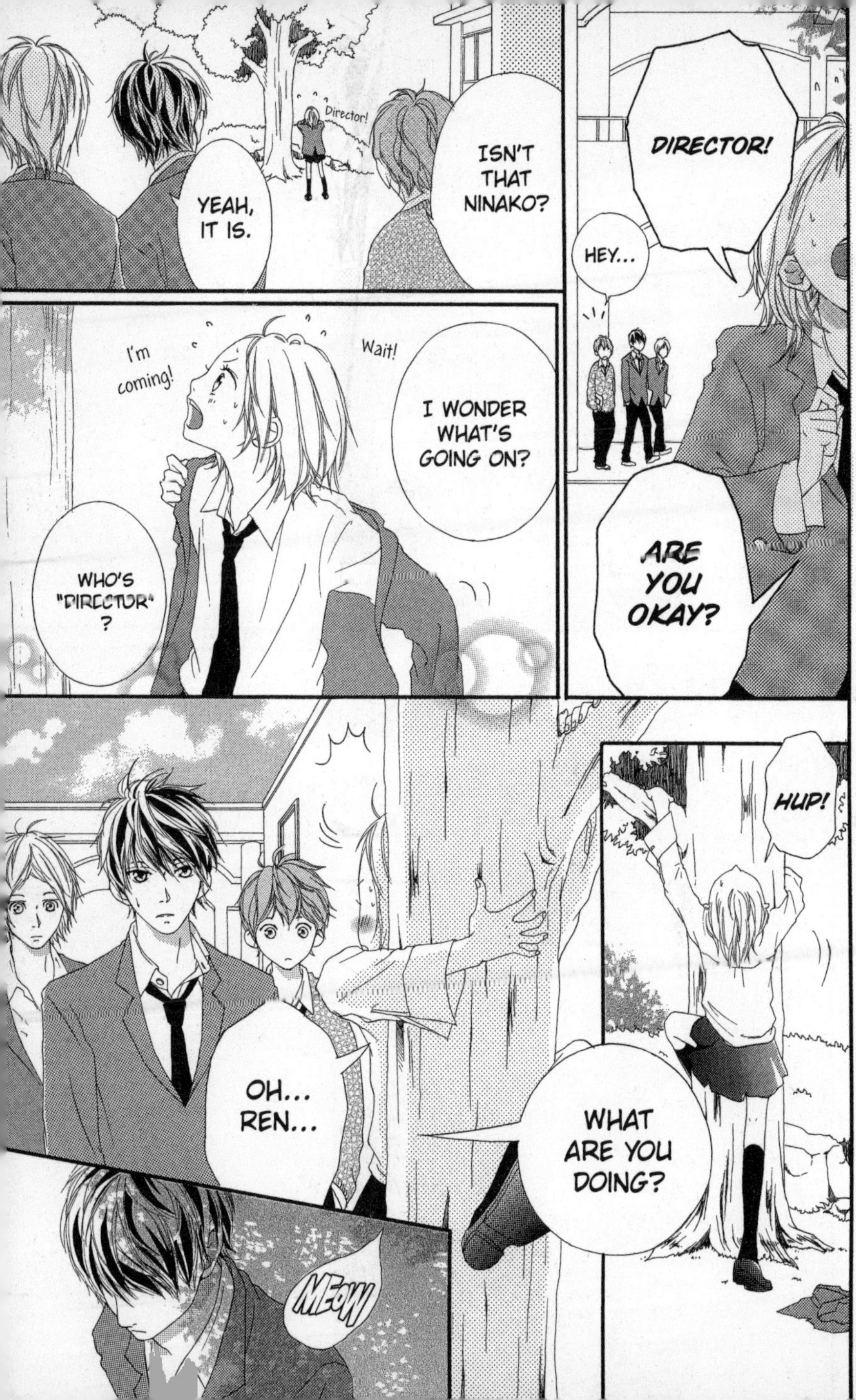
DIRECTOR!
HEY...
ARE YOU OKAY?
ISN'T THAT NINAKO?
Director!
YEAH, IT IS.
I WONDER WHAT'S GOING ON?
Wait!
I'm coming!
WHO'S "DIRECTOR"?
HUP!
WHAT ARE YOU DOING?
OH... REN...
MEOW

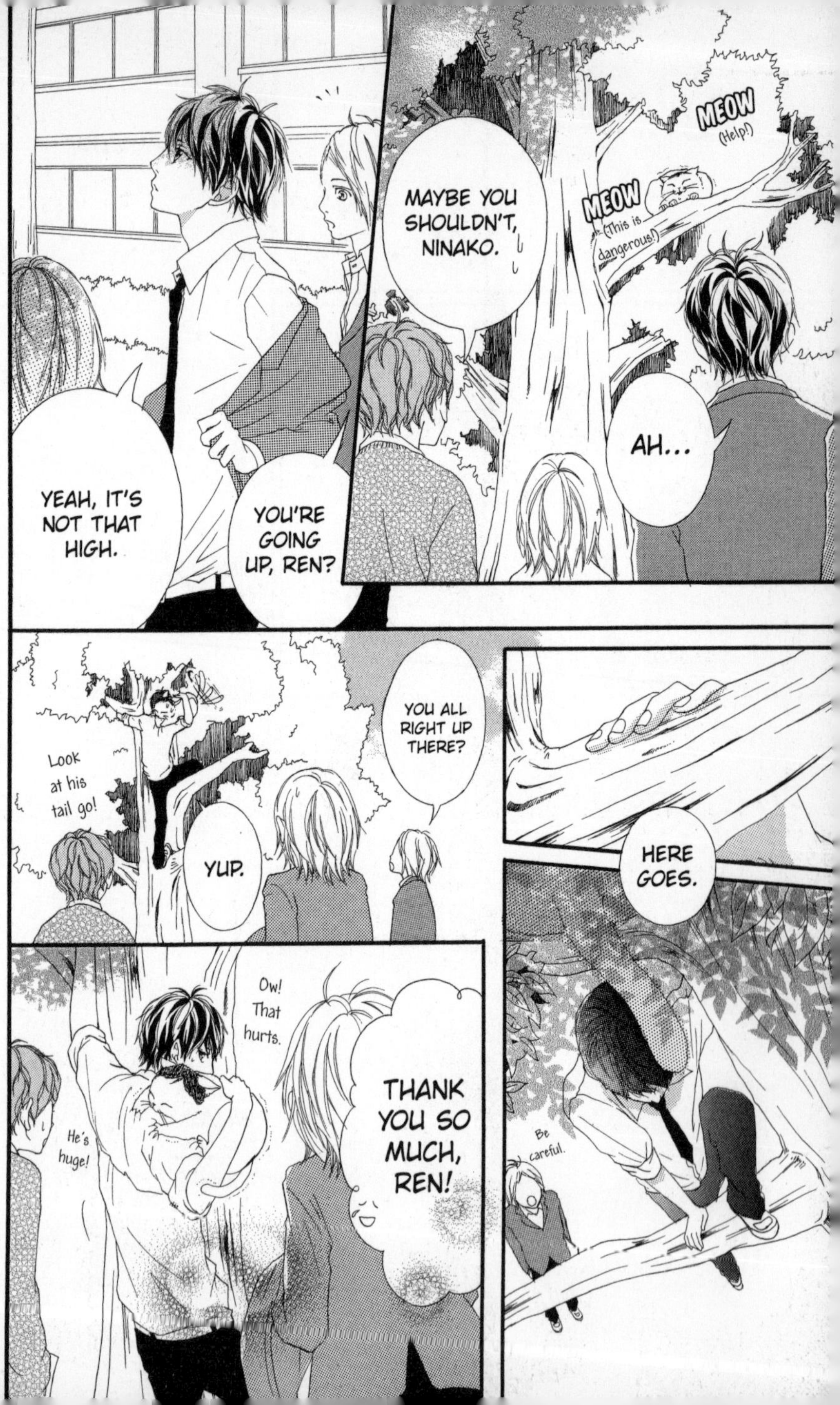

MEOW
(Help!)
MEOW
(This is dangerous!)
MAYBE YOU SHOULDN'T, NINAKO.
AH...
YOU'RE GOING UP, REN?
YEAH, IT'S NOT THAT HIGH.
HERE GOES.
Be careful.
YOU ALL RIGHT UP THERE?
Look at his tail go!
YUP.
THANK YOU SO MUCH, REN!
Ow! That hurts.
He's huge!

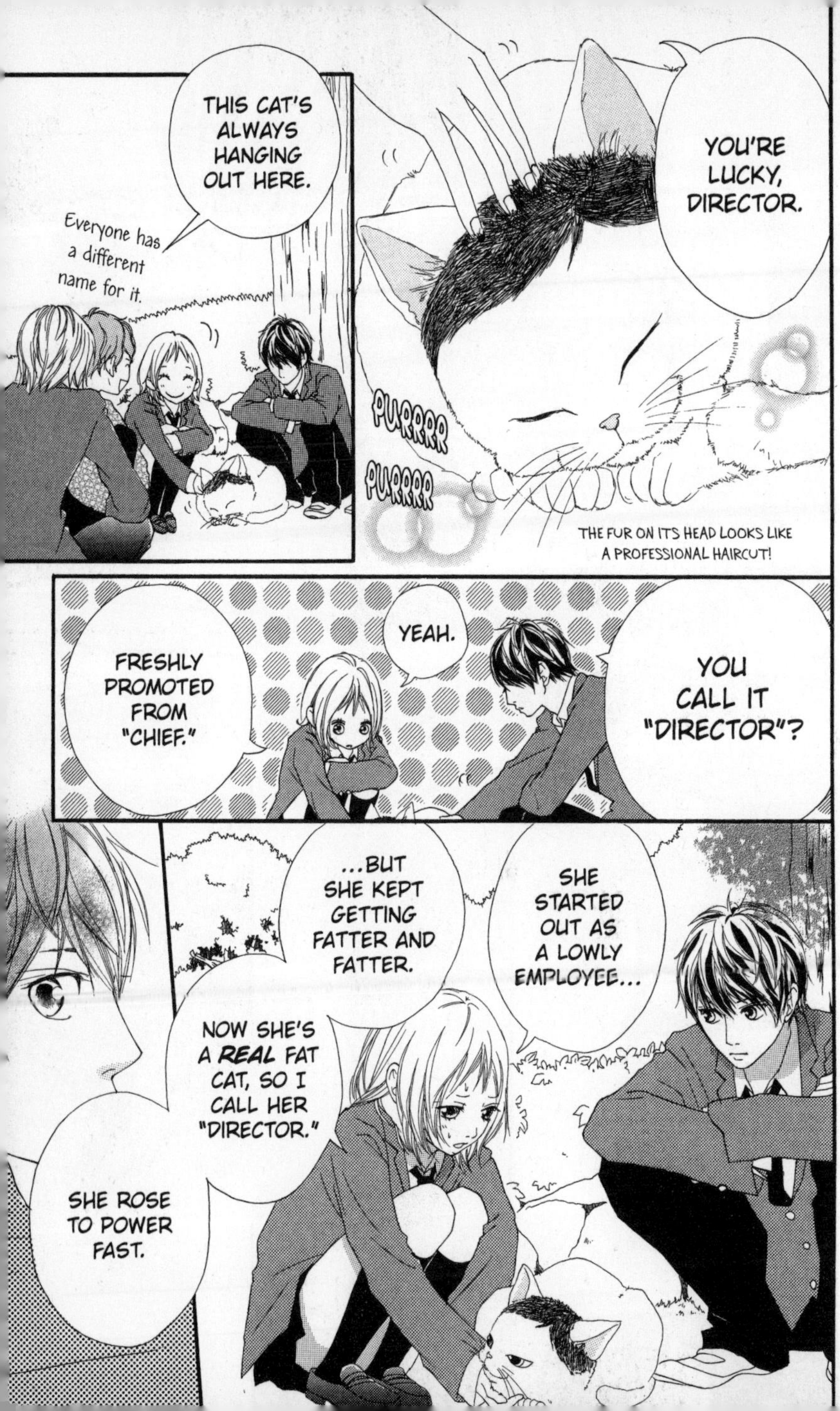
YOU'RE LUCKY, DIRECTOR.
PURRRR
PURRRR
THE FUR ON ITS HEAD LOOKS LIKE A PROFESSIONAL HAIRCUT!
THIS CAT'S ALWAYS HANGING OUT HERE.
Everyone has a different name for it.
YOU CALL IT "DIRECTOR"?
YEAH.
FRESHLY PROMOTED FROM "CHIEF."
SHE STARTED OUT AS A LOWLY EMPLOYEE...
...BUT SHE KEPT GETTING FATTER AND FATTER.
NOW SHE'S A *REAL* FAT CAT, SO I CALL HER "DIRECTOR."
SHE ROSE TO POWER FAST.

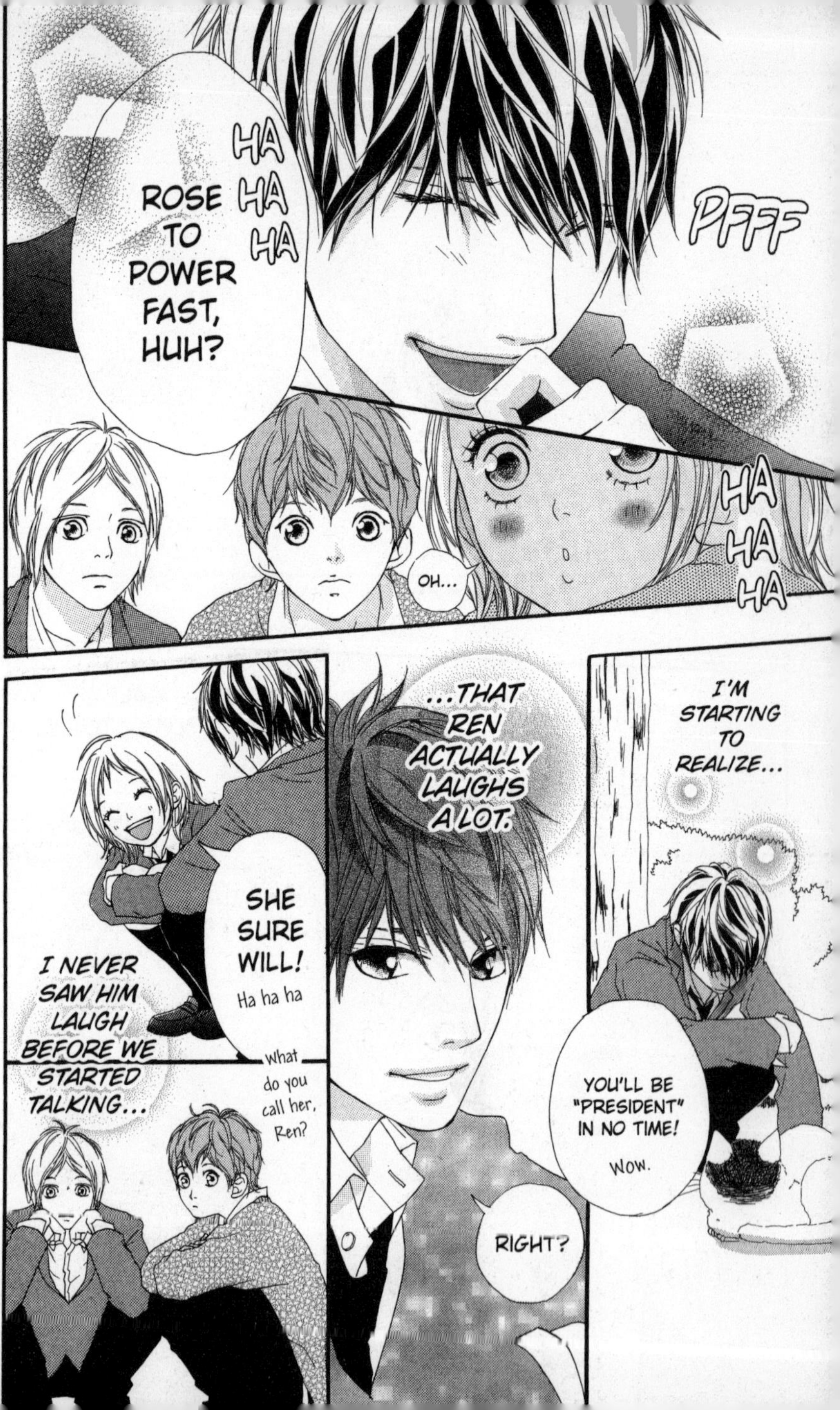
PFFF
HA HA HA
ROSE TO POWER FAST, HUH?
HA HA HA
OH...
I'M STARTING TO REALIZE...
YOU'LL BE "PRESIDENT" IN NO TIME!
Wow.
...THAT REN ACTUALLY LAUGHS A LOT.
RIGHT?
SHE SURE WILL!
Ha ha ha
I NEVER SAW HIM LAUGH BEFORE WE STARTED TALKING...
What do you call her, Ren?

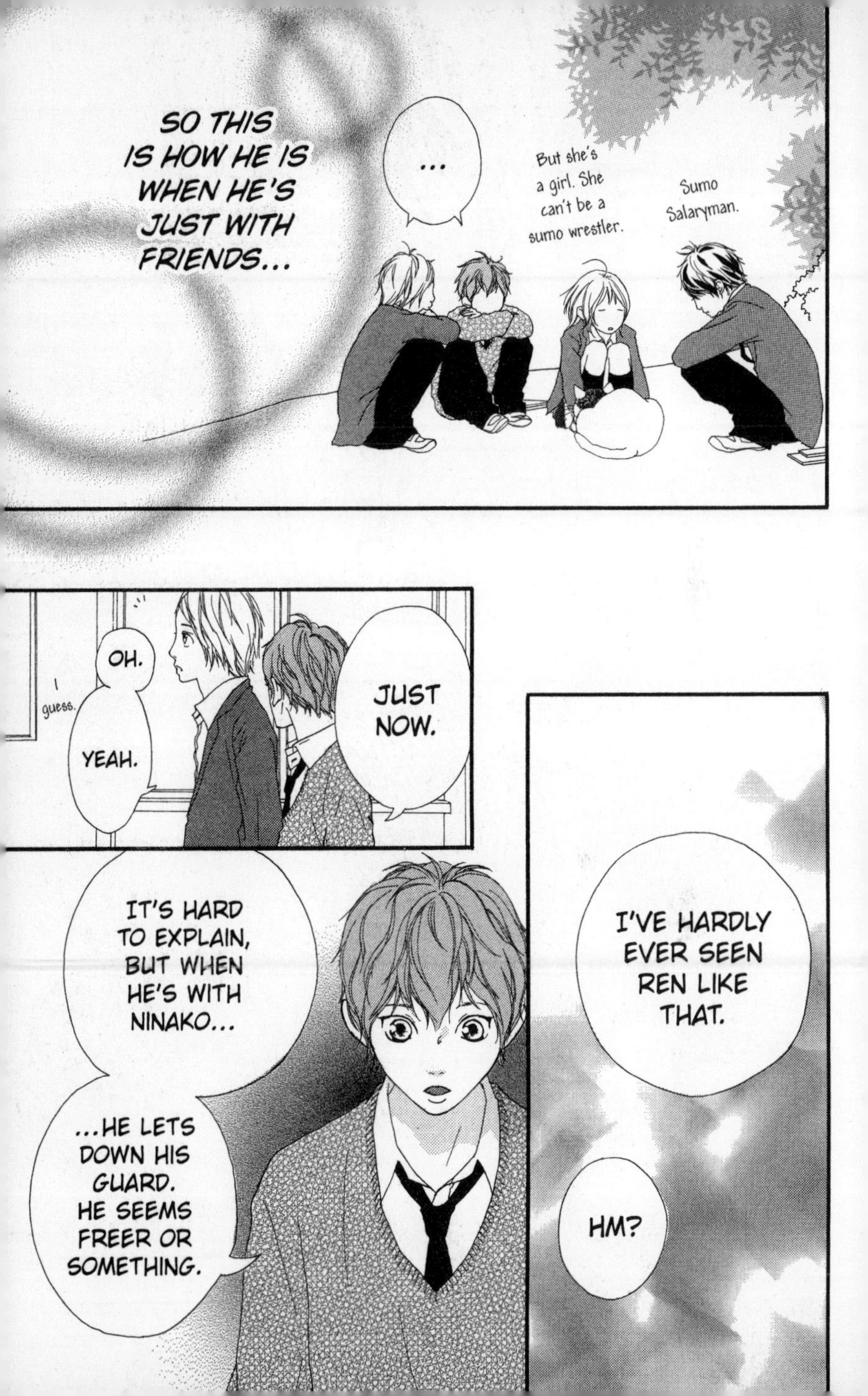
Sumo Salaryman.
But she's a girl. She can't be a sumo wrestler.
...
SO THIS IS HOW HE IS WHEN HE'S JUST WITH FRIENDS...
JUST NOW.
OH.
YEAH.
I guess.
I'VE HARDLY EVER SEEN REN LIKE THAT.
HM?
IT'S HARD TO EXPLAIN, BUT WHEN HE'S WITH NINAKO...
...HE LETS DOWN HIS GUARD. HE SEEMS FREER OR SOMETHING.

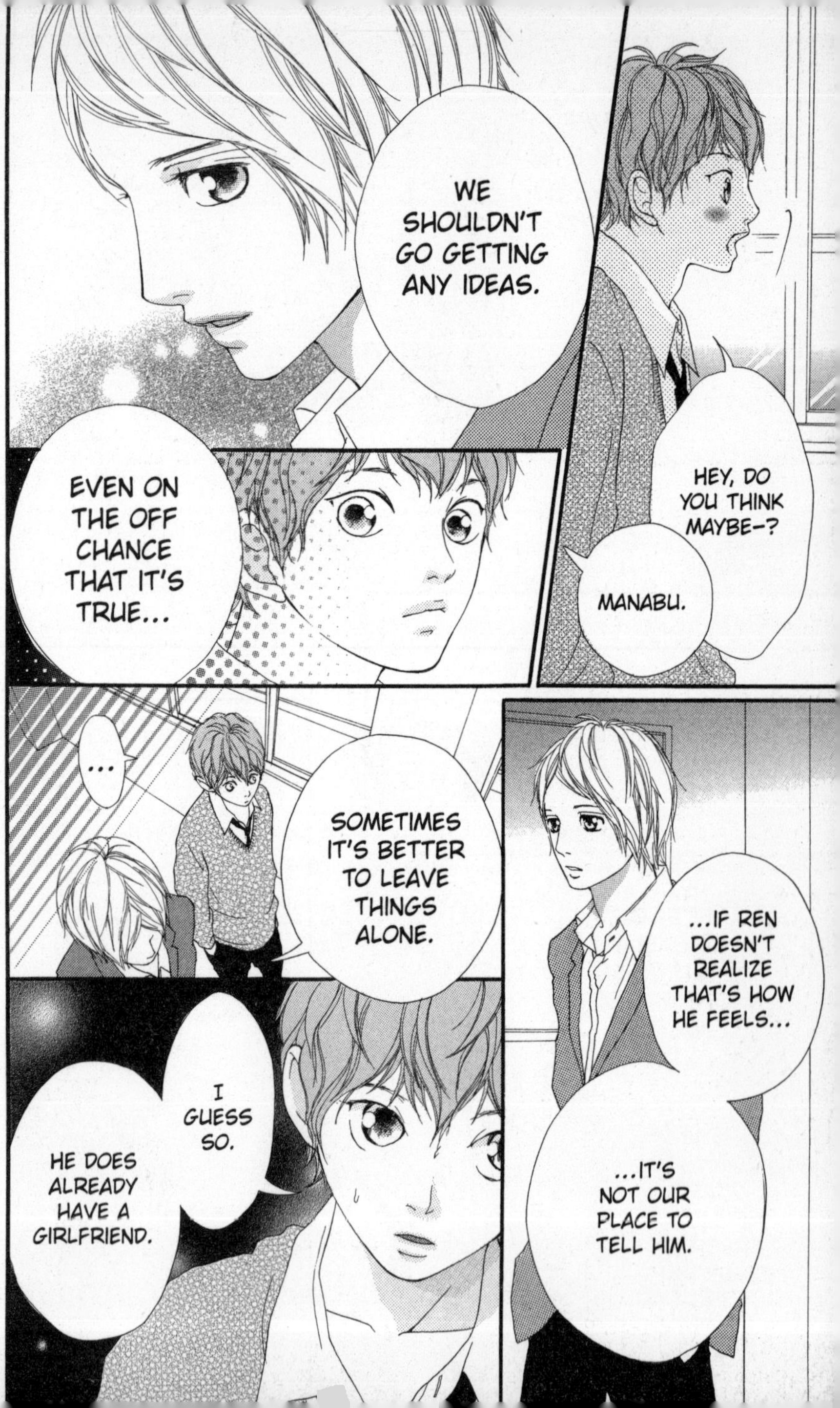
HEY, DO YOU THINK MAYBE-?
MANABU.
WE SHOULDN'T GO GETTING ANY IDEAS.
EVEN ON THE OFF CHANCE THAT IT'S TRUE...
...IF REN DOESN'T REALIZE THAT'S HOW HE FEELS...
...IT'S NOT OUR PLACE TO TELL HIM.
...
SOMETIMES IT'S BETTER TO LEAVE THINGS ALONE.
I GUESS SO.
HE DOES ALREADY HAVE A GIRLFRIEND.

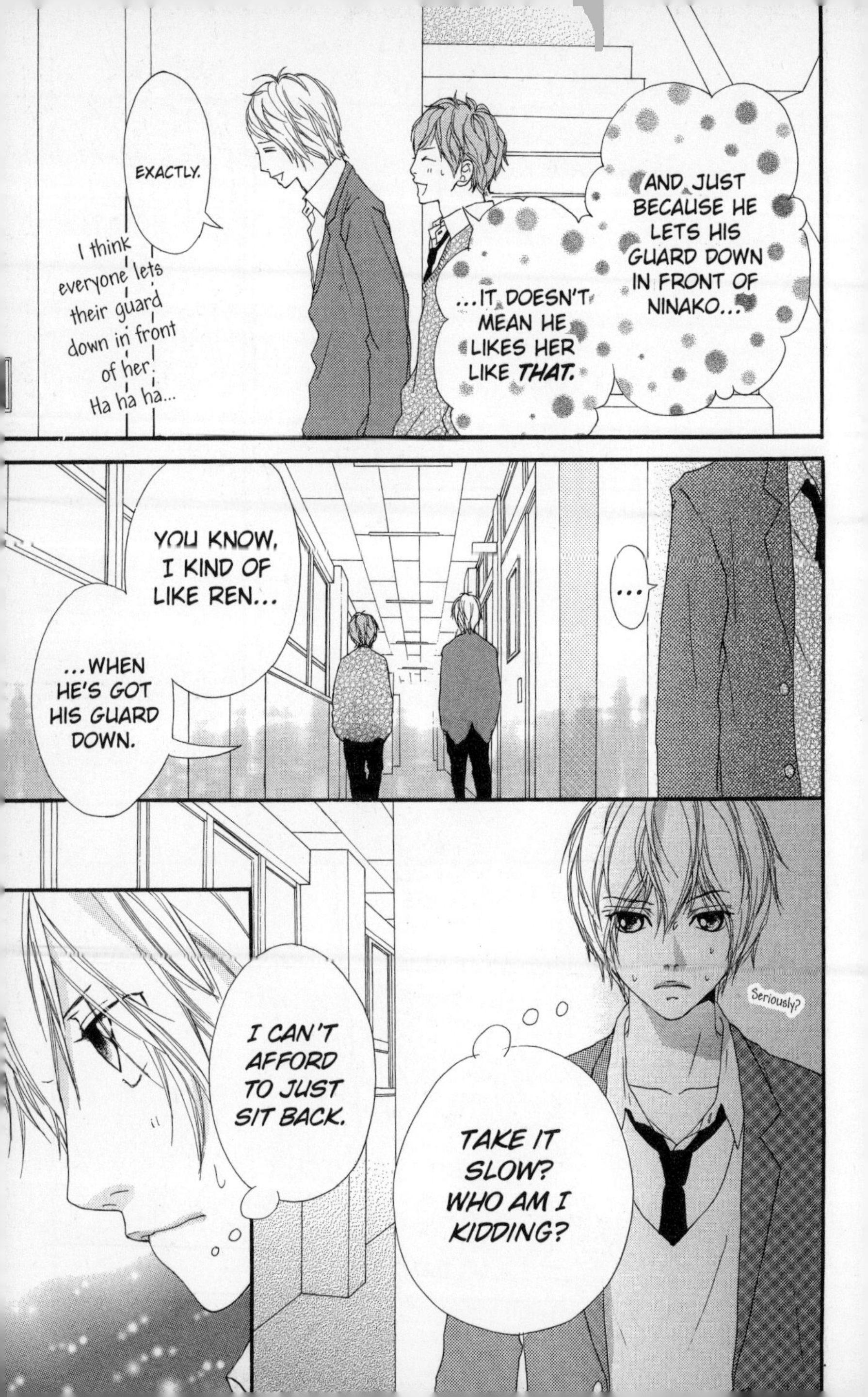
AND JUST BECAUSE HE LETS HIS GUARD DOWN IN FRONT OF NINAKO...
...IT DOESN'T MEAN HE LIKES HER LIKE *THAT.*
EXACTLY.
I think everyone lets their guard down in front of her. Ha ha ha...
...
YOU KNOW, I KIND OF LIKE REN...
...WHEN HE'S GOT HIS GUARD DOWN.
Seriously?
TAKE IT SLOW? WHO AM I KIDDING?
I CAN'T AFFORD TO JUST SIT BACK.

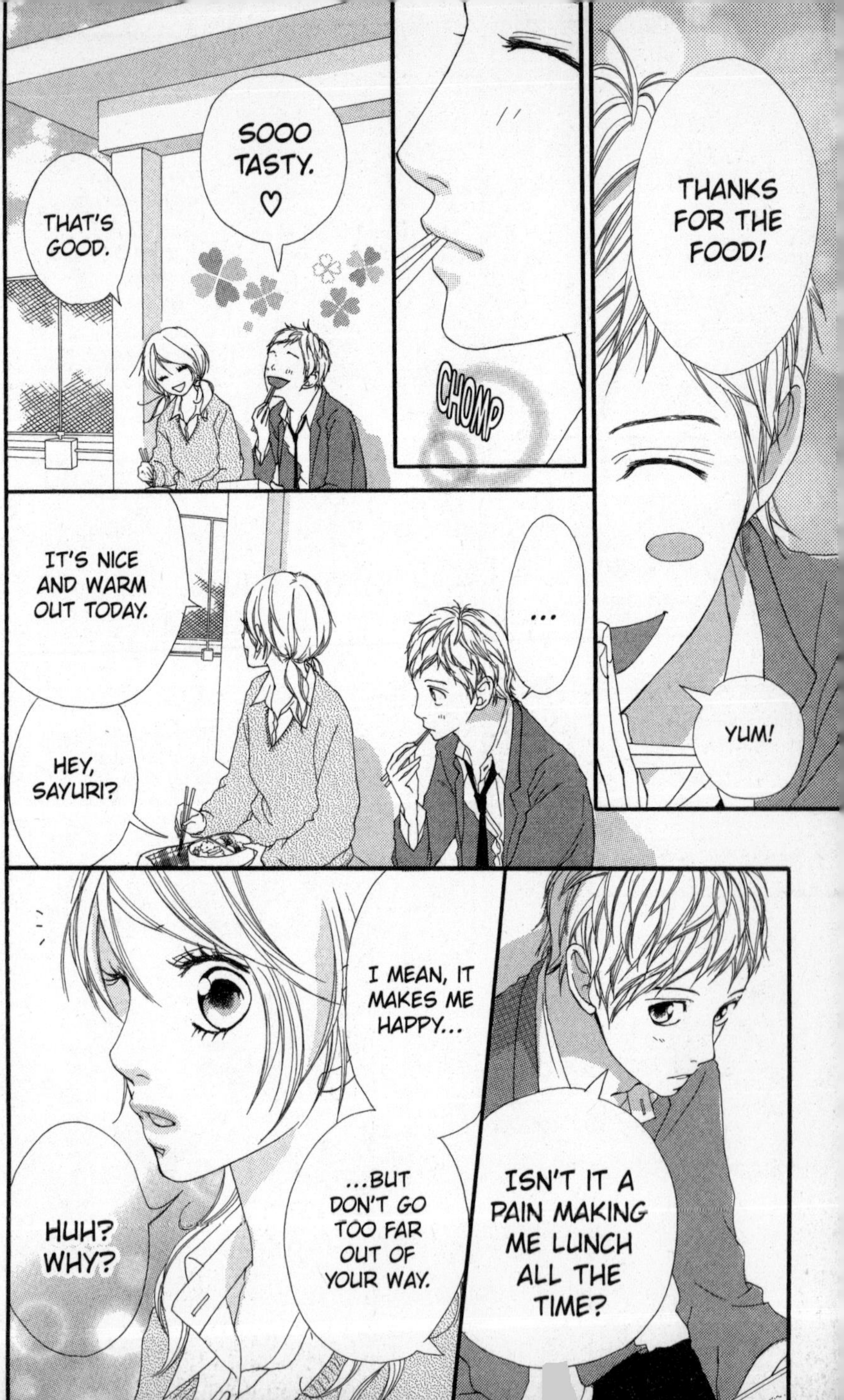
THANKS FOR THE FOOD!
YUM!
CHOMP
SOOO TASTY. ♡
THAT'S GOOD.
...
IT'S NICE AND WARM OUT TODAY.
HEY, SAYURI?
ISN'T IT A PAIN MAKING ME LUNCH ALL THE TIME?
HUH? WHY?
I MEAN, IT MAKES ME HAPPY...
...BUT DON'T GO TOO FAR OUT OF YOUR WAY.

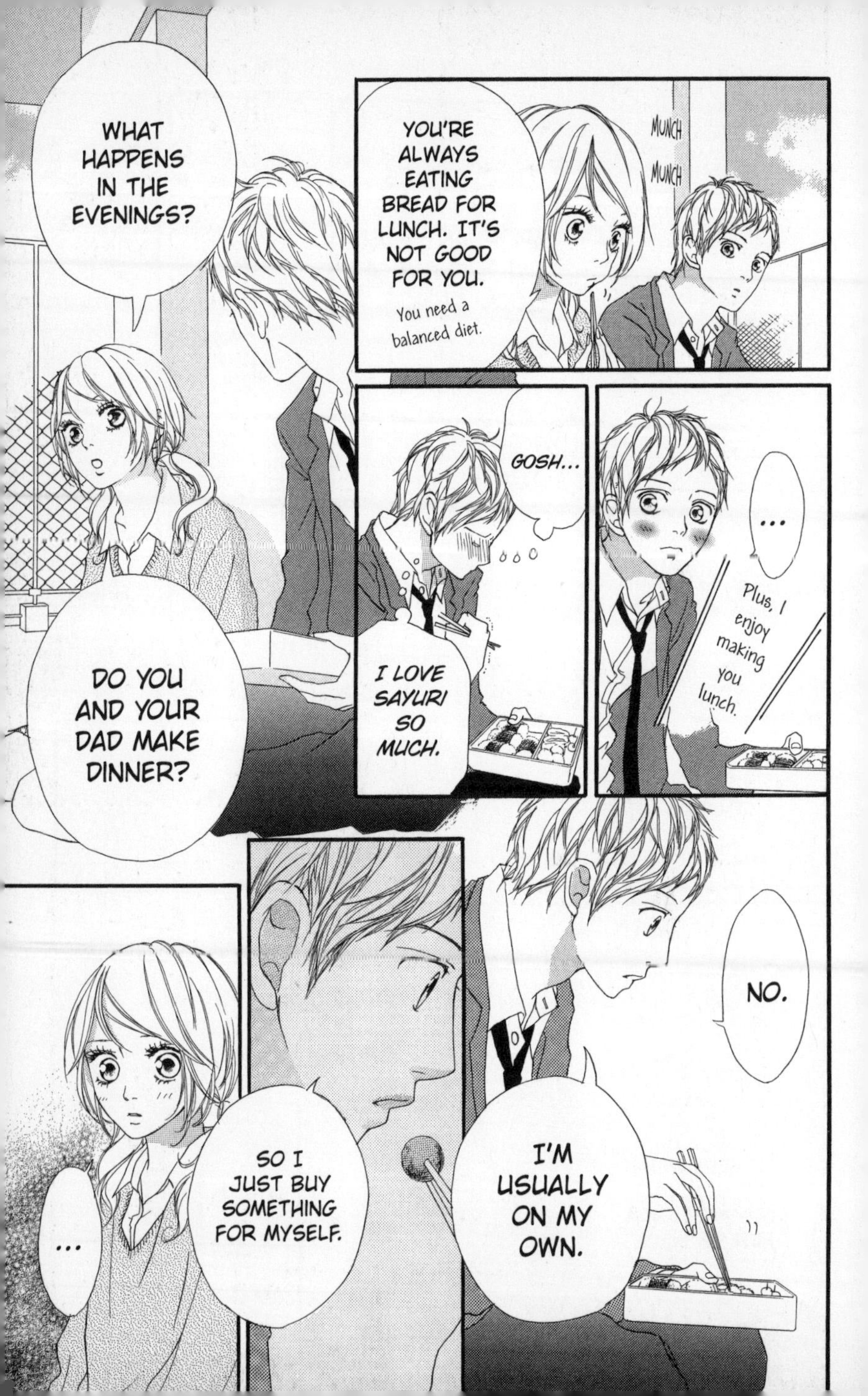
MUNCH MUNCH
YOU'RE ALWAYS EATING BREAD FOR LUNCH. IT'S NOT GOOD FOR YOU.
You need a balanced diet.
...
Plus, I enjoy making you lunch.
GOSH...
I LOVE SAYURI SO MUCH.
WHAT HAPPENS IN THE EVENINGS?
DO YOU AND YOUR DAD MAKE DINNER?
NO.
I'M USUALLY ON MY OWN.
SO I JUST BUY SOMETHING FOR MYSELF.
...

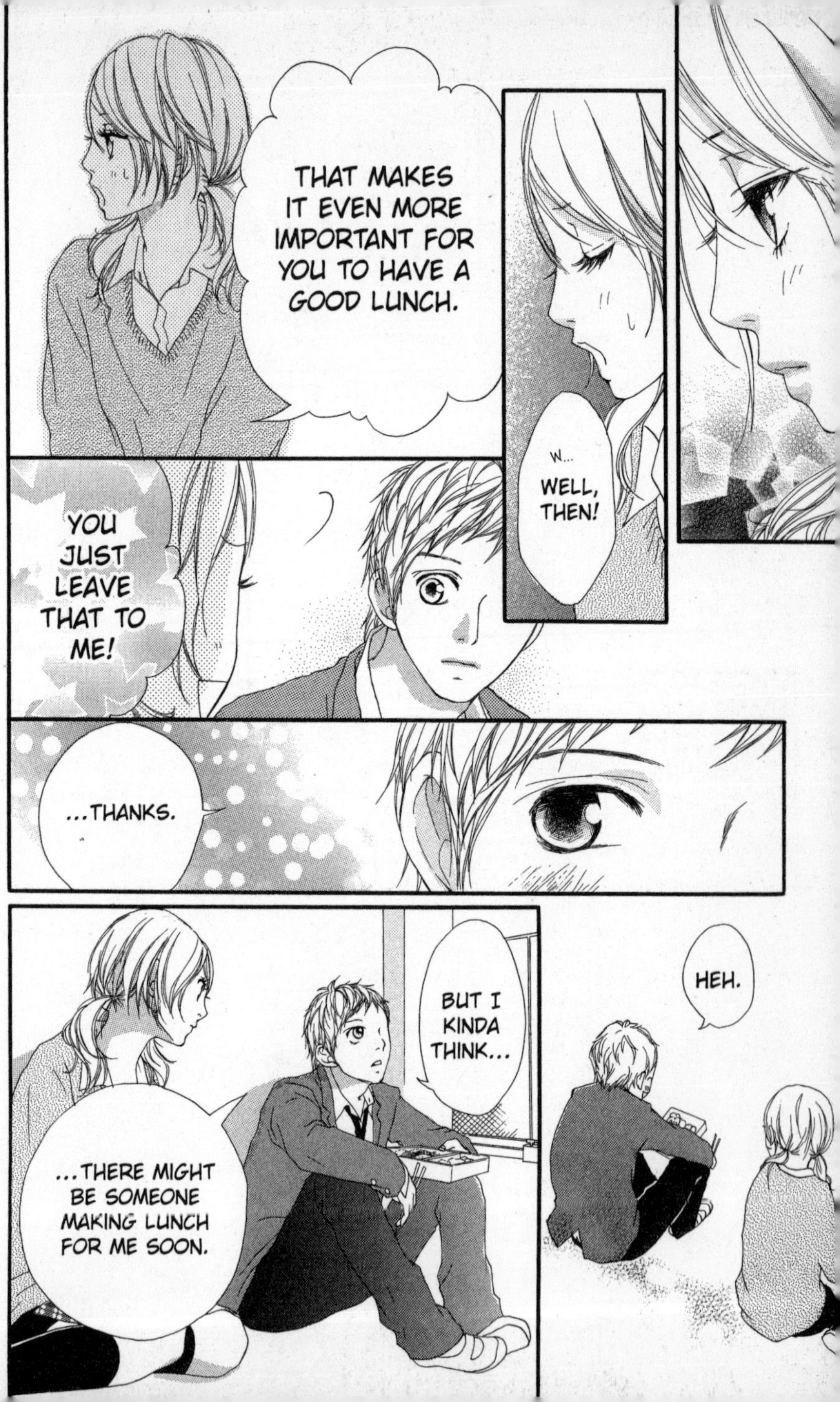
W... WELL, THEN!
THAT MAKES IT EVEN MORE IMPORTANT FOR YOU TO HAVE A GOOD LUNCH.
YOU JUST LEAVE THAT TO ME!
...THANKS.
HEH.
BUT I KINDA THINK...
...THERE MIGHT BE SOMEONE MAKING LUNCH FOR ME SOON.

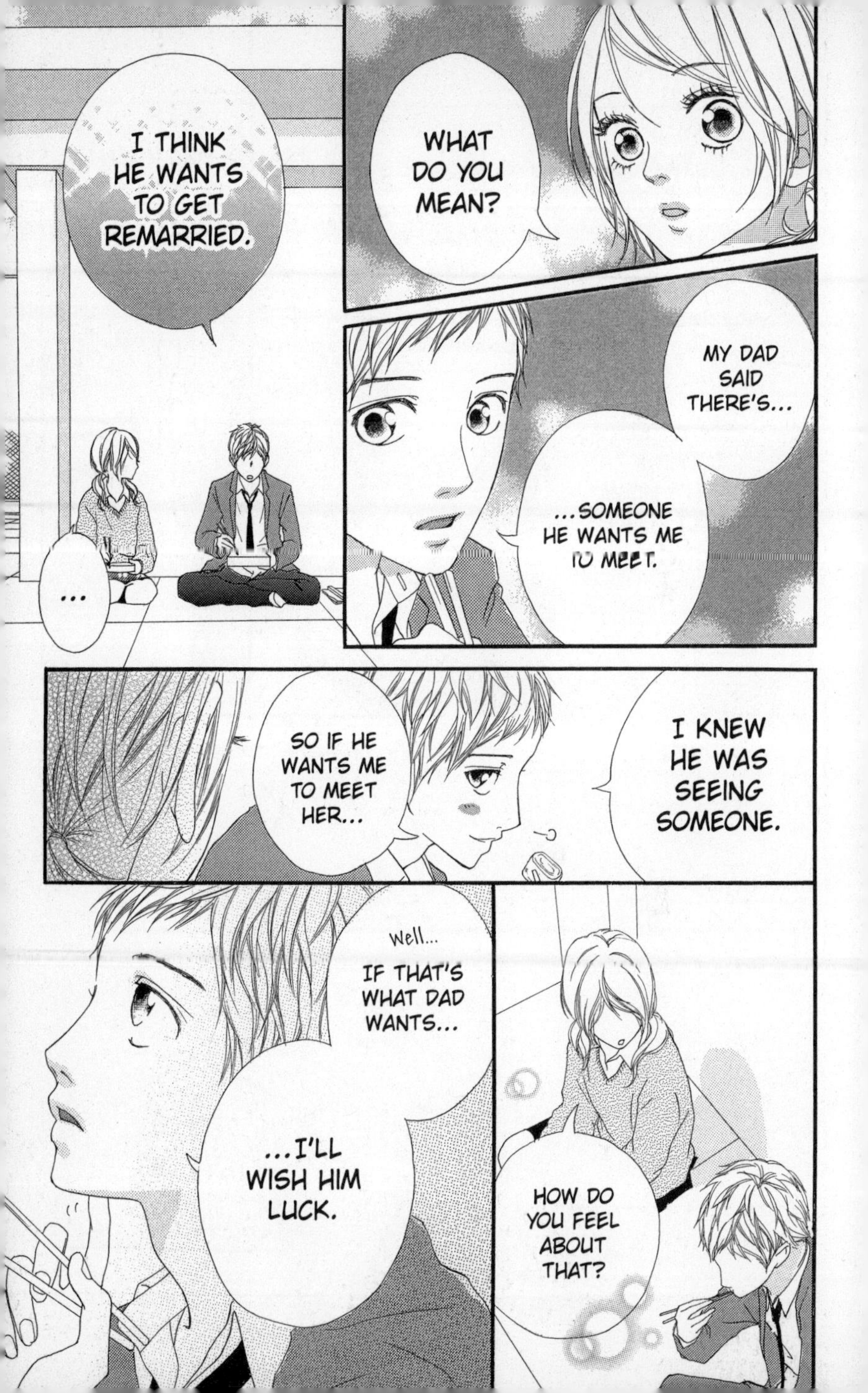
WHAT DO YOU MEAN?
MY DAD SAID THERE'S...
...SOMEONE HE WANTS ME TO MEET.
I THINK HE WANTS TO GET REMARRIED.
...
I KNEW HE WAS SEEING SOMEONE.
SO IF HE WANTS ME TO MEET HER...
HOW DO YOU FEEL ABOUT THAT?
Well...
IF THAT'S WHAT DAD WANTS...
...I'LL WISH HIM LUCK.

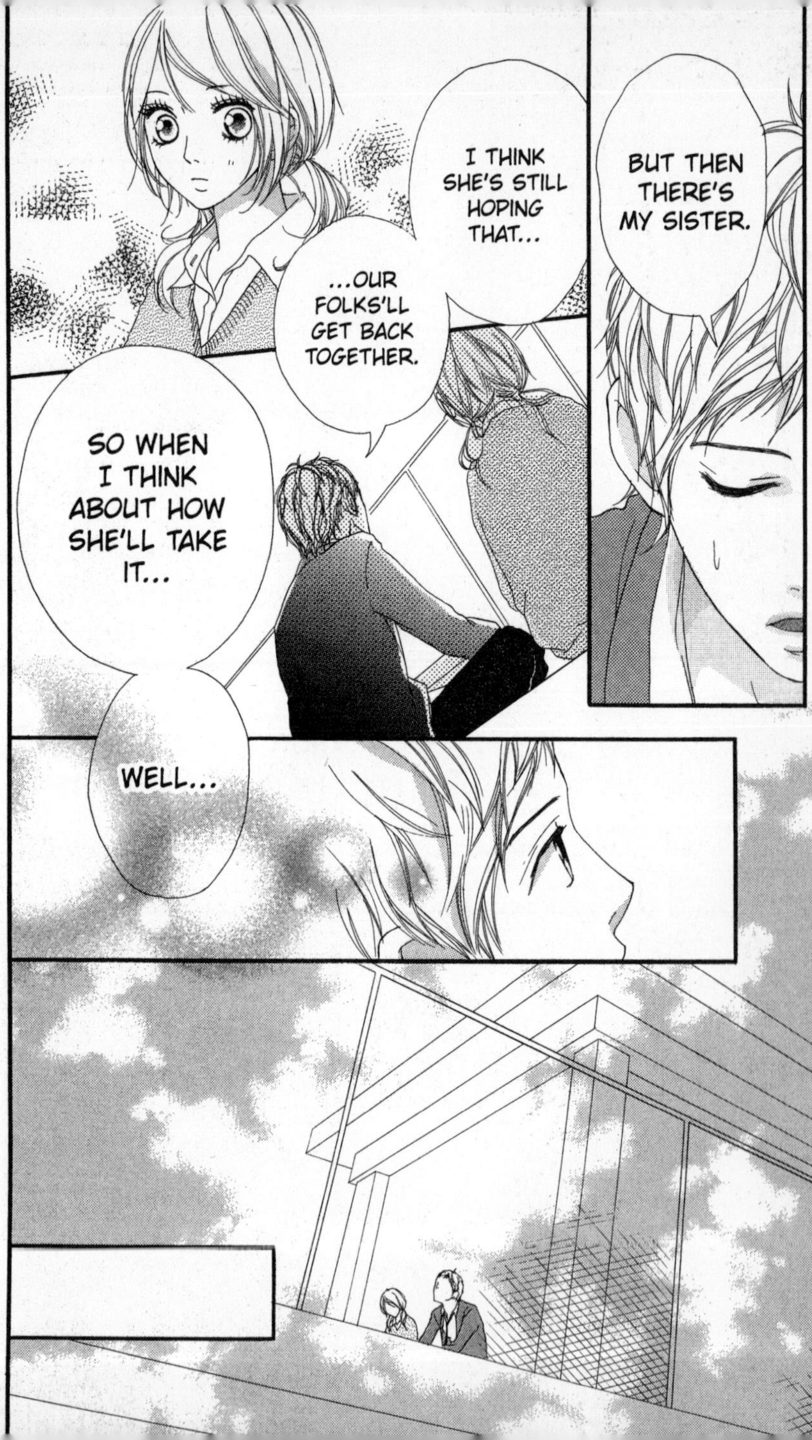
BUT THEN THERE'S MY SISTER.
I THINK SHE'S STILL HOPING THAT...
...OUR FOLKS'LL GET BACK TOGETHER.
SO WHEN I THINK ABOUT HOW SHE'LL TAKE IT...
WELL...

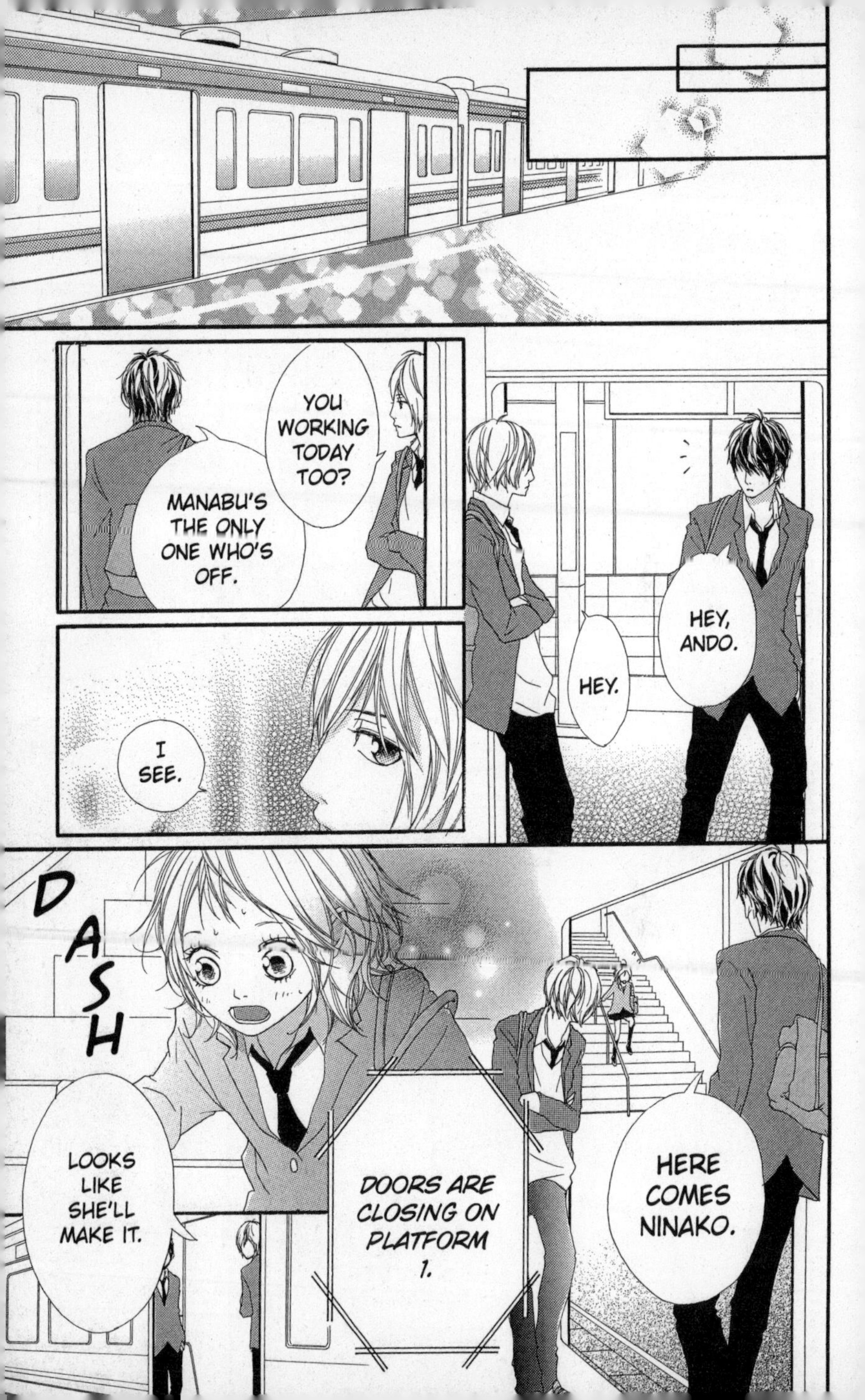
HEY, ANDO.
HEY.
YOU WORKING TODAY TOO?
MANABU'S THE ONLY ONE WHO'S OFF.
I SEE.
HERE COMES NINAKO.
DOORS ARE CLOSING ON PLATFORM 1.
DASH
LOOKS LIKE SHE'LL MAKE IT.

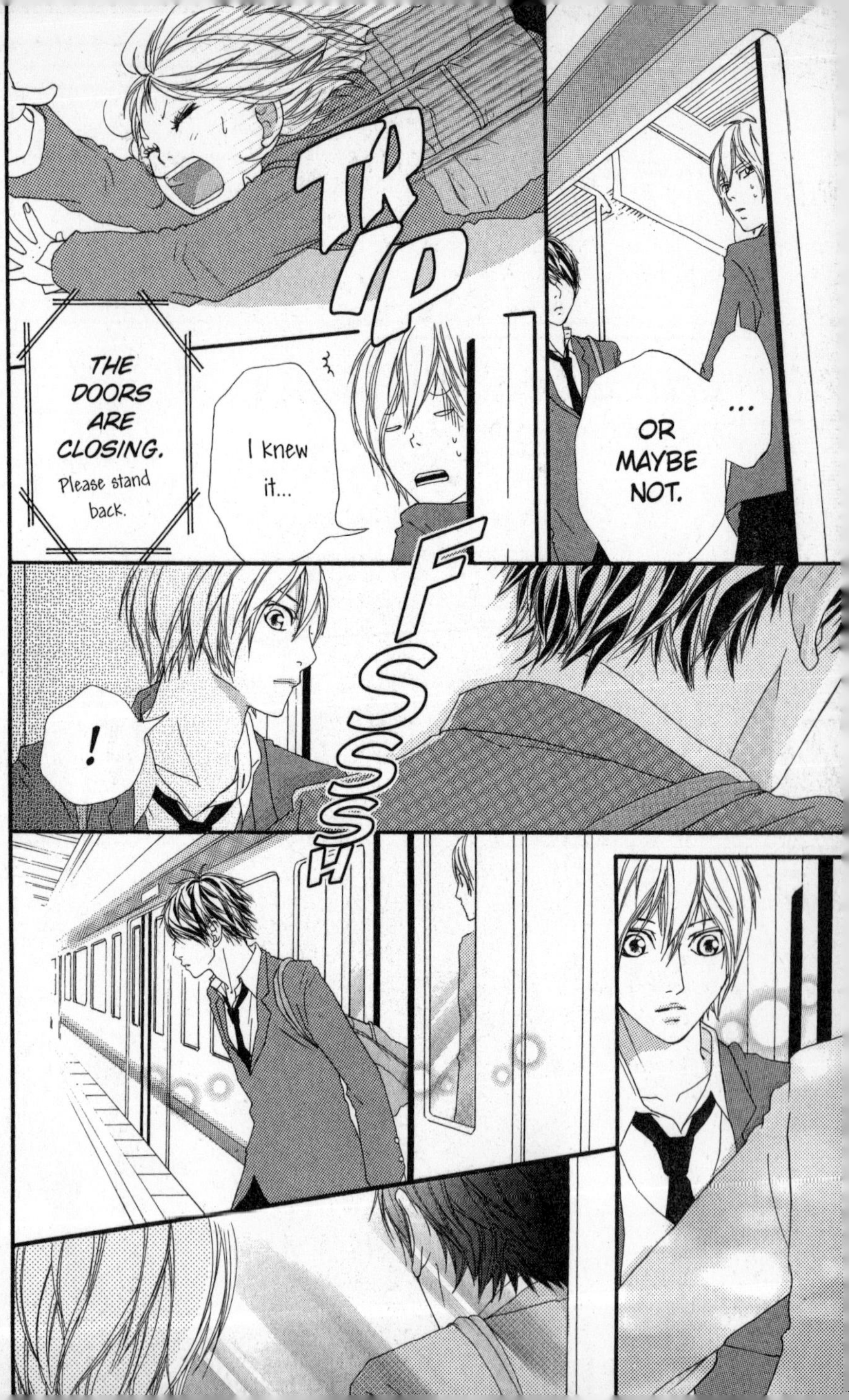
...
OR MAYBE NOT.
TRIP
THE DOORS ARE CLOSING. Please stand back.
I knew it...
FSSSSH
!

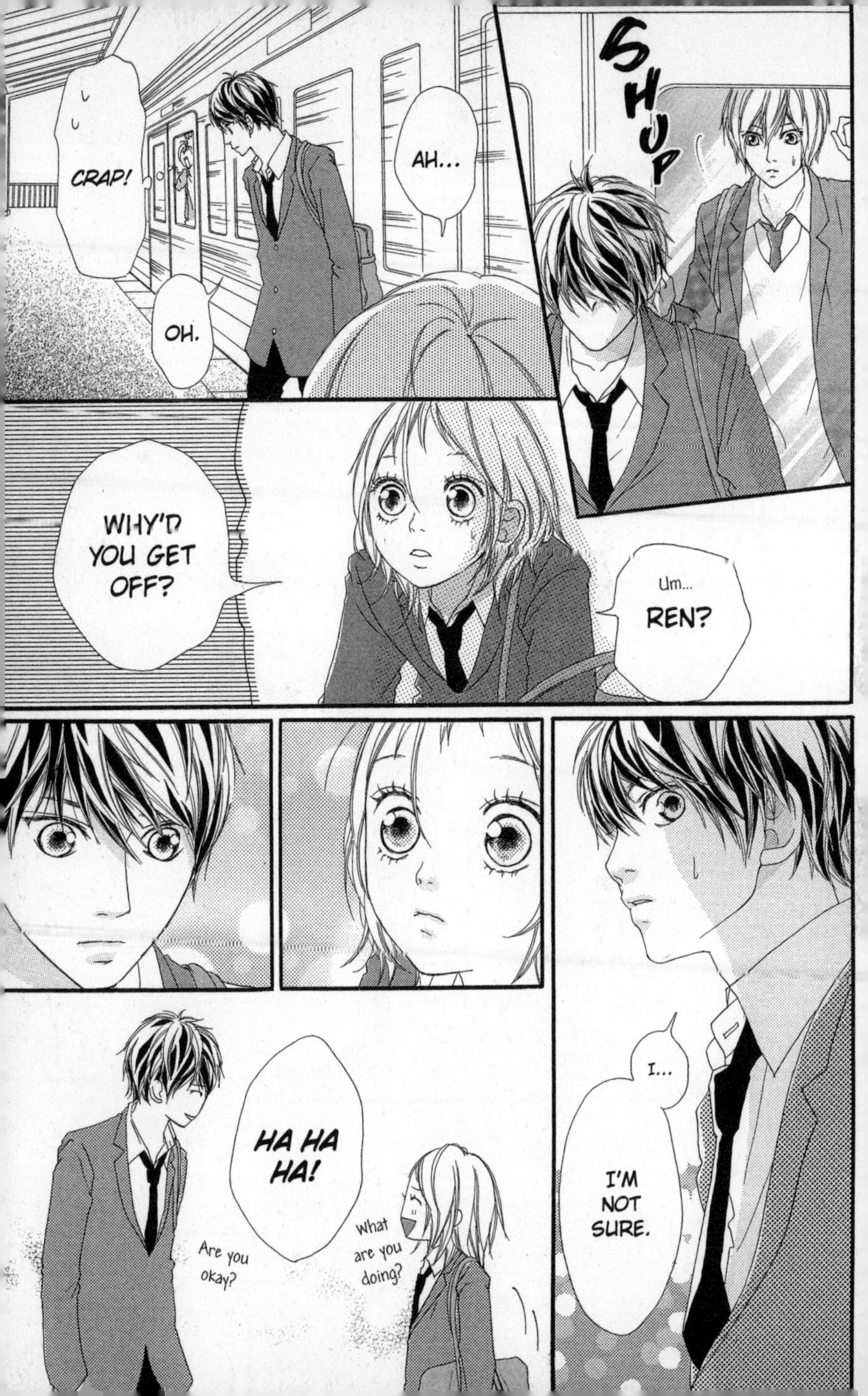
SHUP
AH...
CRAP!
OH.
Um... REN?
WHY'D YOU GET OFF?
I...
I'M NOT SURE.
HA HA HA!
What are you doing?
Are you okay?

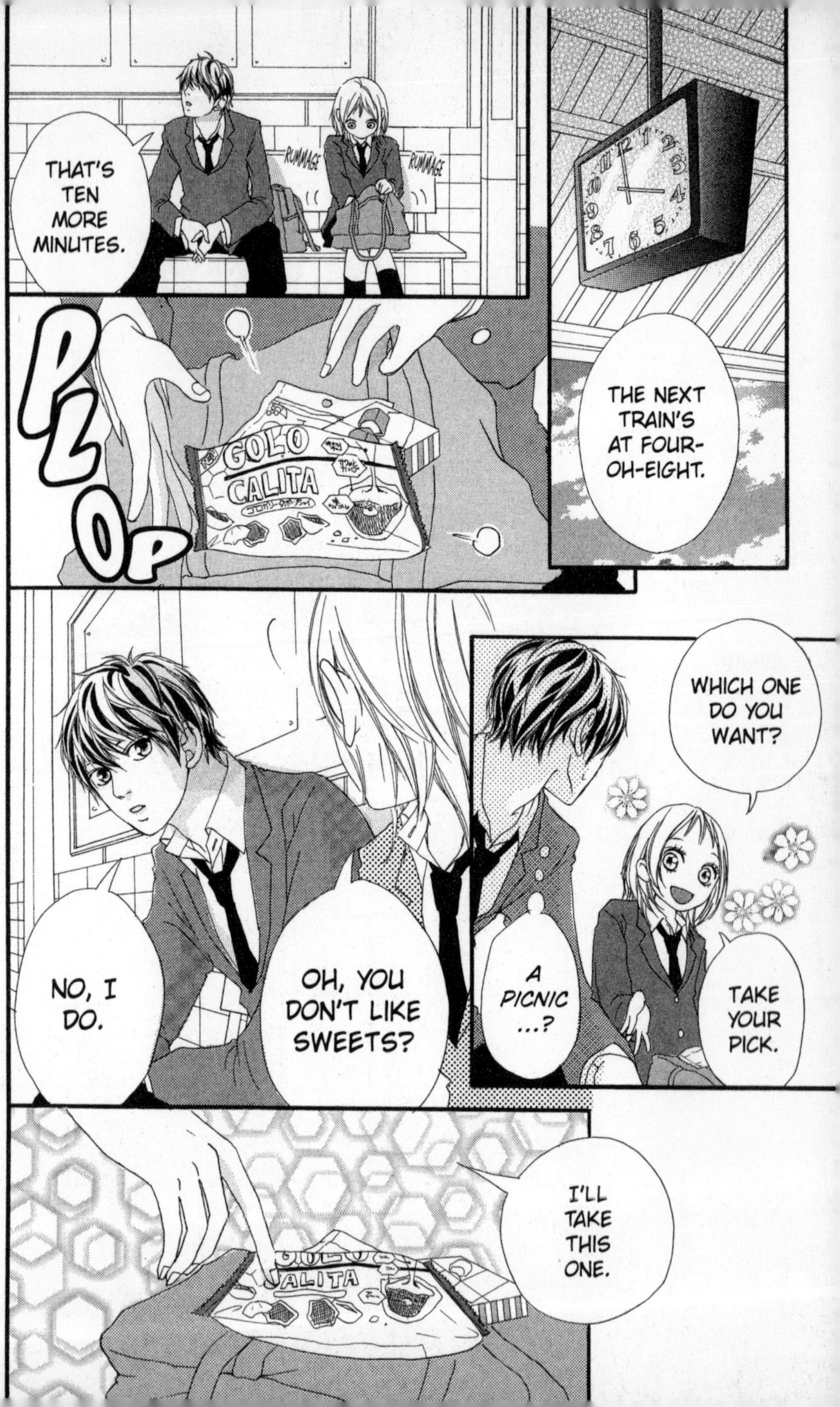
THE NEXT TRAIN'S AT FOUR-OH-EIGHT.
THAT'S TEN MORE MINUTES.
RUMMAGE
RUMMAGE
PLOP
GOLO CALITA
WHICH ONE DO YOU WANT?
TAKE YOUR PICK.
A PICNIC ...?
OH, YOU DON'T LIKE SWEETS?
NO, I DO.
I'LL TAKE THIS ONE.

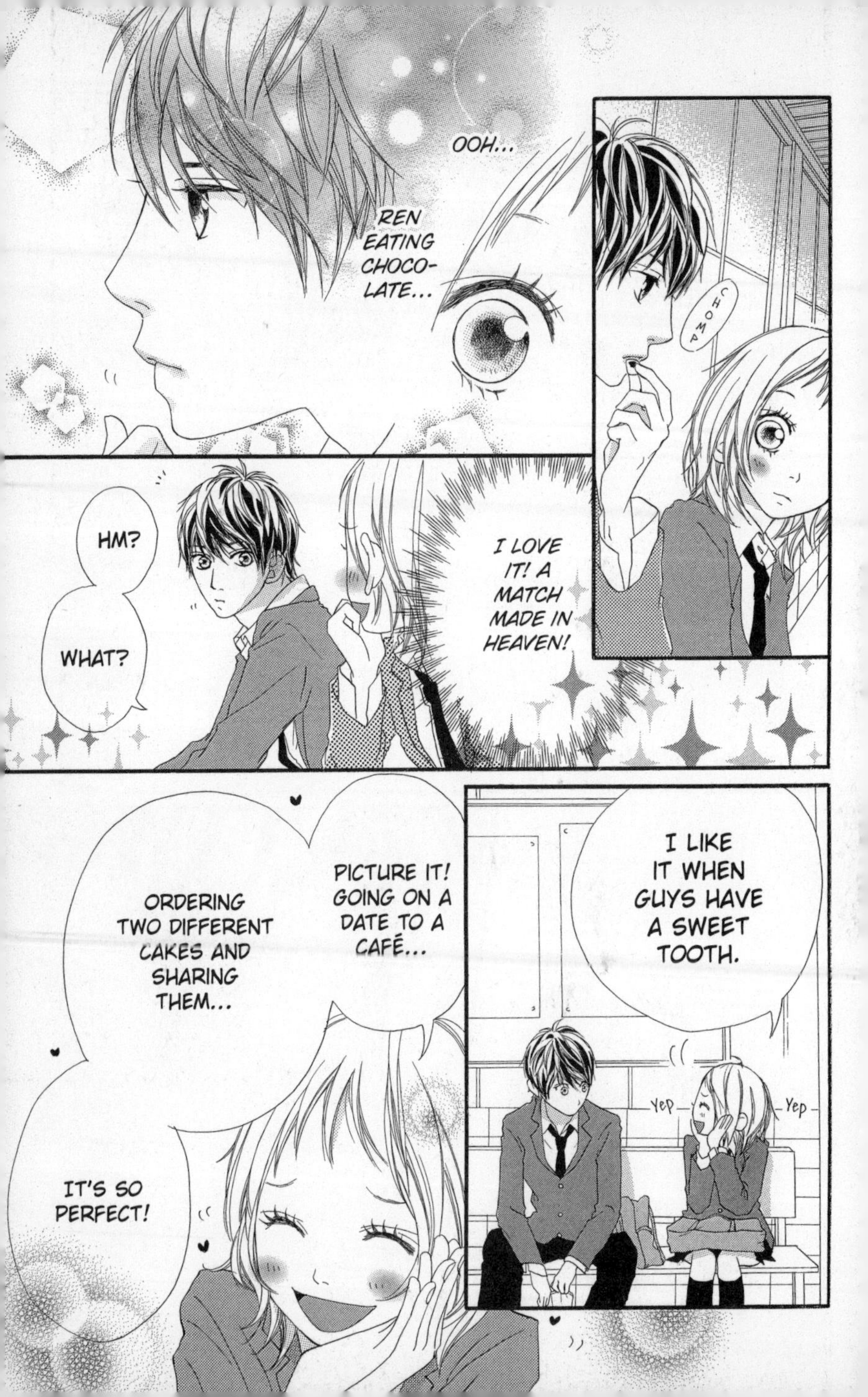
CHOMP
OOH...
REN EATING CHOCO-LATE...
I LOVE IT! A MATCH MADE IN HEAVEN!
HM?
WHAT?
I LIKE IT WHEN GUYS HAVE A SWEET TOOTH.
Yep
Yep
PICTURE IT! GOING ON A DATE TO A CAFÉ...
ORDERING TWO DIFFERENT CAKES AND SHARING THEM...
IT'S SO PERFECT!

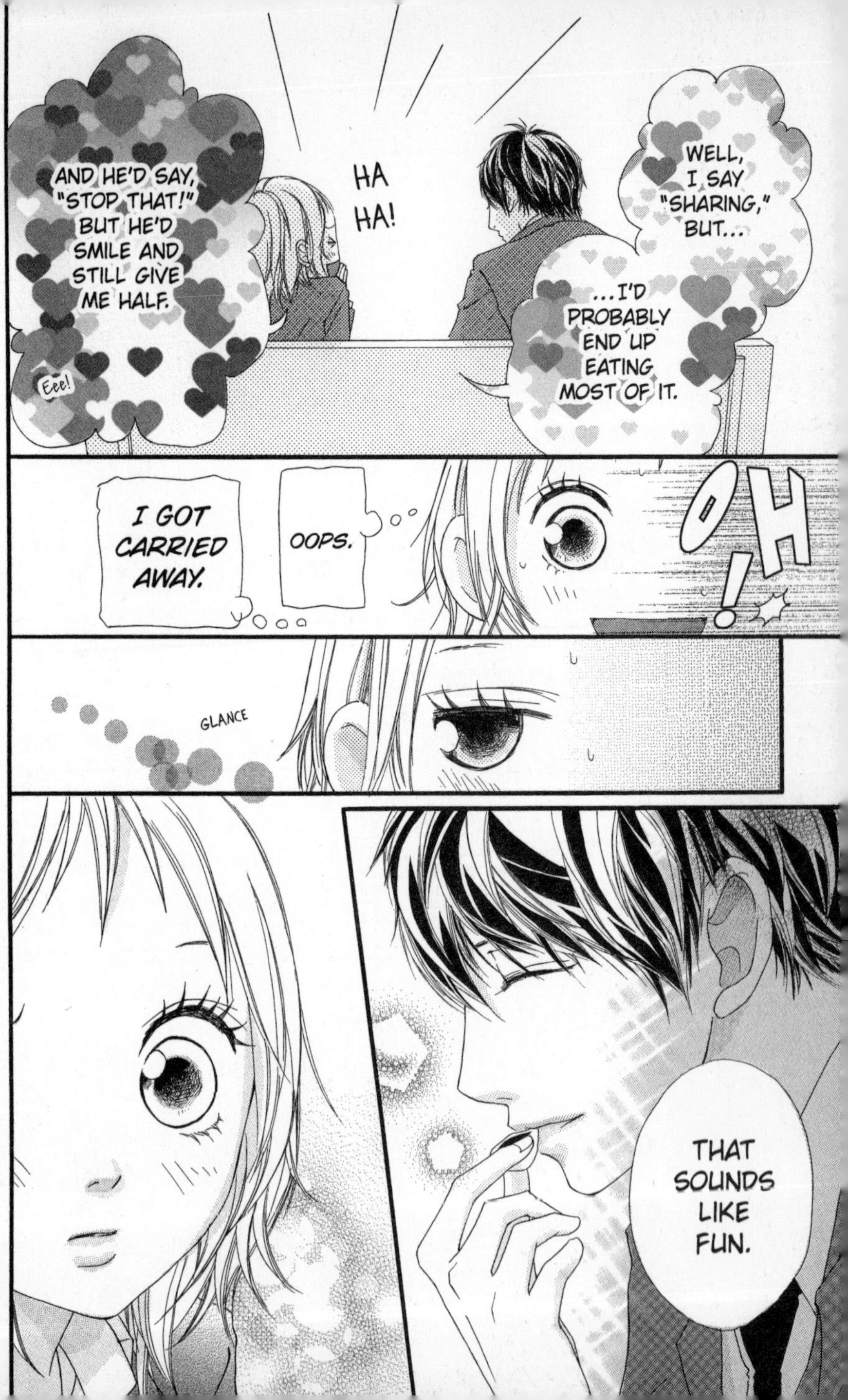

WELL, I SAY "SHARING," BUT...
...I'D PROBABLY END UP EATING MOST OF IT.
HA HA!
AND HE'D SAY, "STOP THAT!" BUT HE'D SMILE AND STILL GIVE ME HALF.
Eee!
OH!
OOPS.
I GOT CARRIED AWAY.
GLANCE
THAT SOUNDS LIKE FUN.

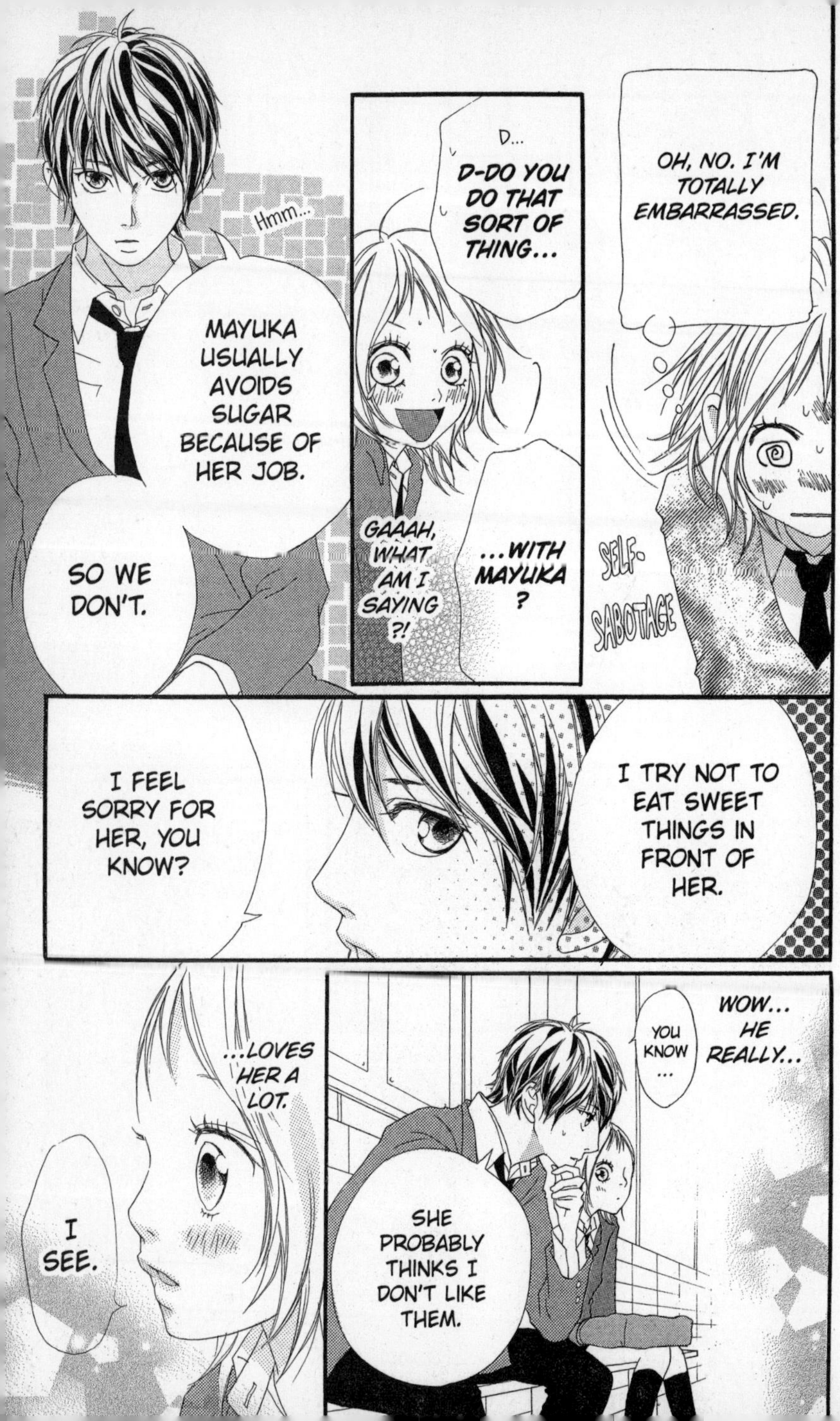
OH, NO. I'M TOTALLY EMBARRASSED.
SELF-SABOTAGE
D...
D-DO YOU DO THAT SORT OF THING...
...WITH MAYUKA?
GAAAH, WHAT AM I SAYING?!
Hmm...
MAYUKA USUALLY AVOIDS SUGAR BECAUSE OF HER JOB.
SO WE DON'T.
I TRY NOT TO EAT SWEET THINGS IN FRONT OF HER.
I FEEL SORRY FOR HER, YOU KNOW?
WOW... HE REALLY...
YOU KNOW...
SHE PROBABLY THINKS I DON'T LIKE THEM.
...LOVES HER A LOT.
I SEE.

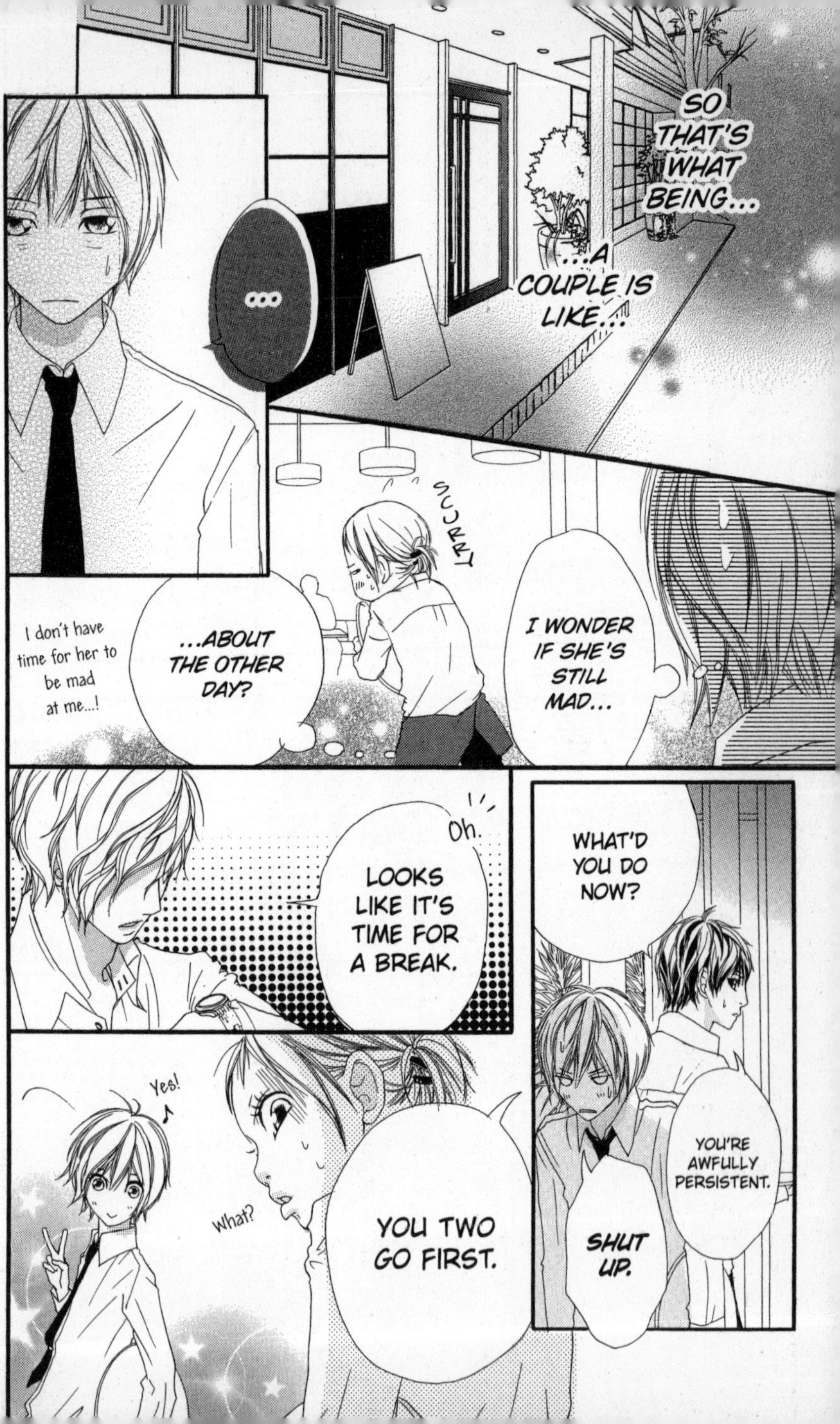
SO THAT'S WHAT BEING...
...A COUPLE IS LIKE...
...
I WONDER IF SHE'S STILL MAD...
...ABOUT THE OTHER DAY?
SCURRY
I don't have time for her to be mad at me...!
WHAT'D YOU DO NOW?
YOU'RE AWFULLY PERSISTENT.
SHUT UP.
Oh.
LOOKS LIKE IT'S TIME FOR A BREAK.
YOU TWO GO FIRST.
What?
Yes!

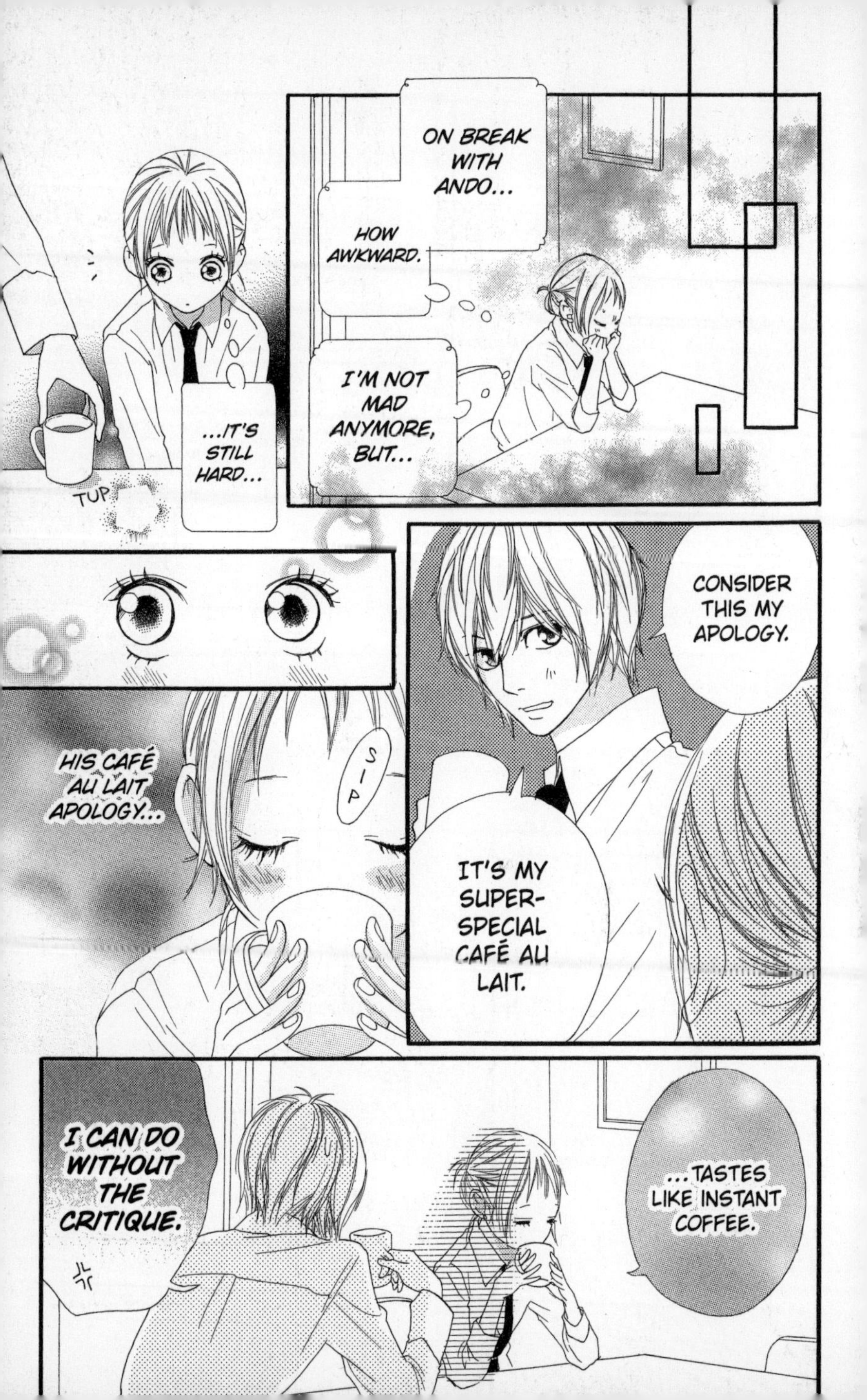
ON BREAK WITH ANDO...
HOW AWKWARD.
I'M NOT MAD ANYMORE, BUT...
TUP
...IT'S STILL HARD...
CONSIDER THIS MY APOLOGY.
IT'S MY SUPER-SPECIAL CAFÉ AU LAIT.
SIP
HIS CAFÉ AU LAIT APOLOGY...
...TASTES LIKE INSTANT COFFEE.
I CAN DO WITHOUT THE CRITIQUE.

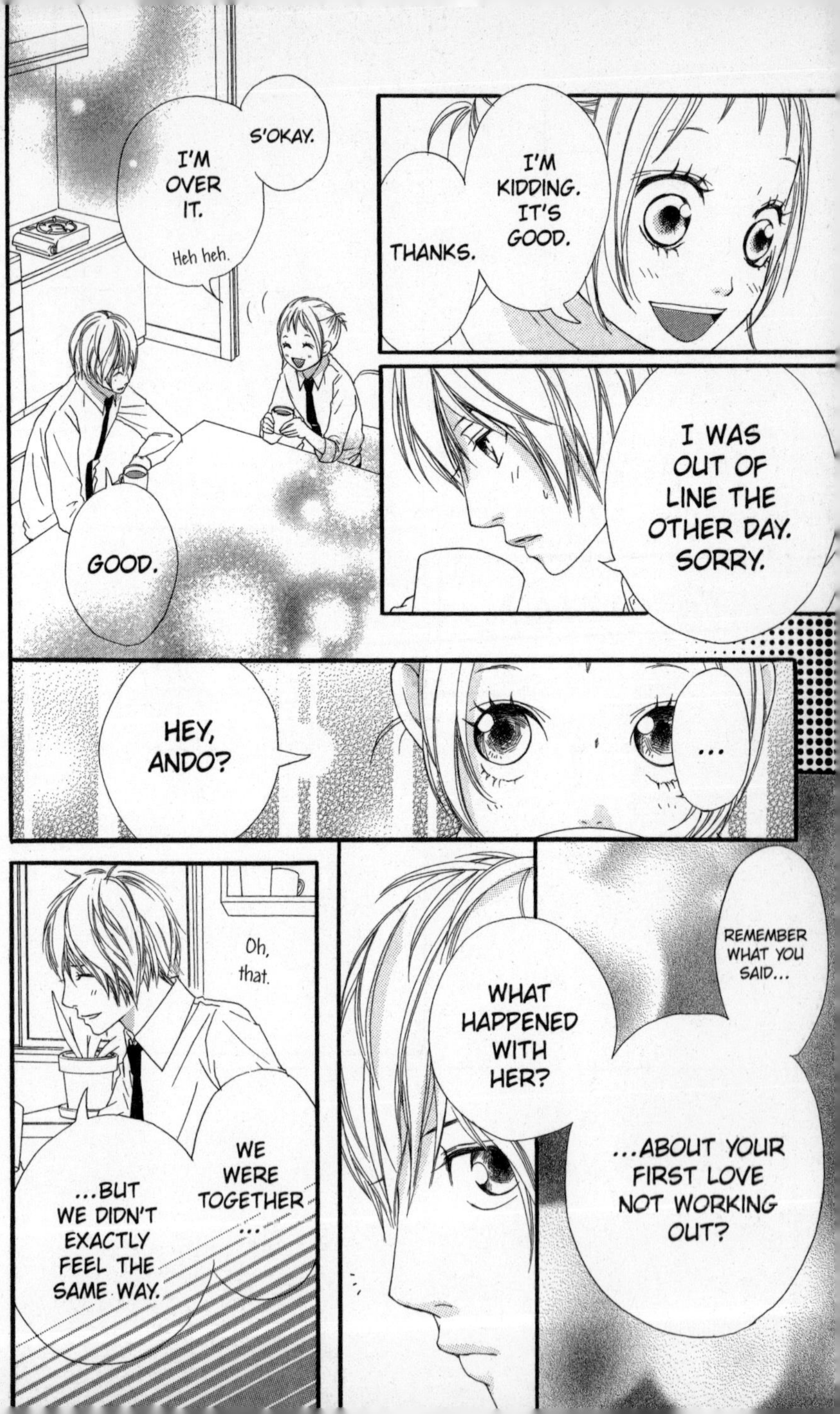
I'M KIDDING. IT'S GOOD.
THANKS.
I WAS OUT OF LINE THE OTHER DAY. SORRY.
S'OKAY.
I'M OVER IT.
Heh heh.
GOOD.
...
HEY, ANDO?
REMEMBER WHAT YOU SAID...
...ABOUT YOUR FIRST LOVE NOT WORKING OUT?
WHAT HAPPENED WITH HER?
Oh, that.
WE WERE TOGETHER...
...BUT WE DIDN'T EXACTLY FEEL THE SAME WAY.

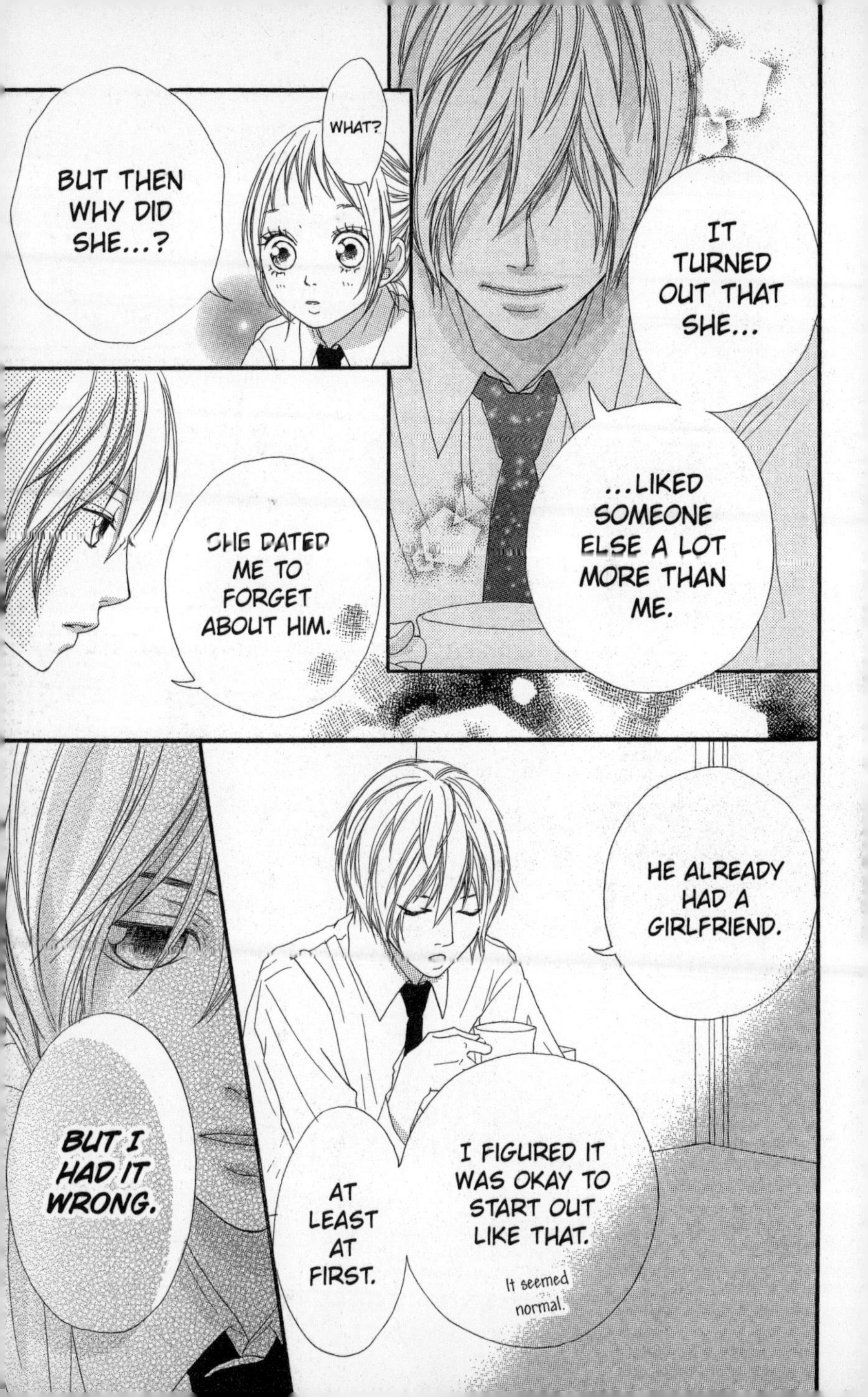
IT TURNED OUT THAT SHE...
...LIKED SOMEONE ELSE A LOT MORE THAN ME.
WHAT?
BUT THEN WHY DID SHE...?
SHE DATED ME TO FORGET ABOUT HIM.
HE ALREADY HAD A GIRLFRIEND.
I FIGURED IT WAS OKAY TO START OUT LIKE THAT.
It seemed normal.
AT LEAST AT FIRST.
BUT I HAD IT WRONG.

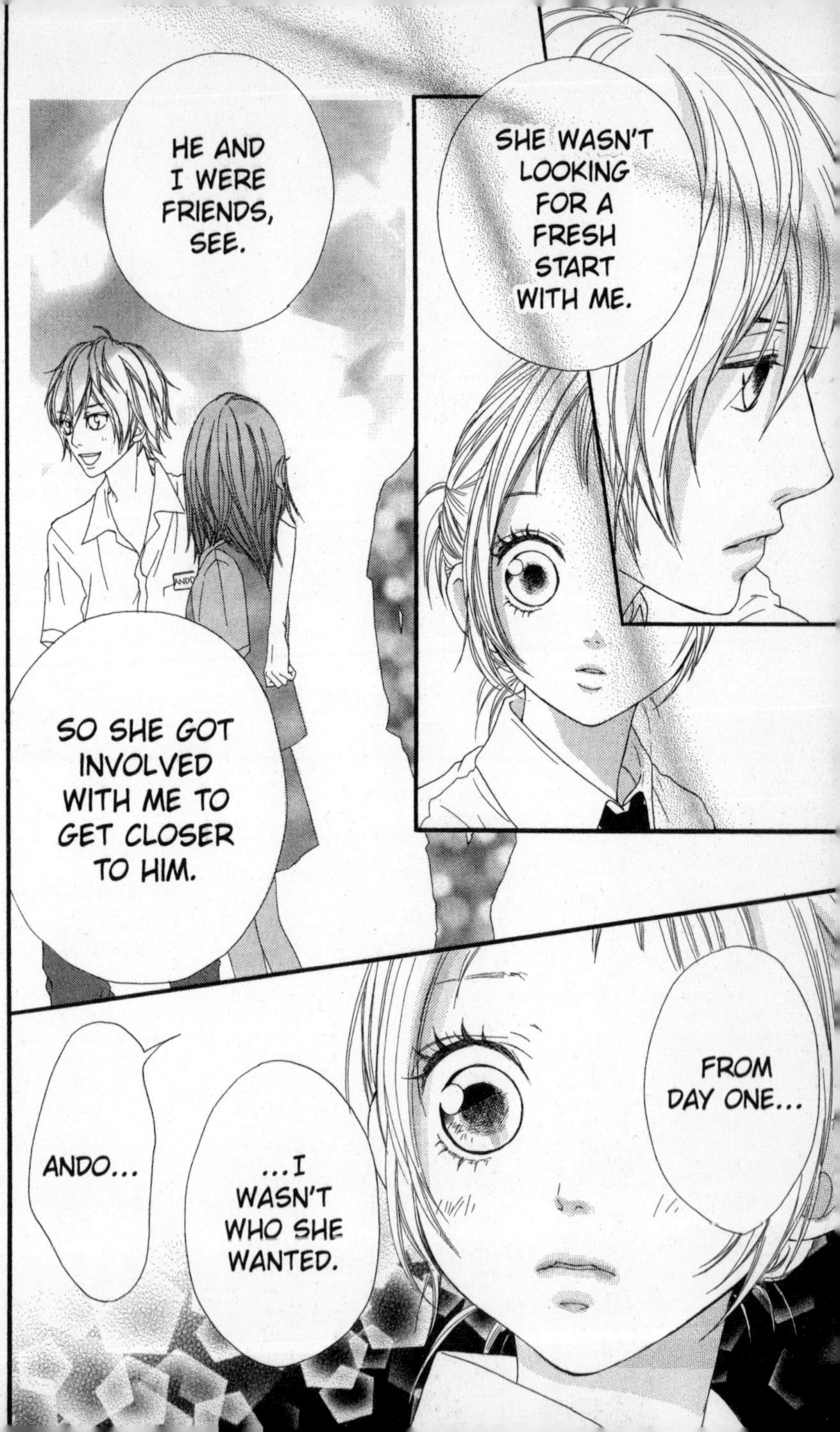
SHE WASN'T LOOKING FOR A FRESH START WITH ME.
HE AND I WERE FRIENDS, SEE.
SO SHE GOT INVOLVED WITH ME TO GET CLOSER TO HIM.
FROM DAY ONE...
...I WASN'T WHO SHE WANTED.
ANDO...

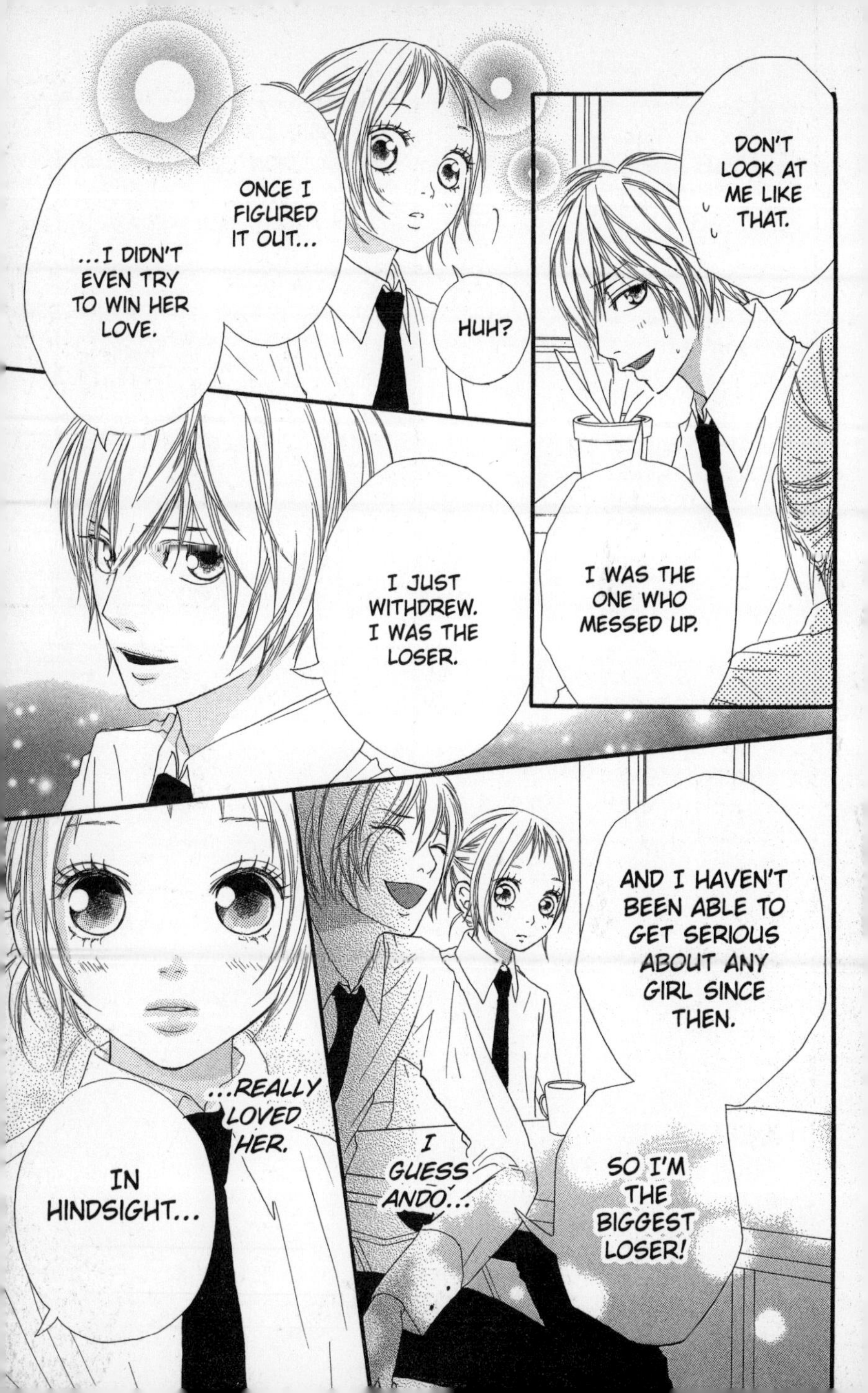
DON'T LOOK AT ME LIKE THAT.
I WAS THE ONE WHO MESSED UP.
ONCE I FIGURED IT OUT...
HUH?
...I DIDN'T EVEN TRY TO WIN HER LOVE.
I JUST WITHDREW. I WAS THE LOSER.
AND I HAVEN'T BEEN ABLE TO GET SERIOUS ABOUT ANY GIRL SINCE THEN.
SO I'M THE BIGGEST LOSER!
I GUESS ANDO...
...REALLY LOVED HER.
IN HINDSIGHT...

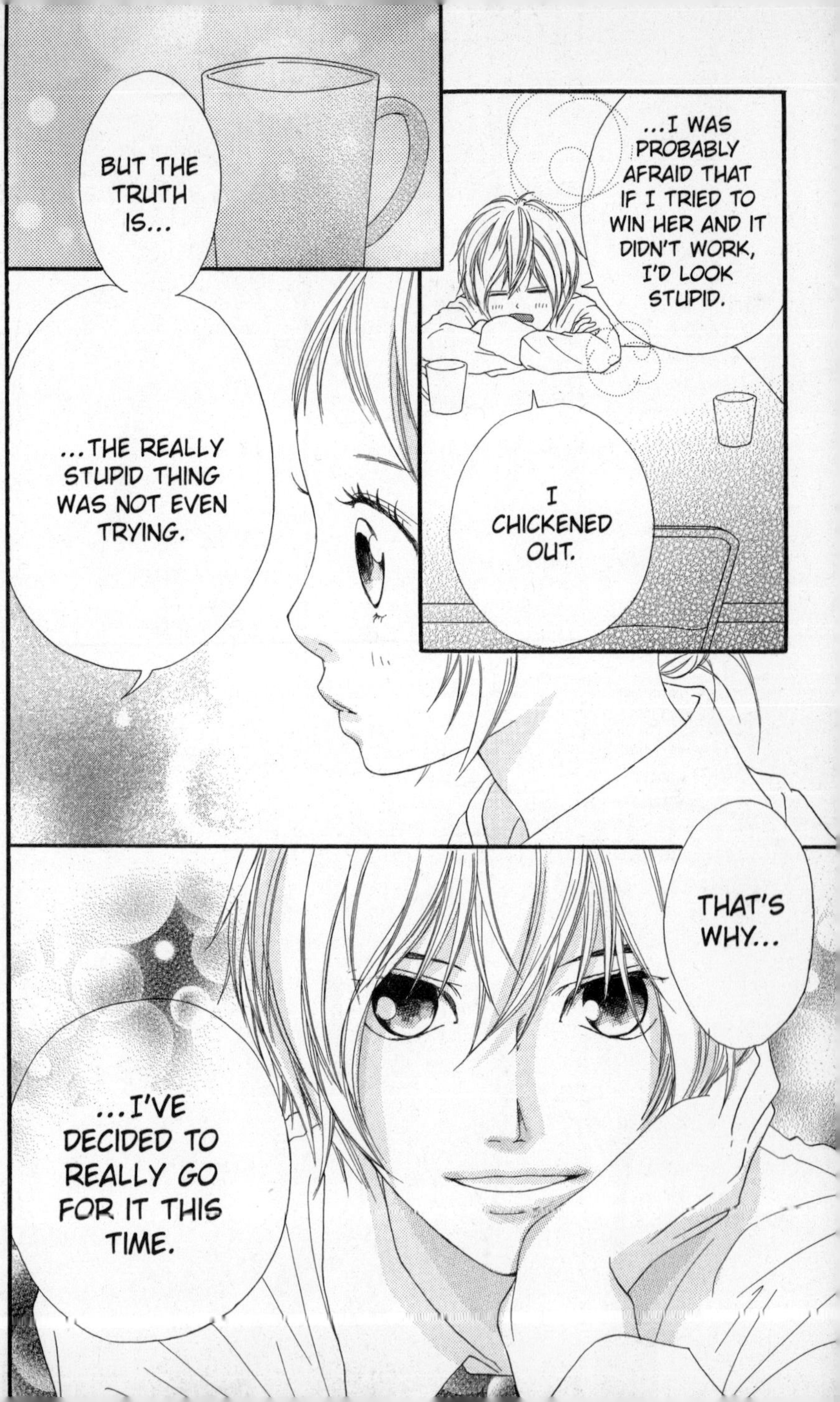
...I WAS PROBABLY AFRAID THAT IF I TRIED TO WIN HER AND IT DIDN'T WORK, I'D LOOK STUPID.
I CHICKENED OUT.
BUT THE TRUTH IS...
...THE REALLY STUPID THING WAS NOT EVEN TRYING.
THAT'S WHY...
...I'VE DECIDED TO REALLY GO FOR IT THIS TIME.

WORKFLOW

~My Particular Method~

(10) SUBMISSION

As soon as I submit my draft, we begin discussing the next chapter. But once we have that conversation, I spend the day not thinking about work at all. I watch TV all day! Yay!

After that, I immediately go back to step 1. That's how it goes. I'm not particularly efficient or professional at any of the steps in this process. Ha ha! I start shaking every time I hear how quickly other artists work. I've tried to resign myself to the fact that this is just my pace, but every time I meet a new artist, I can't help asking how much they can draw in a day.

★ ★ ★ ★ ★

These lovely people helped me with this volume:

Umi Ayase

Moto Harui

Naomi Minamoto

Thank you so much!!!!!

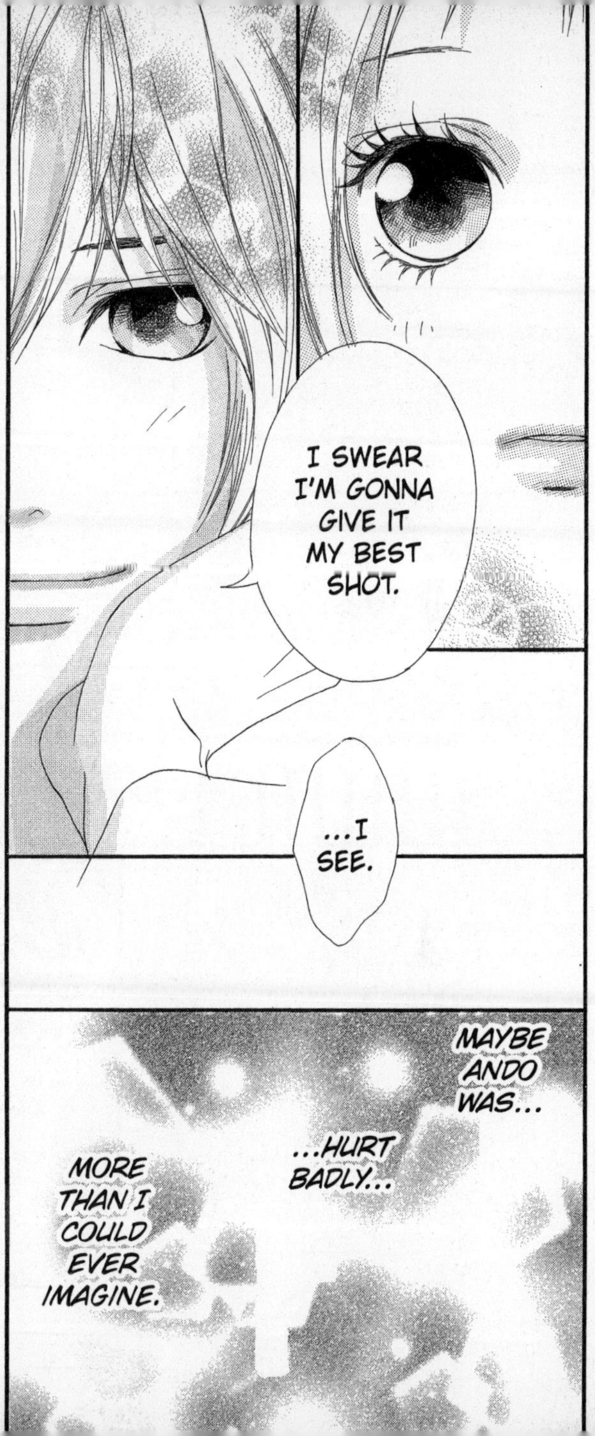

I SWEAR I'M GONNA GIVE IT MY BEST SHOT.
...I SEE.
MAYBE ANDO WAS...
...HURT BADLY...
MORE THAN I COULD EVER IMAGINE.

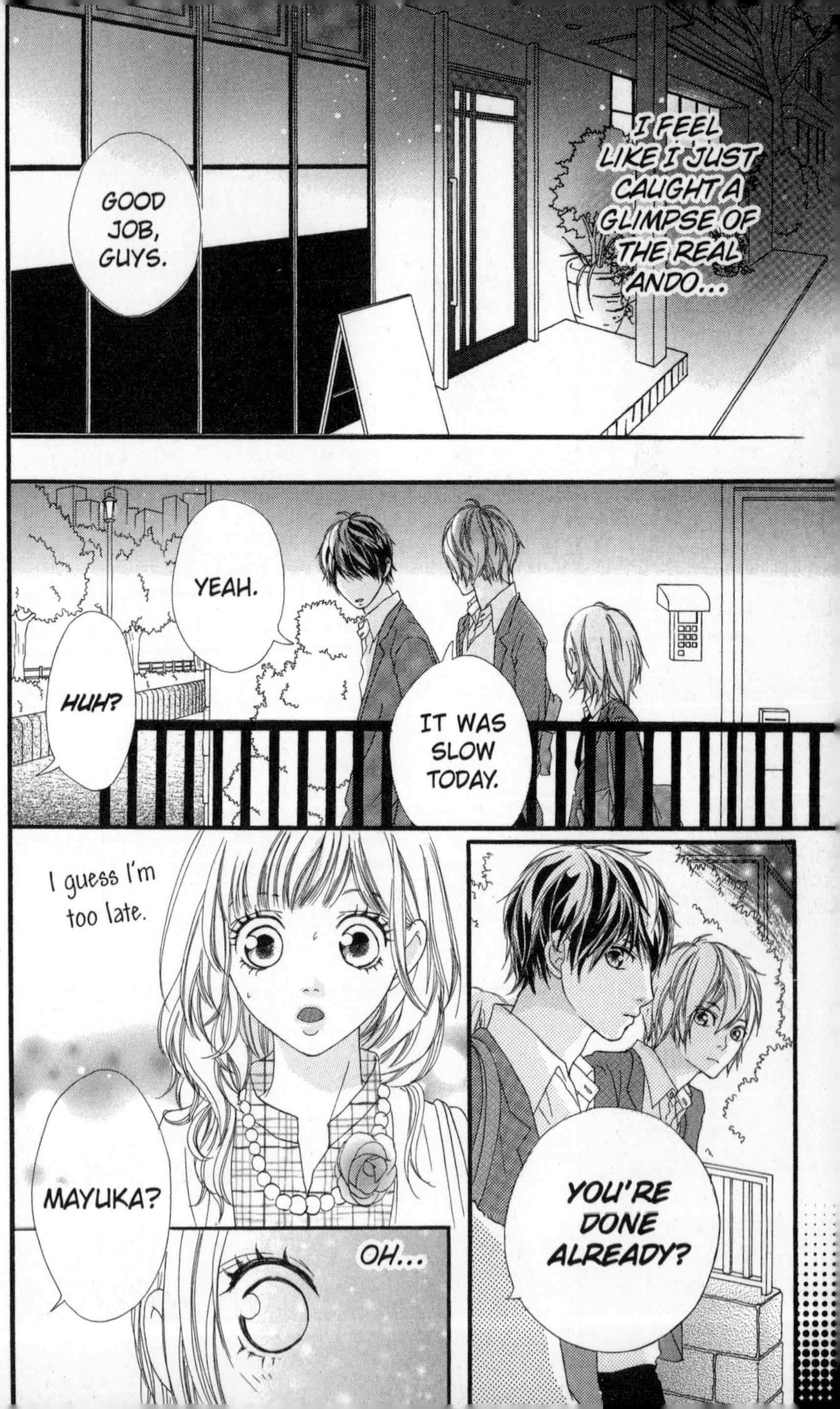
I FEEL LIKE I JUST CAUGHT A GLIMPSE OF THE REAL ANDO...
GOOD JOB, GUYS.
IT WAS SLOW TODAY.
YEAH.
HUH?
YOU'RE DONE ALREADY?
I guess I'm too late.
MAYUKA?
OH...

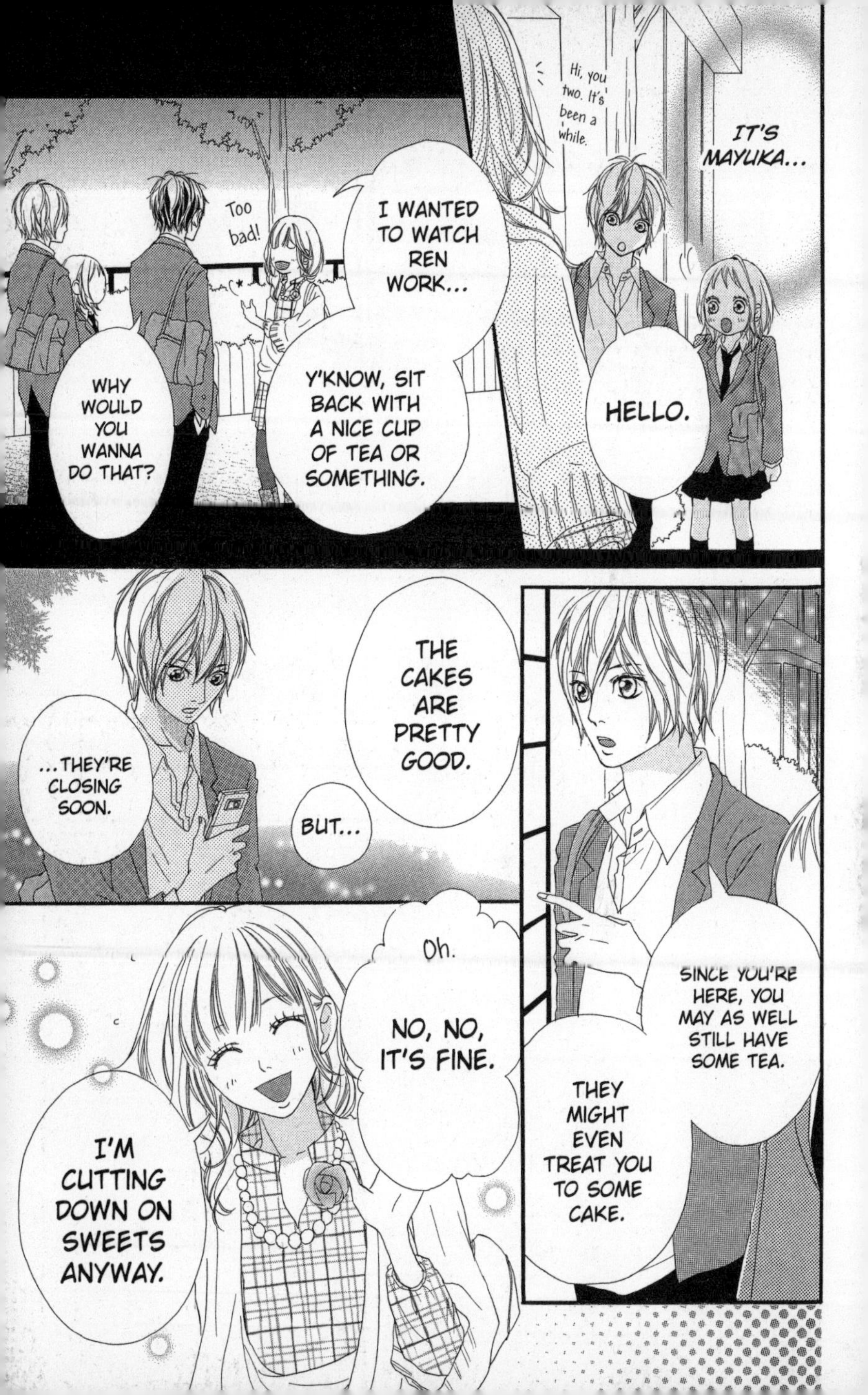
IT'S MAYUKA...
Hi, you two. It's been a while.
HELLO.
I WANTED TO WATCH REN WORK...
Y'KNOW, SIT BACK WITH A NICE CUP OF TEA OR SOMETHING.
Too bad!
WHY WOULD YOU WANNA DO THAT?
SINCE YOU'RE HERE, YOU MAY AS WELL STILL HAVE SOME TEA.
THEY MIGHT EVEN TREAT YOU TO SOME CAKE.
THE CAKES ARE PRETTY GOOD.
BUT...
...THEY'RE CLOSING SOON.
Oh.
NO, NO, IT'S FINE.
I'M CUTTING DOWN ON SWEETS ANYWAY.

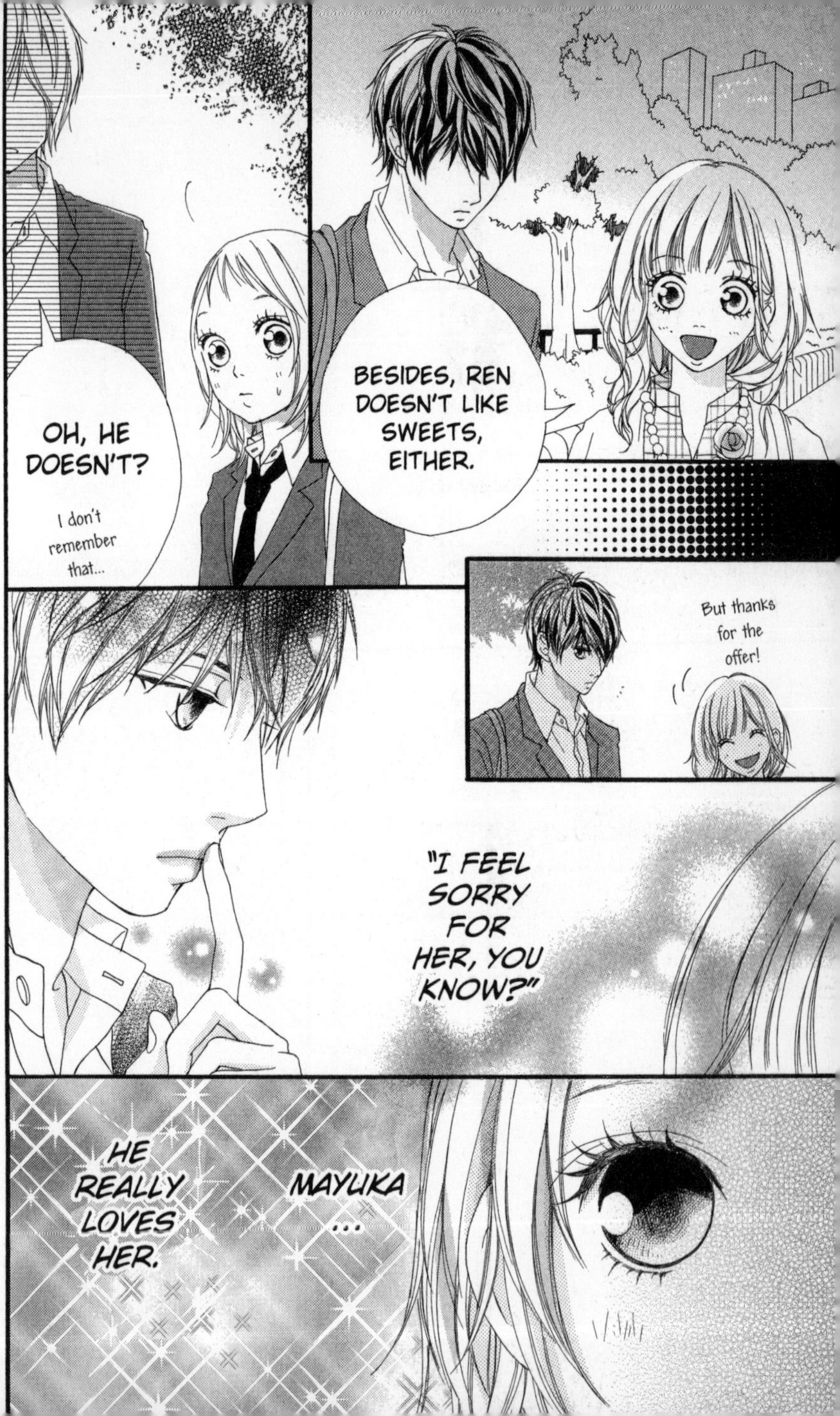
BESIDES, REN DOESN'T LIKE SWEETS, EITHER.
OH, HE DOESN'T?
I don't remember that...
But thanks for the offer!
"I FEEL SORRY FOR HER, YOU KNOW?"
MAYUKA...
HE REALLY LOVES HER.

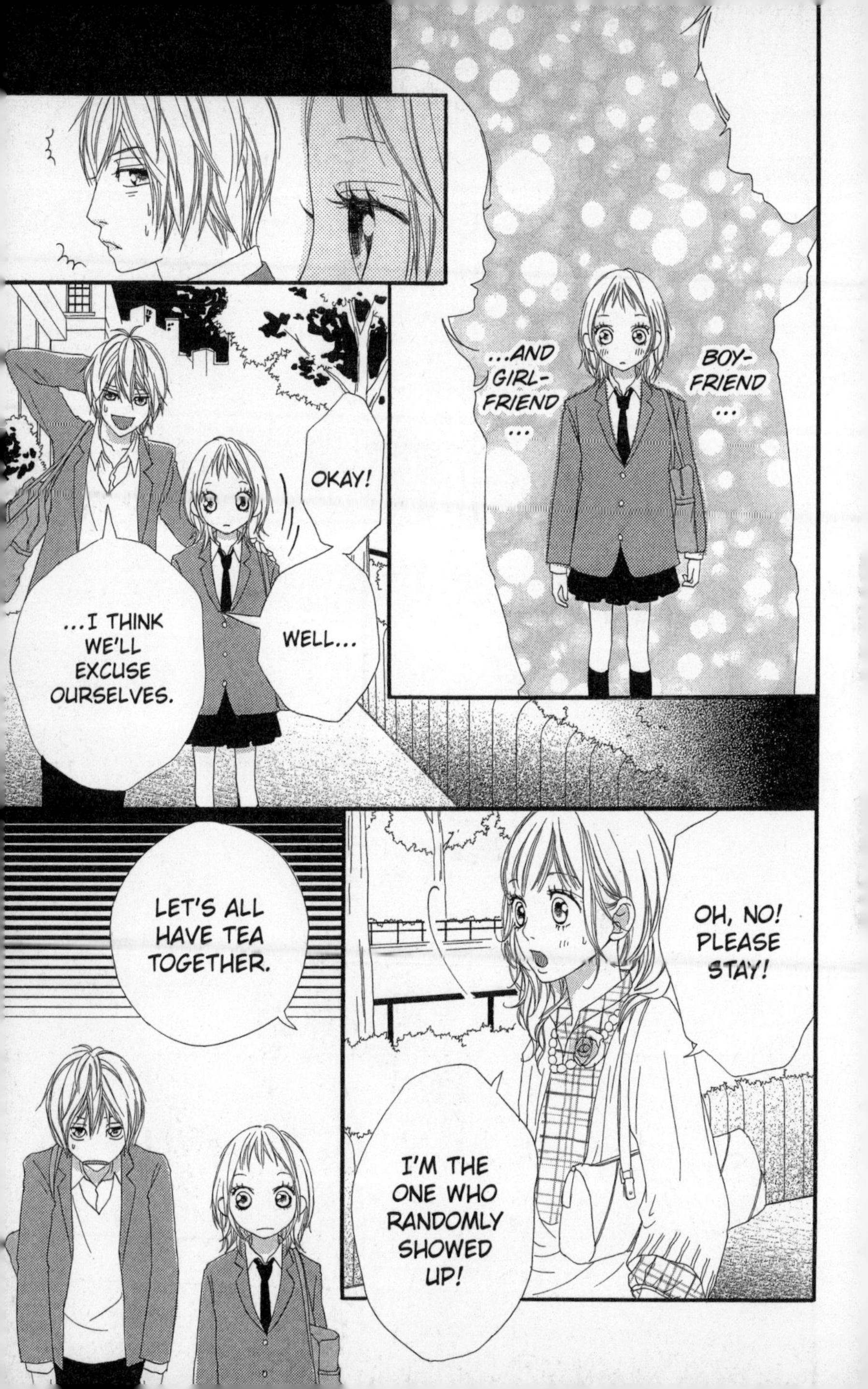
BOY-FRIEND...
...AND GIRL-FRIEND...
OKAY!
WELL...
...I THINK WE'LL EXCUSE OURSELVES.
OH, NO! PLEASE STAY!
I'M THE ONE WHO RANDOMLY SHOWED UP!
LET'S ALL HAVE TEA TOGETHER.

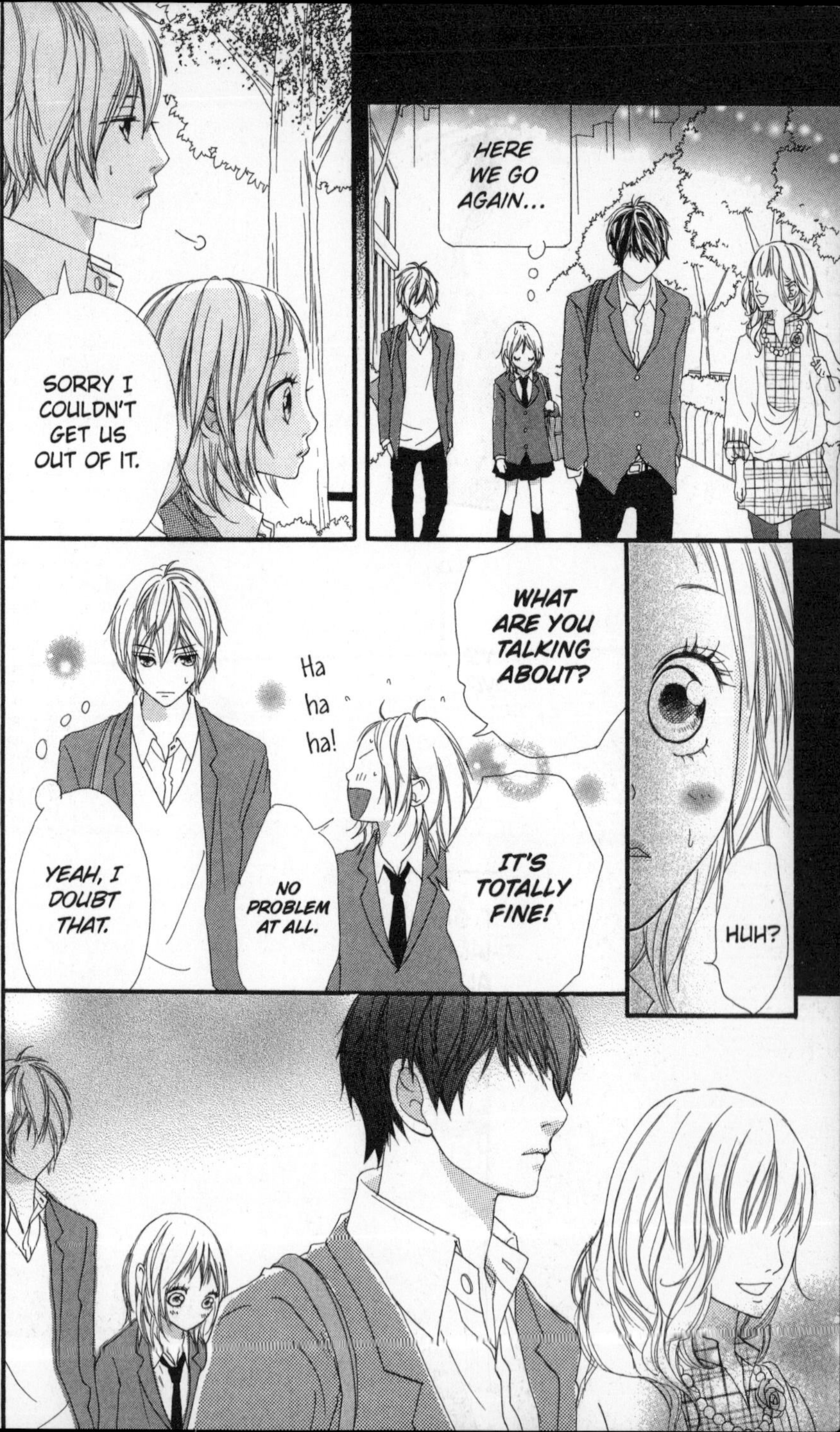
HERE WE GO AGAIN...
SORRY I COULDN'T GET US OUT OF IT.
HUH?
WHAT ARE YOU TALKING ABOUT?
IT'S TOTALLY FINE!
Ha ha ha!
NO PROBLEM AT ALL.
YEAH, I DOUBT THAT.

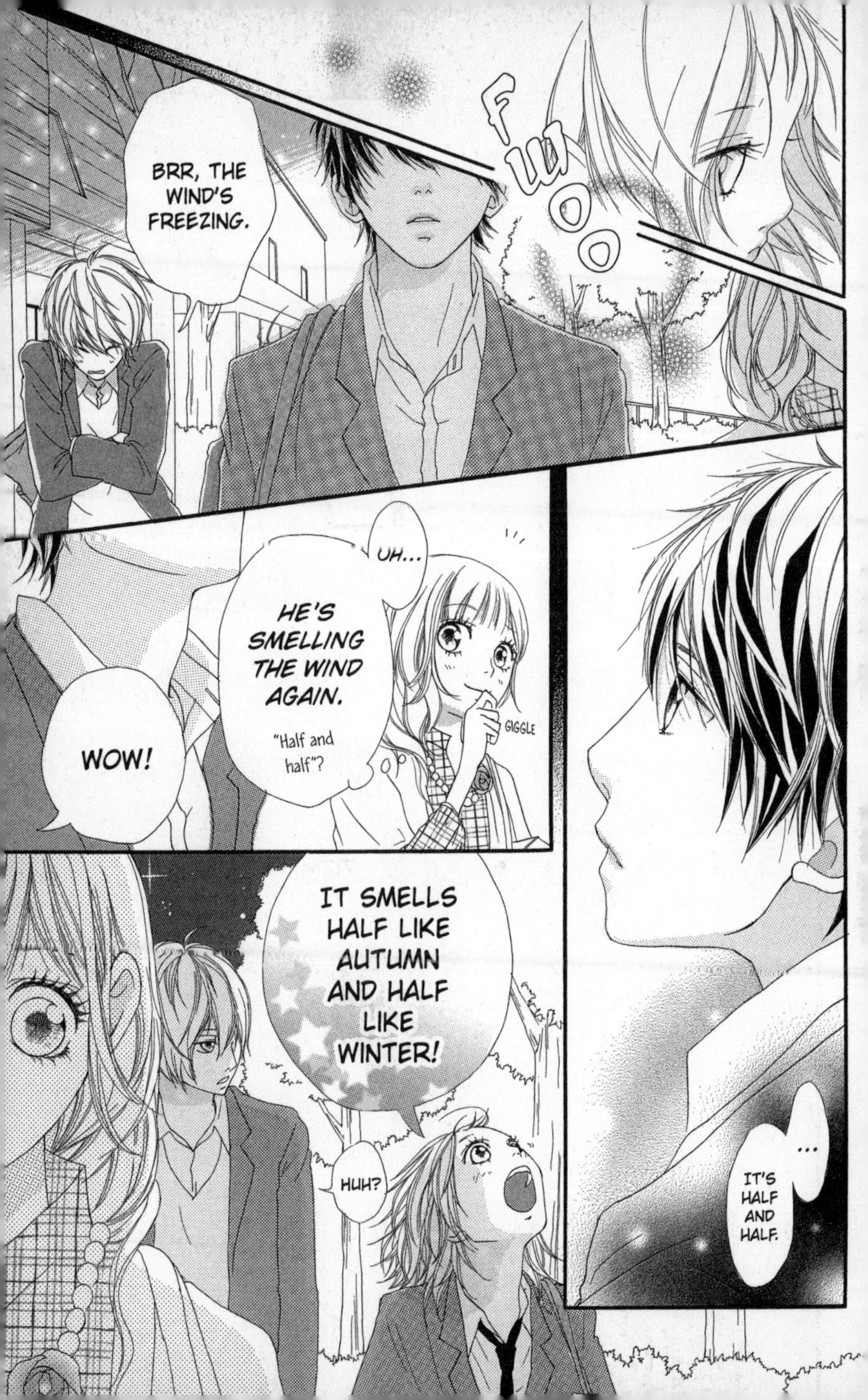
FUWOO
BRR, THE WIND'S FREEZING.
...
IT'S HALF AND HALF.
UH...
GIGGLE
HE'S SMELLING THE WIND AGAIN.
"Half and half"?
WOW!
IT SMELLS HALF LIKE AUTUMN AND HALF LIKE WINTER!
HUH?

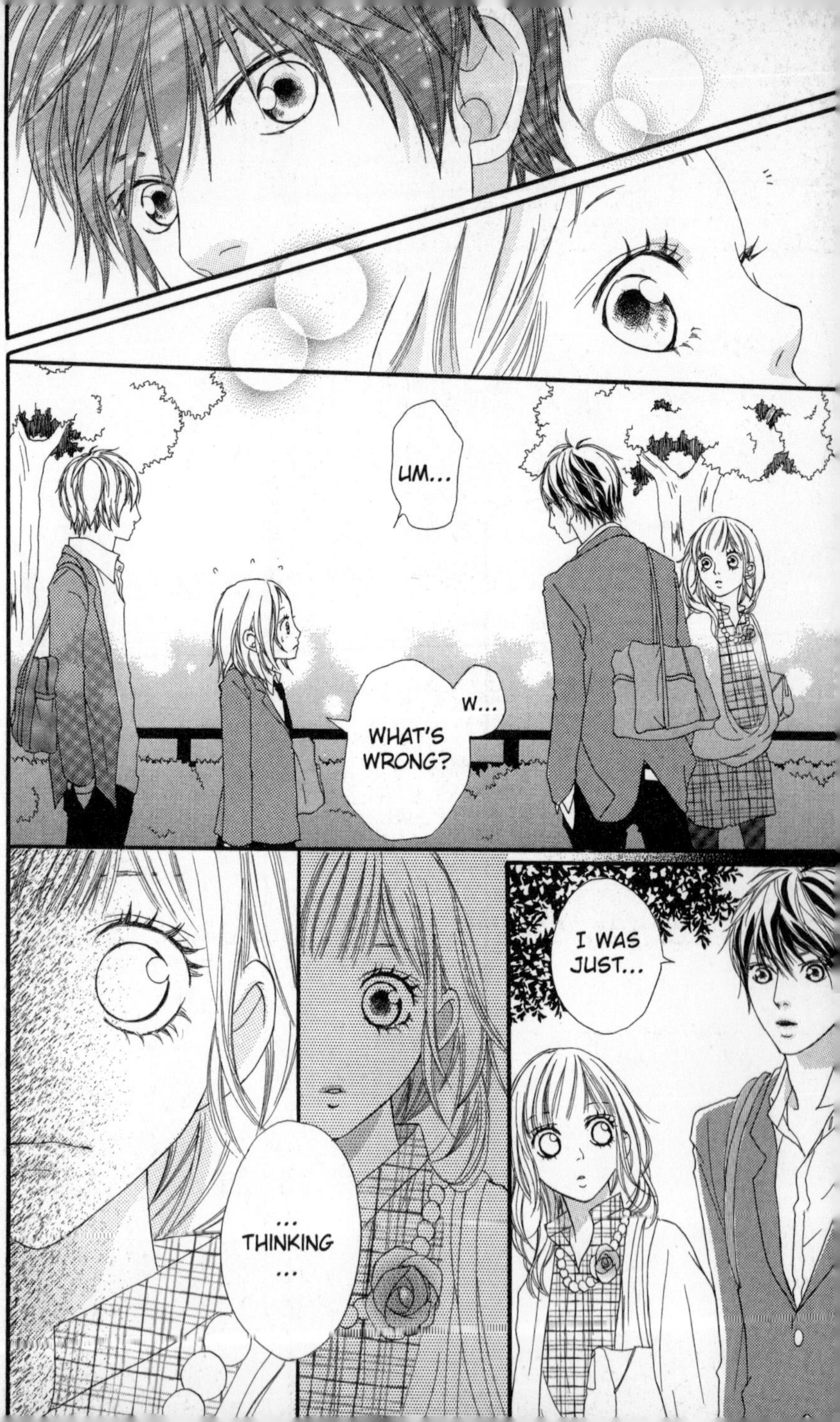
UM...
W... WHAT'S WRONG?
I WAS JUST...
... THINKING ...

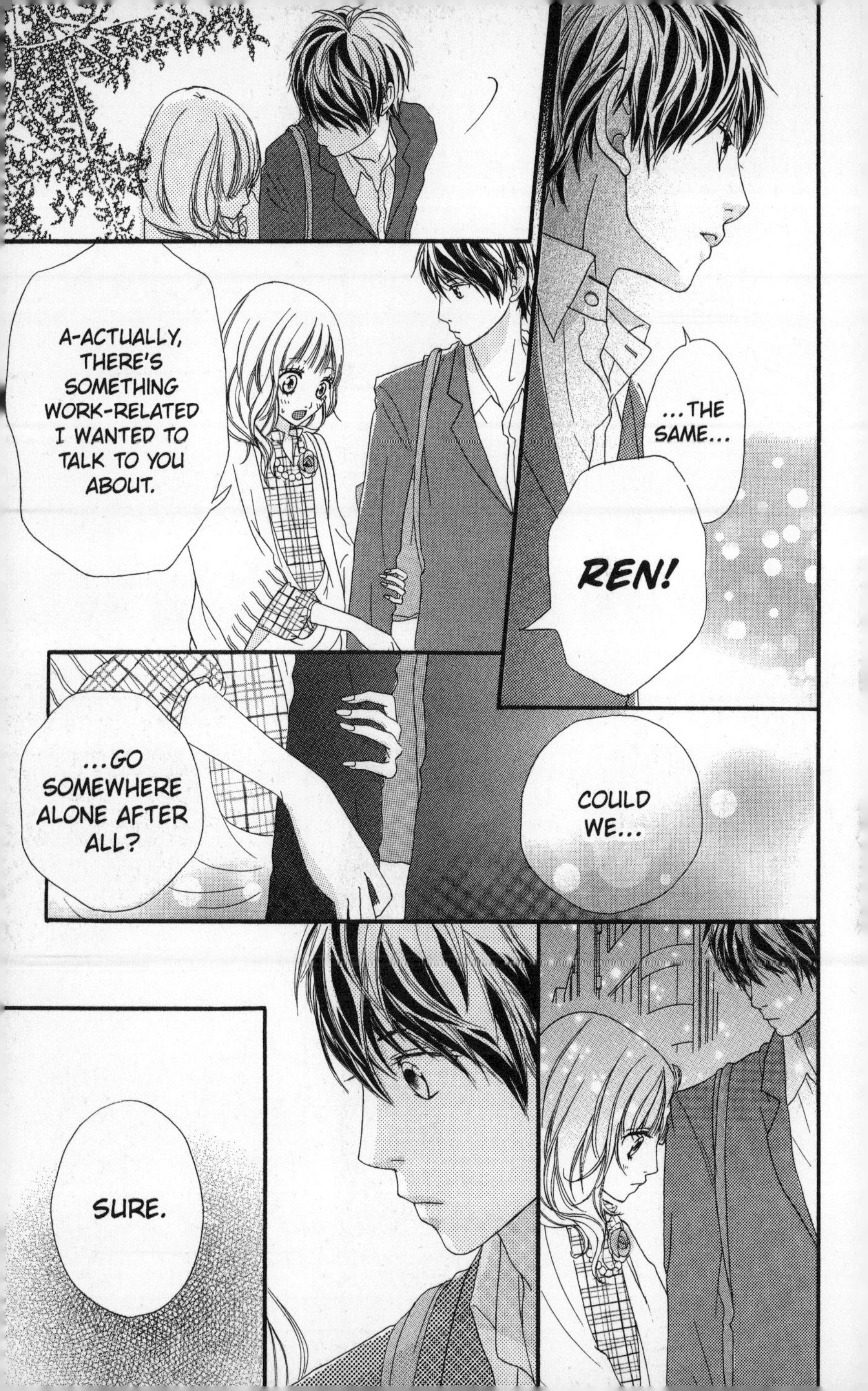
...THE SAME...
REN!
A-ACTUALLY, THERE'S SOMETHING WORK-RELATED I WANTED TO TALK TO YOU ABOUT.
COULD WE...
...GO SOMEWHERE ALONE AFTER ALL?
SURE.

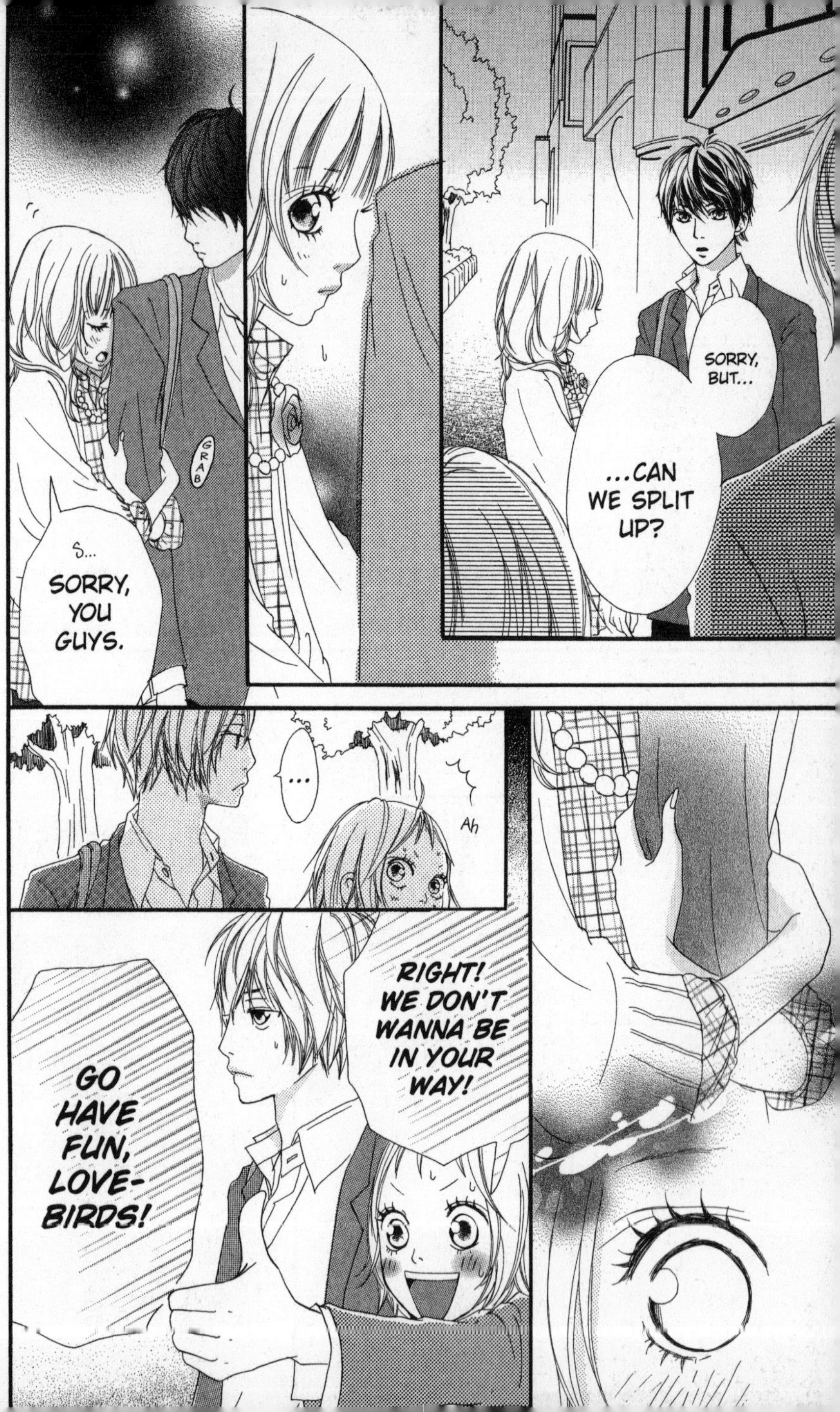
SORRY, BUT...
...CAN WE SPLIT UP?
GRAB
S... SORRY, YOU GUYS.
...
Ah
RIGHT! WE DON'T WANNA BE IN YOUR WAY!
GO HAVE FUN, LOVE-BIRDS!

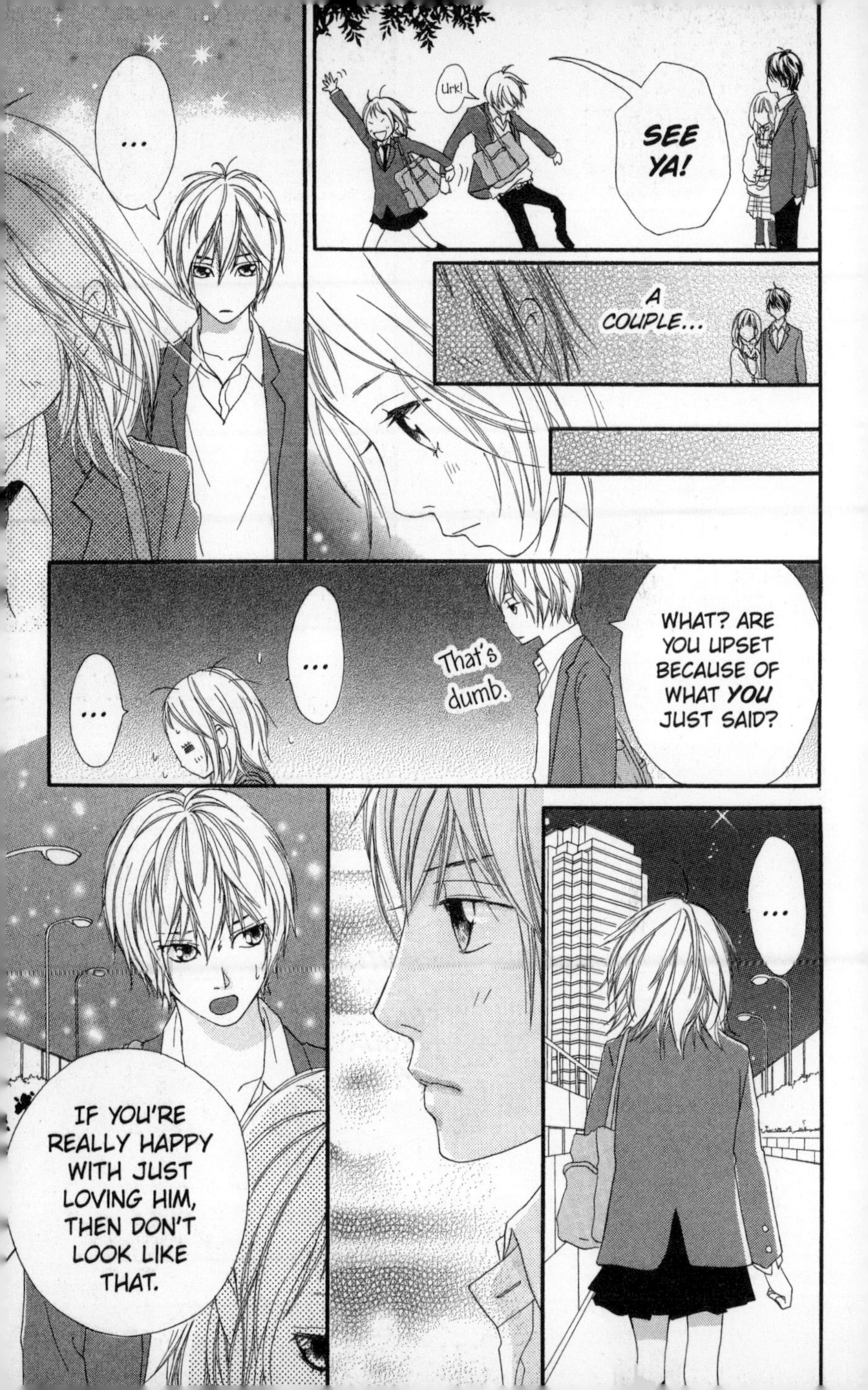
SEE YA!
Urk!
A COUPLE...
...
WHAT? ARE YOU UPSET BECAUSE OF WHAT *YOU* JUST SAID?
That's dumb.
...
...
...
IF YOU'RE REALLY HAPPY WITH JUST LOVING HIM, THEN DON'T LOOK LIKE THAT.

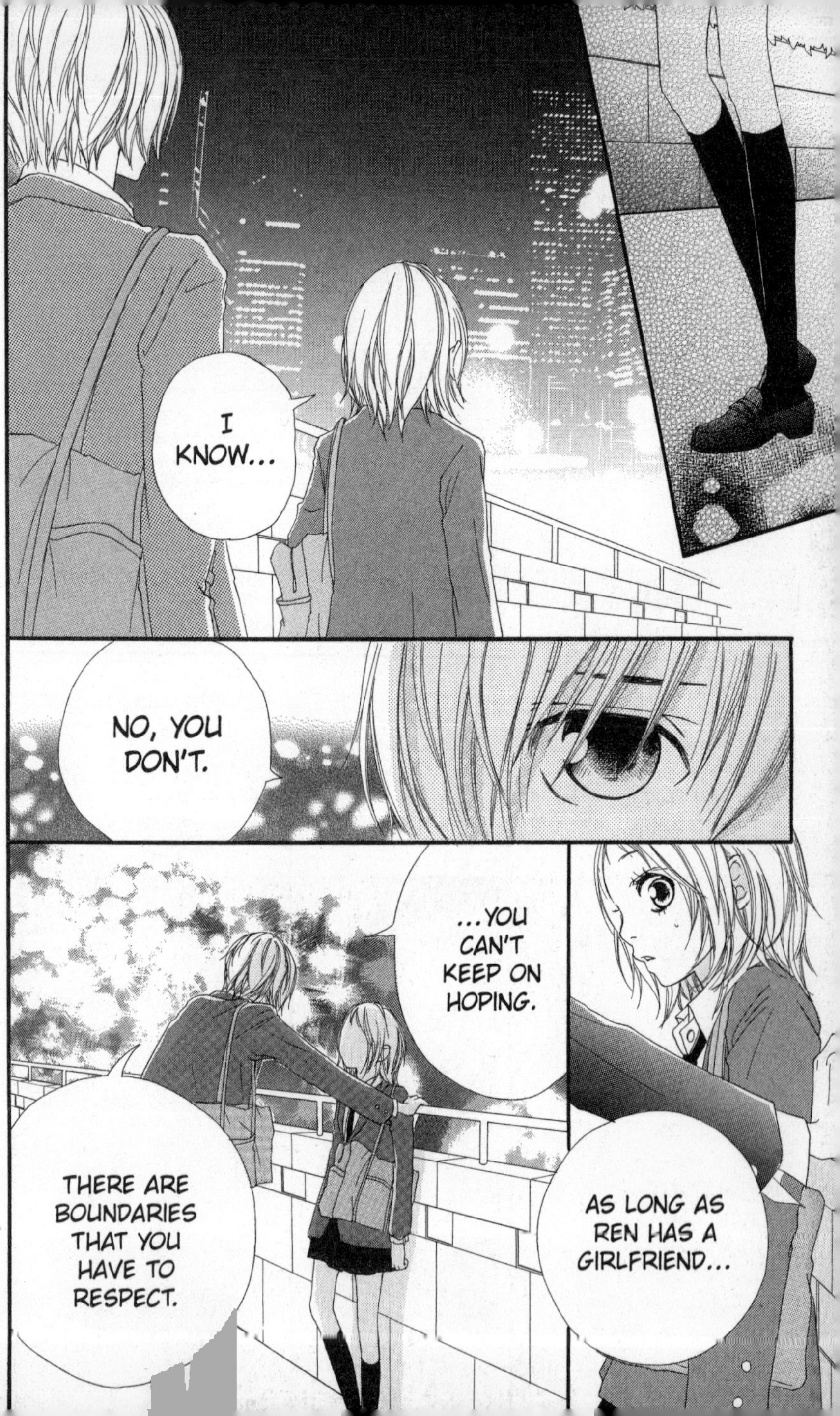
I KNOW...
NO, YOU DON'T.
AS LONG AS REN HAS A GIRLFRIEND...
...YOU CAN'T KEEP ON HOPING.
THERE ARE BOUNDARIES THAT YOU HAVE TO RESPECT.

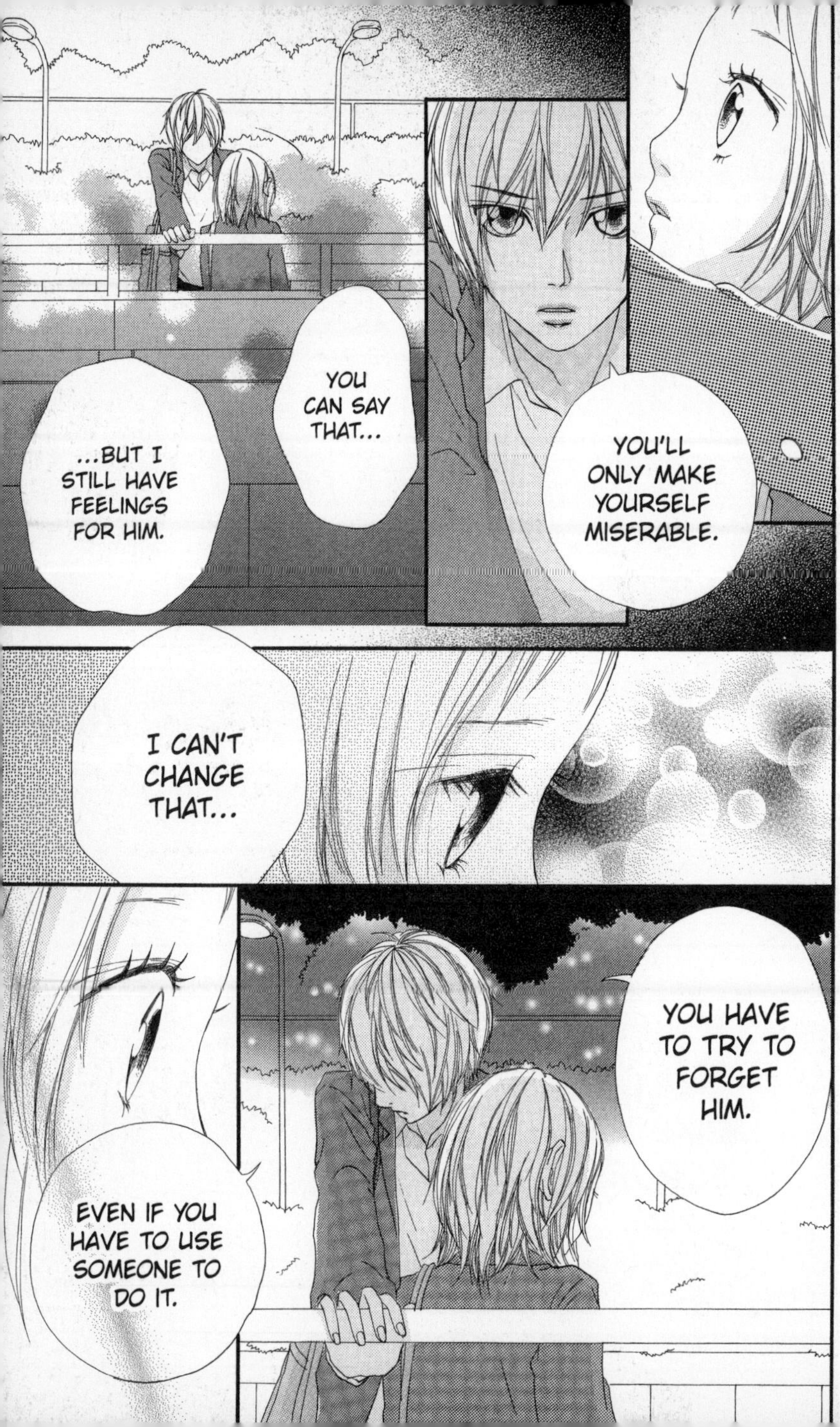
YOU'LL ONLY MAKE YOURSELF MISERABLE.
YOU CAN SAY THAT...
...BUT I STILL HAVE FEELINGS FOR HIM.
I CAN'T CHANGE THAT...
YOU HAVE TO TRY TO FORGET HIM.
EVEN IF YOU HAVE TO USE SOMEONE TO DO IT.

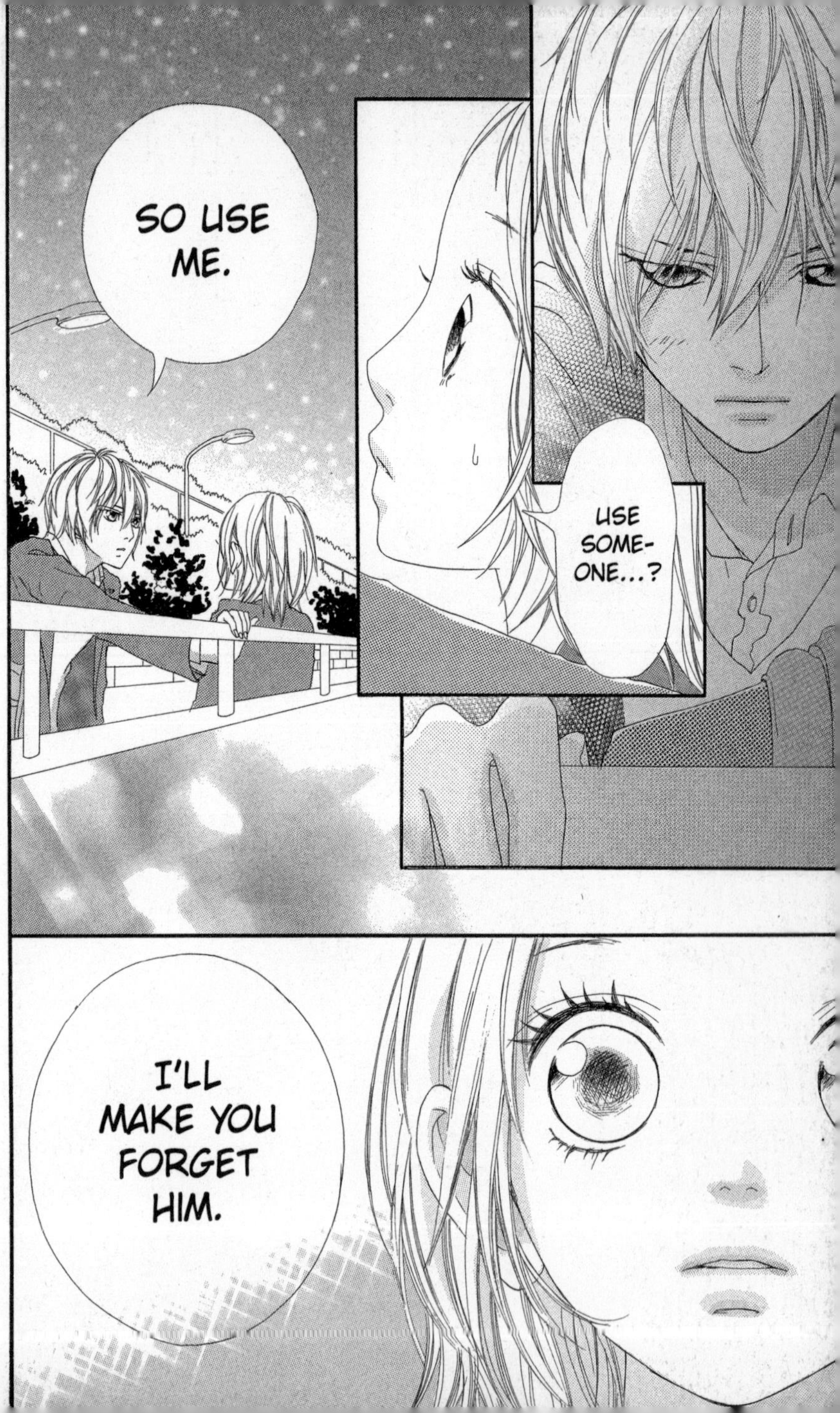
USE SOME-ONE...?
SO USE ME.
I'LL MAKE YOU FORGET HIM.

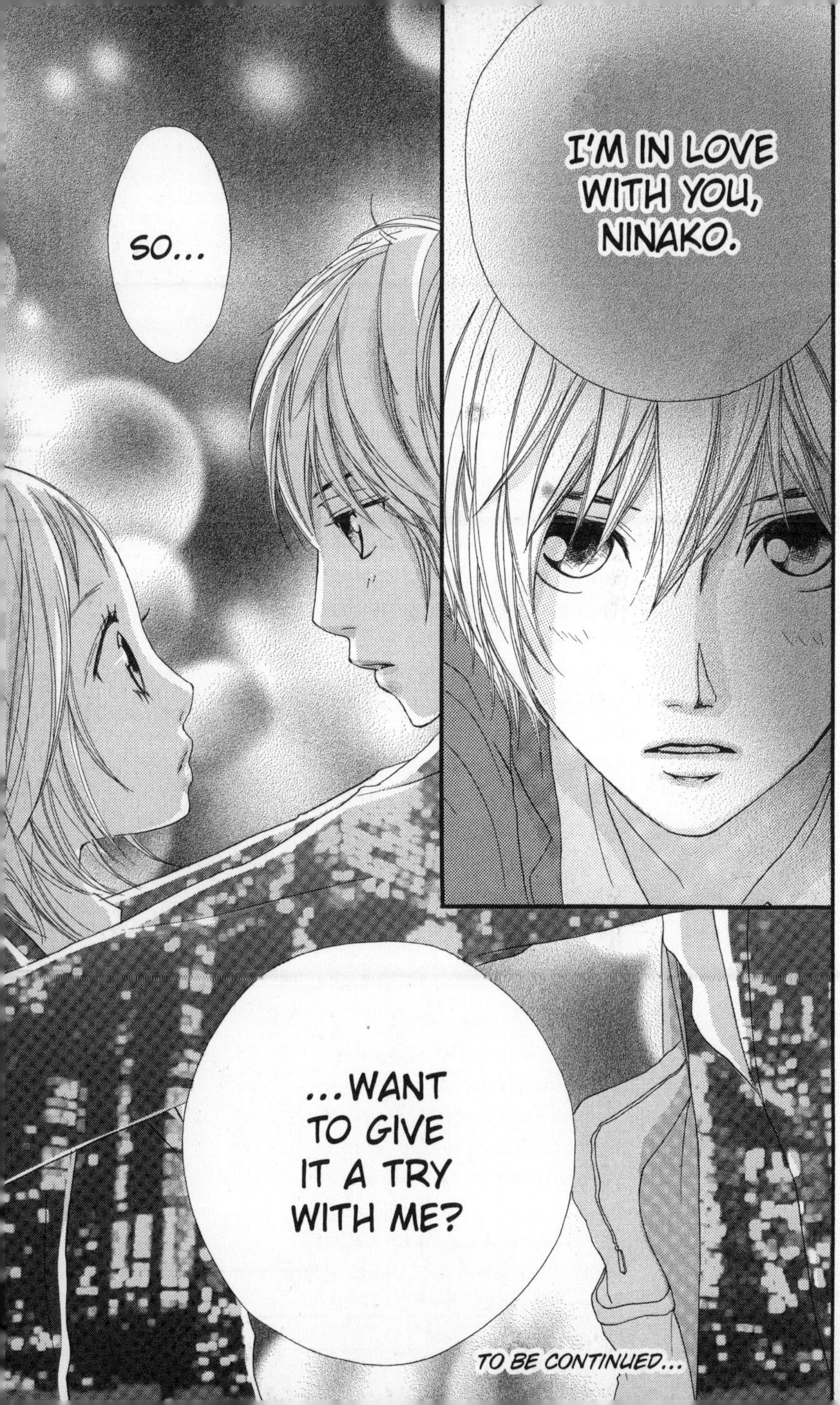
I'M IN LOVE WITH YOU, NINAKO.
SO...
...WANT TO GIVE IT A TRY WITH ME?
TO BE CONTINUED...

To be
continued...

...in
volume 4 ★

My pet chinchillas (small
animals) don't like heat or
humidity, so I must have air
conditioning in the summer.
They also occupy one whole
vacant room. What a luxury.
Meanwhile, my assistants
and I are slaving away in a
tiny, cramped workspace. But
when I see them sleeping so
contentedly, oblivious to the
world, I find myself forgiving
them just about anything—
even clawed-up wallpaper.
I shall forgive!

—Io Sakisaka

Born on June 8, Io Sakisaka
made her debut as a manga
creator with *Sakura, Chiru*. Her
works include *Call My Name*,
Gate of Planet, and *Blue*. Her
current series, *Ao Haru Ride*, is
currently running in *Bessatsu
Margaret* magazine. In her spare
time, Sakisaka likes to paint
things and sleep.

STROBE EDGE
Vol. 3
Shojo Beat Edition

STORY AND ART BY
IO SAKISAKA

English Adaptation/Ysabet MacFarlane
Translation/JN Productions
Touch-up Art & Lettering/John Hunt
Design/ Yukiko Whitley
Editor/Amy Yu

Printed in the U.S.A.

Published by VIZ Media, LLC
P.O. Box 77010
San Francisco, CA 94107

10 9 8 7 6 5 4 3 2 1
First printing, March 2013

www.viz.com www.shojobeat.com

PARENTAL ADVISORY
STROBE EDGE is rated T for Teen and is recommended for ages 13 and up. This volume contains suggestive themes.
ratings.viz.com

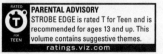

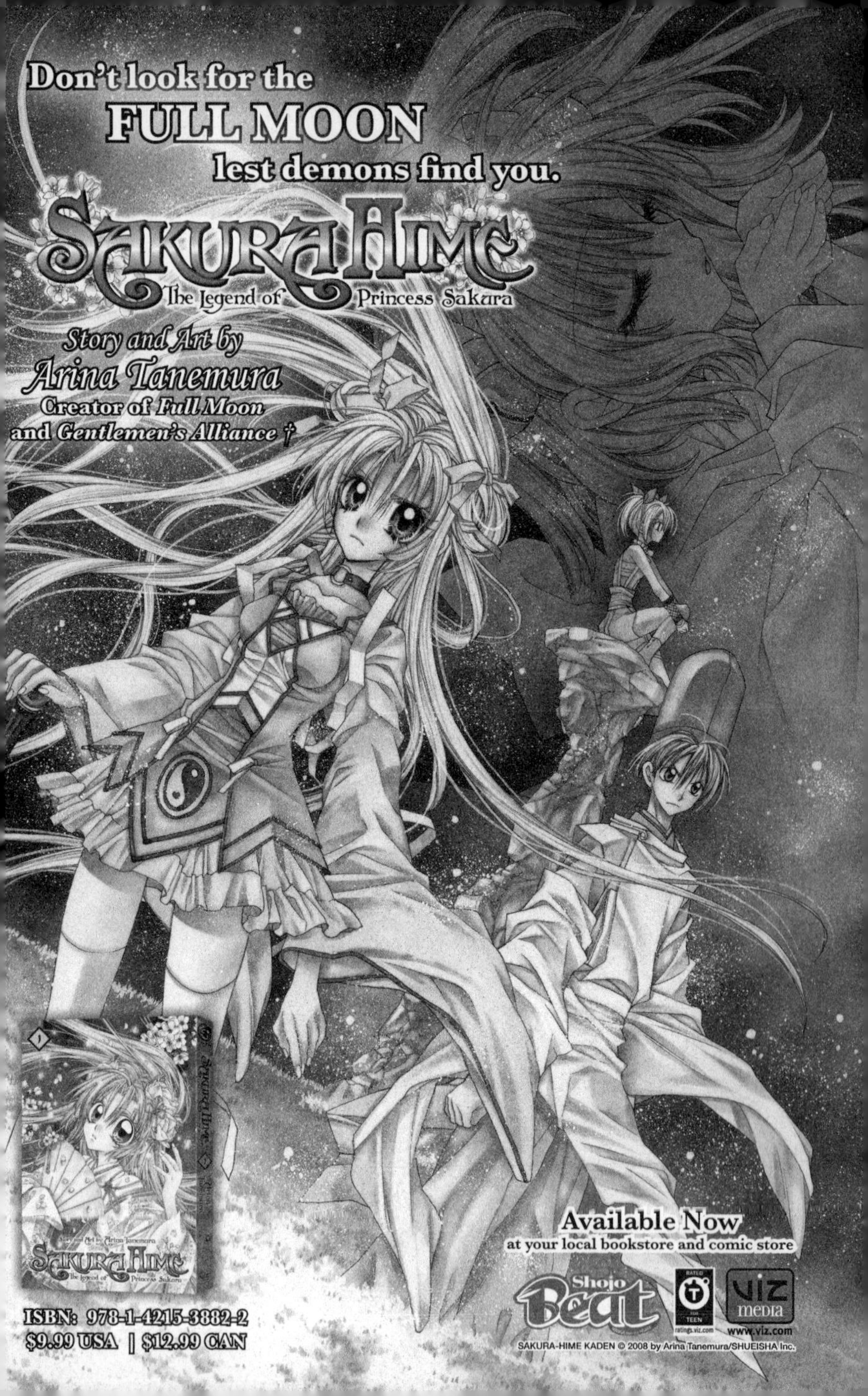
Don't look for the
FULL MOON
lest demons find you.
SAKURA HIME
The Legend of Princess Sakura
Story and Art by
Arina Tanemura
Creator of Full Moon
and Gentlemen's Alliance †
Available Now
at your local bookstore and comic store
ISBN: 978-1-4215-3882-2
$9.99 USA | $12.99 CAN
Shojo Beat
RATED T FOR TEEN
ratings.viz.com
VIZ media
www.viz.com
SAKURA-HIME KADEN © 2008 by Arina Tanemura/SHUEISHA Inc.

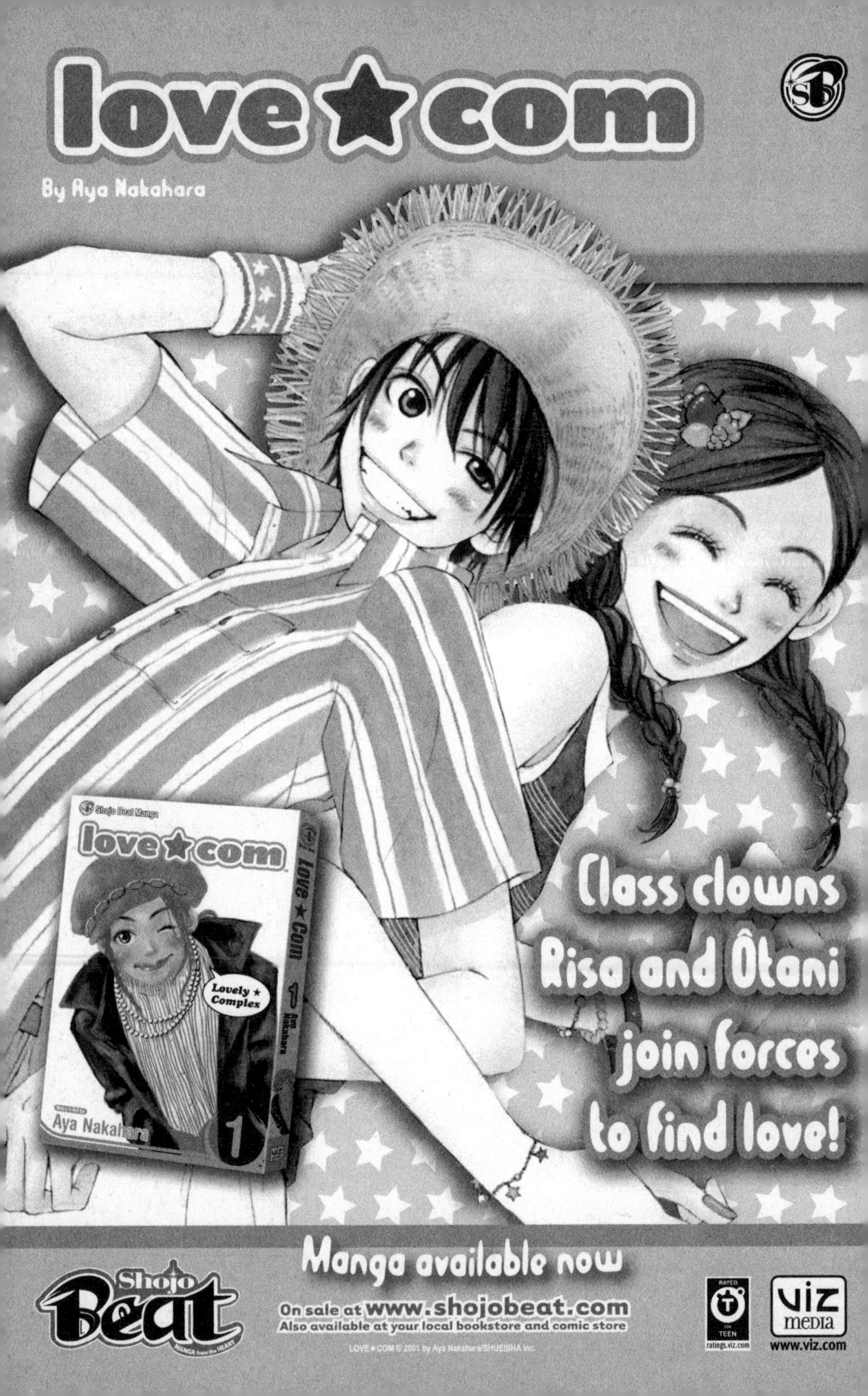
love★com
By Aya Nakahara
Shojo Beat Manga
love★com
Lovely ★ Complex
Love★Com
1
Aya Nakahara
Class clowns Risa and Ôtani join forces to find love!
Manga available now
Shojo Beat
On sale at www.shojobeat.com
Also available at your local bookstore and comic store
LOVE★COM © 2001 by Aya Nakahara/SHUEISHA Inc.
RATED T FOR TEEN
ratings.viz.com
VIZ MEDIA
www.viz.com

VIZMANGA

Read manga anytime, anywhere!

From our newest hit series to the classics you know and love, the best manga in the world is now available digitally. Buy a volume* of digital manga for your:

- iOS device (**iPad**®, **iPhone**®, **iPod**® touch) through the **VIZ Manga** app

- Android-powered device (**phone or tablet**) with a browser by visiting VIZManga.com

- **Mac or PC computer** by visiting VIZManga.com

VIZ Digital has loads to offer:

- 500+ ready-to-read volumes
- New volumes each week
- FREE previews
- Access on multiple devices! Create a log-in through the app so you buy a book once, and read it on your device of choice!*

To learn more, visit www.viz.com/apps

* Some series may not be available for multiple devices.
  Check the app on your device to find out what's available.

viz.com/apps

Surprise!
You may be reading the wrong way!

It's true: In keeping with the original Japanese comic format, this book reads from right to left—so action, sound effects, and word balloons are completely reversed. This preserves the orientation of the original artwork—plus, it's fun! Check out the diagram shown here to get the hang of things, and then turn to the other side of the book to get started!

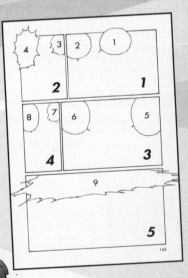